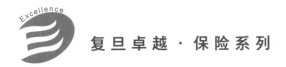

复旦卓越·保险系列

国际寿险架构
理论与实践

LICA国际寿险架构师协会 ◆ 主　编

编委会主任 ◆ 高华声　张婧媞　文小龙

International Life Insurance

免责声明

本书提供的信息不是,也无意构成法律意见;相反,本书中提供的所有信息、内容和材料仅是为了提供概括信息。本书中可能未包含最新的法律规定或其他信息。

本书的读者应该联系他们的律师,以获得有关任何特定的法律问题的建议。本书的读者在未事先征求相关司法管辖区律师的法律意见之前,不应根据本书中的信息采取任何行动或不采取任何行动。只有您的个人律师才能保证本书包含的信息,以及您对本书的理解,适用或适合您面临的特定情况。使用本书,并不会在读者和本书的作者、内容贡献者,或内容贡献者所在的律师事务所之间形成律师-客户关系。

对于基于本书内容所采取或未采取的行动,特此明确免责。

教材概述

本书旨在帮助财富从业者"打破边界、放眼国际",并且通过寿险、税务和信托等工具的使用形成寿险架构思维,从不断提升业绩转变为以客户利益为导向,走上成为有运用能力的优秀国际寿险架构师(Life Insurance Counselor,LIC)道路,建立起保险业的全球视野。

第一章概述国际财富和风险管理,并探讨各种情况下人寿保险的作用,以建立对人寿保险全貌的概念。

第二章介绍人寿保险的主要参与者,以及每个角色的职责、权力、利益/权利,为各位国际寿险架构师学员理解人寿保险奠定基础。

第三章探讨各种类型人寿保险的特点和应用。在之前章节的基础上,通过本章进一步的讲解,各位国际寿险架构师学员将熟悉常见的人寿保险产品类型。

第四章定义人寿保险合同中的重要术语,以确保各位国际寿险架构师学员能够在实践中理解保险合同。

第五章介绍全球不同司法管辖区的人寿保险市场和主要寿险产品,令各位国际寿险架构师学员能够详细了解全球不同市场的特点和产品。

第六章讨论与人寿保险相关的税务问题——这是高净值人士重点关注的方面之一。各位国际寿险架构师学员应具备人寿保险相关的基本税务知识。

第七章解释人寿保险信托架构。该架构将人寿保险和信托相结合,为高净值人士提供了满足其需求的复杂而精妙的解决方案。

第八章介绍人寿保险在高净值人士企业场景中的应用,使国际寿险架构师学员掌握人寿保险在企业中的应用知识,满足客户企业相关的需求。

第九章和第十章专注于有丰富投资经验者需要的人寿保险产品——私募寿险(Private Placement Life Insurance,PPLI)。该类产品专用于为高净值人士提供财富管理解决方案。

第十一章探索保险市场的结构和监管机制,使国际寿险架构师学员充分理解寿险参与各方的合规义务。

第十二章介绍除人寿保险产品外,保险公司在不同司法管辖区发行的其他产品,以补充各位国际寿险架构师学员关于其他相关产品的知识。

附录 A 为美国税务律师对美国税务相关问题的分析和解答。

附录 B 为加拿大税务律师对加拿大税务相关问题的分析和解答。

附录 C 为澳大利亚注册会计师对澳大利亚税务相关问题的分析和解答。

附录 D 为英国税务律师对英国税务相关问题的分析和解答。

附录 E 为日本税务律师对日本税务相关问题的分析和解答。

序言一 | Preface

"架构何可当,架构溯斯堂。"架构思维起于建筑,建筑即使复杂也能稳定;以架构思维应对难题,即使问题复杂,也能理清本质抓住核心。架构思维应用于财富传承也成为近年来财富管理领域的新课题。中国改革开放数十年,中国企业不断发展,逐步强大,"2024胡润全球富豪榜"中我国以814位十亿美元企业家的总数荣登世界第一。中国企业家也开始面对财富传承等复杂问题。继国际信托架构认证2021年在国内开展以来,国际寿险架构也孕育而生。近年来,我国财富管理市场迎来爆发式增长,给相关行业带来历史性机遇。2020年中国个人金融资产规模已达人民币200万亿元,成为全球第二大财富管理市场。随着中国国内生产总值(GDP)稳健增长带来居民收入增长以及资本市场发展带来资本增值,预计中国居民的家庭总资产将进一步增加。国家推行的"房住不炒"政策也将促使居民在资产配置中减少对房产的投资,转而增加金融资产的配置。据麦肯锡测算,中国个人金融资产规模将保持约11%的高速增长,至2025年达到332万亿元。

人寿保险在财富管理领域扮演着核心角色,尤其在财富传承、资产保全和税务规划方面展现出其独特的优势。在"大财富管理"背景下,寿险行业供给侧结构性改革势在必行。从供给端来看,各大金融机构正在积极参与到这一波大财富管理的竞争中,寿险行业各类主体将与全市场参与者,包括银行、券商、信托、基金、第三方财富管理机构、互联网财富平台等玩家在更广阔的平台上竞争;需求端方面,富裕及以上群体的保险渗透率仍有很大提升潜力,高净值客户的财富需求更加多元及广泛,涵盖从基本保障到财富的保值增值、传承与社会责任等方面。然而,当前国内保险产品功能单一,更多侧重保障类需求,无法满足高净值客户在财富增值和税收规划方面的附加需求。在不远的将来,寿险行业必将在清理低端产能、升级专业化队伍、丰富产品供给能力等方面迎来重大变革。洞悉不同法域寿险市场与产品特点,为高净值客户量身定制全球化资产配置方案,国际寿险架构师必将成为寿险行业内大受欢迎的高端职业选择。

复旦大学国际金融学院专注于高端金融人才培养和金融领域学术智库研究,力争切实回答并解决金融行业发展的重大现实问题。针对当下寿险行业转型需求,学院携手国际顶级师资团队与国际寿险架构师协会强强联合,推出《国际寿险架构理论与实践》一书。本书将从基本概念出发,介绍寿险的主要参与者、各类寿险的特点和应用场景、合同关键术语,以及不同司法管辖区的市场与产品特点,旨在为读者提供全面的寿险知识;在此基础上,本书将深入探讨寿险相关的税务问题、信托架构、企业场景应用、私募寿险等进阶内容,并为学员提供必要的合规指导。本书的目标是帮助财富从业者培养架构思维、拓展国际视野,从不断提升业绩到以客户利益为导向,最终成长为具备运用能力的优秀国际寿险架构师。

高华声
复旦大学国际金融学院副院长、教授
2024 年 4 月

序言二 | Preface

Dear Readers,

It is with great pleasure that I introduce the inaugural Chinese language edition of **"International Life Insurance: Theory and Practice"** (this "textbook"), published by the International Life Insurance Counselors Association ("LICA"). As an independent organization founded by experts with a combined 100 years of experience in the life insurance industry, LICA is committed to advancing the understanding and practice of international life insurance structures while fostering collaboration among practitioners worldwide.

In an increasingly interconnected global economy, understanding the international markets for life insurance and related products cannot be overstated, as the need for comprehensive wealth and risk management solutions transcends borders and jurisdictions. This textbook represents a culmination of expertise and insights from leading professionals in the field, offering a comprehensive guide to navigating the complexities of international life insurance.

Having spent over 25 years in the international life insurance industry and having been lucky to contribute in a small way to its growth from its nascent stages to what it is today, I've witnessed how knowledge regarding these products has spread. Initially confined to carriers and select advisors, this knowledge is now accessible to advisors worldwide. However, possessing knowledge alone, without the ability to implement it effectively, can pose risks. This understanding led to the founding of LICA, with the primary objective of educating future generations of insurance professionals. At LICA, we recognize the imperative for practitioners to understand theoretical concepts and practical applications to serve their clients effectively in today's dynamic global marketplace. That's why we designed the Life Insurance Counselor ("LIC") program, a comprehensive professional certification initiative that revolutionizes continuing education in the life insurance field.

The LIC program breaks down traditional life insurance certification and training boundaries between countries, insurance carriers, and product lines, incorporating more specialized concepts of international life insurance, trust, and taxation related to wealth management. At the center of the LIC program is this textbook, co-authored by more than a dozen professionals with extensive experience in international insurance product design, distribution, and sales, that provides a global viewpoint on the role of insurance in wealth preservation, enabling advisors to employ a systematic, professional approach towards international life insurance planning.

This textbook consists of twelve modules designed to provide a holistic understanding of the complexities of international wealth and risk management and the role life insurance products can play. From the features and applications of various types of life insurance products to an exploration of advanced wealth management solutions to a discussion of products offered in various jurisdictions beyond traditional life insurance, the textbook covers a wide range of topics essential for practitioners seeking to excel in the field of international life insurance. In addition to providing education to build technical expertise, the textbook emphasizes the utmost importance of compliance with jurisdictional laws and regulations. Compliance is not just a legal obligation but a cornerstone of ethical practice in the field of international life insurance and the key to earning consumer trust.

As the global economy undergoes rapid transformations and families' wealth and holdings span boundaries and jurisdictions, the demand for skilled professionals capable of navigating the complexities of international life insurance planning has never been greater. Through this textbook and the LIC certification program, LICA is proud to support practitioners in meeting this demand, equipping them with the knowledge, skills, and tools necessary to thrive in today's dynamic marketplace.

In closing, I invite you to embark on a journey of exploration and discovery as you delve into the pages of "International Life Insurance: Theory and Practice." May this textbook, the LIC program, and the ongoing training provided by LICA serve as invaluable resources in your pursuit of professional growth and success in the exciting world of international life insurance.

Sincerely,
Andy Man
Chairman, Co-Founder
International Life Insurance Counselors Association (LICA)

序言三 | Preface

人们都梦想拥有财富,求财恨不多。

殊不知,手中有了余钱,喜中亦带忧。

因为我们的父辈祖辈一穷二白,勉强温饱度日,没有给我们留下财富管理与传承的奥秘。让我记忆犹新的是,我1994年参加工作的第一项任务是起草信托法,记得有人问及我时,对此嗤之以鼻:人们哪来的财产做信托哦?

由于理财经验的断层,财富易快速集聚又快速溃散,例如富人排行榜,境外的相对稳定,而我国则频繁更替。同时,财富在人们手中常常无法发挥它的价值和效能,甚至财多伤人并拖累子孙后代。因此,当人们富起来后,需要补上"财富管理与传承"这一课。

对财富拥有者而言,"创富"之后面临的是"守富"和"传富"。"守富"的目的是防止财富缩水,我们需要大智慧,否则财富来了,我们是留不住它的。"我们一不小心或不择手段抢下了第一桶金,这里有自身的精明,也有天时、机遇,切不可自得,这里我们最好冷静一下,内省体味一下:我们接住了它,但抱得住吗?享得了吗?"①"传富"的目的是希望家族长盛不衰,我们需要先见之明,提前构筑财富延续的基石。但我国早就有"富不过三代"的说法,"中国历史上根本没有家族财富传承的成功案例可以借鉴,有的只是一个个富有家族不断衰败、受难的悲剧故事和传说"②。因此,经济社会发展到了今天,我们在富足之余,就要认真思考"守富"和"传富"的方法和途径,不断追求卓越。特别是当今世界金融工具不断丰富,金融产品层出不穷,更需要我们掌握一些常识性的知识,与时俱进。

对财富从业者而言,则是要帮助财富拥有者"守富"和"传富"。因为创富一代有其主业,其家族后人往往也有自己的兴趣和爱好,不可能在实现"守富"和"传富"的过程中处处专注且专业。我认为,要实现财富的最佳管理和处置,需要具备的条件和因素很多,其中,专业资产管理能力最为重要。它包括资产管理的经验和技能,也包括资产管理的资格和资质等这种能力,财富拥有者通常并不具备,"故将自有财产交由他人打理成为一种趋

---

① 刘钟海、韩冰:《财富论》,经济管理出版社,2017年版,第19~20页。
② [美]比尔·邦纳(Bill Bonner)、威尔·邦纳(Will Bonner):《家族财富》,机械工业出版社,2013年版,第Ⅷ页。

势,并发展成为国际通行做法"[①]。术业有专攻,这就需要财富从业者为财富拥有者提供专业的服务。特别是当今世界经济一体化、金融全球化的趋势明显,财富也开始在全球范围内寻求跨区域的资产配置。我非常赞同教材中关于财富从业者要"打破边界,放眼国际"的提法。我过去曾从事银行、证券、信托、基金等法律的起草工作,足迹遍及欧美亚等地的十多个发达国家和地区,长期从事资产管理与财富传承方面的研究和实践。我发现,境外的金融机构能够为财富拥有者提供综合金融服务,而我国由于分业经营,在这方面明显有短板,因此,财富从业者不可偏安一隅,还应大力提升自己的能力。

国际寿险架构师教材的付梓,无疑非常及时,其内容涵盖保险、信托、税务等方方面面。单拿我自己来说,也需要加强这方面知识的学习。

是为序。

蔡概还[②]

2024 年 5 月 9 日

[①] 蔡概还:《资产管理与财富传承》,中国金融出版社,2023 年版,第 3 页。
[②] 中国慈善联合会慈善信托委员会主任,曾担任《中华人民共和国信托法》《中华人民共和国证券投资基金法》执笔起草人,参与《中华人民共和国保险法》的起草工作。

目录 | Contents

1 国际财富与风险管理 ... 1
  1.1 财富管理概述 ... 1
  1.2 高净值人士 ... 2
  1.3 身故风险与财务影响 ... 3
  1.4 人寿保险与财富管理 ... 4
  1.5 风险管理策略 ... 4
    1.5.1 风险规避 ... 5
    1.5.2 风险抑制 ... 5
    1.5.3 风险自留 ... 5
    1.5.4 风险转移 ... 5

2 人寿保险中的重要角色 ... 6
  2.1 保险公司 ... 6
    2.1.1 传统人寿保险公司 ... 7
    2.1.2 再保险公司 ... 7
    2.1.3 私募人寿保险公司 ... 8
  2.2 投保人 ... 8
  2.3 被保人 ... 9
    2.3.1 单一被保人 ... 10
    2.3.2 多被保人 ... 10
    2.3.3 联合保险 ... 11
  2.4 受益人 ... 12
    2.4.1 可撤销受益人 ... 13
    2.4.2 不可撤销受益人 ... 13
  2.5 各角色的责、权、利 ... 14
    2.5.1 保险公司 ... 14
    2.5.2 投保人(保单持有人) ... 14

  2.5.3 被保人及受益人 15

3 人寿保险的种类 16

3.1 定期人寿保险 16
  3.1.1 什么是定期人寿保险 16
  3.1.2 定期人寿保险的类型 17
  3.1.3 定期人寿保险的特点 17
  3.1.4 定期人寿保险的应用 18

3.2 储蓄保险 19
  3.2.1 什么是储蓄保险 19
  3.2.2 储蓄保险的类型 20
  3.2.3 储蓄保险的特点 20
  3.2.4 储蓄保险的应用 20

3.3 终身寿险 21
  3.3.1 什么是终身寿险 21
  3.3.2 终身寿险的类型 21
  3.3.3 终身寿险的特点 26
  3.3.4 终身寿险的应用 27

3.4 万能寿险 28
  3.4.1 什么是万能寿险 28
  3.4.2 万能寿险的类型 29
  3.4.3 万能寿险的特点 30
  3.4.4 万能寿险的应用 31

3.5 指数型万能寿险 31
  3.5.1 什么是指数型万能寿险 31
  3.5.2 指数型万能寿险的运作方式 32
  3.5.3 指数型万能寿险的特点 35
  3.5.4 指数型万能寿险的应用 35

3.6 投资型万能寿险 36
  3.6.1 什么是投资型万能寿险 36
  3.6.2 投资型万能寿险的特点 36
  3.6.3 投资型万能寿险的应用 37

3.7 私募寿险 37
  3.7.1 什么是私募寿险 37

3.7.2　私募寿险的特点 ·· 37

4　人寿保险合同 ··· 39
4.1　定义 ··· 39
　　4.1.1　有效人寿保险合同的一般要素 ··· 39
　　4.1.2　披露义务 ··· 40
　　4.1.3　担保与陈述 ··· 41
　　4.1.4　重大失实陈述 ··· 41
　　4.1.5　弃权和禁止反言 ·· 41
4.2　人寿保险合同中的常见条款 ··· 41
　　4.2.1　完整合同 ··· 42
　　4.2.2　保费 ·· 42
　　4.2.3　保单价值 ··· 43
　　4.2.4　分红条款 ··· 43
　　4.2.5　保险金 ·· 44
　　4.2.6　保单持有人权利 ·· 46
　　4.2.7　冷静期 ·· 46
　　4.2.8　宽限期 ·· 46
　　4.2.9　不可抗辩和自杀条款 ··· 47
　　4.2.10　误报年龄及/或性别 ··· 47
　　4.2.11　取款和退保 ·· 48
　　4.2.12　保单贷款条款 ·· 48
　　4.2.13　失效 ·· 49
　　4.2.14　自动保费贷款 ·· 49
　　4.2.15　复效 ·· 49
　　4.2.16　转让 ·· 49
　　4.2.17　索赔 ·· 50
　　4.2.18　背书 ·· 50
　　4.2.19　其他 ·· 50

5　不同司法管辖区的寿险市场和主要寿险产品 ··································· 51
5.1　美国 ··· 51
　　5.1.1　美国寿险市场概述 ··· 51
　　5.1.2　定期寿险 ··· 53

		5.1.3	终身寿险	53
		5.1.4	万能寿险	54
	5.2	加拿大		55
		5.2.1	加拿大寿险市场概述	55
		5.2.2	定期寿险	57
		5.2.3	终身寿险	57
		5.2.4	万能寿险	58
	5.3	中国香港特别行政区		58
		5.3.1	储蓄分红险	60
		5.3.2	万能寿险	61
		5.3.3	定期寿险和两全保险	62
	5.4	新加坡		62
		5.4.1	新加坡寿险市场概述	62
		5.4.2	定期寿险	64
		5.4.3	终身寿险	64
		5.4.4	指数型万能寿险	65
		5.4.5	储蓄险	65
		5.4.6	投资连结险	65
	5.5	离岸产品		66
		5.5.1	离岸寿险市场概述	66
		5.5.2	指数型万能寿险	67
		5.5.3	分红型终身寿险	69
		5.5.4	分红型储蓄险	70
		5.5.5	指数型储蓄险	71
	5.6	中国内地		72
		5.6.1	中国内地寿险市场综述	72
		5.6.2	定期寿险	73
		5.6.3	终身寿险	74
		5.6.4	两全保险	74
		5.6.5	万能保险	74
		5.6.6	分红保险	75
6	人寿保险与税务			76
	6.1	税务居民身份		77

目 录

  6.1.1 常见司法管辖区的个人税务居民身份认定标准 ………… 77
  6.1.2 常见司法管辖区的公司/企业税务居民身份认定标准 …… 81
  6.1.3 常见司法管辖区的信托税务居民身份认定标准 ………… 83
6.2 私人财富规划领域的税务问题 ………………………………………… 85
  6.2.1 所得税 …………………………………………………………… 85
  6.2.2 资本利得税 ……………………………………………………… 86
  6.2.3 预提税 …………………………………………………………… 86
  6.2.4 遗产税和赠与税 ………………………………………………… 87
6.3 人寿保险的相关税务问题 ……………………………………………… 87
  6.3.1 现金价值 ………………………………………………………… 87
  6.3.2 现金提取 ………………………………………………………… 88
  6.3.3 保单转让 ………………………………………………………… 88
  6.3.4 保单贷款 ………………………………………………………… 88
  6.3.5 身故赔偿金 ……………………………………………………… 88
  6.3.6 保单持有人/受益人身份变化引起的税务问题 ………………… 89
6.4 人寿保险的税收筹划方案与反避税总原则 …………………………… 89
  6.4.1 加拿大人寿保险的税务政策 …………………………………… 89
  6.4.2 与美国人寿保险相关的一般反避税规则 ……………………… 90
  6.4.3 澳大利亚的合格境外人寿保单 ………………………………… 91
  6.4.4 保单相关的金融信息交换 ……………………………………… 93
6.5 案例分析 ………………………………………………………………… 93
  6.5.1 案例背景 ………………………………………………………… 93
  6.5.2 案例分析 ………………………………………………………… 93

7 信托与寿险 ……………………………………………………………………… 95

7.1 信托的概念和特征 ……………………………………………………… 95
7.2 信托的主要角色 ………………………………………………………… 96
  7.2.1 设立人 …………………………………………………………… 96
  7.2.2 受托人 …………………………………………………………… 97
  7.2.3 保护人 …………………………………………………………… 97
  7.2.4 受益人 …………………………………………………………… 98
7.3 信托的主要功能与底层逻辑 …………………………………………… 98
  7.3.1 资产保护与风险隔离 …………………………………………… 98
  7.3.2 财富传承与家族治理 …………………………………………… 99

	7.3.3 税务优化	99
7.4	信托与寿险的组合应用	100
	7.4.1 信托作为保单持有人	100
	7.4.2 信托作为保单受益人	101
	7.4.3 信托作为保单付款人	101
	7.4.4 常见的信托与寿险架构组合	101

8 人寿保险与企业传承 · 103

8.1	企业类型	103
	8.1.1 个体经营户	104
	8.1.2 合伙企业	104
	8.1.3 公司	105
8.2	人寿保险在企业中的应用	105
	8.2.1 重要人士保险	105
	8.2.2 买卖协议	106
8.3	企业持有人寿保单的税务事宜	111

9 私募寿险(一) · 113

9.1	为什么高净值人士需要私募寿险	113
	9.1.1 风险管理	114
	9.1.2 税务筹划	115
	9.1.3 投资规划	115
9.2	私募寿险的发展	116
	9.2.1 私募寿险的市场需求	116
	9.2.2 寿险内投资范围的创新	117
9.3	私募寿险内的投资选择与税务优惠	119
	9.3.1 私募寿险内的投资选择	119
	9.3.2 私募寿险在税务筹划方面的优势	120
9.4	美国对私募寿险的监管	122
	9.4.1 美国对私募寿险保险公司的监管	122
	9.4.2 美国对私募寿险保单的监管	123
	9.4.3 美国对私募寿险内投资的监管	123

10 私募寿险（二） 126

10.1 如何构建私募寿险 126
10.1.1 保费支付方式 126
10.1.2 现金价值和身故赔偿金 127

10.2 私募寿险信托 128
10.2.1 比较私募寿险和信托 128
10.2.2 私募寿险信托 130
10.2.3 私募寿险的不同保单持有人 131

10.3 私募寿险架构中的服务提供者 134
10.3.1 顾问团队——国际寿险架构师配合律师或会计师 134
10.3.2 投资经理 134
10.3.3 保险公司 134
10.3.4 再保险公司 134
10.3.5 托管银行 135

10.4 如何为高净值家庭设计私募寿险架构 135
10.4.1 保单持有人 136
10.4.2 被保人 136
10.4.3 受益人 136
10.4.4 保费 136
10.4.5 保单资产配置 136
10.4.6 税务后果 136
10.4.7 费用 137

11 保险市场结构及监管机制 138

11.1 保险公司 139
11.1.1 核保 139
11.1.2 客户实名认证及反洗钱流程 139
11.1.3 投资监管 140
11.1.4 《共同申报准则》和《海外账户税收合规法案》 141

11.2 保险申请人 143
11.2.1 居民身份 143
11.2.2 健康状况和财务资格 146

11.3 保险中介人 147
11.3.1 保险中介人的资格认证 147

11.3.2　保险中介人的监管机制 ······················· 152
　　11.3.3　保险中介人的长期后续服务 ··················· 154
11.4　保险推荐人 ······································ 156
　　11.4.1　保险推荐人和转介绍活动的认定 ··············· 156
　　11.4.2　对保险推荐人和转介绍活动的监管 ············· 158

12 不同司法管辖区人寿保险公司的非寿险产品 ············ 159
12.1　美国 ·· 160
　　12.1.1　固定收益年金 ······························· 160
　　12.1.2　指数型年金 ································· 161
　　12.1.3　投资型年金 ································· 162
12.2　加拿大 ·· 163
　　12.2.1　年金 ······································· 163
　　12.2.2　分隔基金 ··································· 165
12.3　中国香港 ·· 166
12.4　中国内地 ·· 167
　　12.4.1　年金保险的功能 ····························· 167
　　12.4.2　年金保险的特点 ····························· 168

附录 A：美国税务意见 ······························· 169

附录 B：加拿大税务意见 ····························· 193

附录 C：澳大利亚税务意见 ··························· 201

附录 D：英国税务意见 ······························· 221

附录 E：日本税务意见 ······························· 241

后记 ·· 255

关于本书

未经国际寿险架构师协会(LICA)事先许可,本书的任何部分都不得以机械、影印、录制或其他方式复制、储存在检索系统中。

国际财富与风险管理

本章要点：
- 介绍财富和风险管理的概念
- 定义高净值人士/客户
- 探讨身故的财务影响和风险
- 介绍人寿保险作为财富管理工具的作用
- 探讨风险管理策略

1.1 财富管理概述

在过去的几十年中，随着全球经济的发展，成功的企业家和商人为自己和家人积累下了相当可观的财富。根据瑞士信贷和瑞银联合发布的《2023年全球财富报告》中的最新数据，截至2022年底，全球共有5 940万名百万富豪（以美元计算）。此外，报告还预计，未来5年全球百万富豪人数有望增至8 600万名，可投资资产超过3 000万美元的超高净值人士有望增至37.2万名。①

财富为什么需要管理呢？对于企业家而言，赢得财富不容易，守住财富更难。得到财富后，仍会面临各种各样的问题。比如，在人的一生中，一定会面对通货膨胀、所得税甚至

---

① Credit Suisse and UBS, *Global Wealth Report 2023*.

遗产税问题;可能会遇到债权人追讨、离婚分割和家人争产;可能会遭遇投资亏损、经营不善。这些可能会带给一个家庭动力和鼓励,也可能会影响和睦。不可否认的是,无论在哪个国家、哪个地区,财富顺利传承到第三代、第四代的比例总是越来越低。所以财富管理行业才会应运而生。

财富管理结合了投资咨询与其他金融服务,通过对富裕客户财富的管理,满足其各种需求。这是一个咨询的过程,在这个过程中,顾问收集有关客户需求的信息,并利用适当的金融产品和服务为客户量身定制财富管理策略。

随着财富的增加,家族财富管理的复杂性也随之增加。财富管理不仅是提供投资建议,它也可以涵盖一个人财务生活的所有方面:从银行服务到信贷产品,从资产管理到另类投资,从保险到慈善,从家族治理到管家礼宾服务,越是庞大的财富越需要多元复杂的财富管理。所以财富管理不是单独一个人、一个机构可以做到的,很多时候需要多个专业团队一起努力来帮助一个富有的家族守住财富,延续优秀的家族文化并代代相传。每个专业团队各司其职,处理各自擅长领域的事务。比如,信托公司受托人搭建家族信托,税务师进行税务规划及申报,移民公司顾问进行家族成员身份规划,投资顾问负责制定和操作投资策略,公司服务商成立离岸公司,保险经纪挑选合适的产品投保等。各个专业团队在工作中既有分工又需要紧密合作,围绕客户的家族提供满足其需求的完善服务。

在财富管理领域里的专业人士可能是一个小规模的机构,比如一家小型律所或者几个人组成的家族办公室,也可能是一个大机构,比如银行、大型资产管理公司。尽管大机构容易得到客户的信赖,但是富裕家族更注重财富管理顾问长久的服务,尽量避免因为某位顾问离开某个机构而终止服务。所以对于财富管理顾问来说,能够长久地陪伴一个家族的财富成长是他们努力的方向。

1.2 高净值人士

说到财富管理就一定会提及高净值人士(High Net Worth Individuals,HNWIs)这一概念,普通收入人士因为资产量及需求的复杂性较低,经常可以自己借助一些简单的投资和理财工具来管理财富;而高净值人士通常因为激增的财富数量、复杂的财务情况和需求,需要财富管理专业人士的帮助。所以不同的财富管理公司会根据净资产或可投资资产的数量对高净值客户进行识别分类,典型的分类如下:

(1) 可投资资产在100万至500万美元之间的个人为高净值人士(HNWIs);

(2) 可投资资产在500万至3 000万美元之间的个人为极高净值人士(Very High Net Worth Individuals,VHNWIs);

(3) 可投资资产超过3 000万美元的个人为超高净值人士(Ultra High Net Worth Individuals,UHNWIs)。

财富管理机构根据可投资资产对高净值人士进行初步分类,是因为专业人士普遍认为投资产品和咨询服务的复杂程度会随着财富数量的增加而增加。超高净值人士的金融和非金融需求更大,也更复杂。所以专业人士根据此初步分类可以判断出客户的大致需求方向,明确其感兴趣的服务,依此进行资源分配。

除了单纯以可投资资产对高净值人士进行分类外,不同的财富管理机构还可能根据高净值人士的住所地、财富来源、行为特征等进行分类。但所有的分类方式都不完美。比如单纯根据可投资资产来识别定义高净值人士可能忽视一些新一代的财富创造者,其可投资资产并不多,但是从所得税角度来看,其收入远高于普通收入人士,缴纳的税额也很高,其获得的收入往往会重新投入事业,导致可投资资产较低。这类需要税务筹划的人士,也应该归类为高净值人士,财富管理专业人士提供的合规税务筹划方案非常有助于其发展。他们同样属于财富管理的目标客户。

1.3 身故风险与财务影响

这是一个不确定的世界,其中财富是不确定因素之一。世界经济前景不确定,发展的不平衡有增无减;世界仍然不安宁,局部冲突和热点问题此起彼伏,国际与地区安全依然存在很大的不稳定性;自然环境不确定,联合国环境规划署《全球环境展望报告》称地球生态承载力已超限,人类生存环境变化,新类型病毒肆虐。生活在这样一个充满不确定性的世界中,即使今天是亿万富翁,也很难说几年后、去世时自己还能拥有多少财富。但是正如本杰明·富兰克林所说,死亡和税仍然是这个不确定的世界中最确定的两件事。既然没有人真正拥有水晶球,能预测未来的自己拥有的财富数量,那么高净值人士其实也应该和普通人一样去思考去世后的问题,而不是认为自己眼前的财富可以帮助自己和家人解决未来可能发生的任何问题,虽然这是很多高净值人士完全不愿意听到的意见。

首先,高净值人士及其家庭往往习惯了比普通家庭更高的生活标准,那么当高净值人士去世后,家人是否还可以维持和从前一样的生活标准是其必须考虑的问题之一。由于高净值人士通常是家庭的主要经济来源,因此他们的存在关系到整个家庭的幸福生活。高净值人士的突然去世可能会对维持家庭生活水平所需现金流产生重大影响。

其次,高净值人士同样需要考虑去世是否会带来债务,比如因业务主要人员的去世致使合同无法完成而被追偿导致的债务。高净值人士去世后可能需要向相关税务机关缴纳大笔的税款,是否准备了足额的现金交付这些税款。无论是高净值人士去世带来的债务还是税负,都会对原有的财富造成重大影响,对财富的保护是高净值人士不应忽视的问题。

最后,高净值人士还需要考虑去世后家人就财富分割可能产生的问题,特别是当自己的愿望与法定继承有较大分歧时如何解决。对于高净值人士来讲,一定不希望去世后的财产分配问题造成家庭的分崩离析。

其实,当一个高净值人士赚到了和他的生活标准相匹配的财富后,他完全有能力拿出一笔钱解决两个问题:活得太短和活得太长。解决这两个问题最好的工具都在保险公司发行的产品里,也只有保险公司会在产品里考虑到死亡率(Mortality Rate),即在特定年龄死亡的概率。保险公司通过产品设计,在人寿保险里,让活得长的人一直交保费,活得短的人则提早得到身故赔偿金;在终身年金里,让活得长的人一直可以获得分配,活得短的人则为活得长的人做出了贡献。这两类产品都可以做到:确定性。

这一切的背后都有一套完整的专业理论与实践在支撑着:精算。精算令一个人在去世时的"身价"变成一个确定值,这个价值往往比他生前花费最多精力所从事的事业的价值更加确定。

1.4 人寿保险与财富管理

作为高净值人士财富管理策略的一部分,人寿保险能够发挥独特稳定的作用,更不必说它是高净值人士进行遗产传承规划的关键工具。人寿保险本身可应用于财富管理行业的所有领域,无论是高净值人士还是工薪阶层。尽管如此,高净值人士因其家庭、企业和资产类别较为复杂,需求会比工薪阶层进一步提升。上文提及的高净值人士去世后的财务影响,其实都可以通过人寿保险解决。

另外,保险公司发行的产品除了可以解决"活得太短和活得太长"的问题外,保险还有稳健投资,即解决投资风险的功能。对于高净值人士而言,在万能寿险(Universal Life,UL)、指数型万能寿险(Indexed Universal Life,IUL)或者终身寿险(Whole Life,WL)保单里可以获得最低保证回报率,投资风险由保险公司而非保单持有人承担。当然,不可否认的是,高净值人士往往并不喜欢这样低风险、低回报的产品,他们往往更喜欢自己来掌控投资。现代保险的发展使得保单可以作为一个"包装",在拥有保额的前提下,保单持有人自行选择投资顾问,由保险公司批准,然后由投资顾问进行投资。有些保险公司还允许用保单来持有有价证券以外的资产,比如房产、股权等一切有评估价值的资产。

不同司法管辖区赋予了保单不同的功能,比如有的司法管辖区允许保单里的资产不受保单持有人的债权人追讨;有的司法管辖区允许保单里的现金价值的增长可以享受延税(Tax Deferred)甚至免税(Tax Free)税务优惠政策。大部分司法管辖区对于身故赔偿金的赔付收入是免所得税的,但是需要注意,无论是人寿保险的隔离保护功能,还是税务筹划功能,最好都要经过投保人、被保人、受益人以及资产所在地的税务律师确认。

1.5 风险管理策略

前文简单阐述了身故带来的风险及财务影响,那么如何对风险进行管理呢?一般来说,无论是何种类型的风险,其管理策略一般分为四类:风险规避、风险抑制、风险自留及风险转移。这四种策略可以单独或结合起来使用,取决于哪种方式最适合用来处理相关的风险。

1.5.1 风险规避

最直接的风险管理策略是风险规避,即自始至终不让自己承受某种风险。例如,高净值人士可以选择不自己开车,而是花钱聘请专职司机,避免自己开车撞人的风险。但不幸的是,只要人活着,就会面临身故的风险,身故的风险是无法用上述方式去规避的,因此需要其他策略来解决。

1.5.2 风险抑制

如果不能直接规避风险,那么可以通过采取相关行动的方式来降低风险发生的概率或严重程度,这被称为风险抑制。例如,那些不想聘请司机、更喜欢自己开车出行的高净值人士,可以通过遵守交通规则、确保汽车车况良好,外加谨慎驾驶来减少发生车祸的风险。同样,高净值人士可以通过保持健康的生活方式(如戒烟、健身)和避免参加一些危险的活动(如不参加跳伞和滑雪项目等),来减少身故的风险。但是,这并不能完全避免身故风险,只会减少意外身故的可能性。因此,需要采取额外的策略来解决其余的身故风险。

1.5.3 风险自留

风险自留,也就是说,接受自己面临风险的事实,并且愿意接受风险降临的后果。风险自留策略适用于严重性较低的风险,即发生风险后对财务的影响在可控范围之内。例如,高净值人士去买车时可以选择是否购买延长保修,一旦选择付费延长保修期,则在延长的保修期内,车子部件损坏,其将获得保修;高净值人士也可拒绝购买延长保修,自己承担风险,则在原保修期到期后,车子损坏,其将自己支付维修或更换费用。毕竟修车的费用对于高净值人士的财务并没有太大的影响。

然而,身故风险通常被视为高危风险。特别是对于高净值人士来说,去世会带来较为严重复杂的影响,因此风险自留策略并不适合身故所对应的风险。

1.5.4 风险转移

风险转移即找到愿意承担风险后果的其他人来代替自己承担,购买保险就是典型的风险转移策略。为了应对身故风险,高净值人士选择支付保费,去世后的财务影响将被全部或部分转移,由保险公司进行赔付,以抵销或减少财务损失。身故赔偿金可以作为现金流帮助高净值人士的家庭维持生活水平,也可以用来清偿债务或缴纳税负。需要注意的是,要起到上述效果是有前提的,即高净值人士购买了足额的人寿保险。只有在购买的人寿保险保额足够的情况下,赔付出来的身故赔偿金才能起到上述作用,否则也只是杯水车薪。这一点也是很多高净值人士容易忽略的,需要财富管理专业人士帮助其制订适合其家庭的保险计划,才能完整地发挥人寿保险在财富管理中的作用。除上述功能外,人寿保险还可以通过指定受益人的方式,有效避免遗产纠纷,维持家庭的稳定和财富的传承。

人寿保险中的重要角色

> **本章要点：**
> - 介绍人寿保险的重要角色
> - 探讨每个角色的责权利

人寿保险保单是保险公司（承保人）和投保人在保险经纪帮助之下签立的合同。典型的人寿保险还会有其他角色牵涉其中，即被保人和受益人。

2.1 保险公司

保险公司（Insurance Company/Insurer），也叫承保人，承担风险并发行保单。保险公司是提供保险产品的机构，也就是承担赔偿义务的机构，同时也是收取保费的机构。无论通过什么方式投保，和客户签署保单合同的都是保险公司。换句话说，所签署的与保单合同直接相关的投保文件，都必须是保险公司的文件。保险公司主要负责研发保险产品、建立维护分销渠道、为保单核保、处理保单理赔，以及提供精算、会计、投资支持等。由于保险公司的责任重大，在全世界各地，保险公司都受到非常严格的监管。一般来说，在各司法管辖区进行商业活动的保险公司均须获得当地政府的许可，受到相关的保险法或其他法律管辖。

人寿保险公司按业务及保费投资方式可分为三类：传统人寿保险公司、再保险公司及私募人寿保险公司。

2.1.1 传统人寿保险公司

一般来说,传统人寿保险公司均为各司法管辖区老牌的保险公司,历史悠久、资本实力雄厚,也是客户最熟悉的、时常听说的保险公司,是以综合性人寿保险为主营业务的保险公司。

传统人寿保险公司由于产品长期性、客户依赖性等优势,较少面临来自市场外部力量的冲击,一直可以保持稳定的发展。但是,传统人寿保险公司发行的人寿保险产品中,投资选项由保险公司把控,客户只能在给出的选项中做出筛选;有些人寿保险产品中,客户甚至完全没有选择的权利,只能依赖保险公司进行投资,所获收益的多少取决于保险公司的管理能力、投资表现和分配意愿。

尽管传统人寿保险公司的产品因投资资金总量庞大,可以做到资产的全球化配置,分散风险,收益也相对稳定,但是这可能无法满足高净值人士的相关需求。所以财富管理专业人士在帮助高净值人士进行保险规划时,仍需要以客户的需求为前提,考量产品本身是否合适,而不能单纯考虑保险公司本身的实力。

2.1.2 再保险公司

再保险指保险公司将自己所承担的保险责任,部分地转嫁给其他保险公司承保的业务。再保险业务中转出保险的一方为原保险公司,接受再保险的一方为再保险公司,再保险公司也被称为"保险公司的保险公司"。再保险公司与本来的投保人无直接关系,只对原保险公司负责。作为保险市场一种通行的业务,再保险可以使保险公司不会因为一次大额赔付而对其履行其他赔偿责任造成影响,从而提高保险公司的承保能力。所谓承保能力,是指保险公司综合考量风险后,接受投保业务的能力。再保险可以使保险公司有能力承担某些原先不能承担的风险。例如,某高净值客户想要购买2 000万美元的大额人寿保险,而保险公司只能承保1 000万美元保额,这个时候,保险公司可以通过再保险的方法,转嫁超出自身承保能力的另外1 000万美元保额至再保险公司,从而满足高净值客户的需求。

再保险对于投保人及保险公司发行的保单没有直接影响,投保人也不需要知道他的保单进行了再保险,这完全属于保险公司和再保险公司之间的事。不论保险公司的财务状况怎样,均需根据相关保单合约的条款,直接对投保人负起全额赔偿的责任,而再保险公司能够协助确保保险公司有足够能力付款。

尽管再保险公司和保险公司发行的保单本身没有太大关联,但是对于高净值人士而言,可能需要购买保额为几千万美元的大额人寿保险,而保险公司出于一次性赔付几千万美元现金可能对其整体投资产生影响,或不能保证资产及时变现赔付等考虑,会将部分保额分保给再保险公司。这对高净值人士的保单本身没有任何影响,反而对保单的赔付有更好的保障作用,特别是高净值人士的私募人寿保险产品,几乎都有再保险公司的参与。

其实在传统人寿保险公司的背后,也都有再保险公司的身影,只是因为再保险公司与客户之间没有直接关联,不发行产品,所以客户并不常听说再保险公司的名字。

2.1.3 私募人寿保险公司

私募人寿保险公司有别于传统人寿保险公司,在某些司法管辖区,其投资完全可以定制化,投资的方向和投资管理人由投保人推荐,经保险公司批准,之后保单内资产的投资均由投资管理人负责,即打破了传统人寿保险公司把控投资选择的局面,对于高净值人士来说,在投资自由度上更具有吸引力。

私募人寿保险公司关注的重点是搭建能发挥隔离保护、税务筹划和准确传承作用的架构,而非作为基础元素的人寿保险,所以私募人寿保险公司和传统人寿保险公司的营销策略不同,对维持较高承保率的追求力度也会相应减少。这类保险公司大多比较年轻,历史不超过 30 年,相较传统人寿保险公司而言,历史和资本较为薄弱,也是因为这个原因,其与再保险公司联系紧密。

关于私募人寿保险的详细知识,会在第 9 章和第 10 章中讨论。

2.2 投保人

投保人(Policy Owner)是与保险公司签立合同、申请购买保单的个人或者法律实体(如公司)。一旦合同成立,投保人即成为保单持有人。保单持有人拥有保单法律所有权,可以行使合同及法律规定的相关权利。第一任保单持有人是与保险公司签立原始合同的人。简言之,保单持有人与保险公司签立合同,并且享有保单的合同权利。保单持有人负责做出保单相关的所有决定,包括指定保单的受益人、支付保费、取消保单或将保单转让给他人等。

保单持有人通常也是保单的被保人,也就是为了自己购买人寿保险;但保单持有人也可以让其配偶、子女或父母等其他人作为被保人拥有保单的所有权。一份保单的持有人可以不止一个,也就是说多人可共同持有一份保单。保单条款中会明确共同持有人各自的权利和责任,包括当他们中的一人去世后保单的变化。

最常见的共同持有方式有两种:分权共有(Tenancy in Common)和联权共有(Joint Tenancy)。

在分权共有的情况下,当保单持有人之一去世后,其所拥有的保单份额将根据其遗嘱或相关继承法规则归于其继承人。举例来说,若 Jim 和 Amy 以分权共有的方式共同持有一份保单,当 Jim 去世后,Jim 所拥有的保单份额就会归于 Jim 的继承人。

在联权共有的情况下,当保单持有人之一去世后,其所拥有的保单份额将自动归于另一在世的保单持有人,而不像分权共有那样归于其继承人。另一在世的保单持有人会成为保单的唯一持有人。举例来说,若 Jim 和 Amy 以联权共有的方式共同持有一份保单,当 Jim 去世后,Jim 的份额就会归 Amy 所有,所以 Amy 就 100% 拥有了该保单。

若保单持有人不是被保人,保单持有人可能先于被保人去世(保单仍然有效)。保单的所有权就会转移给新的持有人。新的持有人可以事先由保单持有人在保单中指定,或通过修改保单实现。事先指定的人在原保单持有人去世后成为新的保单持有人,该人被称为继任保单持有人(Contingent Owner)。若原保单持有人没有明确继任保单持有人,则新的保单持有人将间接来说是其遗产的受益人。这可能会与原保单持有人的意愿不符。因此原保单持有人事先考虑是否要指定继任保单持有人是一件很重要的事情。

正因为保单持有人对保单拥有相当大的权利,个人作为保单持有人可能无法有效将保单与个人风险隔离,比如无法与个人的税务问题相隔离。高净值人士在购买人寿保单时,可以不用个人名义持有,而是通过公司、信托等架构持有。在这样的情况下,保单持有人并非高净值人士个人,而是公司或者受托人,以此将个人风险与保单隔离,起到更好的资产保护作用。关于保单持有结构的知识将在第 7 章中详细阐述。

2.3 被保人

被保人(Insured)是指其生命被保,寿险合同基于其生命的人。若被保人在人寿保险期内去世,则保险公司必须支付身故赔偿金。投保人也可以是被保人,但并非必须如此。一份保单保多人的生命也不鲜见。为了确保人寿保险的有效性,投保人必须对被保人有可保利益(Insurable Interest)。

可保利益指的是保单持有人对其所投保标的具有法律承认的权益或利害关系,即在保险事故发生时,可能遭受损失或失去利益。例如,一个人对自己的生命、其子女后代、配偶、受赡养人、雇员等均有可保利益。如果保单签发时不存在可保利益,则保单一般被认为无效。但是大部分司法管辖区,例如美国、加拿大、新加坡、中国香港等,可保利益仅需要在保单发行时存在即可。如果保单持有人与被保人之间的关系发生变化,以致可保利益不再存在,则该保单仍然有效。例如,丈夫 John 以妻子 Mary 的生命为标的,购买了一份人寿保险,几年之后 Mary 与 John 离婚,即 John 不再对 Mary 的生命有可保利益,但是之前购买的保单仍然有效。①

那么是不是所有保单都必须有可保利益存在呢?这取决于各个司法管辖区的法律规定。加拿大的法律规定,如果被保人以书面形式同意将自己的生命作为被保标的,即使没有可保利益,保单也可生效,当然实操上仍需要有让保险公司认为是合理的理由。通常,此类被保人须在投保申请书上签字,以确认其同意。但是其他司法管辖区,比如中国香

---

① 一般来说,不管是在普通法系国家还是大陆法系国家,夫妻关系的变更导致的可保利益的缺失并不会影响保单本身的有效性;夫妻离婚对保单可能带来的影响是保单利益分割的问题。

港、新加坡等地的法律并没有类似的豁免条款。

有些司法管辖区要求保单持有人在行使某些权利时要得到被保人的同意。比如，如果被保人不同意，保单持有人就不可以随意更改受益人。但在其他司法管辖区，绝大多数人寿保险的相关权利，比如更换受益人、用保单抵押贷款等，均属于保单持有人，且无须经过被保人同意即可行使。

由于保单是以被保人的生命作为标的，核保也是以被保人的健康状况为依据的，一般常见的人寿保险是不可更改被保人的。但是，随着保险产品的不断发展，部分产品，比如储蓄型保险、私募寿险产品，保单成立与否和被保人的健康状况关系不大。因此近年来部分保险公司的部分产品提供了"更改被保人"的选择，从而可以让保单存续的时间更长，更好地实现财富传承。值得一提的是，某些司法管辖区的指数型万能寿险也已经出现能够变更被保人的功能，这是传统寿险产品上的一大突破。

2.3.1 单一被保人

大多数保单是单一被保人人寿保险，也就是说被保人只有一个。只有当此人在保单期限内身故时，身故赔偿金才会被支付。

2.3.2 多被保人

除了单一被保人人寿保险外，还有两种多被保人人寿保险，即基于多人生命的寿险：联名首故（Joint First-to-Die）和联名后故（Joint Last-to-Die）。

2.3.2.1 联名首故

在联名首故的保单中，对两个或两个以上的被保人提供单一保额的保险，并在其中一人去世后，就支付身故赔偿金。当两个或两个以上人士共同承担同一债务的情况下，可适用该类保险。对于家庭来说，联名首故保单是夫妻希望不管谁先去世，仍确保家庭获得照顾的理想解决方案。

举例来说，Jack 和 Rose 是夫妻，一起贷款 100 万美元购买了一栋别墅，共同还款。如果两人之一意外去世，收入缺失，在世的一方就很难负担该还款。为了确保在世的一方在上述情况发生时，可以继续安稳地住在别墅里，不为贷款发愁，夫妇俩购买了一份保额为 100 万美元的联名首故保单，受益人为在世的一方。如果 Rose 去世，Jack 就可以获得身故赔偿金，付清贷款；如果 Jack 去世，则 Rose 将获得身故赔偿金，付清贷款。

对于企业来说，联名首故保单也常被用于买卖协议中，作为高净值人士的企业股权退出方式。我们在第 8 章会对此做详细讨论。

联名首故保单通常要比两份分别承保且总保额相同的单一被保人人寿保险便宜。这是因为在联保的情况下，保险公司只承担支付一份身故赔偿金的风险，而如果购买两份单独的保单，则保险公司需要支付两份身故赔偿金。但是同等情况下，联名首故保单的保费又会比下一节中所述的"联名后故"保单贵。

> **例 2.1**[①]
>
> John 和 Mary 为夫妻。John 45 岁，Mary 43 岁，均不吸烟，两人购买某保险公司的 1 000 万美元保额的保单，保费支付 20 年。保费情况如下：
>
> 联名首故：37.7 万美元/年
>
> 联名后故：27 万美元/年
>
> 由此可见，在同等情况下，联名首故的保费明显高于联名后故的保费。在 1 000 万美元保额的情况下，每年的保费相差超过 10 万美元。

2.3.2.2 联名后故

在联名后故保单中，对两个或两个以上的被保人提供单一保额的保险，并在最后一位被保人去世后，才支付身故赔偿金。当对应的风险将在被保人都去世后才产生的情况下，可适用该类保险。这种保单是为受益人建立或保护遗产的一个良好解决方案，保险收益可以用来支付因身故可能产生的税负，来减轻遗产价值受到的税收侵蚀。在很多司法管辖区，夫妻财产在一方去世时会自动转给另一方，等在世的配偶去世时才会涉及遗产视同售出，计算资本增值税和进入遗产认证程序。

> **例 2.2**
>
> David 和 Cindy 夫妇在 20 年前买了一栋度假屋，增值极大。他们想在去世后将这栋度假屋留给他们的孩子。如果 David 先去世，基于转传规则（Rollover Rules），属于他的份额将转移到妻子 Cindy 名下，并不会产生资本增值税。然而，当 Cindy 也去世后，该度假屋的巨大增值就会被课税。联名后故保单可以确保其遗产中有足够的钱支付这笔税款，使得度假屋可以顺利传承到孩子手中。

对于高净值人士来说，若其重视慈善捐赠，则购买这种保单是一种有效的方法，以夫妻共同的名义，为其喜爱的慈善机构或母校提供善款。

2.3.3 联合保险

联名人寿保险需要与联合保险相区别，联合保险其实是一个市场概念。一些保险公司允许在一份保险合同中购买多份独立的保单，每份保单均有不同的被保人。在这样的保险合同中，每个人都是独立的被保人，任何一位被保人去世，保单都会根据该被保人购

[①] 举例中涉及报价仅为教学参考用。

买的保额赔付给保单受益人。如果有两位被保人,当两位被保人同时去世,联合保险合同就支付两笔单独的身故赔偿金。如果只有一个被保人去世,则另一个被保人在保险合同中的保单仍将继续。

举例来说,John、David、Peter 是同一家公司的三位股东,各自作为被保人,分别投保 200 万美元、800 万美元、1 000 万美元的保单,但放在同一保险合同里,受益人是他们三位的公司。若 David 去世,则 800 万美元赔给公司,但是 John 的 200 万美元保额的保单和 Peter 的 1 000 万美元保额的保单继续保留在合同里。这样做的好处是相对于投保三份单独的保单而言,只需要支付一份管理费,并且可能在保费上有些许折扣。

2.4 受益人

受益人(Beneficiary)指的是当被保人去世后,获得身故赔偿金的人。受益人可以是一个自然人或多个自然人,也可以是法律实体(如公司),还可能是法律关系(如信托)。关于信托作为受益人的安排将在第 7 章中详细讨论。

在受益人的指定方面,部分产品可以指定继任受益人(Contingent Beneficiary)。所对应的情况如下:当身故赔偿金赔付之时,若原受益人已故,那么继任受益人将获得身故赔偿金。这可以避免身故赔偿金赔付给保单持有人或保单持有人的遗产可能引起的税务问题。

若受益人是未成年人①,保险公司就不会直接将身故赔偿金赔付给他,而是需要指定一位受托人,这位受托人可以代表未成年的受益人接受并管理赔付的身故赔偿金,直到其成年。若没有指定受托人,则身故赔偿金将支付给未成年受益人的监护人;若没有监护人,则将支付给法院,法院可能会任命一位监护人/受托人或者由相关公务人员来管理这笔身故赔偿金。该受托人可以是自然人,也可以是一个由持牌信托公司担任信托受托人的家族信托。

举例来说,有一对夫妻生前购买了人寿保险,但是在一场意外中双双英年早逝,一共获赔 1 000 万美元的身故赔偿金,他们的儿子是保单的唯一受益人,但是赔付时儿子只有 10 岁。若在保单中任命了受托人,保险公司就会将 1 000 万美元的身故赔偿金赔付给受托人,由受托人代表 10 岁的儿子接受并管理,比如根据其需求,取出部分支付其生活教育等费用,并在其成年后,将剩余部分转给他。若保单中没有任命受托人,事先父母也没有为儿子指定监护人,保险公司就会将 1 000 万美元赔付给法院,让法院按照具体情况进行相关安排。

指定被保人的配偶、子女、孙子女或父母为保单的受益人不但可以保护身故赔偿金,

---

① 每个司法管辖区对于未成年人的定义不同,比如中国香港、新加坡的规定为未满 18 岁;加拿大是由各省的法律规定的,有些省份为未满 18 岁,另一些省份为未满 19 岁;美国的情况和加拿大大致相同,每个州有不同的规定,同样均为未满 18 岁或 19 岁;澳大利亚为未满 18 岁;百慕大为未满 18 岁;中国大陆为未满 18 岁;中国台湾为未满 20 岁。

还能保护保单本身不受法院裁决的执行和扣押。以上人士通常被称为"受保护的"或"家属类别"受益人，即优先受益人（Primary Beneficiary）。但是在不同司法管辖区，对于保单中现金价值部分是否可以防债权人追讨有不同的规定。

在加拿大，一般来说，若保单的受益人为优先受益人或保单的受益人为不可撤销受益人（Irrevocable Beneficiary），则现金价值可防债权人追讨；若不是以上情况，则现金价值可能会被债权人追讨成功。[①] 而在美国，每个州对于保单中的现金价值防债权人追讨都有各自的规定，每个州对现金价值的保护程度也不一样。[②] 例如，纽约州和佛罗里达州的法律对于保单中的现金价值的保护力度较强；而其他州，比如加利福尼亚州，对其保护力度就较弱。

此外，对于保单中现金价值部分是否可以规避离婚情况下的配偶追索，不同司法管辖区有不同的规定。

举例来说，John 和 Mary 结婚 15 年后离婚，但 John 在离婚前购买过大额人寿保险，并为保单缴纳了不菲的保费，也因此保单里累积了大量的现金价值。在 John 和 Mary 离婚的过程中，保单里的现金价值是否可以作为 John 的个人资产而不被分割，主要取决于保单或保单中的现金价值在该司法管辖区是否被视为婚姻财产。若被视为婚姻财产，则需要分割；若不被视为婚姻财产，则不需要分割。

在中国内地，总体上，保险产品在离婚财产分割时，如果是用婚内财产购买的保险，就属于共同财产；如果是婚前财产或者认定的个人财产购买的保险，就属于个人财产。在美国和加拿大，一般来说，保单或保单中的现金价值会作为家庭资产被分割，但是相关的官司仍然屡见不鲜。中国香港和台湾地区也大致相同，均可能分割。

2.4.1 可撤销受益人

受益人可以是可撤销的，也可以是不可撤销的。除非现有的受益人被指定为不可撤销的，否则保单持有人按照保单中规定的程序，可以在保单签发后变更保单受益人，而且不需要获得现有受益人的同意。

2.4.2 不可撤销受益人

如果保单持有人指定的受益人是不可撤销的，如果保单持有人想更改受益人、从保单中提取现金、转让保单、办理保单贷款或退保，就必须事先获得不可撤销受益人（Irrevocable Beneficiary）的同意，这通常需要向保险公司提交一份书面声明。此外，指定不可撤销受益人的好处是，即使不可撤销受益人不属于优先/受保护的受益人类别，保单也仍可能免受法院裁决的执行和扣押。

[①] 加拿大魁北克省关注的是被保人和受益人的关系，其他省份关注的是保单持有人和受益人的关系；除了关系之外，保单申请的目的、各省的家庭法规定等均可能影响保单中现金价值防债权人追讨的效果。

[②] https://topwholelife.com/can-your-cash-value-life-insurance-be-taken-by-creditors.

2.5　各角色的责、权、利

2.5.1　保险公司

除保单中所述的责任外,保险公司还须根据普通法或成文法承担责任。一般来说,保险公司在处理任何交易时都应对保单持有人履行诚信和公平交易的义务,也有义务如实调查和履行有效的保险索赔。

公平交易——保险公司的诚信和公平交易的责任意味着它必须始终以客户的最大利益行事。这一责任在所有保险合同中都有暗示,防止其在涉及索赔交易中采取不诚实的行为。如果保险公司违反了这一责任,保单持有人就有权起诉要求赔偿损失。

一般的职责——保险公司有法律责任对索赔进行全面调查。它还必须向保单持有人或受益人提供所有必要的信息,以便相关人士可以根据保单条款顺利完成索赔流程。此外,保险公司必须对沟通做出回应,如果索赔被认定有效,则需立即支付赔偿金。

履行保险合同——保险公司必须履行保险合同中列出的任何责任。若保险合同中明确相关人士有超出法律规定外的某些权利,则保险公司有责任履行这些额外的责任。

承保人除了以上义务之外,相对应地也拥有权利。在可争议期(一般可争议期是在人寿保险生效后的一到两年),保险公司可以对在核保过程中所陈述的任何内容进行重新评估。可争议期的存在是为了保护保险公司不受欺诈。如果保险公司发现在申请中有重大错误,保险公司就可以选择调整保费、添加免责条款或取消保单。一旦可争议期结束,该保单就被认为是不可争议的。这意味着除非出现未支付保费或欺诈性的虚假陈述,保险公司不能因为任何其他原因取消保单。除此之外,保险公司当然还有收取保费等保险合同中明确的权利。

2.5.2　投保人(保单持有人)

投保人的义务就相对简单很多,在申请保单时,投保人必须诚实地回答保险公司的问题,并提供真实的佐证文件,以便保险公司进行核保,若存在欺诈行为,则极可能影响保单的有效性以及之后的身故赔偿金的赔付。另外,保单签署发行后,投保人有义务支付保费,以保证保单有效。

当然,投保人可以选择不支付保费,这属于投保人各类权利之一,即退保或终止保单。投保人的权与利一般在保单中均会明确。最常见的有使用现金价值、更改受益人、转让保单、退保、保单贷款、终止保单、恢复保单等。这些在本书第4章和第11章中有详细讨论。需要注意的是,投保人在保单发行后的一段时间内有解除权,即可以选择把保单退回给保险公司以取消保单,获得全额退还已支付的保费。这段时间的长度因司法管辖区及保险公司而异,一般为10~15天,非常类似于我们日常生活购物中的"X 天内无理由退货"政策。同时,投保人有权利获得保单相关的年报,或任何相关信息,以及在提出索赔后,保险公司调查所获得的任何信息。

2.5.3 被保人及受益人

被保人和受益人的权利一般会有前置条件,并不像保险公司和保单持有人那么普遍。

被保人通常只是人寿保险被保生命的标的,没有权利,但是,就像前文提到的,在某些司法管辖区,保单持有人需要其同意才能行使权利,即被保人可以被动否决保单持有人行使相关权利。

普通受益人除了获得身故赔偿金的权利之外,并没有其他权利,但是若受益人为不可撤销受益人,前文同样也提到,当保单持有人想要变更受益人,或做出某些影响保单内利益及有效性的决定时,则都需要不可撤销受益人的同意。

人寿保险的种类

本章要点：
- 介绍不同类型的人寿保险
- 介绍各种类型的人寿保险的特点
- 探索每一种人寿保险的应用

3.1 定期人寿保险

3.1.1 什么是定期人寿保险

定期保险最早出现在1750年左右，是历史上最悠久的人寿保险产品之一，也是目前各司法管辖区人寿保险产品的基础和雏形。定期人寿保险是一种人寿保险的类型，旨在满足保单持有人在一定时期内对保险的需求。定期人寿保险通常会提供10年、20年、30年或至特定年龄（如65岁）的保障期限，部分公司还允许保单持有人自行选择定期保险的期限（Pick-a-Term Insurance），以满足客户个性化、阶段性的保障需求。

保单持有人在选择的保单期限内按时支付保费，若被保人在该期限内身故，则保单的受益人有权领取全额身故赔偿金；反之，保单在到期没有发生任何赔偿，且保单持有人不再支付保险公司核准的续期保费的情况下终止，保费也不会退还。

3.1.2 定期人寿保险的类型

3.1.2.1 定额定期人寿保险

定额定期人寿保险(Level Term Life Insurance)即在保险合同约定期限内的保费不变、保额不变。保险公司一般会在保单起始初期收取高于寿险成本的保费,以此确保期限内的保费固定。被保人在约定期限内去世,指定受益人会获得确定的身故赔偿金。绝大部分保险合同中通常也会包括保证续保条款(Guaranteed Renewable Clause),即定期保险合同到期时不会因被保人的身体健康状况等因素而被拒绝续保或额外增加保费,仅根据续保时被保人的年龄正常调整费率。保单持有人在签订保险合同时应悉数了解和明确有无这一条款。

定额定期人寿保险主要包括:
- 5 年定期险
- 10 年定期险
- 15 年定期险
- 20 年定期险
- 25 年定期险
- 30 年定期险
- 到某特定年龄的定期险

3.1.2.2 逐年续保定期人寿保险

逐年续保定期人寿保险(Yearly Renewable Term Life Insurance)没有明确的投保期限,保费起点较低,但根据被保人的年龄逐年增加。伴随被保人的年龄逐年增长,保费可能会变得非常昂贵甚至难以维持。因此其总体成本要高于固定年限的定期寿险,仅适用于需要极短期保障的客户。目前该类型的保险在市场上的占有率较定额定期寿险也要小很多。

3.1.2.3 降额定期人寿保险

降额定期人寿保险(Decreasing Term Life Insurance)是可续保的定期寿险。保费固定不变,但保额随着时间的推移而逐步降低。因为其总体保费要比同等期限的定额定期寿险便宜,所以它比较适合随时间推移债务减少或未来保障需求逐步降低的人士,比如希望在偿还一定期限房屋贷款时有所保障的人士。

3.1.2.4 退还保费定期人寿保险

退还保费定期人寿保险(Return of Premium Term Life Insurance),是保单到期且没有理赔的前提下,退还保单持有人所支付的保费。当然,因为保险公司会在保单到期退还保费,因此也会就此类保单收取相对于其他定期寿险更高的保费。

3.1.3 定期人寿保险的特点

(1)简单。

保单条款易于理解,保单持有人按期支付保费,在保障期限内被保人过世即可获得身故赔偿金。

(2) 可负担。

定期人寿保险通常又被称为"消费型人寿保险",其保费不会参与投资,因此保单无现金价值,保额也不增长;同时,定期人寿保险仅提供一定阶段的人身保障,所以相对于其他终身寿险的保费更便宜。

(3) 特定需求。

可通过最低的成本满足一定阶段/期限内明确的保障需求,如偿还房屋贷款、维系家庭开支、履行未成年人抚养义务、公司重要员工保障等。

(4) 灵活。

定期人寿保险可以作为独立的保险产品购买,也可以在终身寿险的附加险选项中选购。定期人寿保险可以随时取消,也可以根据保险合同中的保证续保条款锁定初始保额和健康核保等级,在保险合同到期前续保,或从短期转为长期,比如10年定期险转为20年定期险或30年定期险。

(5) 可转换。

大部分定期人寿保险在保障期限内可随时转为终身寿险,而无须重新核保,从而可以根据客户家庭的财务状况满足其传承需求。

3.1.4 定期人寿保险的应用

3.1.4.1 家庭财务保障

定期人寿保险侧重通过支付较便宜的保费,满足一定阶段的家庭保障需求。因此它适用于对家中财富制造者(Breadwinner)的人身保障,或房贷、家庭债务的如期偿付,以确保不会因任何意外风险导致家庭成员的正常生活水平遭受影响。

3.1.4.2 持续的商业保护

(1) 核心员工保护(Key Person Protection)。

定期人寿保险可以将失去核心员工对公司正常运营的影响降到最低,而且成本较低。通过为核心员工购买定期人寿保险,在其去世的情况下,公司可以尽快招募和培训替代人员,缓解因失去他们而给公司带来的财务压力。为公司的核心员工购买定期人寿保险,也可以作为公司的一项福利来吸引和留住人才。

(2) 商业债务/贷款保护(Business Debt/Loans Protection)。

通过购买定期人寿保险并转让给债权人,也可以使债权人确保贷款偿还不会因企业主的意外情况而损失。

> **例3.1**
>
> Henry和Susan是一对夫妇,有两个小孩:5岁的Joshua和2岁的Sara。目

前，Susan 在家里照顾孩子，Henry 在 XYZ 公司担任高级运营经理。出于对孩子未来教育的考虑，这个家庭刚刚搬到一个新城市，并购买了一套 100 万美元的联排别墅，首付为 30 万美元。房产抵押贷款是在 Henry 的名下。

① Henry 购买了一份 20 年的定期人寿保险，保额为 100 万美元。他既是保单持有人，也是被保人，他指定他的妻子和孩子为受益人。如果 Henry 去世，则该保单将作为抵押贷款的保护，同时也是对未成年子女的支持。

② 作为 XYZ 公司的核心员工，Henry 作为被保人还有一份 10 年期的定期人寿保险，身故赔偿金为 200 万美元，XYZ 公司被指定为保单持有人和受益人。XYZ 公司可以将这笔身故赔偿金用于任何目的，包括在 Henry 去世后招聘和培训替代者。

客观地说，基于定期人寿保险的主要特征（见表 3.1），对于高净值人士在家族财富的保全、代际传承以及税务筹划上的需求，定期人寿保险更多是阶段性的桥梁作用。高净值人士仍然需要通过与其他终身寿险的结合设计和使用，方可实现其自身和家庭多方面的综合需求。

表 3.1 定期人寿保险的优点和缺点

优 点	缺 点
• 保单条款简单，易于理解 • 保单便宜可负担 • 在特定时期内提供有保证的保护 • 保单有一定的灵活性，可续保并可转换	• 与永久人寿保险相比，缺乏灵活性 • 续保时费用较高，随着年龄的增长可能会变得更加昂贵 • 超过一定年龄保障就停止了 • 保单在期满后没有价值

3.2 储蓄保险

3.2.1 什么是储蓄保险

储蓄保险（Endowment Insurance）是一种特别的保险产品，当保单到期或被保人身故时，保险公司将会支付一笔金额给到保单持有人或其受益人。储蓄保险将人寿保险保障和储蓄功能结合在一起，通常扮演储蓄计划（Savings Plan）的角色。保单持有人可以选择保费的支付频率和金额，以及保单到期的时间。根据支付的保费，保单到期后，保单持有人将获得一笔保证付款（如本金和利息），和银行定期存款有类似的特点。如果被保人在保单存续期内身故，则根据合同的规定，获得一笔身故赔偿金，这具有寿险保障的特色。

相较于以保障身故风险为主的定期人寿保险,储蓄保险更偏向于一种储蓄计划,并附加少量人寿保险成分。两者的保单期限也是不同的。

在过去的几十年里,北美地区的储蓄保险由于相关税法的变化可能带来的税务问题,受欢迎程度明显下降,大多数人寿保险公司已不再提供此类保险产品。在亚洲国家,并没有上述问题,储蓄保险仍比较流行。

3.2.2 储蓄保险的类型

除了普通的储蓄保险以外,还有以下两类较常见的储蓄保险变体。

3.2.2.1 定期生存储蓄保险

定期生存储蓄保险(Pure Endowment Insurance)通常要求被保人在保单到期时仍然存活,方可支付保证支付金,如果被保人在保单规定期限内去世则无权获得赔偿金。定期生存储蓄保险通常与定期人寿保险组合销售,变成所谓的"两全保险"。

3.2.2.2 定期派息储蓄保险

相对于其他储蓄保险,定期派息储蓄保险(Anticipated Endowment Insurance)每隔一段时间会支付一笔金额给保单持有人,最后的到期保证支付金或身故赔偿金不会受定期派息影响,倘若保单到期或被保人中途身故,保险公司在已经派息的基础上仍会支付保证支付金或身故赔偿金。

3.2.3 储蓄保险的特点

(1)保障期是保单发行以后的一段有限时间;

(2)保单到期或被保人身故,保险公司将会支付一笔到期保证金或身故赔偿金;

(3)现金价值增长较快,在一段时间后即可退保兑现;

(4)身故赔偿金一般为保单的实时现金价值,除非另有规定;

(5)产品分为参与型或非参与型,参与型的储蓄保险将能获得分红,其身故赔偿金等于原始保额加上分红(具体分红原理请参考3.3节)。

3.2.4 储蓄保险的应用

3.2.4.1 子女教育

储蓄保险经常被用作子女的教育金,大多数情况下,保单的被保人是孩子本身,而保单的投保人和所有人则是父母。和一般储蓄保险一样,在保单到期时或孩子不幸身故时,保险公司将一次性支付保证金或身故赔偿。

3.2.4.2 储蓄/投资目的

储蓄保险因其快速累积现金价值的特点,经常被用作储蓄或投资;储蓄保险在让投保人为特定目的进行储蓄的同时也能使其家庭在面临具体人身风险时获得保障。

3.3 终身寿险

3.3.1 什么是终身寿险

终身寿险（Whole Life Insurance）为被保人的整个生命阶段提供保障。终身寿险保单中会包含现金价值的积累。具体来说，就是保单持有人缴付的保费在支付保险成本之后，剩余的部分转换成保单的现金价值。保险公司会根据公司的盈利情况派发收益/红利，伴随时间的推移累积为保单中的现金价值和身故赔偿金，因此可以帮助客户实现资产传承的意愿。

3.3.2 终身寿险的类型

终身寿险可以分为两大类：参与型分红终身寿险和非参与型分红终身寿险。

参与型分红终身寿险含有保证利益部分和非保证利益部分。保单持有人支付的保费将共同置于由保险公司统一管理的资金池中进行投资。当保单中产生收入盈余时，保险公司将首先按照当地保监会对于保单准备金的监管要求，将其中部分盈余放入保单准备金留存。然后，选择将剩余盈余的全部或部分以年度红利的形式派发给每位分红保险保单持有人。年度红利使保单持有人有机会分享保险公司的利润。年度红利为非保证红利，每年由保险公司宣布是否派发、派发红利的利率及相应金额。保单持有人可以使用年度派发红利积累保单的现金价值或购买更多的保额。有关红利选项详见本章后续介绍。

如果保险公司对其参与型分红终身寿险的设定回报未达到预期，并导致收入不足（Revenue Shortfall），则由保险公司独自承担收入不足的负担，而保单持有人无须承担此项风险，也不会因此被要求额外支付保费或降低保额。

非参与型分红终身寿险与参与型分红终身寿险最大的区别就是：参与型分红终身寿险的保单持有人有可能通过保单年度红利的派发，分享保险公司的收入盈余（Revenue Surplus），而非参与型分红终身寿险的持有人则无法分享。当非参与型分红终身寿险产生收入盈余时，保险公司也是首先按照当地保监会对于保单准备金的监管要求，将其中部分盈余分配进入保单准备金留存。然后将剩余盈余部分作为利润进入保险公司的留存收益（Retained Earnings），从而增加公司股东的权益，及/或作为应课税股东分红支付给保险公司股东。同参与型分红终身寿险一样，如果保险公司对非参与型分红终身寿险的设定回报未达到预期，并可能产生收入不足，则保险公司将自行承担该收入不足的负担，而不会对保单及保单持有人的利益造成影响。

由于参与型分红终身寿险相对于非参与型分红终身寿险而言，有机会参与分配保险公司的收入盈余，因此参与型分红终身寿险所收取的保费也相比同类非参与型分红终身寿险要高一些。本节主要介绍在各司法管辖区保险市场占有率更高的参与型分红终身寿险。

(1) 终身寿险保费的构成及定价。

终身寿险的保费定价基于对死亡率成本(Mortality Cost)、费用(Expense)和保费预计投资回报(Investment Return)的长期假设。

死亡率成本,或纯保险净成本(Net Cost of Pure Insurance, NCPI),大致相当于保险公司支付保单身故赔偿金的成本。保单的年度死亡率成本是通过将保单的面额乘以被保人在一个保单年度内的死亡概率来计算的。由于身故赔偿金是在被保人一生中的某个时间点支付的(除非被保人提前退保),保险公司在计算终身寿险保单的保费时,会将累积的年度死亡成本分摊到预期的人寿保险合同期内。

保险公司运营费用包括营销费用、工资、佣金、承保费用、签发和管理费用、索赔调查费用、索赔支付、股东红利等。保费定价还会考虑保险公司在保单有效期内对保费进行长期投资的预计投资回报。

(2) 终身寿险的保费支付。

终身寿险通常有两种保费支付的方式。

① 一次性支付保费。保单持有人可以选择一次性支付保费,或称趸交(Lump-sum Pay),且保单终身有效。由于在高税负司法管辖区采用趸交会受到该司法管辖区税法对于保单中现金价值累积额度的制约而产生税务问题,因此趸交在离岸地司法管辖区的终身寿险保单中比较常见。趸交也是比较受高净值人士青睐的一种保费支付方式。因为高净值人士希望通过趸交达成保单初期现金价值最大额度,并随时间推移更高速地积累,从而可以通过保费融资溢价获得保单现金价值和身故赔偿金的最大杠杆效应。

② 期交保费。期交保费选项允许保单持有人选择在规定的期限内支付一定次数的保费,如10年或20年,或支付到特定的年龄(如65岁或100岁),保单终身有效。

(3) 影响参与型分红终身寿险红利派发的因素。

参与型分红终身寿险保单的保费进入分红账户(Par Account)——这是一个专门的资金池,由保险公司管理和投资。根据分红账户的投资回报和其他因素(包括保单索赔率、退保率、管理费等),保险公司决定是否支付红利以及每个保单周年的红利金额。

参与型分红终身寿险保单通常的运作方式如图3.1所示。

分红账户的进项有:保单持有人缴纳的保费、投资收益、保单持有人的贷款还款和贷款利息。

分红账户的出项有:派发给保单持有人的分红、股东分红、投资亏损、运营支出、税项、保单持有人的借款、支付给受益人的保险赔偿。

影响分红的因素有:投资表现(利差)、死亡率(死差)、支出和税项(费差)。

① 利差。

若保险公司在设计保险产品时,预期利率为4%,在年末结算时实际投资回报率是7%,则3%就是利差益;反之则为利差损。

3 人寿保险的种类

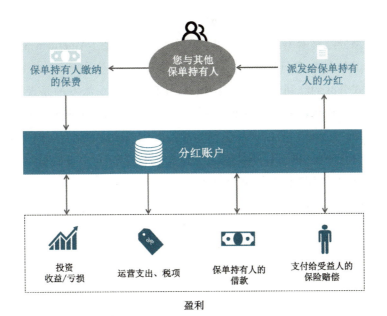

图 3.1 参与型分红终身寿险保单通常的运作方式

② 死差。

若保险公司预期今年每 1 万名客户中有 20 人身故,需理赔 2 000 万美元,但实际只有 15 人身故并理赔了 1 500 万美元,则剩余的 500 万美元为死差益;反之则为死差损。

③ 费差。

若保险公司预期今年行政管理支出为 1 000 万美元,实际只花了 800 万美元,省下的 200 万美元则为费差益;反之则为费差损。

某司法管辖区分红账户红利影响因素如图 3.2 所示。从图中可以看出,在影响分红高低的因素中,死差和费差的占比份额都较小,主要决定因素是保险公司的投资管理专业水平及长期整体经营机制。

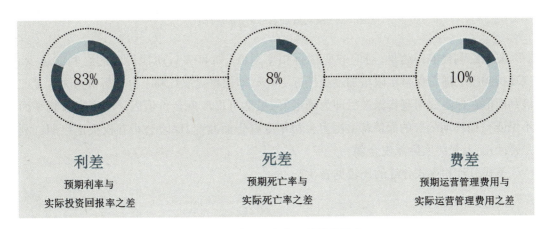

图 3.2 某分红账户红利影响因素

· 23 ·

(4)参与型分红终身寿险的分红类型。

通常,参与型分红终身寿险的分红可以区分为美式分红(American Style Dividends)和英式分红(British Style Dividends)。

简言之,美式分红的红利称为现金红利(Cash Dividend),派发的是现金;英式分红的红利称为复归红利(Reversionary Bonus),派发的是面值(Face Value)。两类分红都拥有终期红利(Terminal Bonus),有的产品也称为额外红利(Extra Bonus),但是美式分红与英式分红的终期红利也有区别。保单持有人可以根据保险合同中有关分红规定(Dividend Provisions)的描述基本判断相关保单的分红类型。

因为美式分红由保险公司以现金形式派发,所以红利可以随时支取,也可用于抵缴保费、累积生息或额外购买保额等。终期红利是用以鼓励保单持有人长期持有保单所派发的一种红利,通常在投保若干年(如第十年)后才开始派发,只有在身故或退保时才可提取。美式分红所派发的红利皆以现金形式存在,公司宣告派发红利后,红利即为确定值,提取时也无须折价。

英式分红每年所派发的复归红利是面值,相当于将派发的红利购买成了额外的保额附加到原保单上(可以理解为股票所派发红利的形式是增派额外的股票),并可以通过分红保单的分红机制衍生额外的红利(可以理解为股票所派发的股息在未来还可继续获取股息)。

单纯从分红机制来看,英式分红的投资效率优于美式分红。不过,由于这部分红利已经转化为保额,不能随意支取,只有在身故或退保的时候才能够取出,因此英式分红的流动性较美式分红差。同时,英式分红在保单早期退保时,红利需要经过一定的折价(见图3.3)。

图3.3 英式分红退保时的折价机制

复归红利提取得越早,对应的变现折扣率越低(如80%),所能提取的红利就越少。变现折扣率会随着保单年限增加逐步接近100%,即保单提取红利不再有折价损失。复归红利面值在保险公司宣告派发后即为确定值(虽然可提取现金价值因浮动变现折扣率而不保证);而终期分红的面值却会随着公司年度宣告而改变,保险公司有权决定终期红利是否派发,及最终实际派发金额。

美式分红和英式分红的比较见表3.2。

表 3.2 美式分红和英式分红比较

	美式分红		英式分红	
	年度分红	终期红利	复归红利	终期红利
频　　次	年度	从某一特定年份	年度	从某一特定年份
派发模式	现金	现金	面额	面额
累积模式	分红累积	不保证宣派	面额增长	不保证宣派
取款时间	任何时间	理赔或退保时	理赔或退保时	理赔或退保时
变现折价	无	无	有	有
现金流灵活性	高	低	低	低
投资回报预期	较低 保守的投资策略	较高 激进的投资策略	较高 激进的投资策略	较高 激进的投资策略

（5）现金红利选项。

参与型分红终身寿险保单持有人有权参与分红的派发，对获得的分红也有多种用途的选择，常见的有如下 5 种选择。

① 增购保额（Paid-Up Addition，PUA），也叫增额缴清保险，即用保单周年日所派发的红利购买额外的保额，而无须再支付额外的保费。这种红利的复式增长可让保单的身故赔偿金和现金价值随时间推移而递增。通常为分红用途的默认选项。

② 优化保额（Enhanced Coverage），也叫提升保额，即在每一个保单周年所获得的红利都将被用来购买年度续保定期保险（Yearly Term Insurance），当分红超过年度续保定期保险的费用后，多出的部分被用于购买增额缴清保险。两者相加的额度等于保单中优化保险的额度。年度续保定期保险将随着时间的推移最终被永久的增额缴清保险取代。优化保险额度拥有终身保证。这意味着即使未来红利不够支付年度续保定期保险，优化保险额度和基本保险额度不变。

③ 现金支付（Cash Payment），即每个保单年度的分红以现金形式支付给保单持有人。因为每年的分红都是拿出来的，所以保额不会增长，维持在基本保证保额。

④ 红利存款（Dividends on Deposit），即保单赚取的红利将自动存入保单中一个类似储蓄存款的账户，保单持有人可以随时提取这些红利。在这个账户中的红利，将按保险公司设定的利率（浮动）每天赚取按年计算的复利。

⑤ 年度保费减免（Annual Premium Reduction），即保费首先需要按年支付，然后通过保单中取得的红利来减免在下个保单年度需要支付的保费。若派发的红利高于年保费，那么多出的额度将存入一个在保单内每天都赚取利息的储蓄账户中，该账户中的资金可以随时取出。

（6）保单现金价值。

参与型分红终身寿险具有现金价值，保单持有人在有生之年可以使用这些现金价值。除非直接从保单中提取，否则保单的现金价值将随时间推移而增长累积，累积后的保单价值即为确定值，即使市场行情下滑，也会得到保护。保单现金价值的使用方式如下。

① 保单贷款（Policy Loan）。保单持有人以保单中的现金价值为抵押向保险公司借钱，通常借款最高额度可达保单退保现金价值（Cash Surrender Value，CSV）的90%。虽然保单没有特定的还款时间，但保险公司按自行设定的利率按天收取利息。保单的保额、现金价值增长及可能派发的红利不受影响。若未清偿贷款，则在保单退保所支付的现金价值或身故赔偿金中，扣除尚未偿还的贷款金额及利息。部分保单贷款可能会触发税务问题，视不同司法管辖区保单贷款的税务原则做相应处理。

② 自动垫交保费贷款（Automatic Premium Loan）。绝大部分参与型分红终身寿险提供自动保费贷款选项，即从保单现金价值中扣除逾期保费以避免保单失效，相当于作为需付利息的保单贷款处理，前提是保单有充足的现金价值。若未清偿贷款，则在保单退保所支付的现金价值或身故赔偿金中，扣除尚未偿还的贷款金额及利息。自动保费贷款可重复使用，直到保单贷款加利息等于保单设定的最高限额（通常为保单退保现金价值的90%~100%），如在30天宽限期后仍然未偿清贷款，则保险公司将扣除贷款及利息后剩余的退保现金价值（如果有）支付给保单持有人，然后保单失效。

③ 第三方抵押贷款（Collateral Loan）。保单持有人以保单中的现金价值为抵押向第三方金融机构借钱。抵押贷款的形式属于债务而非保险合同的选项，所以不会影响保单自身现金价值和身故赔偿金的持续增长，也不会触发税务问题。抵押贷款需根据申请人的财务健康状况决定贷款额度，通常最高贷款额度不超过当期保单现金价值的85%。保单持有人每年需支付贷款利息，但贷款本金将在身故赔偿金中一次性扣除。

④ 直接取款（Withdrawing Directly from a Policy）。直接从保单支取现金价值相当于部分退保（Partial Surrender），是一种保单处置。因此当支取金额超过保单当期调整后成本基数（Adjusted Cost Base，ACB）的部分，会有可能作为应课税收入进行年度申报。这种方式会减缓保单内现金价值和身故赔偿金累积增长的速度，因此并非最佳选择。需视保单持有人的个人税务身份所在司法管辖区、直接支取金额、当期的基准利率（Prime Interest Rate）等因素综合考量该支取方式的最佳适用时点。

⑤ 减额缴清（Reduced Paid-Up）。减额缴清允许保单持有人使用保单中已累计的现金价值作为一次性保费，买断已缴保费所对应的保额，买断后不再需要支付保费，同时保证一定保额的终身额度。可买断的保额取决于退保现金价值的多少和被保人年龄。减额缴清时不需要重新核保。

3.3.3 终身寿险的特点

（1）终身保障。

顾名思义，相对于定期保险，终身寿险提供的是终身保障。

（2）多重保证。

终身寿险所提供的多重保证涵盖保证及固定保费、保证身故赔偿金以及最低保证现金价值。

（3）潜在分红。

参与型分红终身寿险有机会参与保险公司的盈余分红，使保单在保证现金价值的基础上逐步累积更多保单价值和与现金价值对应的非丧失性福利（Nonforfeiture Benefit），供保单持有人灵活使用（详见本章后续讲解和第4章）。

（4）投资托管。

终身寿险的保费去除支付的保单成本外，余下的由保险公司的专业团队统一负责投资方向和策略调整，无须保单持有人自行管理，省心省力。

（5）税筹功能。

对于高税负司法管辖区所签发的终身寿险保单，现金价值在保单中的累积增长作为应计收入可以税务递延。

当然，由于终身寿险的上述特点，它成为在人寿保险产品中同等保额下保费最高的产品，固定保费和缴期也限制了其灵活性。

3.3.4 终身寿险的应用

终身寿险由于其保证特性，随时间推移可实现保单现金价值和身故赔偿金的累积增长。在某些高税负司法管辖区利用终身寿险保单可实现税务筹划功能，通常用于满足高净值人士家庭财富延税且稳健增值，以及代际传承规划方面的需求。特别是在征收代际传承税（包含遗产税）的司法管辖区，终身寿险中累积增长并免税赔付的身故赔偿金，可以实现与其他形式家庭资产增值的匹配，从而最大化地降低其他形式资产在人过世时视同处置的资本增值税（Deemed Disposition Capital Gain Tax）。另外，通过对保单现金价值的支取（高税负司法管辖区的终身寿险需结合税务设计支取方式），也可作为退休收入的补充或安全投资杠杆等使用，可谓中高净值人士不可或缺的"福利"（见例3.2[①]）。

> **例3.2**
>
> John现年50岁，健康状况良好，丧偶，有两个孩子——20岁的David和15岁的Emily。多年来，John成功地经营着自己的生意，还通过购买几处商业地产和通过金融机构投资来积累家庭财富。根据他的家族健康史，John认为他至少可以活到85岁。他计划在60岁时退休，并考虑购买一份分红型终身寿险，主要

[①] 示例数字均为教学使用，不代表任何地区、保险公司、具体产品；相关税务效果也只能作为案例参考，不同地区有不同的税务政策。

出于以下目的。

① 遗产规划：John 估计在他过世后可能会有大约 2 000 万美元的视同处置资本增值，包括他企业的公平市场价值（Fair Market Value，FMV）和他的个人资产（如投资物业和基金）。如果是这种情况，则可能会有至少 500 万美元的最终纳税责任。

② 退休收入补充：John 希望在退休后能保持他的生活方式和标准。除了来自投资组合的每年固定收入外，他希望能够利用保单的现金价值每年额外获得 10 万美元。

③ 税务优化：除了利用保单的现金价值来补充他的退休收入外，John 还想利用现金价值作为他投资组合中的节税杠杆。

④ 不被挑战和不被攫取的遗产：John 想把他的保单身故赔偿金的 10% 留给儿童医院基金会，他自己的孩子在童年时曾受益于此。利用有指定受益人和指定比例的人寿保险可能是确保 John 的遗产既不会受其继承人质疑，也不会被其债权人扣押（如果受益人是优先受益人或不可撤销受益人）的方法之一。

在与他的顾问讨论后，John 购买了一个分红型人寿保险计划，保额为 350 万美元，年保费为 25 万美元，支付期为 10 年。

这个计划可以负担 John 的最后纳税责任，并满足他的退休收入补充需求。按照这个计划，预计从 61 岁到 85 岁，他可以每年提取 10 万美元来满足他的退休收入需求；在他 85 岁时，保额将增加到 550 万美元，所以可以用 500 万美元支付他的税款，并留下 50 万美元给儿童医院基金会。

此外，John 可以通过抵押贷款或其他方式——如即时融资安排（Immediate Financing Arrangement，IFA）——使用保单中的累积现金价值，以达到税务优化效果，因为贷款利息可以 100% 作为投资收入（资本增值收入除外）的费用扣除。最后，John 希望通过该人寿保险计划实现他的传承不被挑战或攫取的意愿。

3.4 万能寿险

3.4.1 什么是万能寿险

万能寿险产生于 1978 年，起源并盛行于美国。万能寿险是一类可提供终身保障并有较大灵活性的永久人寿保险。虽然和终身寿险一样同属于永久产品，但通过购买万能寿险产品，在保单中累积的现金价值可维持支付保单成本的情况下，客户可以根据其投资目标和风险承受能力灵活选择保费成本的支付方式、身故赔偿金的支付方式和投资选项。

3.4.2 万能寿险的类型

3.4.2.1 传统型万能寿险

传统型万能寿险(Traditional UL)的基础资产主要投资于各种债券。资产配置由保险公司管理,一般与市场利率挂钩,具体收益率由保险公司决定,并按利率计入保单。保险公司通常为这种万能寿险保单提供最低的保证回报率。如果保险公司的年度市场回报率高于保证回报率,保单持有人就可以获得相应的利益;如果保单持有人未能按时支付保费,保险公司就会从保单的现金价值中扣除保费。

3.4.2.2 指数型万能寿险

指数型万能寿险(Indexed UL,IUL)与各种指数的表现挂钩,投资收益有上限,下跌有保底。通常,这种类型的万能寿险保单有两个账户:固定账户和指数账户。指数账户与股票指数或一些指数的组合挂钩,使保单具有更大的上升潜力(详见第3.5节)。

3.4.2.3 投资型万能寿险

投资型万能寿险(Variable UL,VUL)也叫变额万能寿险,此类产品允许保单持有人在保险公司提供的各种与市场挂钩的投资组合中选择和管理自己的投资,包括互惠基金、债券和股票,或者他们可以委托投资经理代为管理。投资回报没有上限或保证回报,所以要求保单持有人有更高的投资能力和更高的风险承受能力,自己充当经纪人的角色(详见第3.6节)。

3.4.2.4 保证型万能寿险

保证型万能寿险(Guaranteed UL,GUL)采用了传统型万能寿险的架构,但去掉了其中的市场风险因素。无论市场如何表现,保费都保持不变,因为在保单持有人签署保单时,该计划的利率已被纳入保费。保证型万能寿险保单是唯一一种保单持有人不必担心支付了保费后有可能失去保障的万能寿险产品。这就是为什么保证型万能寿险也被称为"无失效保证万能寿险",以对冲传统型万能寿险的保单失效风险,即保单内的现金价值无法支付保险成本和费用,因为投资利率一直低于保单开始时的初始利率,或者因为保单持有人未能及时支付保费。传统型万能寿险中的现金价值部分通常通过不同的投资策略来积累,而保证型万能寿险保单通常现金价值很少或没有。在这一点上,保证型万能寿险与定期人寿保险最为相似。

定期人寿保险只为被保人提供一定年限的保障,通常是10年、20年或30年,而保证型万能寿险的期限则持续到被保人的生命终止。因此,它的主要特点是以较低的保费为被保人提供终身保护。例如,为被保人购买一份保证型万能寿险保单,保额为1 000万美元,保费支付期限为10年,年保费为25万美元。只要保费如期支付,无论市场是崩溃还是上涨,也无论被保人在什么时候去世,受益人都将获得1 000万美元的身故赔偿金。保证型万能寿险保单不提供灵活的保费支付或身故赔偿金支付选项。然而,对于那些主要寻求终身保护、不太关心现金价值的"投资"部分的人来说,它是一个不错的选择。

3.4.3 万能寿险的特点

3.4.3.1 透明性

对于定期寿险和终身寿险来说,保费中的死亡率成本、费用和投资回报是捆绑式定价的,保单持有人无法知道保费中各项构成的比例。参与型分红终身寿险也是由保险公司每年决定是否派发红利及派发金额。万能寿险保单会披露保费中死亡率成本和费用支出的计算方式,以及适用于保单的任何投资形式的回报率计算依据。传统万能寿险保费运作原理如图3.4所示。

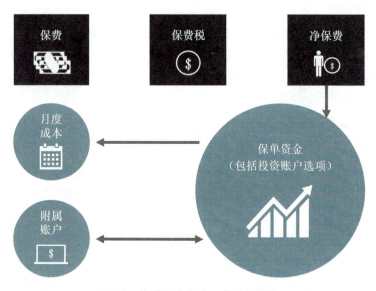

图3.4 传统万能寿险保费运作原理

3.4.3.2 灵活性

保单持有人可以根据家庭财富在不同阶段的管理需求,以及投资风险的承受能力等灵活选择保险成本的支付方式、身故赔偿金的支付方式和投资选项等,定制符合自身家庭需要的万能寿险计划。

(1)身故赔偿金支付方式选项。

① 固定性身故赔偿金(Level Death Benefit)。其身故赔偿金在购买万能寿险产品时已约定好固定不变,在确保保费如期支付且保单有效的情况下,保单受益人将获得约定的身故赔偿金或账户价值,两者中取高者。

② 增长性身故赔偿金(Increasing Death Benefit)。其身故赔偿金总额为购买万能寿险时的初期身故赔偿金,加上现金累积的价值。不同司法管辖区的万能寿险保单还可以设计更多身故赔偿金的支付方式选项,如身故赔偿金赔偿时同时返还累积交付的保费(Death Benefit Plus Cumulated Premiums),或身故赔偿金赔偿时涵盖抗通胀功能(Indexed Death Benefit)等。当然也可以视客户财务状况或保障需要,选择降低身故赔偿金的支付。

(2)自主投资选项。

部分万能寿险产品,如指数型万能险和投资型万能险提供了较为广泛的投资选项。保单持有人可以根据自己对投资收益的预期及风险承受能力,选择在万能寿险保单中投一个或多个标的,并将保费予以不同比例的分配,保险公司会根据不同的投资选项收取管理费用。

(3)可更换被保人选项。

在某些司法管辖区,部分万能寿险保单允许更换被保人,这对公司客户来说特别有利。由于公司的关键人物或股东可能因各种因素而改变,这种选择为公司客户提供了灵活性,以确保公司的持续运营,以及家族企业的传承。

3.4.3.3 流动性

部分万能寿险产品可以在保单生效后即提供较高的现金价值,保单持有人可在需要时获取其现金价值。为避免产生税务问题及损害到保单现金价值的累积,通常可以将保单作为抵押品/担保给金融机构和/或债权人,根据保单价值来进行杠杆融资或保费融资以扩大家庭财富的积累,也可作为商业贷款为家族企业发展所用。

3.4.4 万能寿险的应用

作为长期寿险的一种,万能寿险因其较高的灵活性和透明性以及相对终身寿险更低的保费而在近些年受到了市场的欢迎。但从市场层面我们也看到,大部分万能寿险的投保人更看重的是其带来的投资功能和背后所蕴含的税务筹划作用。万能寿险衍生出多个分支类型,各个司法管辖区的万能寿险的内在含义和使用场景也并不一致。比如美国不同的万能寿险产品几乎可以满足所有传统上对寿险产品的需求,而加拿大则更偏重自主投资的部分,中国香港则经常把万能寿险和保费融资结合起来使用。不同类型和不同司法管辖区的万能寿险的应用场景将在相应的章节详细阐述。

3.5 指数型万能寿险

3.5.1 什么是指数型万能寿险

指数型万能寿险是万能寿险的一个衍生产品,于1997年正式出现。指数型万能寿险具有现金价值,并在身故赔偿金和保费支付方面有一定的灵活性。如果保单持有人的需求或预算发生变化,则可在一定范围内调整身故赔偿金和保费支付金额。简言之,它可以视作一种混合形式的寿险,既具备传统万能寿险的基本特点,又兼顾投资型万能寿险的上行机会,并可规避下行风险。

指数型万能寿险保单中通常包含两个账户:固定账户(Fixed Account)和指数账户(Indexed Account)。所支付的保费在扣除保费成本后,会根据保单持有人意向任选一个账户投入或按比例分配至两个账户中。指数型万能寿险保单的现金价值增长与股票市场的指数挂钩,如标普500指数、恒生指数和欧洲斯托克指数等,也可以与几个指数的组合挂钩,当然也可以仅选择固定账户进行投资。需要注意的是,尽管保单现金价值的增长是基于指数的表现,但不代表保单直接参与任何二级市场的股票或基金投资。事实上,指数型万能寿险还是主要投资在各类债券中,相关挂钩的指数只是计算现金价值收益的参数,并且指数型万能寿险会提供一个现金价值的保底保障(Floor Rate)并限定收益上限(Cap Rate)。

3.5.2 指数型万能寿险的运作方式

3.5.2.1 固定账户

与传统的万能寿险类似,指数型万能寿险的固定账户会公布一个固定利率,保单当年现金价值收益基于该固定利率计算,之后每年公布当年利率,并可调整上浮或下降区间,大部分指数型万能寿险产品的固定利率账户的最低保证率为2%~3%。

3.5.2.2 指数账户

进入指数型万能寿险指数账户的保费所产生的收益将与指数表现挂钩,根据指数的涨跌对比计入收益。保险公司可以选择并设定所挂钩指数的组合及各个指数的参与率和收益封顶率,也可由保单持有人自行选择不同的参数。需要注意的是,指数型万能寿险中的收益率主要有以下3个指标,与指数的实际表现有所差异。

(1)封顶收益率(Index Cap Rate)。

封顶收益率用于计算指数账户的最高利率。保险公司在每个计息周期前针对每个指数计息分段的封顶收益率进行公布并有权调整。不同司法管辖区、不同保险公司及不同指数策略所采用的封顶收益率均不相同。2023年发行指数型万能寿险产品的相关市场公开的封顶收益率通常为8%~12%。这也意味着即使指数市场暴涨,也并不代表保单的现金价值同步无限增长,因为会受限于保险合同中有关封顶收益率的约定(见图3.5)。

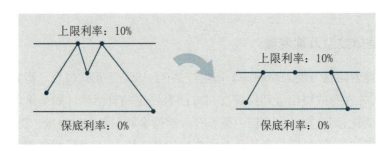

图3.5 指数策略上限原理

(2)保底收益率(Index Floor Rate)。

保底收益率指用于计算指数账户的最低利率。指数账户会按照保单承诺的收益保底利率进行保障托底,市面上的保底利率一般是0~1%,即如果指数暴跌,也会托底为不低于0%。但这并不意味着为保单失效托底,当保单中累积的现金价值因利率持续低于预期,而被持续支付的保费成本和费用消耗殆尽时,保单持有人仍有可能需要补缴保费方可维持保单的效力。

(3)指数参与率(Participating Rate)。

指数参与率指计算指数账户收益率时每个指数的参与比例。保险公司也有权在每个指数周期前针对每个指数计息分段的参与率进行调整,但调整幅度不得低于保险合同中约定的指数最低参与率。目前市场上的指数参与率一般介于25%~140%。

如图3.6所示,某指数挂钩的保单周年收益率通过参与率计算后,为6%×60%=3.6%。

图3.6 某指数挂钩的保单年收益率计算

少数指数型万能寿险保单中还会有一个约定的利差进入保单最终收益率的计算。举例来说,如果指数上涨10%,但保险合同中规定有4%的利差,那么指数最终收益率为6%。如果该指数今年仅上涨2%,由于涨幅小于利差,则按下限利率做收益托底。

指数值的涨跌按设定的不同周期点对点进行比较,最终得到账户的指数收益率。比较常见的有年度点对点(Annual Point-to-Point)、月度点对点(Monthly Point-to-Point)、多指数点对点(Multi-Index Point-to-Point)这3种方式。

① 年度点对点。即以保费进入账户开始投资的时间为初始点,与一年后的指数值对比涨跌。如果指数上涨,则以不超过封顶收益率的数值作为指数收益率;反之,如果指数下跌,则以不低于保底收益率的数值作为指数收益率。有些指数型万能寿险产品会设定周期为2年的指数涨跌对比,相应也会约定更高的封顶收益率或参与率。

② 月度点对点。即封顶收益率以每个月为单位,以每月固定时点与过去1年对应月份的固定时点对比涨跌。如果指数上涨,则以不超过月封顶收益率的数值作为指数收益率;但如果指数下跌,下不保底,则之后以周期1年为限将12个月收益率加总求和。若总和为负值,则收益率为0%(即下限利率);若总和为正值,则为实际指数收益率。

某指数策略每月的封顶收益率为2%,每月无下限利率,则指数年收益率为3.11%(见图3.7)。

③ 多指数点对点。即以12个月为一个指数周期,根据各项指数表现的绩优等级对应分配由高到低的参与率。比如,以与3个指数挂钩,参与率100%举例,选取最佳绩优指数比重为50%,第二绩优指数比重为30%,第三绩优指数比重为20%,再汇总为当年指数收益率,并受制于保险合同中有关封顶收益率、下限利率以及参与率的约定(见表3.3)。

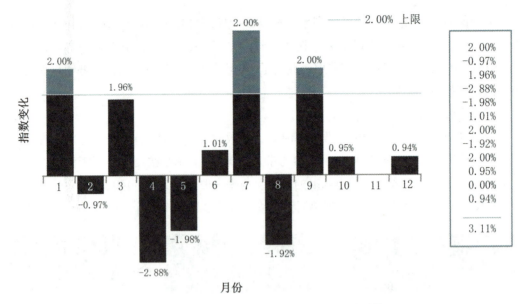

图 3.7 某月度点对点指数策略的年收益率计算

表 3.3 某多指数点对点指数策略的年收益率计算

标普 500 初值	1 000.00
标普 500 末值	925
指数变化	−7.50%
罗素 2000 初值	1 000.00
罗素 2000 末值	1 200.00
指数变化	20.00%
欧洲斯托克 50 初值	2 000.00
欧洲斯托克 50 末值	2 100.00
指数变化	5.00%
最优指数	50%×20.00%
第二优指数	30%×5.00%
第三优指数	20%×(−7.50%)
综合变化值	10.00%
上限利率	11.00%
参与率	100.00%
指数收益率	10.00%

3.5.3 指数型万能寿险的特点

指数型万能寿险属于终身寿险的范畴,因此它具有传统寿险的基本保障功能。同时在确保保单有效的前提下,保单中现金价值的累积也可以供保单持有人支取使用。

除以上终身寿险的一般特点,指数型万能寿险还有以下特点和优势。

（1）更灵活。

保单持有人可以根据自己的风险承受能力选择投资策略,也可根据个人情况调整保额的大小,还可定制适合自己的保单附加条款。保费支付频率和金额方面也比较灵活。

（2）收益有保证。

当市场环境下,股指下跌成负数时,保险公司仍可承诺0~2%的保底收益。

（3）有指数上行的回报潜力。

指数型万能寿险的产品特点就是追踪指数走势,在市场上行时有较高的增长潜力。过去90年间标普500指数年均回报率接近10%,因此增长潜力较大。相比之下,分红型终身寿险提供的分红利率因采用的投资策略不同而偏低。

（4）有税务优化选项。

指数型万能寿险的保单持有人不会因为保单现金价值随时间推移增加而需要支付保单增值税（Policy Gain Tax）,在支取保单现金价值时也可以通过贷款的形式最大限度规避税收问题。因此,可以将指数型万能寿险作为带有终身保障的退休计划账户使用。

任何事物都有两面性,需要提示的是,指数型万能寿险产品结构相对于终身寿险和传统万能寿险更为复杂,其保单实际指数收益率受封顶收益率、保底收益率、指数参与率的影响,同时不同保险公司所采取的指数策略、计算方式、年度利率调整策略也不尽相同,因此指数型万能寿险收益率存在更多的不确定性。指数型万能寿险保险计划书所演示的收益率仅基于未包含指数股息分红的历史回报来假设推算而出,并且封顶收益率也在市场上行时限制了保单获得更多回报的潜力,因此保单持有人应该在对指数型万能寿险产品有充分认知的基础上参与投保,以降低保单实际收益与预期收益不符的落差感。

3.5.4 指数型万能寿险的应用

指数型万能寿险通常被认为是较先进的人寿保险产品,因其保单设计灵活、同等保额下保费较终身寿险便宜、兼具保单收益托底等特点,适用于很多方面,如终身保障、退休收入规划、资产保护、保险信托、财富传承、遗产规划等领域。不同司法管辖区、不同保险公司的指数型万能寿险产品,也有不同的性能表现和适用领域。综合来说,指数型万能寿险适合的群体包括:

① 希望参与股市和股指投资,但是不想直接承受股票亏损的风险,寻找保底保障的人士;

② 希望在世灵活取钱补充退休收入,去世后留下大笔免税现金遗产给家人的人士;
③ 希望通过指数型万能寿险进行保费融资、放大资金杠杆、最大化提高保单资金利用效率的人士;
④ 有家族企业及财富需要进行保护和有效传承的高净值人士。

3.6 投资型万能寿险

3.6.1 什么是投资型万能寿险

投资型万能寿险,又称变额万能寿险,也是万能寿险的一种衍生产品,它结合了传统万能寿险的保障功能和证券市场的投资账户功能,是一种内置投资性质的终身寿险。投资型万能寿险允许保单持有人在一定条件下改变保费和身故赔偿金的金额,适用于希望自行管理保单内投资,并获得保单现金价值累积的人士。

投资型万能寿险保单可以有一个托管账户,也称子账户。通常该托管账户与传统寿险保费的资金池是分开的,保单持有人或其指定的投资经理会负责账户投资组合的绩效,并自行承受由于市场波动而带来的可观回报或重大损失。当市场上行时,收益上不封顶,保单中现金价值在支付每年的保险成本及费用后,可以累积到更多的收益;保单持有人可以通过保单贷款或直接取款(可能会有税务问题)来从保单提取资金。反之,当市场下行时,投资下不保底,如果现金价值账户在金融市场亏损过大,那么保单持有人就必须追加更多的资金或降低保额以维持保单有效。因此投资型万能寿险对保单持有人和投资经理自身的投资水平和风险承受能力要求比较高。

3.6.2 投资型万能寿险的特点

投资型万能寿险最大的特点就是灵活性。

保单持有人可以灵活选择保费支付的金额和年限。比如,对于有充足现金流的高净值人士来说,可以选择在保单早期年份最大化地投入充足资金,从而能够在扣除保险成本和托管账户管理费用后,加速保单内现金价值的投资收益累积。一方面可以负担持续的保单成本以维系保单的效力,另一方面也可以通过贷款的形式支取保单现金价值,进而选择资金杠杆再投资。

另外一个灵活性就是投资选项的灵活性。保单中的托管账户允许参与绝大多数投资组合,如股票、债券、互惠基金等(对冲基金、私募股权等投资形式在部分司法管辖区产品中相对受限),保单持有人也可以指定账户投资管理人。不同的投资表现会直接影响保单收益及保险成本的持续支付能力,若使用得当,投资型万能寿险就会比传统万能寿险和终身寿险产品拥有更大的灵活性及投资回报增长潜力。当然,投资型万能寿险也缺少了指数型万能寿险、传统万能寿险和终身寿险在市场下行时的托底保障。

3.6.3 投资型万能寿险的应用

和指数型万能寿险指数收益率"上有封顶,下有保底"的特性恰恰相反,投资型万能寿险由于赋予保单持有人在投资选项上更大的灵活性,因此在可能获市场高回报的同时,也将面临高风险,投资回报"上不封顶,下不保底"。因此投资型万能寿险更适合看重保单的投资功能、具有丰富的投资经验并且投资策略偏激进的客户;而对于风险承受偏好较保守的客户,传统万能寿险或者指数型万能险可能是更好的选择。

3.7 私募寿险

3.7.1 什么是私募寿险

私募寿险诞生于20世纪90年代的美国。过去数十年,对冲基金为美国的超高净值人士带来了丰厚的回报,但高回报也意味着需要缴纳高昂的所得税。对于超高净值人士而言,他们最关心的不仅是投资的现时收益,而且包括如何更有效地把家族财富传给下一代。因此,私募寿险这一财富传承的工具便伴随超高净值人士的税务需求应运而生。通过合理的安排,私募寿险不仅可以帮助超高净值人士规避投资收益产生的所得税,而且可以有效地减少传承时产生的赠与税和遗产税。

私募寿险可以理解为保险公司提供的一种寿险法律结构,由两个账户"篮子"构成。一个篮子持有不同形式的投资资产,一个篮子持有人寿保险。保单持有人将资产置入私募寿险保单中,并负责选择后续的管理及监督方式。通过私募寿险这种独特的寿险结构设计,不仅可实现不同形式资产的税务优惠,而且可以为投资人实现资产的保护和增值、自我管理和控制(受限于不同司法管辖区私募寿险的规定),以及资产的流动性等多项功能。因此私募寿险作为一种为全球超高净值人士进行财富规划的核心保险解决方案,近年来越来越受到市场的关注。

3.7.2 私募寿险的特点

(1)保费支付及管理有别于传统寿险保单。

私募寿险的保费支付不再是单一的现金,还可以是出租物业或股票基金等形式,比如客户可以将其在其他金融机构的金融资产作为保费平移到保单中;并且保费的管理形式不同,不再是由保险公司统一管理,而是可以根据所在司法管辖区私募寿险的要求自主选择可行的管理机构及方式。

(2)有更广泛的投资标的。

传统寿险的投资范围是相对受限的,而私募寿险内的资金可以持有并投资于对冲基金、大宗商品、股票、房地产(视司法管辖区规定)等各类资产,不仅可以使投资更分散,而且可以获得更高的投资收益潜力。

（3）有更充分的投资主动权。

保单持有人或代表保单持有人的投资顾问可以选择投资经理,当保单持有人或投资顾问认为投资经理的投资管理收益不理想时,有权更换投资经理。

（4）有较好的流动性。

保单持有人可以通过直接提取或贷款的形式从私募寿险获得流动资金,这取决于私募寿险所属司法管辖区的税收法规。

（5）有与信托相结合的双重保护。

私募寿险保单可以与信托结构相结合,通过指定信托作为私募寿险保单的受益人,从而为资产提供额外的保护,进一步满足家族资产风险隔离及定向传承的需求。

（6）简化税务及《共同申报准则》信息互换。

保单内不同形式的投资资产可以合并为单一形式申报,从而简化相关监管机构及《共同申报准则》[①](Common Reporting Standard,CRS)所要求的申报流程和申报内容。

需要提示的是,超高净值人士在考虑使用私募寿险时,还需结合其家庭成员的税务身份进行规划,并充分了解相应私募寿险保单所属司法管辖区的各项法律要求。比如美国的私募寿险,需要满足 7702 条款人寿保单测试的需求,方可实现私募寿险税务筹划的主要功能,以及私募寿险的投资账户需满足投资品种分散及账户控制管理要求等。相对来说,对于离岸地的私募寿险,相关法律要求较为宽松。

---

① 《共同申报准则》是经济合作与发展组织(OECD)制定的用于金融账户信息互换的标准。承诺实施 CRS 的国家或地区,都要将非居民金融账户信息进行交换。中国于 2014 年 9 月经国务院批准承诺将实施这一标准。2018 年 9 月,中国的国家税务总局与其他国家或地区税务主管当局第一次实现了信息交换。

4 人寿保险合同

本章要点：
- 定义人寿保险合同中的重要术语
- 详细解释保险金、保费、保单价值、身故赔偿金、抗辩期、退保和取款、保单贷款、宽限期、失效、复效、转让和其他术语
- 解释如何进行索赔，以及潜在的相关问题

4.1 定义

人寿保险合同，又称人寿保单，是指投保人和保险公司一致认可，由投保人支付保费，以被保人的生命为保险标的，并由保险公司在保险期间基于被保人生存或死亡支付保险金的一种合同。

4.1.1 有效人寿保险合同的一般要素

人寿保险合同适用订立一份有效合同的一般性原则，主要包括以下6项。

（1）要约的提出及接受。

人寿保险合同中的一方（投保人）填写一份包含明确提案的申请表（有时还包括初始保费），即为要约（Offer）；合同中的另一方（保险公司）同意合同条款，或同意接受经过相关修改的要约，并签发保单，即为接受要约。

(2) 对价。

对价是一方为获得另一方在合同中的承诺而支付的价值。在人寿保险合同中,对价是指投保人向保险公司支付的初始的和未来的保费,以换取保险公司在被保人死亡时履行承诺并支付保险金。

保险合同中的对价条款还包括保费支付期、支付频率以及相应的金额(详见第4.2.2小节)。

(3) 订立合同的能力。

合同双方都必须具有完全的行为能力。在人寿保险合同中,投保人需要具备与保险公司订立合同的法律资格;如果被保人是未成年人、有精神疾病、受酒精/麻醉品影响或破产,就没有资格成为投保人来申请合同,也没有资格使自己受合同约束。如果保险公司获得了其所在司法管辖区监管部门的许可或授权,就被认为有能力订立合同和签发保单。

(4) 法律目的。

合同必须具有合法的法律目的,否则签订的合同被视为无效。人寿保险合同始终被认为具有合法的法律目的。

(5) 可保利益。

可保利益是法律目的的一个组成部分。当投保人与被保人不为同一个人时,投保人和被保人之间需要存在可保利益,否则,保单可能无效。需要注意的是,可保利益只需要在申请人寿保险保单时存在即可,而无须在保单生效期间和/或在索赔时存在。关于可保利益的更多信息详见第2章。

(6) 一致同意和最大诚信。

投保人/被保人与保险公司需要根据合同法的基本法律要求,彼此保持最大诚信(*Uberrima fides*)。简言之,投保人需要向保险公司披露相关事实和信息;与之相应,保险公司需要确保与保险产品有关的任何说明文件、产品手册和营销材料的内容与最终保险合同的内容相一致,并且不隐瞒任何信息。相关的宣传材料、产品申请表和合同内容通常需要以书面形式提交给行业监管部门审核并得到批准。

4.1.2 披露义务

投保人有义务向保险公司披露所有可能影响保险公司决定是否签发保单的信息,包括其他已有保单的金额、保单是否被加费/拒保、完整的个人和家庭健康史、生活习惯、旅行史、职业和家庭财务状况信息。所有这些都是保险公司在决定提供寿险保障、保单适用的评级和相应的保险费率时会考虑的重要事实。例如,在寿险保单申请中,吸烟习惯对保险公司来说是一项重要事实,吸烟或不吸烟将导致保险公司以不同的保险费率签发保单。

投保人应注意可能会有以下两种违反诚信的形式:

其一,无辜不披露:投保人未提供其不知道的信息。

其二,故意/欺诈性不披露:投保人故意不提供重要信息,或故意提供不正确的信息。

举例来说,投保人不知道其祖父死于心脏病,因此在申请时没有在家庭健康史中披露这一信息,这就属于无辜不披露;相反,如果投保人知道这一重要事实,但选择不向保险公司披露,就属于故意/欺诈性不披露。如果在保单生效后或在索赔时发现故意/欺诈性不披露的情况,则保险公司有权取消保单或拒绝索赔;相反,如果被认为是无辜不披露的情况,则保险公司可以根据与承保风险的关联程度,选择收取额外保费或维持保单原状。

4.1.3　担保与陈述

担保(Warranty)由投保人做出,保证所提供各方面信息都是真实准确的。担保是实质性的,是保险合同的一部分,保险公司有权根据担保的真实性来决定是否取消保单。

陈述(Representation)是指投保人做出的声明,声明所提供的信息在其所知范围内是真实和准确的。这是保险公司决定是否签发保险合同的依据。与担保不同,陈述不属于合同的一部分,只有当投保人的陈述构成重大失实并与保单的风险直接密切相关时,保险公司才有权决定是否取消保单。

4.1.4　重大失实陈述

在保险合同中,重大失实陈述(Material Misrepresentation)是指投保人做出的、将影响保险公司改变保费费率或签发保单与否决定的不实陈述。如果在保单生效后发现该重大失实陈述为故意不披露,则保险公司有权撤销保单或拒绝索赔。这通常有1~2年的抗辩期,抗辩期的期限可能因保险合同条款不同而有所不同。在抗辩期之后,保险公司将需要对欺诈性失实陈述进行证明,方可对合同提出异议。更多细节详见第4.2.2小节。

4.1.5　弃权和禁止反言

弃权(Waiver)是指对已知合法权利的自愿放弃。如果保险公司自愿放弃保单的某项条款,则其以后不能以违反该条款为理由拒绝索赔。禁止反言(Estoppel)与弃权密切相关。禁止反言是指根据合同法的诚信原则,承诺人所做出的承诺具有约束力,不得出尔反尔,并须强制执行。例如,若投保人在保单申请中未披露某项医疗信息,而保险公司忽略了信息披露要求并签发了保单,该行为即为弃权;如果发生索赔,则保险公司不得以未披露为理由拒绝理赔,此为禁止反言。

4.2　人寿保险合同中的常见条款

尽管不同签发地的人寿保险合同需接受当地相关行业管辖部门的监管,但是作为一种合同形式,不同签发地的保险合同往往具有一些共同的条款。本节将介绍人寿保单中的常见条款。

4.2.1 完整合同

完整人寿保险合同包括完整的保单申请表、相关背书文件及保险合同,以避免投保人与保险公司之间对申请中所提交的信息产生异议和分歧。一旦保险合同确定,未经投保人同意,保险公司不得更改任何合同条款或相关文件。

4.2.2 保费

保费是指投保人为了使保单生效,根据其申请时确定的保费费率向保险公司支付的费用。人寿保单的保费通常基于当地的死亡率表,外加其他费用,如税费、管理费和保单费用等。保费金额因保单类型、计划和支付期而异。国际保单被精算师划分为不同的风险等级,这一般取决于客户的居住国。精算和保费计算是根据相应国家人口的生命周期(死亡率)表进行的。此外,监管和会计标准的差异及其他因素也会导致保单费率的不同。以下将以美国为例,与离岸地进行比较,看看哪些因素导致了保费成本的差异。

(1)准备金标准和合规性。

① 美国。精算师为在美国注册的公司设定法定准备金时必须遵守适用的法律法规和准则。这些规则经常变化,在各州之间也不一致。《人寿保险单估值示范条例》(Valuation of Life Insurance Policies Model Regulation)就是一个例子,该条例改变了许多人寿保险产品的准备金规则。精算准则以其多样的要求使准备金领域进一步复杂化,精算师也被要求使用保守的死亡率和利息假设。

② 离岸地。离岸地寿险公司需要根据一般公认会计原则(Generally Accepted Accounting Principles,GAAP)来计算法定准备金和其他财务项目。这些原则可能是国际会计准则、加拿大标准或其他地方规定的原则。一般来说,类似美国公认会计原则的准备金,或按照公司独立审计师和保险监督员批准的其他方法计算的准备金通常是被接受的。国际标准和加拿大标准通常要求使用最佳估算假设,并辅以不利偏差准备金。寿险的国际标准仍处于发展阶段。

在大多数情况下,离岸地比美国具有更大的灵活性,且更依赖精算判断。相较于设定大量的法律法规和准则,离岸地对保险公司的立法目标更偏重促进业务和尽量减少繁文缛节,同时确保公司的偿付能力。

(2)精算测试和认证。

① 美国。一旦修订后的《精算意见和备忘录条例》(Actuarial Opinion and Memorandum Regulation,AOMR)获得批准,所有在美国注册的人寿保险公司每年都必须进行现金流测试并且由精算师签署一份关于资产充足性的证明。

② 离岸地。离岸精算证明通常是一些措辞简单的文件,证明保险公司为保单的偿付

义务做了适当的准备，或证明保险公司的实际负债在财务报表上得到了正确的反映。在许多司法管辖区，这些证明可能只是几句话。

4.2.3 保单价值

保单价值通常存在于终身寿险中，一般分为当前现金价值和退保现金价值。当保单持有人退保取消保单时，保险公司会收取一定的退保费用，所剩余的退保现金价值即为保险公司会向保单持有人支付的金额，因此当前现金价值减去退保费用等于退保现金价值。退保费用会在保单生效一定年份后降为零，退保收费期视产品不同，一般在 5~15 年。

4.2.4 分红条款

4.2.4.1 年度分红

对于分红型人寿保险保单，如果保单有效且没有逾期未付的保费，则保单持有人有权享受保险公司的可分配盈余。是否分红以及红利的数额由保险公司决定。因此，保险公司并非每年都保证分红，只有分红宣派后，该笔金额才获得保证。红利派发选项规定包含在保险合同中。关于终身寿险红利派发选项的更多信息，请参考第 3 章。

4.2.4.2 复归红利

在一些司法管辖区，分红型保单会派发复归红利而非年度分红。复归红利也是由保险公司根据盈利情况酌情派发的，且不保证每年都有，但一旦派发即为保证。派发至保单的复归红利可以用于购买更多的保额，也可以选择提取现金。在提取保单价值时，复归红利的计算方法在不同司法管辖区有所不同。例如，在某些司法管辖区，复归红利受制于现金价值折扣系数，这意味着复归红利的票面价值必须经过折扣后才会被纳入保单的总现金价值。兑现的折扣率是非保证的，但在保单生效一定年限后将达到 100%；而在某些司法管辖区，复归红利只是作为年度红利的替代品，一旦派发即为保证，无须折算，直接进入保单价值和身故赔偿金部分。

4.2.4.3 期满红利

某些司法管辖区发行的分红保单中还可能派发期满红利。如果被保人在经过一定年限的保单周年纪念日（通常为 10 年）后身故或完全退保，保险公司就会支付期满红利。与年度红利不同，该红利是属于保单可额外享受的保险公司可分配盈余的一次性福利。保险公司在年报中提供的期满红利信息并不会构成增购。

期满红利的金额可能增加或减少，保险公司全权决定在身故或完全退保时是否支付期满红利，实际支付红利金额也可能多于或少于年度报告中所述金额，保险公司也可随时更改或撤销该期满红利。

4.2.4.4 额外红利

对应期满红利，部分司法管辖区发行的分红保单会以额外红利替代。两者的共同点是均为被保人身故或保单退保时可能派发的一次性非保证红利，由保险公司视保单盈利状况决定是否派发,并且实际派发金额可能高于或低于演示金额。

不同处主要体现在保单退保时,额外红利同样引入变现折扣率的因素,即在保单退保支取现金价值时,额外红利的面值需经折算,方可支取;而期满红利没有这一折算要求。

4.2.5 保险金

人寿保险金通常包括非罚没权益和身故赔偿金。

4.2.5.1 非罚没权益

定期人寿保险没有现金价值,所以投保人在保单取消或到期时将无权获得该种利益。另外,终身寿险通常提供非罚没权益,即使投保人停止支付保费,也能获得一些收益。正如上一节所讨论的,终身寿险中的退保现金价值会随着时间的推移而积累,积累的退保现金价值越高,非罚没权益的效果越显著。非罚没权益的主要形式包括自动保费贷款、保费抵扣、取款、保单贷款、抵押贷款、减额缴清保险、展期定期保险等,因各地保险法规的运作、条款的形式以及可选项的不同而不尽相同。

4.2.5.2 身故赔偿金

当被保人去世时,通过保险公司的理赔标准和程序,将会对投保人指定的受益人以对应比例分配身故赔偿金。不同类型的人寿保险身故赔偿金的组成也不相同。保险合同中通常也会根据不同的保险产品约定相应的身故赔偿金选项。本节将介绍分红型终身寿险、万能寿险和私募寿险的保险合同中的身故赔偿金选项。

(1) 风险净额。

风险净额(Net Amount at Risk,NAAR)指保险公司所要承担的实际风险净值。

一份保单在任意一年的风险净额通常等于保单的身故赔偿金减去其账户价值,这是由适用的法规决定的。对于终身寿险保单,累积账户价值将随着时间的推移而积累,从而减少保险公司所要承担的风险量(如图4.1所示)。

风险净额=身故赔偿金-账户价值

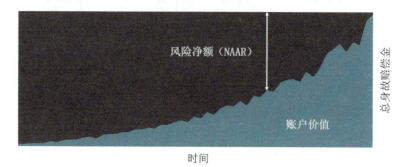

图 4.1 风险净额演示

(2) 分红型终身寿险的身故赔偿金选项。

在分红型终身寿险中：

风险净额＝总身故赔偿金－总退保现金价值

分红型终身寿险会有一个保证的身故赔偿金金额，也称为面值或面额。面值是首次购买保单时在人寿保险申请书上注明的初始金额，旨在作为身故赔偿金支付给保单受益人。在分红型终身寿险中，面额是有保证的，不会因保单的投资而改变。

如果被保人在保单有效期内身故，则保险公司将根据合同条款向指定受益人支付身故赔偿金。自被保人确定身故日期支付的金额为：

面值

加　一切累积年度红利/复归红利（不同司法管辖区发行的保单，构成有所差异）

加　一切期满红利/额外红利（不同司法管辖区发行的保单，构成有所差异）

减　一切债务（未付保费、未偿清贷款、利息）

(3) 万能寿险的身故赔偿金选项。

万能寿险的身故赔偿金组成很复杂，有多种选择。

① 保额加账户价值。在该选项中，身故赔偿金是初始的保额加上保单内的现金价值账户的余额。现金价值也可以称为账户价值。

② 恒定保额。在该选项中，身故赔偿金保持不变，随着保单账户价值的增加，保险公司的风险净额减少，因此收取的保险费用也相应减少。

③ 恒定保额加指数增长。该选项允许保额每年按一定比例增加。保险公司会对指数化的保额设置一个上限，通常上限为保额的3倍。每次保额增长后，根据新保额计算保险成本，并按每年续保直至100岁的方式收费。

④ 恒定保额加退还保费。在该选项中，理赔时除了将获得保额，还将获得已缴纳保费的退还。保单成本根据新保额计算，并按每年续保直至100岁的方式收费。

⑤ 恒定保额加调整后成本基数。该选项适用于那些对于人寿保险的某些组成部分征税的国家所签发的保单。除保额之外，在理赔时还将获得保单调整成本。保单成本根据新保额计算，并按每年续保直至100岁的方式收费。

调整后成本基数＝已付总保费－纯保险净成本（NCPI）

导致保单调整后成本基数增加的因素包括已付保费、贷款利息和提款金额的应纳税部分。导致保单调整后成本基数减少的因素包括从保单账户中取款或贷款、附加保障扣除的保险成本费用、纯保险净成本和保单终止前的一切身故赔偿金调整。

此外，万能寿险中还有两种典型的永久型寿险：指数型万能寿险和投资型万能寿险。与传统的万能寿险不同，指数型万能寿险和投资型万能寿险的身故赔偿金都是灵活可调的，保额可以随时减少或增加（需要符合核保要求及相应的税务规定）。

（4）私募寿险的身故赔偿金选项。

关于私募寿险的更多信息，请参见第 9 章和第 10 章。

由于私募寿险的保额取决于保单账户余额，通常为 1%~5%，但可以扩大到与传统人寿保险相当，以满足特定规划需求。在这种情况下，身故赔偿金将是保额加账户价值（如图 4.2 所示）。

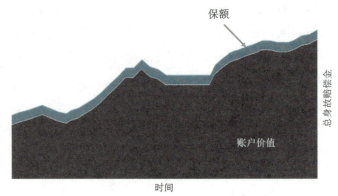

图 4.2　私募寿险的身故赔偿金构成

4.2.6　保单持有人权利

保单持有人是唯一有权在被保人生前行使保单规定的权利或权益的人（指定不可撤销受益人的情况除外）。保单持有人的权利或权益包括：

① 将保单所有权转让给新保单持有人；

② 指定一个继任保单持有人，如果原保单持有人在被保人之前身故，保单就自动由其持有；

③ 受益人的更换和撤销（指定不可撤销受益人的情况除外）；

④ 行使保单下的一切其他权利。

4.2.7　冷静期

保险合同冷静期通常为 10 天或更长（如离岸地保单通常有 30~60 天的冷静期）。在冷静期，如果投保人对保单的条款和/或条件不满意，则可以取消并退还保单，并获得全额保费退款。

4.2.8　宽限期

如同信用卡有免息还款宽限期一样，人寿保险保费逾期也会有宽限期。在宽限期内将保费缴清，就不会有利息产生。通常宽限期为 30~31 天（自然日），有的离岸地区的保单规定为 60 天。如果宽限期过后仍未缴清保费，对于有现金价值的保单，可以用现金价值贷款来支付保费，以免保单失效；但对于没有现金价值的保单，比如定期保险，保单将失效。

4.2.9 不可抗辩和自杀条款

根据不可抗辩条款,如果发现投保人在保单申请上有重大失实陈述,则保险公司有权在保单生效后的特定时间(通常为 1~2 年)内取消保单;在此期限后,保险公司不能仅以投保人提供重大失实陈述为由取消保单,并须按约定支付身故赔偿金,除非有充分证据证明投保人在保单上有欺诈性失实陈述。

根据自杀条款,如果被保人在保单签发或复效之日起的指定期限(通常是 1~2 年)内自杀,保单就被宣布无效,保险公司将不承担任何赔付责任,而只需退还投保人从保单生效日或复效日起支付的所有保费。然而,一旦过了规定的期限,即使被保人自杀身亡,保险公司也必须进行赔付。

以下是一些主要司法管辖区的国际人寿保险关于不可抗辩和自杀条款的例子。

4.2.9.1 美国保单

所有免责条款都要遵循各州的法律。具体的免责条款可能因保险公司而异,所以还要注意保单本身的条款。当保单处于抗辩期(通常是 1~2 年,因州而异)时,如果保险公司发现投保人欺骗或隐瞒信息,则可以取消保单或拒绝索赔。所有的保单都有抗辩期,即使是那些已经提出索赔的保单。例如,如果某人没有披露自己有高血压,并在与高血压无关的车祸中死亡,只要死亡发生在抗辩期内,并且保险公司可以证明该人没有披露高血压的信息,那么保险公司可以拒绝索赔。如果被保人在保单生效后 2 年内自杀,则保险公司不必支付身故赔偿金,只需退还为保单支付的保费。

4.2.9.2 加拿大保单

在不可抗辩条款方面,加拿大法律规定,保险公司不能以任何理由宣布已生效 2 年以上的人寿保险合同"无效"。但是,保险公司有权在任何时候以欺诈为由质疑保单和相关修改的有效性。

若被保人于保单生效日或任何复效日(以较迟者为准)后的 2 年内自杀,无论其当时神志正常或失常,身故赔偿金就只限于退还已缴纳的保费。

4.2.9.3 其他地区

其他国际保单,如中国香港、新加坡或离岸地的保单,通常也有类似的条款和条件,但各保单类型之间仍有差异,投保人需要了解清楚相关条款和条件。

4.2.10 误报年龄及/或性别

如果保单申请文件中的年龄和/或性别有误,则保险公司将对保险金或保单利益的支付进行适当调整,并有权在支付身故赔偿金或保单利益时核实被保人的真实年龄。

如果被保人根据正确的年龄和性别需要支付更高的保费,则保险公司将调整保单利益,使实际支付的保费与以正确的年龄或性别购买相同保障所需保费相一致;反之,保险公司将退还多收的保费(不计利息)。如根据被保人正确的年龄和性别,其已不符合受保范围和要求,则保险公司有权取消保险合同,并在扣除可能的保单欠费后,退还已付保费(不计利息)。

4.2.11 取款和退保

4.2.11.1 取款

分红型保单只支持从保单的现金价值中取款。从保单中取款时,投保人需要计算取款金额是否超过保单的调整后成本基数;如果超过了,则取决于保单发行地的税收政策,可能会有应课税收入。一旦提取分红,相应增加的保额就会减少。

4.2.11.2 退保

如果终身寿险或万能寿险的投保人取消了保单,这通常被称为完全退保。投保人完全退保时,会收到保险合同下的保单现金价值(减去一切欠款),并放弃保险合同下的所有权利,包括身故赔偿金。投保人也可以部分退保,即在每份保险合同规定的最大提取金额内提取部分保证现金价值。在这种情况下,保险合同的权利继续存在,但保额通常会减少,身故赔偿金将在被保人身故后按调整后的金额支付。

需要注意的是,取决于保单签发地的不同,无论保单是全部还是部分退保,都可能对投保人有税收后果。

4.2.12 保单贷款条款

理论上,如果保单有现金价值,投保人可以通过保单贷款条款向保险公司申请贷款。以下是香港某保险公司的合同中对保单贷款条款的阐述:

"您可以申请保单贷款,但贷款金额(包括一切尚未偿付的贷款金额)不得超过负债前净现金价值的90%。您将被告知本公司确定的利率,该利率可能会不时变化。因此,在某些情况下,如退保或到期时,应付价值会减少。"

保单贷款的最高金额是:

<u>保单年度的总现金价值(分红保单为保证现金价值+年度红利/复归红利)</u>

减　按现行贷款利率计算的1年利息

减　一切逾期保费

减　一切债务

大多数保险公司也会设定一个最低贷款额度。

保险公司将向保单持有人收取保单贷款利息。贷款利息按日累计,如未在每个保单周年日偿还,利息就自动进入贷款额中累加,直至所有贷款全部偿清后停止计息。保单贷款年利率由各司法管辖区保险公司视不同的基准厘定并浮动。

保单持有人可以随时部分或全部偿还贷款,若贷款在保险公司支付任何赔偿或利益时尚未偿清,则贷款加利息的金额将优先从应付给受益人的款项中扣除。

国际寿险保单的主要代表司法管辖区也有类似的条款,但在可贷款额度、厘定贷款利率方式及税务后果上又有差异(详见第 3 章介绍)。

4.2.13 失效

保单持有人有义务按时支付保费,但如果保费逾期,且宽限期已过,保单就会失效。如果是定期保险,没有现金价值,则直接失效;然而,如果是终身寿险保单,因为有现金价值,则进入自动保费贷款计划。

4.2.14 自动保费贷款

自动保费贷款指在保费逾期且宽限期已过的情况下,保单的现金价值被自动转换为保费贷款以支付基本保费。当自动保费贷款的数额大于保单的现金价值时,若不及时还清,则保单将失效。自动保费贷款会产生利息,补交保费时需要将利息一并付清。自动保费贷款的好处是,它可以保护保单不立即失效,使其保持有效状态。需要注意的是,如果自动保费贷款耗尽了保单的所有现金价值,则保单仍然会失效。

如果保单失效,则保险合同立即终止,保险公司将不会支付未来的身故赔偿金。

4.2.15 复效

保单失效后会发生什么?每家保险公司都会允许一定的复效期,通常是 2 年,也有些司法管辖区允许的复效期长达 3~5 年。在保单失效后 6 个月内,通常只需要一份书面申请和补齐未付保费即可复效,而不需要任何额外的核保。如果保单在 6 个月后复效,可能需要核保,经保险公司批准后方可复效。在这种情况下,保单的抗辩期和自杀免责期将从复效日重新计算。

4.2.16 转让

保单持有人可以选择将其保单中的部分或全部权利转让给其他人。

4.2.16.1 保单的绝对转让

在保单的绝对转让的情况下,保单持有人将保险合同的法律所有权,包括所有权利和义务,全部转让给受让人。一旦交易完成,原保单持有人就不再对保单拥有任何控制或经济权益。一般来说,保单中会明确规定保单绝对转让的要求。

4.2.16.2 保单的部分转让

使用保单作为贷款的抵押品要求投保人进行抵押转让(Collateral Assignment)。这通常是以部分转让的方式进行的,即受让人(通常是贷方)并不成为保单的所有人,保单持有人仍然拥有保单。然而,这样的转让允许贷方阻止投保人进行任何破坏抵押品价值的行为,例如从保单中取款,或者不支付保费。

若贷款在被保人身故时仍未偿还,则贷方对身故赔偿金享有优先权,可以从中优先获得未偿还的贷款金额。如果投保人在被保人在世时拖欠贷款,则贷方可以强制退保并收回未偿贷款余额。

4.2.17 索赔

在被保人身故后,保单的受益人或继承人(在未指定受益人的情况下)将成为索偿人(Claimant)。通常,保险公司要求索偿人在切实可行的情况下,及时提交被保人的身故证明及符合要求的索赔表等系列文件。

4.2.17.1 索赔表及相关证明

保险公司要求提供索赔表,以便理赔审查员核实信息,确认保单的生效状态,并及时核证相关证明文件。对于身故索赔,主要证明文件包括被保人的死亡证明,保单正本,遗嘱认证函(如果遗产被指定为保单受益人),主治医生声明(Attending Physician's Statement, APS),被保险人的年龄和性别证明,保单受益人/受托人、遗嘱执行人的身份证明,以及保险公司合理要求的一切用于审批索赔的文件。

4.2.17.2 受益人的确认

理赔审查员需要确认索偿人是保险公司记录中的保单指定受益人,或者是被保人的遗嘱中的受益人。如果第一受益人先于被保人身故,则保险公司在向继任受益人支付身故赔偿金之前也会要求提供第一受益人的死亡证明;如果没有指定继任受益人,则保险公司将向遗产支付身故赔偿金。

4.2.18 背书

背书是对保单的修订,也是保险合同的一部分。背书可以扩展或限制保险合同所承诺给付的利益。例如,在保单上增加或删除某项附加条款或排除性条款都需要背书,当保单进行转让时也需要背书。保险合同中的背书内容各不相同,重要的是要确保投保人对保险合同中的背书内容充分知情。

4.2.19 其他

人寿保险通常包含各种其他的保险条款、额外利益、保险公司的行政信息等。

不同司法管辖区的寿险市场和主要寿险产品

CHAPTER 5

> **本章要点：**
> - 以美国、加拿大、中国香港、新加坡、离岸地和中国内地为例，介绍各司法管辖区的主要寿险产品

5.1 美国

5.1.1 美国寿险市场概述

人寿保险最早起源于18世纪四五十年代的伦敦。当时的人寿保险要求投保人每年按年龄投入一定量的资金，到年底如果投保人死亡，则把其他投保人聚集起来的钱理赔给死者的家庭，费用的制定就是依照当时的生命周期表。彼时伦敦海上运输非常发达，因此人寿保险首先从船员和商人发展起来。至今，所有国家和地区的人寿保险还是沿用这个原始概念。

18世纪60年代在美国以费城和纽约作为起源地，美国人根据这一概念设计出类似产品并开始面向市场发售。美国寿险市场经过百年发展愈加成熟，产品线不断迭代升级，因此可以较全面地满足寿险客户在不同人生阶段、伴随自身需求变化的保障需求调整和适配。到目前为止，美国保险市场是产品类型最齐全、功能最强大、创新能力最强的保险市场之一，在现代保险行业中占有重要的地位。根据国际保险监理官协会（International

Association of Insurance Supervisors,IAIS)发布的2021年全球保险市场报告披露的数据,美国市场占到全球总保费规模的38.1%,是全球最大的单一保险市场,占比比排第二至第六位国家的总和还要多(详见图5.1)。

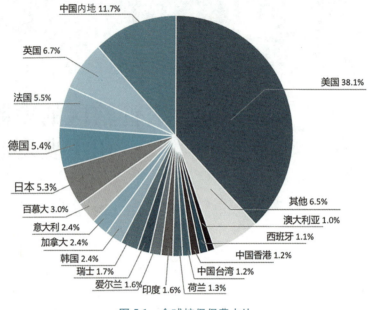

图 5.1　全球核保保费占比

来源：IAIS SWM 2022。

从历史上来看,美国的寿险产品只对本国居民开放,但近年来有部分美国保险公司也允许符合资格的外国人进行投保,其基本要求是在美国本土进行销售、体检、签单等全部动作,并且投保人/被保人还需满足一定的"美国关联"要求,外国人购买的保单以指数型万能寿险产品为主。

美国全国保险委员会协会(National Association of Insurance Commissioners,NAIC)在其发布的《人寿保险和意外伤害保险行业分析报告》中指出,2022年美国748家人寿保险公司的总承保保费规模达到了1.17万亿美元,其中人寿保险承保保费为2 135亿美元。从产品类型来看,终身寿险依然在销量上高居榜首,而指数型万能寿险已经大幅超越传统型万能寿险和投资型万能寿险,成为最受欢迎的万能寿险产品。

目前,美国市场上的人寿保险从大类上主要分为以下几类:
- 定期寿险
- 终身寿险
- 万能寿险
    - 投资型万能寿险
    - 指数型万能寿险

美国人寿保险发展史详见图5.2。

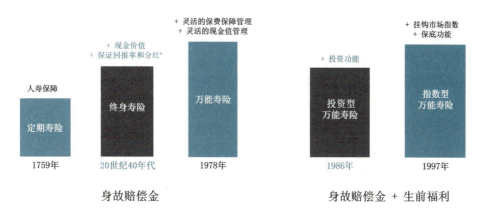

图 5.2　美国人寿保险发展史

注：分红不保证每年都派发，也不保证派发金额，视保单收益决定。

5.1.2　定期寿险

从 1913 年开始，受到法律规范监管的定期寿险开始在美国市场盛行。定期寿险通常有 5 年、10 年、15 年、20 年、30 年期限选项，在保险合同期限内保费固定不变。但随着投保人年龄增加，保费成本及续保保费也会大幅增加。此外，市场利率、保险公司的财务状况和各州法规也有可能影响保费费率。定期寿险基于"其通过低廉保费，就可获得一定期限内高杠杆身故保障"的特性，受到中低收入阶层人士的广泛青睐。美国大部分保险公司提供条件优厚的"免体检"定期寿险产品，在满足一定年龄和其他要求的前提下，投保人可免体检购买最高至 200 万~300 万美元保额。

5.1.3　终身寿险

定期寿险具有多种优点，但其提供非终身保障及纯消费险的局限性也不容忽视，因此保险公司在 20 世纪 40 年代前后推出了终身寿险，其可以说是定期寿险的一种延续和补充。其引入了现金价值的基础概念，为之后美国市场上其他类型寿险产品的发展奠定了基础。

美国的终身寿险产品中，当所缴纳的保费支付保险成本之后，剩余部分就进入现金价值账户。每年保险公司会根据公司盈利情况决定是否派发红利及派发金额，保单内的现金价值因而伴随时间的推移累计增长。保险公司通常会对终身寿险保单的现金价值承诺一个保障收益率，如年最低收益率保证为 2.5%~4%，并且有机会获得保险公司的额外红利。终身寿险产品的最大特点及主要优势就是保费终身固定，并提供 100% 终身保障和身故赔偿金；同时，保单内现金价值的保证收益及额外分红不断累积，也可以使投保人有机会使用保单资金及实现税务优化的功能。不过任何事物都有两面性，由于终身寿险承诺终身保障，保费固定且费率较高，在保费支付周期及支付金额上也缺乏灵活性，因此，在 1978

年前后,万能寿险开始在美国市场出现,以灵活的保费支付方式弥补终身寿险的不足。

5.1.4 万能寿险

万能寿险相当于一个有现金价值功能的终身定期寿险,保费往往介于定期寿险和分红型终身寿险之间,一经推出即以保费、保额和保单其他条款的灵活性为主要卖点,受到市场的关注和欢迎。美国的万能寿险又叫传统型万能寿险或固定型万能寿险,保单投资的自由选择权较小,保单收益根据保险公司厘定的固定利率来计算,不与特定资产挂钩。保险公司会参考整体利率环境及自身投资组合的情况,每隔一段时间重新厘定最新的利率,但保单中往往也有最低利率的相关规定以保护保单持有人的权益。

伴随美国投资市场的变化以及客户对投资预期的需求变化,万能寿险又出现了不同类型的衍生品,其中最有代表性的是保证型万能寿险(详见第3章)、投资型万能寿险和指数型万能寿险。保证型万能寿险的保费相对便宜,是所有险种中保费最低的终身人寿保险产品。美国市场上的保证型万能寿险的价格,在全球同类型终身寿险险种中,也最具有竞争力。

5.1.4.1 投资型万能寿险

投资型万能寿险于20世纪80年代在美国市场出现,源于美股牛市对当时主要投资于长期债券市场、年化收益3%~5%的保险产品所造成的巨大冲击。保险公司不甘于看到大量客户将资金投入股市或将保险账户的资金取出来转战股市,因此适时在传统型万能寿险的基础上推出了投资型万能寿险,也称为变额万能寿险(VUL)。

投资型万能寿险赋予了投保人更大的灵活性。投保人可以在美国国税局允许的保单免税额度内最大化地将资金投入保单中,并在保险公司提供的投资对象中自行选择、自我管理,保单收益直接与投资市场挂钩。在支付基本保费成本、维持万能寿险的保障属性之上,更突出保险的投资属性。但投资型万能寿险上不封顶、下不保底,这就意味着高回报和高风险。投资型万能寿险一度非常盛行,直至2008年全球金融危机股市暴跌,其后流行起了指数型万能寿险(IUL)。

5.1.4.2 指数型万能寿险

指数型万能寿险的概念发源于20世纪90年代的美国,1997年由全美人寿(Transamerica)正式以产品形式发行引入人寿保险市场。20世纪90年代美国股市依然火热,但伴随着1994年债市危机、2000年互联网泡沫破裂,直至2008年美国次贷危机波及全球,不少投资型万能寿险账户持有者的资金在股市中几经沉浮后遭受重创,甚至由于保单现金价值已不足以支付基本保单成本而导致保单失效,投保人方才清醒并意识到收益保障的重要性,指数型万能寿险才得以再次大规模地回到市场的关注中。

指数型万能寿险与投资型万能寿险最显著的区别就是所投入保费只是追踪指数趋势,而非直接投资到股票市场;同时在保单收益上设定为上有封顶、下有保底。在市场环境不好的时候,保单不会获得保底保障;作为交换,当市场大涨的时候,保单当个计息周期所获得的收益将会有封顶上限,封顶收益率由保险公司约定。2023 年,美国市场的指数型万能寿险的封顶收益率大概在 8%~12%。另外需要注意的是,指数型万能寿险保单中约定的"上有封顶、下有保底"只是针对保单收益而言——正如第 3 章中所述,并不是保证保单不会失效,当保单中累积的现金价值因利率持续低于预期,而被持续支付的保费成本和费用消耗殆尽时,投保人仍有可能需要补充保费方可维持保单的效力。因此在美国发行的指数型万能寿险产品中,通常可以采用几种措施来防止保单失效,比如:选择在最少基本保额下最大化保费供款,以加速保单内现金价值累积;在指数型万能寿险中加上附加险,包括身故赔偿金保证赔偿额、超额贷款保护、生前福利、收益增强、保单避免失效条款等。

客观地说,在过去 20 多年中,指数型万能寿险在美国人寿保险市场得到了高速发展。目前,美国市场上有 50 家以上的保险公司在发行以不同指数策略设计的指数型万能寿险产品。人寿保险和市场研究协会(Life Insurance and Market Research Association,LIMRA)在早些年的美国寿险市场预测中就指出,指数型万能寿险已经成为寿险产品中较为成功的典范,未来仍有销量上升的空间。据人寿保险和市场研究协会的 2022 年美国寿险不同产品保费显示(详见图 5.3),这一预测是正确的。

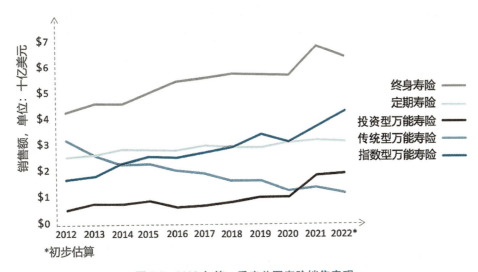

图 5.3　2022 年第一季度美国寿险销售表现

来源:2022 Life Insurance Sales Match Record Set(LIMRA)。

5.2　加拿大

5.2.1　加拿大寿险市场概述

人寿保险行业在加拿大已发展了近两个世纪,经营超过百年的加拿大人寿保险公司有数十家。鉴于加拿大有历史悠久且相对全面完善的金融保险行业的监管体系,其人寿保险公司对于不同的风险,如死亡率、地区风险、从业道德风险等,都有一套完整数据及监控运作系统。

人寿保险业也是加拿大金融体系中非常重要的组成部分,在经济领域甚至社会职能方面发挥着重要的柱石作用。据加拿大人寿和健康保险协会 2020 年数据报告,约八成的人寿保险由个人通过保险代理或顾问购买,其余则通过公司、工会或协会等团体计划获得。

加拿大人寿和健康保险协会(Canadian Life and Health Insurance Association,CLHIA)的数据报告显示,2022 年全加拿大的人寿保险公司为 2 200 万加拿大人提供了人寿保险产品,实现总保费收入 1 450 亿加元,其中人寿保险保费收入超过 275 亿加元(详见图 5.4)。同时,加拿大也是一个开放型自由市场,主张保险公司在有序监管体系下的公平、公开竞争,因此保险公司能够根据市场需求,向大众提供多种类且保费定价合理的产品。加拿大的参与型终身寿险是加拿大最具有代表性的产品,以长期稳健的分红而著称(详见 5.2.3)。

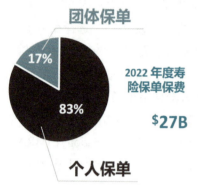

图 5.4 2022 年度加拿大寿险市场个人和团体保单保费占比

来源:CLHIA2022 年数据报告。

目前加拿大保险公司在加拿大本地市场发行的寿险产品主要分为三大类:
- 定期寿险
- 终身寿险
- 万能寿险

2022 年加拿大寿险市场各类产品保额的占比如图 5.5 所示。可以看出,个人人寿保

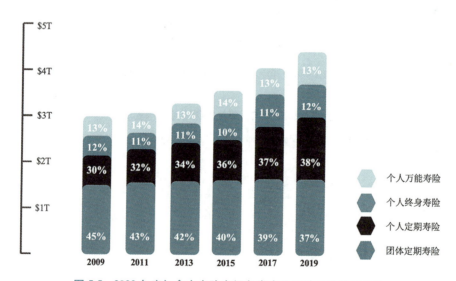

图 5.5 2022 年度加拿大寿险市场各类产品累计保单数量占比

来源:CLHIA 2022 年数据报告。

险(非团体保险)占比从2012年的58%上升至2022年的65%——主要是源于定期寿险的销售增长。在加拿大,虽然没有税法明文规定的遗产税,但是有代际传承税,即个人名下资产在去世时要视同售出(Deemed Disposition),如果有增值,则需要清税后才能进入遗产认证和遗产分配程序。因此对于有资产代际需求的中高净值客户来说,必须通过永久性寿险才能实现资产的最大化传承。加拿大永久性寿险的主要代表产品为终身寿险和万能寿险。

5.2.2 定期寿险

单从已生效保单数量来看,定期寿险(个人加团体)占据了加拿大寿险市场的75%。定期寿险之所以在加拿大人寿保险市场占较大的份额,与其本身的产品特点及使用功能息息相关(具体可参考第3章的详细描述)。加拿大有多种类型且具有相当性价比的寿险产品,一般来说保障期限可分为10年、15年、20年甚至30年,保额最高可达2 000万~2 500万加币。部分加拿大保险公司也提供无须体检即可购买的定期寿险,以两家加拿大国民保险公司的产品为例,如果保额在7.5万~10万加币,则仅需回答相关健康问题且满足其他特定条件,即可无须进行体检获批10年期定期寿险。

5.2.3 终身寿险

以保险公司处置保单投资的盈余为区分,终身寿险分为参与型和非参与型。参与型终身寿险可以算作加拿大终身寿险中的一款明星产品,它不仅可以提供终身保障,而且可以通过复利分红积累现金价值,从而与其他形式的家庭资产增值匹配,并最大化地减少身故时的税负,因此参与型终身寿险也被称为分红寿险。加拿大税务体系完整且严密,分红寿险可以说是本地居民特别是中高净值人士不可或缺的"福利"。加拿大分红寿险中的分红类别既不是英式分红,也不是美式分红(详见第3章),更像是两者兼而有之。

加拿大保险公司法(Insurance Companies Act)461节规定保险公司每个财务年度宣派分红的2.5%~10%可分配给股东,余下部分则需分配给保单持有人。但为了保护保单持有人获得分红权益,通常保险公司会把股东分配比例控制在2.5%~2.7%,从而最大化让利给保单持有人。加拿大分红寿险的回报利率素来以稳健见长,依托的是保险公司专业投资团队的长线投资策略和审慎管理思维,以及分红账户资金池庞大的可投资资金体量。同时,为了减少各种因素带来的波动性,达到长期稳定的红利派发,保险公司通常会采用平滑策略(Smoothing Strategy),即将投资回报较好的年份的一部分收益留在分红账户中作为盈余,用以在投资回报不好的年份派发稳定的红利。图5.6为加拿大某分红寿险产品的分红利率(Dividend Scale Interest Rate,DSIR)与加拿大通胀指数、股指、10年政府债券和5年期定期存款利率的比较,从中可看出分红利率的波动性非常小。

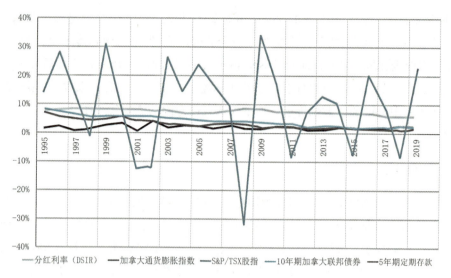

图 5.6　加拿大某分红保险产品分红利率与加拿大通货膨胀指数、股指、10 年联邦债券和 5 年期定期存款利率的比较

来源：https://www.sunnet.sunlife.com/files/advisor/english/PDF/810-3827.pdf.

5.2.4　万能寿险

全球主流司法管辖区均有万能寿险，绝大多数万能寿险产品共同的特点就是赋予投保人灵活的选择，投保人可以选择保费的金额、缴费周期、身故赔偿金金额，但在衍生产品和投资选择上不同司法管辖区的万能寿险却不尽相同。加拿大本土市场还未出现和发行投资型万能寿险和指数型万能寿险产品，加拿大的万能寿险与大家所熟知的美国万能寿险（或者叫固定型／传统型万能寿险）不同，反而具有相当多投资型万能寿险的特点。例如，加拿大的万能寿险允许保单持有人从一系列投资标的如利息账户（Daily Interest Accounts）、保证投资账户（Guaranteed Investment Accounts）、指数基金、互惠基金中自由建立投资组合。

由于万能寿险中的投资组合是由投保人自行选择和管理，若投资回报远低于预期，则可能需要补充保费以避免保单失效，因此万能寿险存在较大的不确定性，需要投保人具有良好的风险意识和承受能力，并对投资领域有一定的认知和把控能力。另外，万能寿险在加拿大企业保单中的运用较终身寿险更为广泛，主要是从企业资本分红账户（Capital Dividend Account，CDA）分配时的税务问题考虑（详见第 8 章）。

5.3　中国香港特别行政区

保险业是中国香港特别行政区（下文简称"中国香港"）最古老的行业之一，至今已有两百多年的历史。中国香港保险业的发展最早可追溯至 1805 年在广州创办的英资谏当保安行(Canton Insurance Society)。1841年在英军占领中国香港后,谏当保安行的总部也跟着搬迁到了中国香港,成为中国香港最早的保险公司。经过近两个世纪的发展后,中国香港已成为全球领先的国际保险中心之一。中国香港保险市场监管制度成熟有效、市场成熟度高,外资机构数量众多,保险公司可全球配置保费资产,发展出了门类齐全的港币、美元和其他主要货币的保险产品。

目前,中国香港的保险业务主要分为一般业务和长期业务。个人人寿保险在中国香港是长期业务中最主要的业务类别。中国香港保险业2022年的毛保费总额达5 380亿港元,其中,个人人寿业务有效保单保费达4 242.89亿港元,占整体保险业务规模的78.87%。作为国际金融和保险中心,境外访客是中国香港个人寿险市场重要的客户来源,其中又以内地访客占比最大。对于境外投保人,中国香港保险公司普遍要求客户必须到中国香港境内签单和体检,否则视为无效保单。截至2022年底,中国香港保险市场的有效个人人寿保险为1 400万份。根据中国香港保监局发布的数据,2022年新造个人人寿业务统计如图5.7所示。

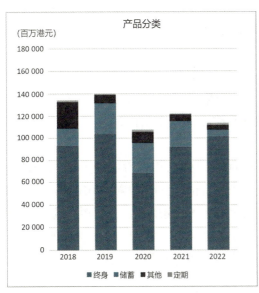
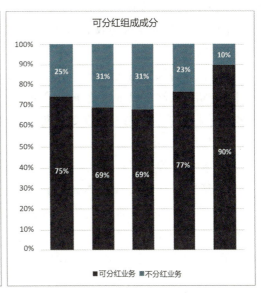

非投资相连业务之保单保费（按产品分类）(百万港元)	2018	2019	2020	2021	2022
终身	92 918.3	102 949.2	68 098.5	91 551.3	100 906.8
储蓄	15 982.8	28 055.6	28 197.0	23 404.7	6 996.4
定期	521.3	727.3	806.5	799.3	549.3
其他	23 771.6	7 689.4	9 738.4	6 005.2	4 168.1

图5.7 新造个人人寿的非投资相连业务保单保费

中国香港寿险市场代表性产品有:
- 储蓄分红险
- 万能寿险
- 定期寿险和两全保险

5.3.1 储蓄分红险

储蓄分红险是中国香港最具特色并且最受欢迎的产品,在中国香港的保险业务中占据了重要的地位。在中国香港保监局的分类里并没有储蓄分红险这一类别,储蓄分红险是对通过长期分红提供储蓄功能的寿险的一种更加直观的说法。储蓄分红险在中国香港保监局统计数据里属于终身寿险的一种,但其与传统意义上的寿险有一定的区别。储蓄分红险具有以下特征。

5.3.1.1 购买年龄及核保要求

储蓄分红险对购买年龄的要求较为宽松,一般投保年龄为 1~80 岁。视供款期不同,部分产品的投保上限会降低到 60 岁左右。储蓄分红险的身故赔偿金大多为其保单现金价值或所缴保费的特定百分比,与传统寿险的高额杠杆区别较大,因此绝大多数储蓄分红险只需进行财务核保而无须进行健康核保。

5.3.1.2 保证收益和非保证收益

储蓄分红险的现金价值有两部分:保证和非保证。保证收益即保险公司承诺一定会给保单持有人的,属于确定收益;非保证收益则是保险公司根据综合情况派发的红利,属于不确定收益。

非保证收益部分的红利派发形式又分为英式分红和美式分红两种(详见第 3 章),在中国香港储蓄分红险保单的设计中,这两种方式均有采用。相对而言,英式分红由于险资更多会投资于权益类资产,从保单长期持有的角度看,表现会更出色些。

5.3.1.3 分红实现率

为了协助投保人了解分红产品非保证收益的派发表现,中国香港保监局于 2017 年 1 月实施了指引 16(Guidance Note16,GN16),要求所有保险公司披露从 2010 年起以及最近 5 年内发出的新保单的分红产品非保证收益的实际分红实现率并公布在官网上,从而给投保人一个合理的预期值。中国香港保监局于近期更新了指引 16,要求保险公司自 2024 年 1 月 1 日起,就 2010 年后发出并且仍有有效保单存在的分红保单或万用寿险保单,都要披露分红实现率和过往派息率。

分红实现率是用来衡量指定时间内实际非保证利益的履行表现,以客户购买计划时建议书内说明的非保证利益所达之百分率表示。例如某产品在计划书上预计派发非保证红利为 100 元,而实际派发时只派发了 80 元,则红利实现率为 80%(=80/100)。

5.3.1.4 退保现金价值的折现率

储蓄分红险的现金价值包括三部分:保证现金价值、归原红利、终期红利。在退保时,其现金价值存在折现率,退保现金价值为现金价值总和(面值)乘以一定的折现率,该折现率一般随着保单年份增长而接近 100%。不同保险公司会制定不同的折现率,如保单生效初期即退保的话,现金价值折现率可低至 30%,平均在 70%~80%。因此,中国香港储蓄分红险短期持有的储蓄功能并无明显优势,退保损失也很大,长期持有才能获得相对较满意的保单年化收益。

5.3.1.5 多元货币

从传统上说,中国香港的储蓄分红险的保单货币主要是港币和美元,近年来多家中国香港保险公司均推出了多元货币计划,进一步将投保货币扩充到了离岸人民币、英镑、欧元、加元、日元、澳元、新加坡元、澳门元(澳门保单)等国际主流货币。保单不仅可在投保时以不同货币支付保费,部分计划也支持在保单生效后进行保单内部的货币转换,以灵活满足客户的外汇需要。

5.3.1.6 可更改和预设投被保人

中国香港的储蓄分红险还有一个比较重要的特征是,多数保险公司近年发行的产品可以更改投保人及被保人,主流产品允许无限次更改,但这也取决于首位被保人的年龄及不同保险合同中的规定。部分产品还支持预设投保人及被保人,从而将保单的生命周期延长。这些功能赋予储蓄分红险类信托的功能,"一张保单,多代人共享"。因此在设计这类保单权益时,可围绕如何稳妥更改投保人及被保人,实现保单内资金的长期持续滚存及跨代传承来综合考量。需注意,不同保险公司的具体规定有所不同,部分保单需要新投保人及被保人和/或老的投保人及被保人亲自赴港完成书面手续,这对实际流程的便利性形成了一定的挑战。

5.3.2 万能寿险

中国香港的万能寿险也叫作万用寿险,比较类似于美国的传统万能寿险或者固定型万能寿险。除了具有灵活缴款、灵活增减保障额、可于固定期限获派发利息、灵活提款等一般特征外,部分保险公司设计的产品还可用于保费融资撬动高杠杆。通常这类万能寿险产品的缴费时间短(平均2~3年),当然短期内保费交付金额高,保单现金价值累积也高。其原理如图5.8所示。

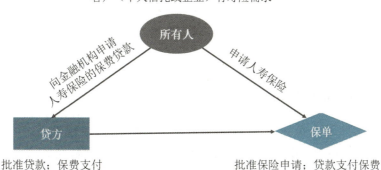

图 5.8 保费融资原理

首先,投保人申请保单,并成功获得核保。同时,在相关金融机构开户,开户手续、贷款审批流程及要求参照各金融机构具体标准执行。通常,保单可抵押贷款的最大额度为首日保单退保现金价值的90%,客户在支付了自付额度及手续费/利息后,金融机构就会将全额保费支付给保险公司,以使保单即刻生效。

如在低息环境下,投保人不仅可以获得一份终身寿险(通常保单内会有不低于2%的保证利息收益),而且可以通过保单撬动的高杠杆融资最大化地提高资金的使用效率。但一旦面临加息环境,投保人就面临很大的利率风险。该类保费融资的操作适合投资经验丰富、善用投资杠杆、资金流充裕的高净值人士了解和使用,需要全面考虑利率风险、汇率风险、派息风险和保险公司主体风险等。

5.3.3 定期寿险和两全保险

中国香港定期寿险的产品设计及功能和美国、加拿大司法管辖区的产品基本一致,增加了更多更灵活的选项。比如在定期寿险发生赔付时,可以根据预先的保单条款约定,选择一次性赔付发放身故赔偿金,也可以选择定期定额发放或定期不定额发放身故赔偿金,以确保受益人将来得到稳定的收入来源,发放款项的年期更可长达30年;也可以在定期寿险的基础上增加多项附加保障选择,包括重疾、医疗、永久残疾及意外保障等。

中国香港两全保险也称为储蓄计划,具有储蓄性和给付性两个特点,即无论被保人在保险合同期间死亡,还是被保人到保险合同期满时生存,保险公司均会给付一笔保险金。中国香港两全保险一方面提供保险合同期限内的人身保障,另一方面通常也会设定一个保单的保证回报率。目前各家发行两全保险的保险公司设计的保证收益率平均在2%~3%,即保险合同期满未就被保人身故赔偿的话,保险公司会给付全额所缴保费及保费产生的收益,保单形式通常以"交2保5""交3保6""交3保8"等组合为代表。因此从某种程度上讲,可以将两全保险理解为一种短期储蓄工具,也类似于一种返还型的定期寿险。中国香港两全保险提供港币(HKD)、美元(USD)及人民币(CNY)等保单货币的产品供客户选择,以对冲保单的外汇风险。

5.4 新加坡

5.4.1 新加坡寿险市场概述

新加坡是亚洲唯一被全球最大的三家信用评级机构即标准普尔(S&P)、穆迪(Moody's)与惠誉(Fitch)给予AAA信用评级的主权国家。政治、经济稳定,货币相对于其他货币长期保持坚挺,因此新加坡一直是亚洲最大的私人财富管理中心,被称为亚洲的瑞士。近年来,随着世界及亚洲经济、政治环境的发展及变化,新加坡市场开始引起众多追求稳健投资及保障的保险客户的关注。根据新加坡人寿保险协会(Life Insurance Association Singapore, LIA)发布的数据,2022年新加坡个人人寿保险和健康保险总加权保费（Total Weighted Premium）较2021年下跌5.2%，为50.98亿新元，除极少部分来自健康保险外，绝大部分保费来自人寿保险。新加坡三大主要寿险销售渠道为保险公司直销代理人渠道、银保渠道和独立经纪人渠道，共占到总销售份额的90%以上。

新加坡逐步成长为亚洲新兴保险市场的代表，主要有两方面原因：一是新加坡对整个金融市场的监管都非常严格。新加坡保险公司由新加坡金融管理局（Monetary Authority of Singapore，MAS）负责监管。为了维护整个新加坡在亚洲金融行业的龙头地位和良好声誉，新加坡保险公司执行了全球最高标准的透明度，比如在保险合同中会公布一些在其他司法管辖区不一定会公布的信息，如保单收取的各项费用，包括代理人佣金等。信息的透明化及严格健全的监管机制有助于客户更有效地选择保险产品。二是新加坡人寿保险的保费也有不错的竞争力。保费计算的主要依据是死亡率，因此较低的死亡率也会获得较低的保费和更高的保额。新加坡作为全球最长寿国家的前三甲（详见表5.1）之一，有理由为发行的寿险产品设计更高、更合理的保障杠杆。此外，近几年来中国香港地区在金融业地位的下降也为新加坡带来了大量资金，其中一部分资金进入了新加坡的寿险行业。

表5.1　2016年和2040年各国平均预期寿命排名

排名	国家	2016年平均预期寿命	排名	国家	2040年平均预期寿命	排名变化（对比2016）
1	日本	83.7	1	西班牙	85.8	▲
2	瑞士	83.3	2	日本	85.7	▼
3	新加坡	83.3	3	新加坡	85.4	不变
4	西班牙	82.9	4	瑞士	85.2	▼
5	澳大利亚	82.5	5	葡萄牙	84.5	▲
6	安道尔	82.5	6	意大利	84.5	▲
7	意大利	82.3	7	以色列	84.4	▲
8	法国	82.3	8	法国	84.3	不变
9	冰岛	82.3	9	卢森堡	84.1	▲
10	卢森堡	82.2	10	澳大利亚	84.1	▼

来源：Institute for Health Metrics and Evaluation Straits Times Graphics。

新加坡人寿保险产品的险种及相应保障条款都非常全面，保单货币以新币和美元为主要代表，也有少部分以欧元、英镑、澳元、港币为保单货币发行的产品，充分满足客户全球资产配置及抵御外汇风险的需求。

新加坡寿险市场的主要产品有：
- 定期寿险
- 终身寿险
- 指数型万能寿险
- 储蓄险
- 投资连结险

5.4.2 定期寿险

新加坡的定期寿险以高性价比著称，保费便宜，保障额度杠杆率高，并可以附加多种保障，如全残、重疾、轻疾等；可接受的投保年龄高至 70 岁，最高保额达 1 500 万新币。

新加坡定期寿险产品一直在亚洲定期寿险市场具有较强的竞争力，这与政府在全民范围内的大力推广有着密不可分的关系。新加坡政府深知全民寿险保障存在缺口，对于家庭经济支柱身故导致家庭保障严重缺损，以及之后可能产生的一系列社会问题，可以在一定程度上通过定期寿险来解决。因此，新加坡金融管理局于 2016 年强制要求每一家保险公司都必须向消费者提供简单、便宜的定期寿险产品，并且推出了一个官方的保险比价网站，以促进行业正当竞争，最终让利于民。

从保险产品开发的角度来看，一个产品的参保者越多、覆盖面越广，其理赔发生率就越容易预测，产品的定价也就更精准。因此，新加坡通过提高全民的定期寿险参保率以及对行业公平透明度的严格监管体制，提高了其定期寿险产品的价格竞争优势。

5.4.3 终身寿险

参与型终身寿险和非参与型终身寿险的介绍详见第 3 章。新加坡终身寿险产品中两种形式均有，以参与型终身寿险的产品更为典型和常见。

与其他章节介绍的参与型终身寿险类似，新加坡参与型终身寿险的保单收益也分为保证利益和非保证利益两部分，并在保单合同中注明。保证利益是在任何情况下，保险公司都必须向客户兑现的；分红基金的投资收益情况，决定了保单持有人能再得到多少非保证利益。同时，新加坡保险公司会采取平滑策略，以避免保单每年的收益因投资市场短期震荡而产生较大波动。

此外，新加坡参与型终身寿险保单的持有货币有新币和美元两种形式。以新币计价的分红寿险保单都需要用 4.25% 和 3.00% 这两个演示收益率来预期分红，不允许私自上调（美元保单暂时无此项限制，绝大部分保险公司是以 5% 和 3.75% 进行演示）。相对于中国香港保单同时兼顾权益类和固收类的险资投资策略，新加坡参与型终身寿险的投资策略整体偏向保守、稳健，当然这也是基于新加坡金融管理局更严格的监管机制。每家保险公司的分红基金中约 55%~70% 投向固收类资产，15%~30% 投向股权类资产，剩余部分则投向地产和其他资产。

5.4.4 指数型万能寿险

新加坡的保险公司除了发行最基本的传统万能寿险产品外,个别保险公司也于近年发行了指数型万能寿险和投资型万能寿险这两种在亚洲寿险市场不常见的万能寿险产品。

如前文所述,指数型万能寿险是在美国寿险市场过去十年迅速发展并日趋成熟的一类万能寿险产品。新加坡保险公司发行的指数型万能寿险产品在设计原理和保单运用上与美国的指数型万能寿险产品类似,也是通过对指数趋势的追踪及"上有封顶、下有保底"的保单收益率调节,获得相对安全也更高的保单增值空间和保障杠杆。从投资策略上看,新加坡指数型万能寿险产品的指数策略较美国单一,可选择的指数策略灵活性较弱;但新加坡指数型万能寿险产品的一大特色是可以更改保单被保人,被保人可以是企业,也可以是个人,企业被保人可以无限次更换,个人被保人最多可以更换2次,从而充分发挥保单资金更长效的传承。这一可更改被保人的保单亮点尚未出现在美国的指数型万能寿险产品中。另外,新加坡的指数型万能寿险不受美国 7702 条款和 MEC 测试(详见 6.4.2)的限制,可以趸交保费。

5.4.5 储蓄险

新加坡的储蓄险也分为非参与型和参与型两种,除了有保值增值的储蓄功能外,也能在出现保单到期前身故的意外情况时提供一定的保障功能。非参与型储蓄险在计划到期时有保证收益和保证的现金价值,但是不像参与型储蓄险在保证现金价值的基础上还可能享受额外红利。市面上的储蓄险以参与型的为主。新加坡的储蓄险和中国香港的储蓄险在产品设计原理和运用功能上基本类似,只是相对来说新加坡的产品在期限设定上偏中长期,像中国香港"交2保5"这类短期产品较少,通常以10年或20年期限的产品最为常见;其产品的保证年化收益率一般略高于新加坡本地银行的定期存款利率,目前在 3%～5%。对于保障期限非终身需要,以及投资风险偏好非常保守的本地客户,这类储蓄险是有一定市场的。

5.4.6 投资连结险

投资连结险(Investment-Linked Policy,ILP)由人寿保险和投资两部分组成。与终身寿险及储蓄险不同之处是,投资连结险的保费将首先用于购买一个或多个子基金单位(Sub-funds Units),然后将其中一些单位出售用于支付相关保险成本及费用,剩余单位进入基金账户用于投资。投资连结险和私募寿险不同,它不是私募的保单,也没有独立的托管专户,应属投资型万能寿险。

投资连结险根据保单条款在约定的期限内为被保人提供身故保障,赔偿额度以保单约定的金额与投资连结险账户价值取高值偿付。投资连结险也可以附加其他保障选项,如重疾、全残险等。保费支付方式可以是一次性支付或定期支付,大部分一次性支付保费的投资连结险所提供的保额要小于定期支付保费的投资连结险,而后者还可以灵活变更保险额度。与投入终身寿险和储蓄险的保费不同的是,投入投资连结险的保费并非由保险公司全权决定投资策略,而是由保单持有人自行选择子基金和决定投资策略;投资连结险账户价值完全取决于基金账户的投资表现,因此投资连结险不会像终身寿险和储蓄险有保证现金价值一说,这也意味着投资连结险的持有人需要对所选基金的投资方向和策略充分了解,也愿意承担在基金表现不佳时的潜在风险和机会成本。

投资连结险因其高度的灵活性而受到部分消费者的关注和青睐。投资连结险提供了一系列适合不同投资目标和风险偏好的基金选择,投资连结险持有人可以根据家庭财务需求变化,减少保障额度(以合同约定最低保额为准),或提高保障额度(以合同约定承保上限及核保要求为准);还可以向保单内追加投资或进行部分提款;也可以通过转换子基金来改变投资策略,降低市场波动风险和/或满足自身退休收入等需求。

需要注意的是,尽管在投资连结险合同期限内每月须支付相同的保费,但保险费用通常会随着年龄、死亡、疾病等风险率的增加而逐年增加。这意味着可能需要出售更多的基金单位来支付保险费用,而留下更少的单位来积累保单现金价值。在保险费用逐年增加、保额维持不变而子基金持续表现欠佳时,就有可能导致基金的单位价值不足以支付保险费用,保单持有人必须通过追加保费投入或降低保额来维持保单的效力。因此,选择投资连结险的客户应充分了解其潜在的投资风险给保单效力带来的不确定性,在综合评估自身的中长期的财务目标、投资专业能力、投资偏好及风险承受度等因素后,再做出选择。

5.5 离岸产品

5.5.1 离岸寿险市场概述

长期以来,讲到全球主要离岸金融市场,公认的代表为开曼、英属维京群岛(British Virgin Islands,BVI)和百慕大。开曼和BVI分别以信托业务和离岸公司业务见长,百慕大则是因保险和再保险业务而声名在外。与大众对离岸地区在合规方面疑虑的想象不同,实际上百慕大拥有非常健全的司法体系和严格的合规准则。作为英国最早的海外领地,百慕大采用普通法体系,现今的政治和司法制度可追溯到17世纪。经过4个世纪的发展,百慕大在金融监管和合规方面已成为一个受到广泛认可的司法管辖区,比如其在保险和再保险领域就先后受到了欧盟《偿付能力监管Ⅱ号指令》和美国全国保险委员会协会"合资格司法管辖区"地位的认可。

百慕大在再保险方面已经是高度成熟的市场,全球前40大再保险公司中,有14家在百慕大持有执照和展业。根据国际保险监理官协会发布的2022全球保险市场报告披露的数据,百慕大占到全球再保险净保费规模的19.1%,仅次于美国,是全球第二大的再保险市场。从保险类型来看,百慕大是全球最重要的单一财产和巨灾保险市场,而以人寿保险、年金、退休金为主的长期保险市场则正处于快速发展阶段。百慕大国际长期保险和再保险协会(Bermuda International Long Term Insurance and Reinsurance,BILTIR)的统计就指出,截至2019年,百慕大长期保险在管总资产为6 670亿美元,较2018年增长35.6%。

由于离岸地区的客户来自全球各地,因此其销售渠道和对客户的签单要求与传统在岸地区都有较大区别。一般来说,离岸地区全球性的保险公司会授权有限的一级保险代理人在世界各地销售其产品,投保客户也无须去保险发行地,而是可以通过保险公司在当地认证的医院完成体检后进行远程签单核保,这与绝大多数在岸地保险公司的要求不同。得益于离岸地区的特殊地理位置和灵活有创新性的立法,保单投保人能以更方便的方式完成投保、核保、签单、付款等全过程,这也是离岸地区保单的一大优势。本节主要以百慕大作为离岸寿险产品发行地的代表做介绍。

百慕大发行的产品种类主要有以下几种:

- 指数型万能寿险
- 分红型终身寿险
- 分红型储蓄险
- 指数型储蓄险

5.5.2 指数型万能寿险

指数型万能寿险的产品原理及指数策略运用等可参考第3章和本章5.1节的详细描述。在离岸国际市场上发售的指数型万能寿险,主要采用的指数有标普500(S&P 500)和恒生(Hang Seng)等。保单币种通常为美元,支付期限灵活,可选择一次性支付保费、多次付款(Multipay),也可在保单有效的情况下停交再复交保费。该保单投保门槛比其他司法管辖区高,也常被称作大额保单(Jumbo Life)、富豪保单。起购保额视产品不同,一般为100万~200万美元,保额最高可申请到2亿美元,受保年龄为0岁至85岁,前提是健康和财务核保都经审批通过。

5.5.2.1 指数及参与率

大多数产品主要挂钩标普500指数,部分产品也会挂钩恒生或欧洲斯托克50等指数。收益计息方式是一年期点对点即计算一年后的指数点位和开始时的指数点位之比,然后乘以参与率,得出该一年期的分段收益率,再用来计算现金价值的增长。

5.5.2.2 封顶收益率和保底收益率

不同指数策略的封顶收益率不尽相同。比如,假设当前封顶收益率为9%,如果实际指数增幅为10%,那就只会将封顶值9%用于计算收益率。封顶收益率由保险公司控制并有权调整,通常离岸指数型万能寿险产品的封顶收益率不低于3%。保底收益率是指数账户的一种保护机制,也就是收益下限。离岸指数型万能寿险产品的保底收益率通常设定为0,即指数下跌时保单不会产生负收益。

5.5.2.3 演示收益率

在实际操作时,保险公司通常会采取所选股指在近25年或近几十年间的历史表现作为演示收益率。比如目前离岸指数型万能寿险产品计划书中不同指数策略采用的演示收益率平均在5%~7%。

5.5.2.4 指数收益率计算

不同的指数型万能寿险产品所采取的指数策略不同,也对应有不同的指数收益率计算方式。计算方式在保险合同中均有明确列示(详见第3章)。

5.5.2.5 指数型万能寿险保单内其他账户的设置

指数型万能寿险保单内除了必要的指数账户之外,通常还设有固定收益账户。客户可以选择将缴纳的保费放在指数账户或者固定收益账户,分配比例也是可以调整的,指数账户中不同策略与固定收益账户加总为100%即可。

指数型万能寿险的固定收益账户每年由保险公司厘定一个固定利率,一旦公布,这个利率在一年内就保证不变。近年来固定回报账户利率在3.6%~4.5%,相对指数账户收益率较低,但略高于在岸地指数型万能寿险产品的固定收益账户。

5.5.2.6 指数型万能寿险保单收费项目

指数型万能寿险保单的收费清晰透明,根据不同保险公司的设置,常见的收费项目如下。

(1) 保费收费(Premium Charge)。

即一次性扣费,从保单现金价值中直接扣除。当每次有新保费交进去时,根据交费时的保单年份,按照既定的收费比例扣取。

(2) 初始保额收费(Face Amount Charge)。

即按月扣费,从保单现金价值中直接扣除。通常保单前15年收取该费用。这项收费以面值中每1 000美元为收费基础,按照对应的比率计算收取。

(3) 保险成本费用(Cost of Insurance Charge)。

这项费用,按月扣除至100岁或保险理赔时,从保单现金价值中直接扣除。这项收费以风险净值中每1 000美元作为收费基础,按照对应的比率计算收取。

(4) 退保费用(Surrender Charge)。

此项收费仅适用于保单取消时。通常保单前10年退保会有退保费用产生,且根据退保时间,收取的费率不等,越往后费率越低。

(5) 其他费用(Other Charge)。

一些指数账户可能有业绩费用(Performance Charge)。这项费用有一个固定的收费率,以每个月末的保单价值为基准。

以上收费项的费率都由保险公司制定,且费率写进保险合同中。

5.5.2.7 指数型万能寿险保单持有结构

在岸司法管辖区的保单通常通过个人、企业或信托(有限制)持有,而离岸保单则有以下 3 种持有方式。

① 个人设立离岸公司持有保单;

② 个人设立离岸信托持有保单;

③ 个人作为保险公司已有的主权信托(Master Trust)的参与者持有保单。

5.5.2.8 为什么选择离岸市场的指数型万能寿险

① 百慕大作为全球三大保险中心之一,历史悠久,监管严格,信誉度高。

② 申请流程及要求相对宽松,无须入境及建立和国外的居住联系(见表 5.2)。

表 5.2 国际销售规则比较

	离岸	美国	中国香港
是否允许通行的新单申请流程	需要	不需要	不需要
需要在保单签发地体检吗	不需要	需要	需要
需要入境保单签发地申请吗	不需要	需要	需要
在何地可以合规推荐产品	居住地以外	只能在美国	只能在中国香港

③ 需要美元配置的保单作养老、储蓄、隔离保护、传承之用。保单可以视为离岸地区的银行账户。保单中累积的现金价值可灵活支配,包括直接支取、保单贷款/抵押贷款,也可根据客户资金流状况做保费融资。

④ 保费支付灵活,保单内投资与指数挂钩,跟着大盘走势获得收益,且不用承担直接投资股市带来的风险。

基于以上优势,离岸指数型万能寿险产品近年来逐步受到市场关注。

5.5.3 分红型终身寿险

百慕大发行的寿险面向全球的高净值人士,多为万能寿险,但随着高净值客户所在地域和家庭财务需求的转变,近几年百慕大也推出了终身寿险。

百慕大的终身寿险主要是分红型终身寿险,与其他司法管辖区发行的分红型终身寿险在产品原理和使用功能上类似。保单内既有保证部分,也有非保证部分;保单中的投资运作和分红由保险公司决定,客户仅能被动享受不保证的分红。保险公司的评级实力、过往分红表现、分红账户运作等是选择分红产品的重要考量因素。

5.5.3.1 产品特点

① 可选择一次性付清、5 年付或 10 年付。最低投保额为 100 万美元。被保人年龄区间为 20~85 岁,保单现金价值由保证现金价值和非保证的分红构成。

② 分红有两类:复归红利和终期红利。终期红利 10 年后开始派发,每年保险公司在年报上公布终期红利的数字,但这个数字可变,只有在完全退保或领取身故赔偿金时才可

以获得实际的终期红利金额。

③ 保单的身故赔偿金也是由保证的起始保额和非保证的增购保额构成的。与其他在岸地在分红用途上的多样性选择不同的是,百慕大的分红用途只有一种,就是增购保额。因分红不获保证,所以分红购买的额外保额也不是固定不变的。当分红被支取后,增加的保额也会相应降低。百慕大的分红型终身寿险保费也是集中在分红账户,由保险公司的专业投资团队统一管理运作,保险公司会根据所属司法管辖区保险法规对分红账户的资产进行长久、稳健、动态的投资管理,同时会对分红保险保单持有人公布分红账户投资组合和策略。目前百慕大分红型终身寿险的基本投资策略有:固定收益类、政府债券、公司债券、房地产类、股票和商业贷款等。

其持有结构同其他离岸寿险一样,请参考第 5.5.1 小节。

5.5.3.2 为什么选择离岸市场分红寿险

离岸分红寿险将离岸寿险市场的优势(详见第 5.5.1 小节)与分红寿险的优势相结合,适合希望获得稳定的保额杠杆和确定传承金额,对保费支付期限和金额有保证需求的客户,也是有兼顾税务筹划需求、家族企业和财富需要传承的高净值人士的备选寿险产品之一。

5.5.4 分红型储蓄险

近年来,百慕大推出了此前只在亚洲当地市场有的分红型储蓄险,此类产品的出现填补了市场的空白,给了全球高净值客户更多的选择。该产品的保单价值从组成上看与其他参与型的寿险产品类似,也是分为保证部分和非保证部分。非保证部分由年度红利(Annual Dividend)和其他红利来实现保单内的财富累积;此外,此类产品还能提供额外的安全性,为客户提供不少于缴纳总保费的身故赔偿金,同时伴有意外身故赔偿的功能。百慕大分红型储蓄险的特点总结如下。

5.5.4.1 财富累积

① 年度红利:每个保单周年日,保险公司将公布非保证年度红利;一旦宣派,它就成为保单累积股息的保证部分,会产生利息。累积的年度红利会产生利息回报,保险公司或会不定时调整利率。

② 终期红利:在保单到期、全额退保、违约或被保人身故的情况下,均会支付终期红利。终期红利虽然每年都计算,但与年度红利不同,计算得出的金额并不能保证保单价值的增加。保险公司可能会增加或减少这个数字,并且不作保证。

5.5.4.2 收益保护

① 现金价值支付:保险公司确保退保时应支付的终期红利不低于保证价值。

② 分红平稳(Dividend Smoothing):为免受市场波动的影响,保险公司对派发红利采用平滑策略。因此业绩好坏不会立即反映在分红的高低上面,以维持稳定的分红金额。

5.5.4.3 世代规划

① 无须健康核保:购买此产品只需要财务核保,无须对被保人的健康做体检和核查,

为身体不好或上了年纪的投保人提供了购买保险产品的选择。

② 可更换被保人：在符合保险公司对新被保人年龄和可保利益要求的前提下，可以无限次更换被保人，使得家族财富可以世代累积。

5.5.4.4 使用现金价值

对于储蓄保险，如何使用保单内的钱尤为重要。该类产品提供 2 种方式。

① 提取（Withdrawing）：直接提取保单内累积的分红（但这将会减少保单的身故赔偿金和退保利益）。

② 退保（Surrendering）：保单有效期内可以提出全额退保或部分退保，某些产品会有起始退保年份的要求，也会有退保收费产生。保单将在保单到期日，通常是第 121 个保单年的第一天到期并终止（自动退保），届时保险公司将支付退保现金价值。

5.5.4.5 身故赔偿

主要身故赔偿金将会是以下两者较高者：

① 累计分红和终期红利之和；

② 支付的保费和应计的分红之和。

需要注意的是，保单的任何贷款、债务或支出都将在分配身故赔偿金之前被扣除。

5.5.4.6 保费支付计划

一次性付清（趸交）、5 年付或 10 年付。

5.5.4.7 产品演算关联因素

此类产品只与投入保费金额、付款期限相关，与年龄、性别、身体状况无关。

从上述产品特点来看，虽然该产品有分红、有现金价值的累计增长，但与分红寿险的最大不同是，保额没有放大保费的杠杆作用，也就是说，身故赔偿金等于投入保费，或者等于保单内现金价值总额。正因如此，保险公司没有需要承担的净风险保额，即没有额外的赔偿风险，所以也无须对被保人进行健康核保。

5.5.4.8 保单持有结构

其持有结构同其他离岸寿险一样，请参考第 5.5.1 小节。

5.5.4.9 适合人群

① 希望被保人可以更换，为家族财富实现世代累积；

② 希望产品在投资储蓄的功能之外又有意外身故赔偿的保障；

③ 健康核保达不到要求的人士；

④ 在家族财富规划中，为用不到的现金资产找到更优存放地的客户。

5.5.5 指数型储蓄险

除了分红型储蓄险以外，百慕大这几年还发明了一个较为新颖的产品类型——指数型储蓄险。从产品名字上即可以看出此类产品仍然是一个储蓄险，但同时结合了指数型产品的特点。我们通过与分红型储蓄险的对比可以对此类产品有一个更清晰的了解。

作为储蓄险中的一种,指数型储蓄险与分红型储蓄险有很多相似点。例如,指数型储蓄险的主要目的仍然是资产的保值、增值和传承,保险公司不会就指数型储蓄险支付一个杠杆较大的身故赔偿金,当被保人身故时受益人获得的是全部保费或者当时的现金价值(两者取较大者),因此指数型储蓄险的被保人在投保时同样无须进行健康核保。此外,两类产品的一些附属功能或者额外条约往往是类似的,例如可更换被保人已经成为各类储蓄险里的一个标准配置。

指数型储蓄险与分红型储蓄险的区别主要有以下3点。

首先,两者的账户价值虽然都分为保证和非保证部分,但非保证部分的收益机制完全不一样。分红型的收益主要来源于保险公司的分红,而指数型产品的收益则是挂钩一个或多个指数,在这一点上指数型储蓄险和指数型万能寿险有高度的相似性,同样会涉及指数的选择、参与率、收益率上限和保底率等。

其次,保单的成本和费用不一样。分红型储蓄险一般没有额外的成本,依靠保险公司的分红逐年提高现金价值;而指数型储蓄险因为涉及挂钩指数以及其他跟投资策略相关的成本,因此保单本身会收一定的费用,如保单支出费用、基本面额收费、指数账户收费和退保费用等。

最后,因为两种产品的收益机制不一样,所以造成了计划书中演示利率的内在含义也有差别。分红型储蓄险的演示利率是依据保险公司对分红的预估情况来设定的,而指数型储蓄险的演示利率则是按照将所选指数代入策略进行回测的真实表现来确定的。从这个角度来说,指数型产品的透明度更好。但两种产品的计划书也都清楚地列明了不同收益状况下保单价值的演示。

5.6 中国内地

5.6.1 中国内地寿险市场综述

中国内地寿险市场是一个充满机遇和挑战的市场,经历了近三十年的快速发展,它已经成为仅次于美国的全球第二大寿险市场。根据中国保险行业协会发布的《2022中国保险业社会责任报告》,2022年全国共有保险法人机构237家,资产总额为27.15万亿元人民币。中国银保监会发布的保险业经营数据显示,2022年保险业实现总保费收入4.70万亿元人民币,同比增长4.6%(其中寿险收入为2.45万亿元人民币,占保险保费收入的52%),保单总件数553.8亿件,同比增长13.27%(如图5.9所示)。

从销售渠道来看,中国内地保险类金融产品的销售主要包括直接销售渠道、保险代理渠道(包括银行保险)和保险经纪渠道。从主要上市保险企业保费收入渠道来看,目前代理人渠道是保险企业获取保费的主要渠道,占比均超过65%。

5 不同司法管辖区的寿险市场和主要寿险产品

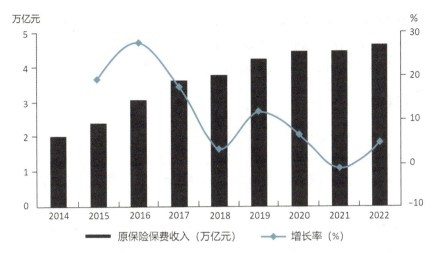

图5.9 2014—2022年中国原保险保费收入及增长率

资料来源：前瞻产业研究院。

寿险行业在中国社会的发展中起到了诸多的积极作用。保险公司通过提供各类保险产品，为人们提供了有效的社会保障；保险产品又通过专业的风险评估和精算技术，为个人和家庭提供风险管理服务。寿险行业的发展也有助于社会稳定，通过提供养老保险等产品，它可以为老年人提供经济保障，减轻社会负担，促进社会和谐。

从产品类型来看，中国监管部门将保险分类为财产险和人身险，人身险中按照保障范围分为寿险、健康险、意外险，而寿险是人身险的基础和核心。寿险主要分为普通型人寿保险和新型人寿保险。普通型人寿保险又分为定期寿险、终身寿险、两全保险、年金保险。新型人寿保险则包含分红保险、投资连结保险、万能保险，三者都带有投资属性，只不过投资收益形式不同，受监管和投资能力限制，大多在投资收益上表现一般。但是除投资连结保险外，都有保本保底条款，相对其他金融投资产品有较高的安全性和稳定性。下文将就定期寿险、终身寿险、两全保险、万能保险和分红保险作详细介绍。

5.6.2 定期寿险

中国内地的定期寿险主要包括定额定期寿险和降额定期寿险。

5.6.2.1 定额定期寿险

与前文所提到的其他地区的同类产品类似，中国内地的定额定期寿险也是为被保险人在指定时间内提供身故保障赔偿。此类产品在中国内地一般保额在400万元人民币以内，保费较低，赔付杠杆很高。保障期间可以分为一年期定期寿险和长期定期寿险。一年期定期寿险的保障期限就是一年。长期的定期寿险的保险期限通常有10年、20年、30年，或到50岁、60岁、70岁等约定年龄的多项选择。

5.6.2.2 降额定期寿险

此类产品的特点是按基本保额逐年减少，直到合同到期时，只剩基本保额（基本保额＝首年保额/保障期限）。降额定期寿险适合分期还款高负债人群,比如高房贷、装修贷和车贷,随着负债额度的减少,保障也逐渐减少。降额定期寿险在中国内地市场产品较少,相对定额定期寿险费率优势不大,常以定额定期寿险替代。

5.6.3 终身寿险

5.6.3.1 定额终身寿险

定额终身寿险承保后保额是终身固定的,因为可以用低保费撬动高保额,通常也叫杠杆寿。定额终身寿险是传统功能的寿险,侧重风险保障功能。突出身故风险补偿作用,利用小额资金,防止在被保人高收入阶段突发身故引发家庭财务崩溃。如果安全健康地生活至老年,百年时保额就赔付给受益人。中国内地的定额终身寿险从某种角度来说类似海外部分国家的非参与型终身寿险,投资增值功能较差,主要依靠较低的保费来满足保障需求。

5.6.3.2 增额终身寿险

中国内地的增额终身寿险是于2013年从中国台湾地区引进的一款寿险产品,保额按照预定利率复利增长。其本金安全,收益稳定;高现金价值可灵活减保,优于年金;具有回本快,利于大额急用资金时的退保需求,小额用款可减保、可高额贷款的特点。从功能上来看,保额和风险杠杆较低,长期储蓄功能更明显。保单现金价值较定额终身寿险更高、回本更快,而且持续增长,便于减保和保单贷款,可作为解决不时之需的流动性安排,是一款很好用的长期现金流规划工具。增额终身寿险适合大众用作安全保本保底的储蓄理财工具;也可用作高净值人士的资金池,利用保单架构设计,作为大额资产管理工具,比定额终身寿险容易核保,手续简单。

在中国近年来连续去杠杆、执行资管新规和不断加强金融监管等政策背景下,各种爆雷跑路事件频发,让中国内地深陷理财荒,倒逼民间资金进入寿险公司的各类储蓄理财型保险,推动了连续三年的增额终身寿险火爆热销。

5.6.4 两全保险

中国内地的两全保险和中国香港的同类产品类似,在保障期间,若被保险人死亡,则保险公司会理赔身故保险金。若保障期间被保险人未出险,且保险期满仍平安生存,则保险公司会按照合同约定给付生存保险金。近年来,单独的两全保险在中国渐渐淡出主流市场,常与重疾险叠加演化为两全型重疾险(返本型重疾险),也有与意外险叠加演化为长期驾乘意外险等。

5.6.5 万能保险

万能保险集保障、储蓄与理财功能于一体,客户可以根据自身的约定来调整万能险中有多少保费用于保险(风险保费),有多少保费用于投资使用,是允许客户自己调整保费结构的寿险,所以它又被称为万能险。

中国内地的万能保险和海外的万能寿险相比,既类似又有很大差别。相似性主要体现在"万能"的部分——可灵活调整保费、灵活付款取款,同时,保底利率、成本透明也是绝大部分万能险的特点;而差异则主要体现在"寿险"的部分——万能险在中国是非传统寿险的一种,主要被当作理财产品来使用,其保障功能较弱,大多数产品的身故赔偿金仅为本金或是当期现金价值。内地市场几乎所有主流万能保险的设计均是注重结算利率而非身故保障;海外的万能寿险则仍注重保障,一般会有较大杠杆的身故赔偿金,同时兼顾投资理财的功能。从另外一个角度来看,中国的万能寿险绝大部分的保费是用于投资,而海外则是更大比例的保费用于身故保障,差额部分才用来投资。

中国内地的万能保险具有手机端操作、缴费灵活、进出方便、有保底利率、一般是日计息月复利、保额随账户数额自动变化等特点。这其实就类似一个存取自由的银行活期账户,保底高于定期存款利率。因此,它被各家寿险公司作为附加投保险来推动主险的捆绑销售。

近几年附加万能险也是增额终身寿险成交中的重要卖点。不过,随着持续的降准降息,中国万能保险产品也会与海外发达市场同步,高保底和固定利率产品会很快退出市场,同时也会更加注重产品的保障功能。

5.6.6 分红保险

分红保险是指保险公司将其实际经营成果优于定价假设的盈余,按照一定比例向保单持有人进行分配的人寿保险。严格来说,分红保险不应该作为一个产品分类,而是一项产品功能。中国内地的分红保险非常类似于其他地区的参与型寿险,但其在中国的应用更为广泛,几乎所有的险种都可以附加分红功能,常见的有分红型年金、分红型寿险、分红险两全险、分红险万能险,甚至还有分红险重疾险。

分红险在为客户提供了更多产品选择和更高潜在回报的同时也引发了一些问题。保险公司热衷分红险的主要原因在于可以通过分红预期设计出高分红利益演示吸引客户,这也是业内一个重要的营销手段。但分红分配具有不透明和不确定的特点,中国内地也还未有类似其他地区强制公布分红实现率的规定,在向客户推荐分红险时应更加全面地评估保险公司和产品功能,避免过度关注计划书不保证部分的潜在收益。

人寿保险与税务

本章要点：
- 介绍如何认定个人、公司/企业和信托的税务居民身份
- 探讨私人财富规划的税务问题，如所得税、资本利得税、分红税、预提税、遗产税和赠与税
- 探讨与现金价值、现金提取、保单转让、保单贷款和身故赔偿金相关的人寿保险的税务问题
- 探讨在加拿大、美国和澳大利亚法律法规下的人寿保险的税务策略

税务优化是人寿保单为人熟知同时也备受关注的一项功能。人寿保单可以从多个方面帮助客户实现税收筹划的目的，比如优化遗产税、递延所得税。在某些司法管辖区，比如澳大利亚，满足一定条件的情况下投保人甚至无须就退保所得缴纳所得税；在某些司法管辖区，如加拿大，可以用公司的未分配利润支付保费，从而实现股东个人层面的税务优化。

在通过国际寿险架构购买综合性人寿保险以实现最优税务筹划前，保单持有人必须首先对其整个家庭的税务状况有准确、综合和全面的了解。

不同税务居民身份的客户，可以持有的人寿保险产品不同，所需承担的税务后果不同，每份保险需符合的税务要求不同，在保险中担任不同角色的影响也不同。因此，必须先了解后规划。一位财富管理顾问必须在充分了解客户背景情况、目标需求和相应的专业知识的基础之上，才有可能协助客户寻找到合适的、必要的专业人士，共同设计、搭建一个能够实现包括但不限于税收筹划功能的国际寿险架构。

基于这个目标,本章将主要介绍为客户开展税务筹划的过程中所需了解的税务基础,以及几个主要在岸国的与保险相关的税务知识。在附录中还可以看到美国、加拿大、澳大利亚等国的税务律师和会计师对相关税务问题的解读(英文原版)。

6.1 税务居民身份

税务居民身份决定了一个主体的纳税义务,因此,确定一个主体的税务居民身份是开展税务筹划的第一步。在一个国际寿险架构中,相关角色的税务居民身份决定着整个架构的合规要求和税务筹划效果。因此,在为客户设计国际寿险架构之前,务必了解相关人士当前的税务居民身份,以及近期甚至远期的身份规划方案。

自然人、公司实体,甚至信托都拥有税务居民身份。概括而言,一个主体的税务居民身份是由该主体与该司法管辖区联系的紧密程度决定的,联系包括国籍、居住时间、居住意愿、家庭、社会联系、经济联系、管理控制等。尽管大致原则是相似的,各个司法管辖区对各自税务居民身份的判断标准仍有所区别。

一个主体可能同时成为两个或两个以上司法管辖区的税务居民。在此情况下,如果各司法管辖区间签有双边税务协定,通常就可以根据双边税务协定来解决这一冲突问题,从而避免该主体同时承担多重纳税义务。但如果相关司法管辖区间并未签有双边税务协定,则相关主体可能需要同时对多个司法管辖区承担纳税义务,甚至需要就同一笔收入双重甚至多重交税。

> **例 6.1**
>
> A 先生持有美国护照,长期在新加坡居住;太太和孩子在加拿大居住生活。根据美、新、加三国的法律规定,A 先生可能同时成为这三个国家的税务居民,并面临较重的税务负担。在此情况下,需要结合相关的双边税务协议(如有)及其个人的生活工作布局,对其税务身份进行梳理与规划,从而合法合规实现其税务责任的优化。

综上所述,高净值人士的税收筹划方案设计,需要从厘清其税务身份做起。

6.1.1 常见司法管辖区的个人税务居民身份认定标准

6.1.1.1 中国内地

满足以下任一条件的个人,属于中国税务居民[①]:

[①] 《中华人民共和国个人所得税法》(2018 年修正)第一条:在中国境内有住所,或者无住所而一个纳税年度内在中国境内居住累计满一百八十三天的个人,为居民个人。居民个人从中国境内和境外取得的所得,依照本法规定缴纳个人所得税。

① 在中国境内有住所。此处,住所指"因户籍、家庭、经济利益关系而在中国境内习惯性居住"①。根据这一规定,如果一个人拥有中国户籍,则大概率会被视为在中国境内有住所,从而被视为中国税务居民。

② 一个税务年度内在中国境内居住累计满183天。

中国内地实行全球收入征税制,这意味着中国税务居民需就其来源于境内外的收入纳税。如果中国税务居民同时是其他司法管辖区的税务居民,则在有双边税务协议的情况下,可以避免就同一笔收入重复纳税。

> **例6.2**
>
> A先生持有中国护照,拥有中国户籍,因为工作原因经常居住在中国香港。A先生的太太和孩子都在中国内地工作生活。在此情况下,A先生大概率属于中国税务居民。

6.1.1.2 美国②

美国税务居民需要就全球收入向美国缴税,同时需履行一系列的税务申报义务,包括但不限于申报海外金融资产、申报海外银行及金融账户等。根据《美国国内税收法典》(Internal Revenue Code,IRC),持有美国护照的美国公民属于美国税务居民。对于外籍自然人,如果通过以下任一测试,则也被视为美国税务居民。

(1)绿卡测试。

如果一个外籍人士是美国的合法永久居民,即取得了美国绿卡,那么这个人就满足绿卡测试,被视为美国税务居民。但此情况下也有例外:一个持有美国绿卡的自然人如果同时是其他司法辖区的税务居民,且该司法辖区与美国签有双边税务协议,那么此时此人或有可能根据协议中的"加比规则"被视为另一司法辖区的税务居民。

(2)实际居住测试。

一个人如果在美国居住的时间同时满足如下31天和183天测试,就被视为满足实际居住测试,并将被视为美国税务居民:

在当年度居住满31天,且本公历年度和过去两个公历年度加起来的三年内在美停留不少于183天,则:

三年内停留天数=本年度在美停留的全部天数+前一年度在美停留天数的1/3
+再前一年度在美停留天数的1/6

---

① 《中华人民共和国个人所得税法实施条例》(2018年)第二条:个人所得税法所称在中国境内有住所,是指因户籍、家庭、经济利益关系而在中国境内习惯性居住;所称从中国境内和境外取得的所得,分别是指来源于中国境内的所得和来源于中国境外的所得。

② http://www.oecd.org/tax/automatic-exchange/crs-implementation-and-assistance/tax-residency/United-States-Tax.

> **例 6.3**
>
> 1. A 先生持有美国护照,但他在加拿大工作和生活,每年仅在美国停留 30 天。此时,A 先生为美国的税务居民。
>
> 2. B 先生持有美国绿卡,他在新加坡生活和工作,每年仅在美国停留 30 天,新加坡与美国之间没有双边所得税协定。此时,B 先生是美国税务居民。
>
> 3. C 女士没有美国护照或绿卡。她 2023 年在美国居住了 120 天,2022 年在美国居住了 120 天,2021 年在美国居住了 120 天。基于实际居住测试的计算公式,C 女士从 2021 年到 2023 年居住的天数不超过 183 天(120 天+120 天×1/3+120 天×1/6=180 天)。根据实际居住测试,C 女士在 2021~2023 年在美国停留的时间少于 183 天,因此,C 女士不是美国税务居民。

6.1.1.3 加拿大

加拿大也实行全球征税制,其税务居民需就其境内外收入交税。此外,加拿大税务居民还需履行包括申报海外收入、海外资产和海外企业在内的税务申报义务。加拿大税务居民包括以下三类(加拿大税法下的税务责任并无区别)。

(1) 加拿大税务居民(Tax Resident of Canada)。

如果一个人拥有加拿大国籍或持有加拿大枫叶卡,同时与加拿大有着紧密的居住联系,比如在加拿大有居所,有配偶或同居伴侣,有需要赡养的人,工作和各种社交活动都在加拿大等,那此人就是加拿大的税务居民。

(2) 加拿大事实居民(Factual Resident of Canada)。

如果一个人事实上在加拿大境外居住,但仍然与加拿大保持着紧密的居住联系,比如是暂时地被外派到加拿大境外工作、在外国教书或上学、在加拿大境外度假等,或因工作或学习而定期(每天、每周或每月)往返于加拿大和另一国家,那此人就被认定为加拿大事实居民。[①]

(3) 加拿大视同居民(Deemed Resident of Canada)。

如果一个人与加拿大并未建立起紧密的居住联系,则可能符合成为加拿大视同居民的条件,比如,一个税务年度内在加拿大居住的时间超过了 183 天(含 183 天)且根据加拿大和另一个司法管辖区签署的双边税务条约,不被视为另一个司法管辖区的税务居民;或是公务员、加拿大部队成员,包括其海外学校工作人员,或在加拿大全球事务援助项目下工作的人员或这些人员的家庭成员。[②]

---

① https://www.canada.ca/en/revenue-agency/services/tax/international-non-residents/film-media-tax-credits/residency-status-determination.html.

② https://www.canada.ca/en/revenue-agency/services/tax/international-non-residents/film-media-tax-credits/residency-status-determination.html.

> **例 6.4**
>
> A 先生持有加拿大护照,但他与家人全年居住在中国香港并在中国香港工作。A 先生并未在加拿大居住,且在加拿大没有任何房产、银行账户或其他资产,也没有缴纳社保。在这种情况下,A 先生大概率是中国香港税务居民。

6.1.1.4　澳大利亚

澳大利亚税务居民个人需要就其全球收入向澳大利亚纳税,还需要履行海外资产和海外企业的申报义务。满足以下任一测试的个人,将被视为澳大利亚的税务居民:

（1）普通法测试(Common Law Test)。

如果该个人居住(resides)于澳大利亚,那此人被视为澳大利亚的税务居民。判断是否构成居住,需要考虑以下因素:

① 居住于澳大利亚的目的和意图;

② 其家庭、事业、雇佣关系与澳大利亚之间的关联程度;

③ 其个人财产的保存地、所在地;

④ 其个人的社会及生活安排。

（2）成文法测试(Statutory Tests)。

满足以下一项或多项条件,即被视为澳大利亚的税务居民:

① 住所(Domicile)位于澳大利亚(除非其永久住所在澳大利亚之外);

② 每年在澳大利亚居住超过一半时间(除非其经常居住地在澳大利亚之外且其并无意图定居在澳大利亚);

③ 该个人是澳大利亚政府雇员养老金的缴费成员,或该成员的配偶,或其未满 16 岁的子女。

> **例 6.5**
>
> Vicky 女士离开澳大利亚到韩国担任英语教师,她的合约为期一年,之后她计划在中国和亚洲其他地区旅游,然后返回澳大利亚重新工作。在韩国期间,她住在一个视她为自己家人的家庭内,并将她澳大利亚的物业出租。Vicky 未婚,她的父母住在不同的州,哥哥移民去了法国。
>
> 尽管她住在韩国,仍会被视为澳大利亚税务居民,因为在定居测试下:
>
> （1）她的定居住所在澳大利亚(一直居住在澳大利亚的居民通常会在海外居住同时保留在澳大利亚的定居住所,除非选择永久移民到另一个国家);
>
> （2）她的永久居住地仍然在澳大利亚。

6.1.1.5 新加坡[①]

新加坡税务居民个人仅需就其来源于新加坡的收入向新加坡纳税。新加坡的税务居民包括：

① 除了短暂、合理原因的离境之外，经常居住在新加坡的个人；

② 一个税务年度内，在新加坡实际停留或者在新加坡务工（除了公司的董事）的时间超过183天（含183天）的个人。

6.1.1.6 中国香港[②]

中国香港税务居民仅需就其来源于中国香港的收入向中国香港纳税。

通过以下任一测试的，将被视为中国香港的税务居民：

① 经常居住于中国香港。经常居住指该人在中国香港有永久居所，习惯性地、经常地居住在中国香港，且有定居在中国香港的主观意愿。

② 某一税务年度在中国香港居住超过183天，或者连续两年在中国香港居住加总超过300天。

6.1.2 常见司法管辖区的公司/企业税务居民身份认定标准

6.1.2.1 中国内地[③]

满足以下任一条件的企业，将被视为中国税务居民：

① 依法在中国境内成立的企业；

② 依照外国（地区）法律成立但实际管理机构在中国境内的企业。

一个企业的"实际管理机构在中国境内"与否，可参考以下要素予以判断：

① 企业负责实施日常生产经营管理运作的高层管理人员及其高层管理部门履行职责的场所主要位于中国境内；

② 企业的财务决策（如借款、放款、融资、财务风险管理等）和人事决策（如任命、解聘和薪酬等）由位于中国境内的机构或人员决定，或需要得到位于中国境内的机构或人员批准；

③ 企业的主要财产、会计账簿、公司印章、董事会和股东会议纪要档案等位于或存放于中国境内；

④ 企业1/2（含1/2）以上有投票权的董事或高层管理人员经常居住于中国境内。

---

① http://www.oecd.org/tax/automatic-exchange/crs-implementation-and-assistance/tax-residency/Singapore-Tax-Residency.pdf.

② http://www.oecd.org/tax/automatic-exchange/crs-implementation-and-assistance/tax-residency/Hong-Kong-Residency.pdf.

③ 《中华人民共和国企业所得税法》（2018年修正）第二条："企业分为居民企业和非居民企业。本法所称居民企业，是指依法在中国境内成立，或者依照外国（地区）法律成立但实际管理机构在中国境内的企业。本法所称非居民企业，是指依照外国（地区）法律成立且实际管理机构不在中国境内，但在中国境内设立机构、场所的，或者在中国境内未设立机构、场所，但有来源于中国境内所得的企业。"

中国内地税务居民企业需要就全球收入在中国缴纳企业所得税。

6.1.2.2　美国①

与复杂的税务居民个人的判断标准相较而言,美国的公司税务居民判断标准则简单很多——看注册地。如果一个公司在美国根据美国的法律注册成立,那么该公司即是美国的税务居民。公司的实际经营管理所在地并不作为判断税务居民身份的标准,一般情况下在美国境外设立的公司不会被视为美国税务居民②。

有趣的是,在一些特殊的美国领土内(比如波多黎各)成立的公司却不会被视为"根据美国或任何州的法律成立的公司",因此,在这些地方成立的公司并不属于美国税务居民。

6.1.2.3　加拿大③

满足以下任一标准的公司,将被视为加拿大的税务居民:

① 在加拿大注册成立;

② 主要管理控制地在加拿大。

此处管理控制地主要指董事会行使职权、举办董事会的地方。

不过,在加拿大境外注册成立但在加拿大境内和境外均有主要管理控制地的公司,如果满足加拿大税收协定中的加比规则,则将被视为加拿大非税居民。

6.1.2.4　澳大利亚

满足以下任一标准的公司,将被视为澳大利亚税务居民:

① 在澳大利亚注册成立;

② 在澳大利亚境外注册成立,但其核心经营管理所在地在澳大利亚,或其掌控有投票权的股东是澳大利亚的税务居民。

此处核心经营管理所在地包括公司管理机构的会面地点、股东会议的召开地、股东登记册的保管地等。

6.1.2.5　新加坡④

新加坡采用管理与控制地的标准判断一个公司的税务居民身份。换言之,如果一个公司的实际管理与控制地在新加坡,则该公司属于新加坡的税务居民。

管理与控制指对公司的重要事项做出决策的行为,比如召开董事会等,因此,一个公司日常召开董事会的地方可能会被视为一个公司实际管理与控制的所在地。

如果一个公司是新加坡税务居民,除了需要就来源于新加坡的收入缴税之外,一般还

---

① http://www.oecd.org/tax/automatic-exchange/crs-implementation-and-assistance/tax-residency/United-States-Tax-Residency.pdf.

② 例外情况请见附录A:美国税务意见。

③ http://www.oecd.org/tax/automatic-exchange/crs-implementation-and-assistance/tax-residency/Canada-Residency-EN.pdf.

④ http://www.oecd.org/tax/automatic-exchange/crs-implementation-and-assistance/tax-residency/Singapore-Tax-Residency.pdf.

需要就来源于境外且已汇入或视同汇入新加坡的收入缴税。①

6.1.2.6　中国香港②

如果满足以下任一条件，则该公司将被视为中国香港税务居民：

① 在中国香港注册成立；

② 在中国香港境外注册成立，但主要管理控制地在中国香港。

此处管理地指公司的日常管理或者经营决策的做出地，而控制地则指最顶层的操控，包括公司经营策略的制定、选择营业融资、评估经营表现等。

中国香港税务居民公司需就来源于中国香港的收入缴纳利得税（Profit Tax）。③

6.1.3　常见司法管辖区的信托税务居民身份认定标准

6.1.3.1　中国内地

在中国内地税法下，税务居民可以分为两类：税务居民个人和税务居民企业。信托作为一种法律关系，暂无明确法律对其税务居民身份的判断标准做出规定，也暂无法律规定对其参考适用企业或者个人的相关规定。因此，中国内地税法对此问题的规定目前还是空白状态。

6.1.3.2　美国

在美国，信托相关的税务问题非常复杂。在一些情况下，信托本身是纳税主体，因此需要对其是否具备美国税务居民身份做出判断。在另一些情况下，信托本身将被视为一个穿透的"流体"，相关的税务责任并非由信托自身承担，而在信托被穿透之后由相关的信托角色承担。

因此，在美国税法下厘清一个信托的税务责任时，我们首先需要判断这个信托是一个被穿透的"流体"，还是一个独立的纳税实体；这就要求我们去判断一个信托是委托人信托（Grantor Trust），还是非委托人信托（Non-Grantor Trust）。二者的区分标准既简单又复杂：简单而言，一个信托有没有委托人即决定了这是不是一个委托人信托；但要认定一个信托有没有委托人，又非三言两语可以概括。这里的"有无委托人"并非指信托中有没有一个签署信托契约、将资产从个人名下转入信托的设立人（settlor），而是指这个信托里有没有一个对信托资产拥有控制权的角色。常见的也相对易懂的标准之一，在于信托设立人是否拥有撤销信托的权利：如果设立人拥有这项权利，这个信托则更有可能被视为拥有委托人，从而被视为一个委托人信托。

对一个委托人信托而言，相关税务责任将由信托委托人承担，如同信托内的资产仍在委托人个人名下。在此情况下，如果委托人是美国税务居民，则该美国委托人需要就信托

---

① https://taxsummaries.pwc.com/singapore/corporate/taxes-on-corporate-income.

② http://www.oecd.org/tax/automatic-exchange/crs-implementation-and-assistance/tax-residency/Hong-Kong-Residency.pdf.

③ https://www.ird.gov.hk/chs/tax/bus_pft.htm.

内的所有收入向美国纳税;如果委托人是非美国税务居民,则除非信托有源于美国的收入,否则该委托人无须就信托内的任何收入向美国缴税。后者即是常为移民到美国的家庭使用的"外国委托人信托"(Foreign Grantor Trust)。在外国委托人信托中,美国税务居民的受益人从信托中获得分配将无须缴纳个人所得税。

对于一个非委托人信托而言,其自身即为一个纳税主体。此时,我们就有必要对该信托是否为美国税务居民做出判断。如果该信托同时满足以下两项测试,则该信托为美国税务居民,属于美国信托(US Trust):

① 法院测试(Court Test):如果美国法院对该信托拥有管辖权,则满足该项测试。
② 控制测试(Control Test):如果该信托由美国人士控制,则满足该项测试。

例 6.6

如果一个非委托人信托约定,该信托由一个美国境外的法院管辖、适用美国境外的法律,且由非美人士对信托进行管理决策,那么这个信托将无法满足上述任一标准,因此大概率将被视为一个非美信托(Non-US Trust),或者相对于美国来说的外国信托(Foreign Trust)。

6.1.3.3 加拿大

如果一个信托满足以下任一条件,那么这个信托就是加拿大的税务居民或事实居民:
① 信托在加拿大设立;
② 信托的受托人是加拿大税务居民;
③ 信托由加拿大税务居民设立;
④ 信托的主要管理与控制地在加拿大;
⑤ 信托内业务的实际发生地在加拿大。

如果一个信托在加拿大境外设立,根据加拿大所得税法(Income Tax Act)第 94 条的规定,满足以下条件,则其仍然有可能成为加拿大税法下的视同税务居民。[①]

① 该信托有税务居民出资人(Resident Contributor),即这个出资人是一个加拿大税务居民,而其在作为税务居民的当时或此前对信托进行了出资。
② 该信托有税务居民受益人(Resident Beneficiary),这里包含两个条件:一是这个信托有关联出资人(Connected Contributor),关联出资人即一个在对信托出资时或者在出资前后 60 个月内是加拿大税务居民的人;二是这个信托有加拿大税务居民受益人。

加拿大本地信托需每年将信托收入分配给受益人,并由受益人申报缴税,否则,加拿大本地信托需按照个人最高税率缴税。

---

① https://www.canada.ca/en/revenue-agency/services/tax/trust-administrators/types-trusts.html#drt.

> **例 6.7**
>
> 1. A 先生是新加坡税务居民,他的儿子 B 及其太太孩子移民到了加拿大。A 先生在新加坡设立了一个酌情信托(Discretionary Trust),不保留任何权利,受益人是他的儿子 B 及其家人。在加拿大税法下,该信托不符合被视为税务居民的标准,因此该信托不是加拿大税务居民信托。这类信托也被称为非居民信托(Non-Resident Trust)或祖母信托(Granny Trust)。
>
> 2. 如果设立信托两年后,A 先生也移民到了加拿大与儿子团聚,那么这个信托将变成加拿大的税务居民信托。

6.1.3.4 澳大利亚[①]

在澳大利亚税法下,满足以下任何一个条件的信托,即为澳大利亚税务居民:
① 在该纳税年度的任意时间里,该信托中至少有一个受托人是澳大利亚税务居民;
② 在该纳税年度的任意时间里,该信托均在澳大利亚进行管理与控制。

澳大利亚本地信托需每年将信托收入分配给受益人,并由受益人申报缴税,否则,澳大利亚本地信托需按照个人最高税率缴税。

6.1.3.5 中国香港[②]

满足以下任一条件的信托,即为中国香港税务居民:
① 受托人是中国香港税务居民;
② 根据中国香港法律设立;
③ 在中国香港域外设立,但信托的管理控制在中国香港进行。

6.2 私人财富规划领域的税务问题

6.2.1 所得税

在私人财富规划领域,针对高净值人士的所得税筹划是重点。个人所得税的常见筹划思路包括以下 3 方面。

6.2.1.1 个人税务居民身份规划

这个筹划思路的重点是改变一个人的税务居民身份,将其从一个高税负司法辖区的税务居民,转变成一个低税负司法辖区的税务居民(比如新加坡、中国香港等地)。如前

[①] https://www.ato.gov.au/Business/International-tax-for-business/In-detail/residency/residency-requirements-for-companies,-corporate-limited-partnerships-and-trusts/?page=1#Trusts.

[②] https://www.ird.gov.hk/eng/pdf/2016/chapter17.pdf.

文所介绍,大部分司法辖区以居住时间作为认定税务居民身份的主要标准。因此,通过这一方式进行税收筹划的,往往要求相关人士对个人生活做出重大调整,要变更自己和家人的经常居住地。由此可知,市面上一些宣称通过获取一本护照或者居住身份即可实现税收筹划的方案,往往是不可行的。

同时需要关注的是,这一税收筹划方案本身也是可能发生税务成本的。以美国为例,如果一个持有美国护照的美国税务居民计划通过弃籍改变其税务居民身份,那么他在弃籍的过程中还需缴纳弃籍税。此外,中国内地也要求其公民在移民前办理税款清算。

6.2.1.2 双边税务协定的运用

为了避免出现多个司法辖区对同一主体进行重复征税的情况,大部分在岸地和中岸地的司法辖区之间签有避免双重征税的税务协定。因此,通过合理设计资产的持有方式与架构,既可以避免重复征税的负累,还有机会享受双边税务协定带来的税务优惠(如优惠的预提税率),从而实现税收筹划的目的。以计划到中国境内开展投资的外国投资者举例:如果通过 BVI 公司投资到中国境内,则未来中国公司对其股东 BVI 公司进行分红时,需要缴纳 10% 的预提税;如果通过中国香港地区公司投资到中国内地,则在该中国香港地区公司确实属于中国香港地区税务居民的前提下,未来中国内地公司对其股东中国香港地区公司进行分红时,有机会享受 5% 的预提税率。

6.2.1.3 变更资产持有主体/持有方式

当资产仍在高净值人士个人名下直接持有时,因该资产的增值和受益所发生的税负责任往往与该个人直接相关。但变更资产持有的结构,比如将资产置入保单架构或信托架构之中,则有机会实现税务递延甚至无须缴税的效果。

6.2.2 资本利得税

在处置股权、土地、资本投资等财产时,可能会产生资本利得税(Capital Gain Tax)。与所得税的筹划相似,资本利得税也可以通过更换税务居民身份,以及变更资产的持有主体/持有方式进行税务筹划。

6.2.3 预提税

预提税并不是一个税种,而是一种征税的方式。通常而言,对于外国税务居民,由于税务征收和执法上的困难,一个司法管辖区通常通过预提的方式,在从本国境内向外支付相关分红、利息、特许权使用费的过程中,要求境内对外支付分红、利息、特许权使用费的主体预先缴纳税费,此即预提税。

一般情况下,一个司法管辖区会制定固定的预提税率;而对于与之签有双边税务协议的司法辖区,则会在此基础上给予一定的优惠税率。充分利用税务协定,是对预提税进行优化的一种常见方式。

6.2.4 遗产税和赠与税

在本书讨论的几大主要司法管辖区中：

① 中国内地、中国香港地区和新加坡目前均无遗产税和赠与税。[①]

② 加拿大没有遗产税或赠与税，但其税务居民去世后，其遗产通过继承方式给予其继承人时，这个过程将视同被继承人售出资产，需要以其遗产缴纳相应的资本利得税。如果通过保单来安排传承，则能在一定程度上降低传承过程中可能产生的税负。

③ 澳大利亚也没有遗产税或赠与税，但如果澳大利亚非居民继承人从澳大利亚居民处继承非澳大利亚应税资产，则需要缴纳资本利得税。同加拿大一样，如果通过保单来安排传承，就能在一定程度上减轻资产在代际传承过程中可能产生的税负。

④ 美国是征收遗产税和赠与税的国家。实践中，在美国通过不可撤销人寿保险信托（Irrevocable Life Insurance Trust, ILIT）加上美国人寿保险的架构安排，能够使保单中的身故赔偿金免于占用联邦终身遗产税免税额（2023年个人联邦终身遗产税免税额为1 292万美元，2024年将增至1 361万美元，超过此额度的部分最高税率可达40%。如果美国国会未将现行法律延长到2026年之后，那么到2026年初，该额度经通胀调整后将降至500万美元）[②]，从而实现一定的税收筹划效果。

6.3 人寿保险的相关税务问题

6.3.1 现金价值

对于有投资属性的保险而言，保单内的现金价值将随着投资的收益波动而变化；由于保单内的投资一般会选择低风险的稳健投资，因此大部分情况下保单内的现金价值都会逐年增长。对于这部分投资增值，保单的一项常见且重要的税收筹划功能是税务递延。一般情况下，对于符合相关规定的寿险保单，如果保单内的投资产生增值或获得收益，则保单持有人并不需要在相关增值或收益产生的当年度即对之进行申报交税，相关增值或收益可以在保单内一直免税累积，直到保单持有人通过部分取消保单等方式实际获得了相关收入。

但需要注意的是：受制于反避税总原则（General Anti-Avoidance Rule, GAAR），如果一张保单被当地的法律穿透视同为一项投资时，这张保单可能就无法实现税务递延的好处了（详细内容请见第6.4节）。

[①] 截至完稿时，中国内地尚未推出遗产税，不过一直有关于遗产税的研究与讨论。2023年7月2日，国务院发展研究中心李建伟在第十七届中国经济增长与周期高峰论坛上表示，"应尽快研究出台遗赠税，弱化财富两极分化走势"。

[②] 详见附录A：美国税务意见。

6.3.2 现金提取

如上所述,虽然保单内的投资在持续增值,但保单通常可以实现延税的功能。那么这部分税务递延到什么时候需要缴纳呢?一般情况下,大部分司法管辖区会规定如果保单持有人通过部分取消或全部取消保单的方式取出现金,此时就可能需要为投资的收益缴税。这个问题并不能通过购买在低税收司法管辖区签发的保单来避免,因为保单持有人有责任缴纳由其税务居民所在地司法管辖区征收的所得税。

各司法管辖区对此的规定及具体的计税方式会有区别,因此,当客户计划从保单中提取现金的时候,国际寿险架构师应当提醒并协助客户对于相关的税务后果做好充分的评估与考量。

6.3.3 保单转让

保单持有人转让保单时,根据当地司法管辖区税法的具体规定,可能会面临个人所得税的问题。因此,如果客户有意将保单转让给他人,国际寿险架构师应当适当提醒客户获取必要的税务意见、充分了解相应的税务后果,从而做出恰当的决定。

6.3.4 保单贷款

常见的保单贷款有两种形式:一种是保单持有人直接向保险公司申请贷款;另一种是保单持有人以保单作为抵押,向银行等金融机构申请贷款。一般情况下,保单持有人获得的贷款不会被视为收入或者资本利得,也因此不会产生税负[①];但如果该贷款是零息或低息且未约定期限的,则在一般反避税原则之下,相关贷款可能会被穿透、被视为保单持有人从保单中获得的收入,从而致使保单持有人需要承担相应的纳税义务。

此外,如果一张保单从本质上被否认其保单的属性,而被视为一项投资的话,保单持有人获得的保单贷款就有可能被视为收入并需要缴税(比如美国税法下的 MEC,详见第 6.4.2 小节)。

因此,如客户有意申请保单贷款,专业顾问就应当帮助其充分了解相关的税务责任,从而进行最优的贷款安排。

6.3.5 身故赔偿金

保单受益人获得身故赔偿金通常免税,但前提是该保单符合相关司法管辖区下"人寿保险"的定义和要求。如果一张保单不被当地法律认可为人寿保险的话,则保单受益人可能需要为其获得的身故赔偿金缴纳税款。这一规定本质上也是对反避税总原则的应用,

---

[①] 但在某些司法辖区也有例外,详见附录 B:加拿大税务意见。

这一部分内容将在第 6.4 节详细讨论①。

6.3.6 保单持有人/受益人身份变化引起的税务问题

在高净值人士群体中,移民是一项很常见的选择。高净值人士在变更自己的国籍和实际居住地的同时,其税务居民身份也往往会发生变化。对于已经购买了人寿保险的客户而言,应当密切关注这一变化对其税务身份、保单、申报纳税义务带来的影响。

举例而言,如果一位中国香港的居民在中国香港购买了保险,受益人是他的家人,随后这位客户全家移民到美国。在移民到美国后,这位客户可能需要根据美国税法的要求对这张保单承担相应的申报责任。此外,这份保单能够实现的税收筹划效果也会发生变化。举例而言,如果这份保单不符合美国税法的相关规定,那么客户申请获得的保单贷款可能就会被视同获得了收入并需要缴税。此时客户可能需要考虑是否继续持有这张保单,或将资金转入新保单。

对于每一位已经配置了人寿保单且有移民计划的客户,专业顾问都应及时提醒客户关注这一变化可能带来的影响,如有需要,还应协助客户就相关问题获取法律意见。

6.4 人寿保险的税收筹划方案与反避税总原则

如前所述,配置人寿保单是一种常见的税收筹划方案,可以协助客户实现税务递延,甚至实现无须缴税的效果。合法、合规、合理的税务优化是为法律所允许的,但如果人寿保险的税收筹划功能被滥用,被作为一个包装去掩盖投资产品的本质,则可能会触及法律的边缘,并被法律所规制。目前,大部分司法辖区都制定了一系列反避税规则,防止保险被滥用,对于表面保险、实质投资的情况,都进行了"穿透"和规制。

6.4.1 加拿大人寿保险的税务政策

加拿大所得税法就人寿保险制定了一套豁免标准。如果一张人寿保单可以满足相关标准,则该保单可被视为一张免税保单(Tax-Exempt Policy),此时保单持有人能够享受税务递延甚至税务豁免的优惠政策。但如果一张人寿保单未能满足这些标准,则该保单将被视为非豁免保单(Non-Exempt Policy),此时保单持有人需要每年就保单内的收入进行申报缴税。

法律制定这一套标准的底层逻辑在于,当一份保单不具备保险最基本的保护功能和特点时,则其本质上即属于一项投资,因此持有该项投资的人应该像持有一般投资一样,对收入进行申报和纳税。

豁免测试适用于两项规则:最高税收精算储备(Maximum Tax Actuarial Reserve,MTAR)限制和反快速供款规则。如果不符合任一规则或者两项规则都不符合,那么相关

---

① 在美国税法下,这一问题更加复杂,详细可参考附录 A:美国税务意见。

保单就被归类为"非豁免保单"。

6.4.1.1 最高税收精算储备限制

这项规则是指，保单内累积的资金（保单的投资部分）的现金价值不得超过最高税收精算储备，即免税保单累积资金的预测现金价值。此外，累积资金的预测现金价值在未来的任何时候都不能超过预测的最高税收精算储备，直到被保人达到特定年龄的那一天为止。

6.4.1.2 反快速供款规则

这项规则又被称为250%规则（The 250% Rule），旨在防止保单持有人在保单生效7周年后向保单进行一次性大额供款。

6.4.2 与美国人寿保险相关的一般反避税规则

为了防止保单被滥用成为包装投资的工具，从而使得相应的税务责任被逃避，美国制定了一系列的标准和规则，以区分真正的寿险保单和保单包装下的投资产品，并对二者的税务后果分别做了规定。以下是最主要的三项反避税规则。

6.4.2.1 7702条款

《美国国内税收法典》7702条款规定了人寿保单的标准，只有符合该标准的保单，才是一张真正的保单。可以说，美国税法7702条款的制定出台，是为了让人寿保单回归本原，确保寿险被真正地应用于对生命风险的保障，而非用于投资收益的避税。

对于符合7702条款规定的寿险保单，投保人将能享受到税务递延（在被取出之前，投资收益都可以在保单内免税增长）的好处，而受益人也无须为身故赔偿金缴纳个人所得税。①

7702条款首先要求人寿保单必须符合其当地法律对于人寿保单的定义，简言之，如果这是美国境外发行的保单，那么根据发行地的法律，这张保单应当属于一张人寿保单。

此外，7702条款还规定了两项测试来判断一张保单是否属于美国税法下的人寿保单。

（1）现金价值累积测试（The Cash Value Accumulation Test，CVAT）。

简单来说，这项测试要求一张保单的退保价值在任何时候都不能超过用来支持这张保单赔偿金的单笔保费（the net single premium that would be required to fund the contract's death benefits）。

（2）基准保费测试（The Guideline Premium Limitation Test，GPL）和现金价值通道测试（Cash Value Corridor Test，CVC）。

简单来说，GPL限制了一张保单的保费上限——不能超出足以支持这张保单身故赔偿金的必要金额，CVC则规定了身故赔偿金与保单现金价值之间的最低比例。

以上两项标准都涉及复杂的计算公式，受篇幅所限，在此不展开介绍。

6.4.2.2 MEC

对于符合上述7702条款的保单，还可以进一步细分为MEC（Modified Endowment

---

① 如果该保单曾经有过交易，则可能导致受益人需就赔偿金缴纳所得税（详见附录A：美国税务意见）。

Contract)和非 MEC 两种类型。虽然二者都可以在身故赔偿金方面享受到税务好处,但对于包含贷款在内的利益分配行为,MEC 的税务待遇则不及非 MEC。

具体而言,如果投保人从非 MEC 中取钱,则相关金额将会被视为从保单中拿回投资,超过部分才被视为收入(这意味着取钱到一定金额的情况下才会触发税务责任);但如果从 MEC 中取钱,则相关金额首先会被视为收入,之后才会被视为取回投资(这意味着从取出的第一分钱开始就可能有税务负担)。

区分 MEC 和非 MEC 的标准也涉及一套复杂的规则,如果用一个不完整但相对简单的方式来总结,则是主要看支付保费的速度:如果付款周期少于七年,那么这张保单就有可能被视为一张 MEC。[①]

6.4.2.3 投资者控制规则

根据投资者控制规则(Investor Control Doctrine),如果保单持有人对保单内的投资拥有实质的控制管理权利,那么美国税法将会认为,是该投保人(而非保险公司)持有保单内的投资产品,从而该投保人需要承担相应的税务负担。

6.4.3 澳大利亚的合格境外人寿保单

6.4.3.1 澳大利亚保单的税筹方案

在 2012 年 7 月 2 日之前,根据海外投资基金规则(FIF Measures),持有境外保单的澳大利亚税务居民,需要每年就保单内的投资收入申报并纳税,无论其是否实际获得相关收入。但从 2012 年 7 月 2 日起,澳大利亚废除了上述规则。

自 2012 年 7 月 2 日起,根据澳大利亚《所得税评估法》第 26AH 条款[Income Tax Assessment Act(ITAA 1936)Subsection 26AH],如果一位澳大利亚税务居民持有一张合格境外人寿保单(Eligible Foreign Life Policy,Eligible FLP),在经过十年的合格周期(Eligible Period)后,如保单持有人通过部分取消或全部取消保单的方式取钱,则其所获得的相关收益(Bonus)将不被计入保单持有人的应税收入中。

这项规则有以下几个要点:

(1)合格境外人寿保单,指在 1982 年 8 月 27 日之后生效的境外人寿保单。

(2)合格周期,自保单生效之日起算,满十年即被视为合格周期届满。需要注意的是,如果任一保险年度支付的保费超过了前一年度的 125%,则合格周期将重新起算。

> **例 6.8**
>
> 1. 某张保单自 2010 年 6 月 1 日起生效,并支付了初始保费 20 万美元,那么合格周期将自 2010 年 6 月 1 日起算,到 2020 年 5 月 31 日后,即已经过十年合

---

① 详见附录 A:美国税务意见。

格周期。

2. 如果这张保单在支付初始保费并生效后的前三个保险年度未支付任何保费（支付保费金额为0），并在2013年7月1日（第四个保险年度）追加支付了25万美元保费，此时，由于25万美元超过了0美元的125%，合格周期将从2013年6月1日起重新起算，要到2023年5月31日后，才算已经过十年的合格周期。此后从保单中通过部分或全部取消的方式取出的钱，将无须纳税。

6.4.3.2 未达合格周期的保单税务问题

如前所述，合格境外人寿保单需要满十年的合格周期后，保单持有人从中取钱才可能无须纳税；而未满十年合格周期的保单，则需按照以下规则纳税：

① 持有保单的第1~8年期间，保单持有人需就从保单中获得的相关金额（Relevant Amount）的全额纳税；

② 持有保单的第9年，保单持有人需就从保单中获得的相关金额的2/3纳税；

③ 持有保单的第10年，保单持有人需就从保单中获得的相关金额的1/3纳税；

④ 持有保单的第11年起，保单持有人无须就从保单中获得的相关金额纳税。

注：根据ITAA第26AH(6)条款规定，应计入应税所得的相关金额，将按此公式计算

$$应税所得=(A/B)[(B+C)-(D+E)]$$

其中：

A＝从保单中提取的金额

B＝取消前的保单退保价值

C＝任何早期保单下支付的金额总和

D＝截至取消日期的总保费（未扣除佣金和管理费等费用）

E＝过往相关金额总和加上根据ITAA的任何其他条款征税（比如，ITAA第26(i)条款）已纳税的一切获利的总和

收益[(B+C)-(D+E)]是指保单价值和已付总保费之间的差额，并对早期提款金额进行了调整。

6.4.3.3 澳大利亚对保单实施的反避税政策

（1）根据一般反避税原则穿透保单。

ITAA中对合格人寿保单缺少详细的定义，这为澳大利亚税局给保单定性留下了空间。即基于反避税等目的，澳大利亚税局有权认定一张表面上的人寿保单并不属于澳大利亚所得税评估法案下的合格海外人寿保单。在此情况下，相关澳大利亚纳税人将无法适用上述税务待遇。

(2)威肯比项目。

根据澳大利亚税局 2009 年实施的威肯比项目(Project Wickenby),如果一个人通过海外人寿保单持有的投资在其个人持有的消极投资中占据了较高比例,或者一个人在保单理赔之前频繁通过部分退保的方式从保单取钱,那么,澳大利亚税局可能会将该保单视为一种避税工具,保单持有人和受益人可能会因此承担一定的税务责任。

6.4.4 保单相关的金融信息交换

6.4.4.1 《共同申报准则》和《海外账户税收合规法案》

无论是在《共同申报准则》还是《海外账户税收合规法案》(Foreign Account Tax Compliance Act,FATCA)的相关规则之下,保险公司均是金融机构,均有义务负责申报保单相关人士的账户信息。两种制度下具体的申报规则,详见第 11.3.4 小节。

6.4.4.2 保险在金融信息交换方面的特点

对于一个信托而言,需要交换的人士包括设立人、固定收益受益人、收到分配收入的可自由支配受益人,以及对信托实施最终控制的人士(如保护人)。对于一张保单而言,在保单有效期内,金融机构仅需要申报保单持有人的相关信息。

此外,保单交换的信息也相对简单。与直接在个人名下同时持有多项资产相较而言,通过保单统一持有多项投资(比如使用私募寿险这一工具)在 CRS/FATCA 下仅需交换保单的现金价值,无须单独就每项投资进行信息交换。

因此,对于希望实现最优税收筹划的高净值人士而言,保单将是一个理想的税收筹划和传承工具。

6.5 案例分析

6.5.1 案例背景

Simon 是澳大利亚公民,他原本和太太孩子一起在澳大利亚生活,去年因为工作被外派到加拿大,一年里有超过一半的时间居住在加拿大。他的家人还在澳大利亚生活。

Simon 在中国香港的银行账户上有一笔现金资产,他现在想用这笔现金进行投资,希望在保留资金流动性的同时,对这部分资产进行传承和税筹规划。

6.5.2 案例分析

6.5.2.1 税务居民身份

由背景信息可知,虽然 Simon 去年有超过一半的时间居住在加拿大,但由于他在加拿大居住只是出于临时的原因,待工作任务结束后仍然会回到澳大利亚,而且他的家人,他主要的社会、经济联系都在澳大利亚,因此,他大概率是一个澳大利亚税务居民。

6.5.2.2 保险架构方案

对于 Simon 而言,如果他希望对目前在中国香港的这笔现金进行传承和税筹规划,则澳大利亚境外保单会是一个理想的选项。

通过购买具有投资属性的澳大利亚境外保单,Simon 将能实现以下目标:

(1) 持有保单期间,免于每年申报与缴税。

如果 Simon 购买了保单,对于保单内投资的增长,Simon 在持有保单期间无须申报缴税。

(2) 经过十年的合格周期之后取钱免税。

经过十年的合格周期之后,Simon 通过部分或全部取消的方式从保单中取钱,将无须就该部分收入缴纳个人所得税。

(3) 持有保单期间,可以通过质押保单进行贷款,保障资金流动性。

如果 Simon 质押保单,并以市场利率向保险公司申请贷款,则 Simon 在持有保单期间可以获得一笔流动资金,除了要承担相应的利息成本之外,并不需要为此承担任何税负。

(4) 身故之后资产可以定向传承给子女。

通过在保单中指定受益人,Simon 将得以定向、定量地将其资产传承给他的子女,并且实现遗产税的优化。

需要注意的是,为了确保该保单符合澳大利亚税局定义的合格海外人寿保险,最好提前请澳大利亚税务局确认;且在保单运行期间不要随意增加缴纳保费,小心触发 125% 相关条例。

信托与寿险

CHAPTER 7

本章要点：
- 介绍信托的概念和主要角色
- 介绍信托的主要功能
- 探讨信托与寿险的结合应用

与寿险一样，信托也是财富规划领域中的常见工具。在搭配合适的情况下，二者能实现一加一大于二的效果。本章内容将向大家介绍信托的基础概念、主要特征、信托角色以及信托的主要功能；在此基础上，本章将介绍信托和寿险的进阶组合应用。

7.1 信托的概念和特征

目前，信托尚无一个通行普世的标准定义，各个司法辖区都有自己对信托的法律定义。想要学习理解信托，我们或可参考《关于信托的法律适用及其承认的公约》(Convention on the Law Applicable to Trusts and on Their Recognition) 第二条的规定：

"在本公约中，当财产为受益人的利益或为了特定目的而置于受托人的控制之下时，'信托'这一术语系指财产授予人设定的在其生前或身后发生效力的法律关系。

信托具有下列特点：

（一）该项财产为独立的资金，而不是受托人自己财产的一部分；

（二）以受托人名义或以代表受托人的另一个人的名义握有信托财产；

(三)受托人有根据信托的条件和法律所加于他的特殊职责,管理、使用或处分财产的权利和应尽的义务。"

从该定义可知信托的几个关键要点:

① 信托是一种法律关系,而非法律实体。换言之,信托不具备独立的法律人格,信托不能持有资产(信托资产由受托人持有),无法以信托名义签约或对外借款。这也是为何在一些司法辖区,信托在税法上是穿透的,其本身并非纳税主体、不承担税务责任;相关的信托收入则穿透信托后被视为某一信托角色的收入,并由该个人承担税务责任。

② 设立信托时,设立人需要将资产从其个人名下转至受托人名下,受托人将为了受益人的利益或特定目的持有、管理或处分信托资产。这体现了信托关系中非常重要的一点:信托设立后,信托资产不再属于委托人,信托资产的法律所有权归受托人享有,信托资产的受益所有权归受益人享有。要注意的是,此时信托财产虽在受托人名下,但信托资产并不属于受托人的自有资产;受托人任何的自有债务都不得以信托资产进行偿付。

③ 信托这个法律关系中包含几个重要的角色,即设立人(财产授予人,有时也称为委托人)、受托人、受益人。在实践中,还会安排保护人的角色。图 7.1 是一个简单的信托架构示意图。下文将详细介绍各个信托角色。

图 7.1 常见信托架构

7.2 信托的主要角色

7.2.1 设立人

信托设立人,又称委托人或者财产授予人,意指以其名下资产设立信托的人,也就是整个信托架构的发起人。

从设立人的条件要求来看,虽然各个司法辖区规定略有区别,但以下4点要求大体一致:
① 应当成年(各个司法辖区对成年的年龄标准规定不一);
② 心智正常(意味着此人从年龄到心智上均具备民事行为能力);
③ 资可抵债(破产人士已不具备设立信托的条件);
④ 对拟用来设立信托的资产拥有所有权和处分权(一个人不得以他人资产设立信托)。

在信托设立过程中,设立人需要挑选信赖的受托人,与之商定并签署信托契约,交付信托财产。设立人还可以指定保护人和信托受益人。

对于设立人而言,最关注的可能是设立信托并将资产交付给受托人之后,自己对信托资产还能保留多少管理和控制的权利。对这一问题,各个司法辖区的立法规定不一,有的比较严格,几乎不允许委托人留权;有的则相对宽松,允许委托人保留较多权利。能保留多少权利、保留了权利之后又会对信托的效力以及资产保护效果及税收筹划效果带来多大影响,这些都是重要而复杂的问题,本章对此不作展开,只强调一项基本原则:少留权则多保护。

需要注意的是,委托人的税务居民身份在很大程度上会影响信托的税务身份及税务负担,因此,作为架构师,应当提醒客户在设计搭建信托架构的过程中获取相应的税务意见。

7.2.2 受托人

受托人是在信托关系中遵守法律规定及信托文件约定持有、管理并分配信托资产的角色。受托人在信托关系中需承担信义义务(Fiduciary Duty),这意味着其一举一动、所作所为都需为了受益人的最大利益着想。

目前实践中常见的受托人,一般是持有当地监管部门颁发的信托牌照、以提供信托服务为业的信托公司。没有牌照的自然人和公司也可以作为一段信托关系中的受托人,但通常当地的法律为了便利监管、维护市场秩序,会限制非持牌受托人以此为业、从中获利。

目前,在一些离岸地还推出了私人信托公司(Private Trust Company)制度。私人信托公司只能服务于一系列关联家族成员,但不能对不特定公众提供信托服务。私人信托公司使得客户能在更大程度上掌握对信托的管理控制权利,但同时需要更多的时间、金钱及人力成本进行维护管理。

作为架构师,可以建议客户从以下几个方面考察选择合适的受托人。

① 受托人所在的司法辖区:从资产保护的角度考虑,建议选择远离风险所在地的受托人;此外,还需要考察其所在司法辖区的信托立法能否满足客户对信托的功能诉求。

② 受托人是否持有牌照:建议选择获得牌照的信托公司担任受托人,以获得更好的监管和保护。

③ 受托人的业界声誉和经验履历:可以通过排行榜、新闻检索等方式了解。

④ 受托人的服务质量与效率:可以通过前期接触了解受托人的服务质量和效率,是否会受时差和语言差异的影响,响应速度如何。

(5) 受托人的配套服务资源:搭建信托架构既与信托相关,又不仅与信托相关,过程中可能涉及税务、公司、婚姻等法律问题,还可能涉及开公司、开户、做投资等实践问题,如果受托人拥有足够丰富、可信的配套资源,就能大大提高架构搭建的效率。

7.2.3 保护人

理论上而言,保护人并非信托关系中的必要角色,但在实践中,保护人是信托中常见的角色。委托人设置保护人的岗位、指定保护人的人选,出发点通常是为了监督受托人的行为、保护受益人的利益。

保护人的权利、义务和责任通常取决于信托文件的约定。保护人能够保留的权利的限度,通常也受制于信托适用法的规定。在留权更友好的司法辖区(如开曼群岛),保护人可以享有的权利也相应地更广泛,比如可以决定分配、增减受益人等。需要注意的是,保护人保留过多权利也可能导致信托面临风险和挑战。在保护人的留权限度方面,其原则和委托人是一样的:少留权则多保护。

保护人既可以是自然人,也可以是公司法人;可以是一个人,也可以是多个人组成的保护人委员会。

作为架构师,如获客户信任,也可以考虑担任信托保护人的职位,长久地为客户提供服务。需要注意的是,保护人在大多数情况下也需要承担面对受益人的信义义务,而有义务就意味着存在违反义务的风险。因此,在接受任命之前,建议充分阅读信托契约,并获取专业意见,充分了解保护人的职责、权利和风险。

7.2.4 受益人

受益人是可以从信托中获得财产分配的角色。不同类型信托的受益人,所享有的权益也有所区别。

在固定利益信托(Fixed Interest Trust)当中,受益人的受益权是确定的,因此,在受托人未依约作出分配的时候,受益人可以主张要求受托人作出分配,甚至可以提起诉讼。对于这部分确定的受益权,受益人甚至可以转让、出售,或者赠与他人。

在酌情信托中,对于作为酌情权对象(The Object of the Discretionary Power)的受益人,其拥有的只是一个获得分配的期待。因为拥有酌情权的主体(如受托人),可以根据其自身的判断,决定什么时候分配、给谁分配、分配多少钱。但没有获得分配的受益人无法起诉要求受托人做出分配,更无法将自己获得分配的期待转让、出售给他人。

在目前的信托实践中,基于资产保护、风险隔离、家族传承以及税务优化等目标,更常见的做法是设立酌情信托,仅给予受益人一个期待,但并不授予其确定的、固定的利益。此举能更好地保护信托资产,避免受益人的债务、婚姻等风险影响信托资产的安全。

7.3 信托的主要功能与底层逻辑

7.3.1 资产保护与风险隔离

信托的主要功能,是资产保护与风险隔离。其底层逻辑在于:当个人直接持有资产时,该个人所面临的风险(包括但不限于债务、婚姻等)都将以该人名下的所有资产承担责任。此时,个人资产是完全暴露在风险之下的。因此,想要实现资产保护的目标,首先应当考虑将个人持有资产的模式改为由架构持有资产的模式。在由架构持有资产且个人对架构没有实质控制权的情况下，个人面临的风险将不再与架构内的资产相关，个人的债权人将无法向架构追索资产偿还债务，个人生老病死也不会发生资产所有权的变更，从而实现了资产保护功能。

从这一底层逻辑也不难理解，为什么少留权则多保护，或者说多留权则少保护：如果一个人对信托架构拥有大量的实质的控制权，虽然资产表面上已经从个人名下转走，却如同在该个人名下持有一般，这些资产仍然需要为个人的风险"买单"。

7.3.2　财富传承与家族治理

在不做任何规划的情况下，一个人的身后财富将根据法定的继承规则进行传承。此时继承人的范围、顺序和比例全部需要依据法律确定，无法体现财富创造者的个人意志。

遗嘱是常见的财富传承规划方式。通过遗嘱，财富创造者可以将指定的财产传递给指定的人，相较于法定继承，能更好地实现财富创造者的个人意志。但需要注意的是，各个司法辖区对遗嘱继承制度均有详细而复杂的规定。比如遗嘱的生效要件：有的司法辖区要求遗嘱需要经过公证或见证方能生效，有的司法辖区也承认自书遗嘱的效力。比如遗嘱的实质内容：有的司法辖区允许立遗嘱人完全自由地处分资产，有的司法辖区则要求立遗嘱人必须按照一定的规则分配遗产。此外，由于一个人可以立多份遗嘱，在一个人身故之后，其继承人很有可能就遗嘱的真假、效力等问题产生分歧，甚至最终需要走进法庭来解决纠纷。对于高净值人士而言，其资产国际化、身份国际化的特征，也必然导致其遗嘱继承的难度增加：A 国人在 B 国立的遗嘱能否决定位于 C 国的资产的传承安排？如果可以，届时又需要经过哪些程序才能最终执行遗嘱？这些都是非常复杂的法律问题。

综上所述，虽然遗嘱是一个不可或缺的财富传承工具，但仅凭其一己之力无法满足高净值人士体量大、分布广、情况复杂的资产的传承规划。

信托，作为财富传承规划的一个进阶工具，将能有效地解决上述法定继承和遗嘱继承过程中面临的很多问题。首先，信托替代个人持有资产之后，个人的生老病死将不再导致资产权属的变化，即不会触发继承这一问题，从根源上避免相关纷争；其次，通过在信托中指定受益人，将能更灵活地实现财富的定向传承，而不受制于法律默认的继承人范围和继承顺序，更能体现并落实财富创造者的个人意志；最后，通过信托来持有资产并在信托层面制定分配规则，将能更好地引导家族后代妥善地使用财富、追求人生价值，比如要求受益人必须获得一定学历、获得一定薪水、获得一定工作履历之后才能得到相应的信托分配。

7.3.3　税务优化

经过妥善设计搭建的信托架构，将有机会实现良好的税务优化功能。常见的优化效果包括：（1）通过设立生前信托，避免触发遗产税；（2）通过信托持有资产，实现资产在架构内的免税增长，起到税务递延的效果；（3）通过特定司法辖区的特定制度（比如美国的外国授予人信托制度和加拿大的祖母信托制度),实现受益人无须为信托分配在当地缴纳税费的效果。

信托税务优化的底层逻辑,则根据不同的优化效果而异,无法一言蔽之。想要设计搭建一个能够实现税务优化效果的信托架构,离不开相应司法辖区的税务专家、法律专家和信托专家的共同努力。

7.4 信托与寿险的组合应用

7.4.1 信托作为保单持有人

以信托作为保单持有人,可以实现增加资产保护和税务优化的效果。

7.4.1.1 加强资产保护功能

人寿保单自身的资产保护功能取决于相关司法辖区的规定。以中国为例,最高人民法院和多地省高院均发布过审判指引,确认保单内的资产可分割、可执行[1];以新加坡为例,由以配偶和子女为受益人设立的信托持有的人寿保单才能免于沦为破产财产[2];在美国,更是可能面临不同州之间的法律规定均有差别的情况。

此时,如果以信托代替个人持有寿险架构,就能进一步加强整体资产架构方案的风险防范效果。对于一个设计得当的信托而言,已经进入信托的资产将不再属于设立人的个人资产;对于已经置入架构中的保单,也不应该再受到债权人的追索。

需要说明的是,上述架构只是一个粗框架的方案,针对具体个案,作为架构师还需提醒并协助客户向专业人士获取意见,判断是否具备搭建该等架构的可行性、最终架构的效果又如何。

7.4.1.2 实现税务优化效果

在某些司法辖区,如果个人直接持有保单,则有可能触发一些税务问题。比如一个美

---

[1] 2023年四川省高院发布的《关于人身保险产品财产利益执行和协助执行的工作指引》规定:
一、执行协助
(一)人民法院因办案需要,依法要求保险机构协助查询、冻结、扣划被执行人人身保险产品财产利益(以下简称保单财产利益),包括现金价值、个人账户价值、红利、满期金、生存金、保险赔款等,保险机构应当积极协助配合。
2021年上海高院发布的《关于建立被执行人人身保险产品财产利益协助执行机制的会议纪要》规定:
三、规范执行与特殊免除
(一)明确被执行人及对应的执行标的
被执行人为投保人的,可冻结或扣划归属于投保人的现金价值、红利等保单权益。
被执行人为被保险人的,可冻结或扣划归属于被保险人的生存金等保险权益。
被执行人为受益人的,可冻结或扣划归属于受益人的生存金等保险权益。
最高人民法院《第八次全国法院民事商事审判工作会议(民事部分)纪要》规定:
婚姻关系存续期间以夫妻共同财产投保,投保人和被保险人同为夫妻一方,离婚时处于保险期内,投保人不愿意继续投保的,保险人退还的保险单现金价值部分应按照夫妻共同财产处理;离婚时投保人选择继续投保的,投保人应当支付保险单现金价值的一半给另一方。

[2] https://io.mlaw.gov.sg/bankruptcy/information-for-stakeholders/information-for-creditors.

国税务居民可能会因为个人持有保单而触发遗产税的问题。此时,以信托作为持有人或可有机会实现这一问题的税务优化(详见下文介绍)。

7.4.1.3 实务操作

以信托作为保单持有人,在实践中可通过两种方式实现:一是从一开始即用信托进行投保,二是在个人投保之后将保单转入信托。二者在效率、效果上各有利弊,需要结合客户的具体情况选择更合适的方式。

7.4.2 信托作为保单受益人

由信托作为保单受益人是市面上最常见的保险金信托。这一安排是为了对寿险保单的身故赔偿金实现更长远、更有序的规划,避免家族成员一次性获得巨额财富后因无法妥当驾驭财富而蒙受损失,尤其是在受益人尚未成年时,这种安排更为必要。

7.4.3 信托作为保单付款人

在信托契约允许的前提下,信托可以用信托资产为信托受益人投保并支付保费。通常情况下,保单的持有人和付款人是统一的,但在个别情况下,如能获得保险公司的同意批准,也可以由第三方为保单支付保费。因此,即便保单并非由信托来持有,也可以单纯地运用信托资产支付保费,让信托受益人从中受益。

需要注意的是,由于信托信义义务的核心是一切为了受益人,所以,在信托层面上,只允许为了受益人的利益支付保费,而不能为其他人支付保费,即便这个人可能是受益人的亲朋好友。

7.4.4 常见的信托与寿险架构组合

7.4.4.1 保险金信托

在狭义层面上,保险金信托指的是将信托指定为寿险保单受益人并以寿险保单的身故赔偿金作为信托资产的信托架构。在广义层面上,保险金信托包含以信托作为寿险保单持有人、以寿险保单作为信托资产的架构。

寿险保单固然可以实现定向传承和定量传承的目标,但财富创造者们不仅关心后代能够获得多少财富,而且关心后代们是否能够正确驾驭财富、妥善使用财富。

如果巨额的身故赔偿金直接进入受益人账户,则可能出现的风险包括:受益人挥霍资产,沾染恶习;受益人正面临债务,赔偿金需立即赔付给债权人;受益人正面临婚姻风险,赔偿金或需与配偶进行分割;受益人身处高税负国家,巨额赔偿金之后产生的任何收入均需承担高额税负……

面对上述风险和问题,经过妥当专业设计的保险金信托或能提供一个理想的解决方案:巨额身故赔偿金将通过信托制定的规则和标准对受益人进行分配、在受益人身处风险时不做分配、针对受益人的税务身份做出相应设计以优化税负。

7.4.4.2 不可撤销人寿保险信托

在美国,常见的信托和寿险的组合是不可撤销人寿保险信托。这个架构的出现,是因为如果一个美国税务居民持有保单,那么在特定的情况下,该保单持有人去世之后,相关的保单受益可能会被视为其遗产,并触发遗产税的问题。

一个常见的情况是,如果保单持有人被认定拥有一张保单,那么保单的受益就可能被视为该人遗产的一部分。这里的"拥有"如何定义?通常指保单持有人有权更换受益人、取消保单、以保单贷款或者以其他方式控制保单。①

通过合理妥当设计的不可撤销寿险信托来持有保单,则有机会避免触发遗产税。

7.4.4.3 集合信托

在离岸地的寿险实践中,还有常见的一个工具是集合信托。这是由保险公司设立的主信托附加为各个客户的保单设立的子信托构成的一个集合。

受制于各保险公司的自身合规需求,部分保险公司不允许个人持有保单,而要求客户个人通过公司或信托持有保单。为了降低客户的持有成本,保险公司即推出了集合信托的方案。这种信托服务通常是免费的,所能实现的功能也相对有限,无法实现家族个性化的信托条款定制,只能进行最基础的对保单的持有功能。

---

① 详见附录 A:美国税务意见。

8 人寿保险与企业传承

本章要点：
- 介绍常见的企业结构：个体经营户、合伙企业和公司
- 探讨人寿保险在企业中的应用，如重要人士保险和买卖协议
- 探讨企业持有人寿保单的税务事宜

人寿保险对于高净值人士，不仅在家庭层面有突出功能，在企业层面同样可以提供出色的帮助。高保额的人寿保险是管理企业风险和规划企业传承的一个简单有效的工具。人寿保险的赔付可以为企业提供用于各种用途的营运资金。例如，公司重要人士去世，人寿保险的赔付可以用来雇佣或者培养替代人员，抵减企业的收入损失，从而减轻对企业的影响；又或是在企业贷款担保人身故的情况下，作为贷款保护使公司免于需要立即偿还贷款的风险。高净值人士通常希望他们企业的存续和发展不会因自己或者其他重要人士的死亡受到影响，人寿保险在其中可以起到重要作用。

8.1 企业类型

在详细阐述人寿保险在企业中的应用之前，我们首先需要简单了解基本的几种企业形式，明确各种企业形式可能面临的风险。本章只关注最基本的三种企业形式，即个体经营户、合伙企业及公司，其衍生的新型企业形式或特殊企业形式并不在讨论范围之内。

8.1.1 个体经营户

个体经营户是最早出现的一种企业形式,即由一个自然人投资创设,企业资产为投资人个人所有,投资人自己作出所有商业决定,企业所有的盈利均归其所有,并以其个人资产对企业债务承担无限责任的经营实体。承担无限责任的意思是,无论这个企业面临多少债务,该投资人均需以个人的所有资产为之承担责任。

由此可见,个体经营户这一企业形式的特点是企业的所有权、控制权、经营权、收益权高度统一,企业经营状况与个体经营户个人的经济利益紧密相连。另外,个体经营户的运营资本仅限于其自身的财富以及投资人可以从其他债权人处借到的资金。个人的资金终归有限,以个人名义借贷的难度也较大,所以个体经营户这一形式对企业的扩展和大规模经营会造成限制。在个体经营户的企业形式下,权力高度统一,这也意味着个体经营户的个人财富风险与经营风险紧密相连,极有可能因为经营风险导致家庭破败。

8.1.2 合伙企业

上文提到,个体经营户的形式下,企业的发展和扩张都会受到限制。随着时代的发展,个体经营户个人之间开始合并,形成了新的企业形式:合伙企业。合伙企业相对于个体经营户而言,可以凝聚更多人的力量:一个合伙企业可以有多个合伙人投资设立,这在一定程度上突破了企业资金受单一个人力量的限制,并使得企业的融资能力增强,扩大了经营资金来源。

常见的合伙企业有两种形式:一是普通合伙,每个合伙人均有权参与企业的管理决策,且均以个人的全部资产为企业的债务承担责任;二是有限合伙,其中普通合伙人(General Partner,GP)对企业有经营管理权,但同时需要以个人资产为企业风险承担无限责任,有限合伙人(Limited Partner,LP)则无权参与企业经营管理,同时以出资为限对企业风险承担责任。

在税务责任上,在大多数司法辖区,合伙企业通常是一个被穿透的实体,即通常由合伙人直接为合伙企业的收入承担纳税责任。

> **例 8.1**
>
> David、Jim 和 Lily 创建了一个普通合伙企业,这意味着,这三个合伙人需要为企业的债务承担无限连带责任。这个企业对外欠债,在用企业资产清偿后,仍存在 100 万美元未偿还债务。此时,三个合伙人均需要以个人资产共同清偿剩余债务,若 David 和 Jim 合计只能清偿 50 万美元,剩余的 50 万美元则全部由 Lily 以个人资产清偿。
>
> 由于在普通合伙企业(区别于有限合伙)中,所有合伙人都有权代表企业从

事经营活动,重大决策都需得到所有合伙人同意,因此很容易造成决策上的延误与分歧。任何一个合伙人破产、死亡或退伙都有可能导致合伙解散,因而其存续期限可能较短。

8.1.3 公司

17 世纪,公司的雏形首次出现——一个人除了可以债主的身份通过借贷的方式向一个公司投资,还可以股东的身份通过注资的方式投资于公司。

与个体经营户及合伙企业相较而言,公司的独立性更强,通常被视为法律下的一个独立法人:可以持有自己的资产、承担自己的负债、签订自己的合同、缴纳自己的税费。

随着经济的发展,现在公司的形式也已经多种多样,以满足不同的商业需求。最常见、最经典的公司类型当属有限责任公司:在有限责任公司中,股东仅以出资为限为公司的债务承担责任。如此一来,股东对于投资创业的责任限度将更加可控。

在决策机制方面,现代的公司机制也可以实现所有权和经营管理权的分离:虽然公司股份的所有权属于股东,但公司的经营管理权可以归属于公司高管,从而能让参与者更有效地发挥各自优势,真正地实现"有钱出钱,有力出力",共同促进公司利润的最大化。

总结来说,公司是更适合现代社会开展经营活动的一种组织形式。

例 8.2

A 公司是一家股份有限责任公司,其股份为 100 美元/股,John 认购了 100 股,此时应支付给公司 1 万美元,但是 John 只支付了 7 000 美元。若 A 公司资不抵债,最终解散,则 John 仍需以 1 万美元为限承担责任,以及除了实际缴纳的 7 000 美元股本金之外,还需补充缴纳 3 000 美元股本金,让公司得以偿付其债务。

8.2 人寿保险在企业中的应用

8.2.1 重要人士保险

如果一个企业主或雇员对企业非常重要,则企业可能会为这个人购买重要人士寿险(Key Persons Insurance)。如果该重要人士去世,则企业将获得免税的身故赔偿金,并可以运用这些资金去招聘和培训继任者、弥补相关收入损失或弥补日常开支直到企业恢复，以此来帮助企业克服重要人士去世给企业带来的影响。

一般来说，企业是保单的持有人，企业主或者重要人士是被保人，企业支付保费，并且同时是保单的受益人。当重要人士去世后，企业获得身故赔偿金。但是也有其他安排，比如保险金分割协议（Split-Dollar Arrangements）。

在保险金分割协议中，保单由企业和重要人士共同所有，两方共同承担保费的支付。在此安排下，可以约定重要人士有权拥有身故赔偿金，而企业拥有保单的现金价值；反之亦可。

在万能寿险保单情况下，身故赔偿金等于保单面值（Face Amount）加上账户价值。通常重要人士享有与面值等额的身故赔偿金，这部分钱会在其去世后支付给指定的受益人，而企业将获得账户价值部分的身故赔偿金。

另一种选择是企业享有与面值等额的身故赔偿金，而重要人士拥有保单现金价值和任何超出面值部分的身故赔偿金。这是最常见的重要人士保险安排。企业需要面值来解决重要人士去世对企业的影响，而重要人士的家人获得余下的收益。

企业和重要人士间的保费支付比例可以依据他们在保单中的经济利益来确定。当企业拥有与面值等额的身故赔偿金时，企业需要承担的保费可以参考对等的定期型寿险的保费，而重要人士则负责剩余保费的支付。

企业为重要人士购买寿险还有一个税务方面的好处，特别是在企业为企业主购买保险的情况下。企业主本身需要购买保险，有两种方式：第一种，以个人身份购买，那么需要用个人税后收入；第二种，以企业身份去购买，那么需要用企业的税后收入。在高税负国家，个人的最高税率一般都高于企业的最高税率。也就是说，对于企业主，特别是高净值人士，基本上需要按照最高税率缴税，所以个人购买保单需要赚取的税前收入比企业购买保单需要赚取的税前收入高很多。

综上所述，对于拥有企业的高净值人士而言，其作为重要人士，由企业购买寿险，不但有益于企业在重要人士身故后的发展，也有益于其家庭。但是需要注意，上述提及的税务筹划作用并非在所有司法管辖区均适用。例如在中国，企业为重要人士购买人寿保险在税务上可能会被视为该重要人士的福利，等同于薪酬，仍然需要缴纳个人所得税；而在美国、加拿大，企业为高净值人购买人寿保险可以起到上述税务优化的作用。

8.2.2 买卖协议

买卖协议（Buy-Sell Agreement）源于北美，是一套成熟的去世股东退出机制，以具有法律约束力的机制来妥当处置股东去世后的股权。通常来说，该类退出机制会明确谁在股东去世后有权利或者责任买下该去世股东所拥有的股份，购买这些股份的价格（可能是固定金额，也可能通过事先决定的方式计算得出），以及购买股份的资金来源。最常见的安排是通过买卖协议，规定股东去世后，该股东必须将股份卖给公司其他股东，或者由公司回购(详细安排及选择见后文),而资金来源则是股东的人寿保险,即以股东作为被保人,去世后产生身故赔偿金的保单。最后,股份归公司或其他股东,股份继承人获得身故赔偿金,以此保证公司的股权结构以及重大经营决策权的稳定,从而达到企业永续经营的目的。

买卖协议也意味着股东不用担心某个不熟悉的人成为公司的共同所有者。在没有买卖协议的情况下,北美地区的股东可以在去世时将其股份留给他选择的任何人,这可能包括他的配偶、子女或者其他人。这些人可能没有能力经营公司,或者与其他在世的股东不合。有了买卖协议,去世股东的股份必须卖给公司本身,即股份赎回计划(Share Redemption Plan),或者卖给其他在世的股东,即交叉买卖协议(Cross-Purchase Agreement)。

买卖协议中最重要的条款是确定交易资金的来源。如果买方没有资金完成交易,交易就不能达成。通过人寿保险来安排买卖协议中所需的资金是最安全有效的方式。

8.2.2.1　股权变动的买卖协议的设计方式

用来控制股东去世后股权变动的买卖协议有两种不同的设计方式。

(1) 交叉购买协议。

在交叉购买协议中,其他股东同意购买去世股东的股份。对于公司来说,这意味着流通在外的股票总数和股票价值保持不变,但是每个在世的股东将拥有更多的股份。

> **例 8.3**
>
> John、Mary、Susan 是公司的三位股东,每人拥有 100 股,每股价值 1 万美元。他们签立交叉购买协议,约定如果其中任意一人去世,在世的股东将以股票现在的价值购买其股份。若 John 去世,则 Mary 和 Susan 每人将以每股 1 万美元的价格购买 John 的 50 股,John 的遗产会获得 100 万美元,Mary 和 Susan 每人会持有 150 股公司股票。在外流通的股票数仍然是 300 股,但是 Mary 和 Susan 各自所占的公司股份份额将是 50%,而不是之前的 33.33%。

(2) 股份回购计划。

通过股份回购计划,公司赎回去世股东的股份,会减少流通的股票的数量,但在世的股东所占的股份比例增加。

> **例 8.4**
>
> John、Mary、Susan 是公司的三位股东,每人拥有 100 股,每股价值 1 万美元。他们以股份回购计划方式签立买卖协议,如果其中任意一人去世,公司就以股票现在的价格赎回其股份,并取消赎回的股份。公司流通的股票数将减少

为 200 股。若 John 去世,则公司将支付 John 的遗产 100 万美元,Mary 和 Susan 每人将仍然持有 100 股,但是公司在外流通的股份将变为 200 股。现在 Mary 和 Susan 每人所占的公司股份份额将是 50%,而不是之前的 33.33%。

8.2.2.2 股东人寿保险购买的方式

接下来讨论的是股东人寿保险购买的两大类:交叉型保险和公司持有保单。

(1) 交叉型保险。

交叉型保险(Criss-Cross Insurance)通常用于为交叉购买型的买卖协议提供资金。在该类安排中,买卖协议的每一方都为协议的另一方购买人寿保险,其保额应足以在另一方去世时履行其购买义务,购买去世股东的股份。

例 8.5

沿用例 8.3 中的情形,假设协议规定,每位股东都要为其他股东购买人寿保险。John 需要为 Mary 和 Susan 各购买 50 万美元的人寿保险,确保足够购买总价值 50 万美元的 50 股股票。

交叉型保险的缺点是,根据各方的年龄和健康状况,要求购买保险的保费可能有显著差异。

例 8.6

沿用例 8.5 中的情形,假设 John 最年轻,只有 32 岁,身体健康;Mary 54 岁,吸烟,有高血压。John 为 Mary 购买 50 万美元人寿保险的保费将远高于 Mary 为 John 购买 50 万美元人寿保险所需支付的保费。

整个流程如图 8.1 所示。

A 和 B 每人拥有 AB 公司 50% 的股份,比如一共 200 股。买卖协议由交叉型保险提供资金。A 不久后去世。

- A 和 B 为对方购买人寿保险并支付保费。
- A 去世,属于 A 的 100 股转给 A 的遗产。
- 保险公司赔付身故赔偿金给 B(B 为 A 买了保险,A 去世后,B 获得赔付)。
- B 用获得的身故赔偿金支付 100 股股份的价格。
- A 的遗产转让 100 股给 B,现在 B 拥有 200 股,即 AB 公司 100% 的股权。

8 人寿保险与企业传承

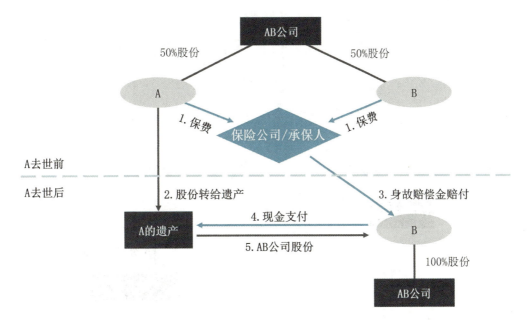

图 8.1 交叉型保险购买流程示意

（2）公司持有保单。

为买卖协议提供资金的另一个方式是让公司为股东购买保险。与股东个人购买保险相比，这有两个潜在的优势：

① 如果每个股东的保险成本（保费）因年龄和健康因素差别很大，那么由公司去购买及持有保单就不会有这个问题；股东们可以查阅公司的财务报表，确保保费的支付，以及保单的有效性。

② 如果保单是股东个人购买，则可能很难确认对方是否购买了保险，并按期交付保费以保证保单的有效性。

公司持有保单不但能为交叉购买协议提供资金，也能为股份回购计划提供资金，所以就会有下述两种流程：

① 为交叉购买协议提供资金：如果交叉购买协议是由公司为公司持有的保单提供资金，通常公司会被指定为保单的受益人。当其中一名股东去世时，在世的股东通常使用承兑票据（Promissory Notes）购买去世股东遗产中的股份。保险公司将向公司支付身故赔偿金。在世股东将指示公司向其支付分红，用来付清承兑票据。流程如图8.2所示。

A 和 B 每人拥有 AB 公司 50% 的股份，比如一共 200 股。公司以公司持有保单的形式为交叉购买协议提供资金。A 不久后去世。

- AB 公司为 A 和 B 的保单支付保费。
- A 去世，属于 A 的 100 股转给 A 的遗产。
- 保险公司赔付身故赔偿金给 AB 公司。
- B 以承兑票据换取 A 的遗产中的股份。

· 109 ·

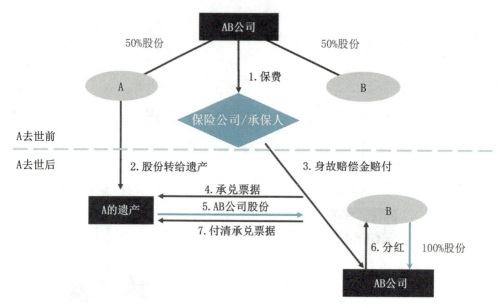

图 8.2　公司持有保单，为交叉购买协议提供资金

- A 的遗产转让 100 股给 B，现在 B 拥有 200 股，即 AB 公司 100% 的股权。
- B 指示 AB 公司对其进行分红。
- B 用获得的分红付清换取股票所用的承兑票据。

② 为股份回购计划提供资金：在股份回购计划中，公司和股东都是买卖协议的签署方。该公司为所有股东购买人寿保险，并作为保单的受益人。其中一名股东去世后，公司会用身故赔偿金回购去世股东遗产中的股份。流程如图 8.3 所示。

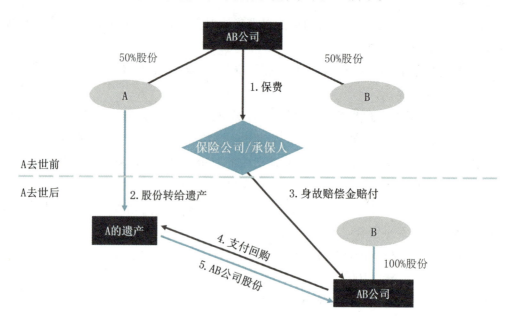

图 8.3　公司持有保单，为股份回购计划提供资金

- AB 公司为 A 和 B 的保单支付保费。
- A 去世,属于 A 的 100 股转给 A 的遗产。
- 保险公司赔付身故赔偿金给 AB 公司。
- AB 公司用这笔钱回购 A 的遗产中的股份,取消股份,使得公司在外流通的股票数量减少为 100 股。
- B 仍然拥有 100 股,但是现在这 100 股代表了 100% 的公司股权。

8.3 企业持有人寿保单的税务事宜

公司持有人寿保单还有一个税务问题。在前面的章节中我们已了解,身故赔偿金赔付出来一般是免税的。在公司拥有保单为交叉购买协议提供资金的安排中,公司获得免税的身故赔偿金赔付后,是否可以同样免税地将身故赔偿金作为分红分配给仍在世的股东,取决于各司法管辖区的法律规定。最典型的例子是加拿大的资本分红账户。

在加拿大,公司使用资本分红账户记录其免税获得的资金,例如税法规定的 50% 的免税资本增值,以及从人寿保险中获得的部分或全部身故赔偿金。公司可以将资本分红账户记录的免税资金作为资本分红同样免税地分配给股东。

需要注意的是,资本分红账户是一个名义上的账户,即并不像银行账户一样实际持有资金,而是单纯从税务角度记录资金。资本分红账户记录了公司可以免税分配给股东资金的额度。当公司的资本分红账户中有足够的额度,且公司也有足够的现金时,可以选择将分配给股东的款项指定为免税资本分红。公司分配资本分红时,会减少同等金额的资本分红账户额度。

对于人寿保险的身故赔偿金而言,只有超过保单调整后成本基数(Adjusted Cost Basis,ACB)的部分才计入资本分红账户,并最终可以以免税资本分红的形式分配;其余部分(即等于保单调整后的成本基数的金额)公司需要缴税。因此,在定期寿险的情况下,调整后成本基数为零,这意味着身故赔偿金可以全额计入资本分红账户。然而,对于终身寿险保单或万能寿险保单,公司实际上需要为身故赔偿金中等于保单调整后成本基数的部分缴税。

在美国,使用有限合伙企业(Limited Liability Company,LLC)持有保单也可以在公司层面享受税务优惠。LLC 在税务上非常灵活,有两种不同的纳税模式:默认情况下,它在税法层面上是一个穿透的实体,即其收入会被穿透视为股东成员的收入,从而直接在股东层面上纳税,无须缴纳企业层面的所得税;如果它选择成为一个独立的纳税实体,那它需要就其收入缴纳企业所得税。

在一个美国税务居民持有的 LLC 作为保单受益人的情况下,如果这张保单能满足特定的需求①,那么此时保单的身故赔偿金将不被视为 LLC 的收入,而直接被穿透视为美国税务居民的收入,此时美国税务居民获得保单赔偿金也是无须缴税的(见例 8.7)。

> **例 8.7**
>
> David 设立 LLC 公司并作为公司的股东成员,这个 LLC 在默认情况下适用税务穿透制度。公司为指定的公司高管被保人购买人寿保险,且公司也是该保单的受益人。当被保人去世后,赔付的身故赔偿金在税务上将直接被穿透视为 David 的收入,公司层面无税务责任。

---

① 需要满足以下要求:(1) 满足《美国国内税收法典》7702 条款的规定;(2) 不是 MEC;(3) 未曾被有对价地交易过;(4) 未受到"投资者控制"。详见附录 A:美国税务意见。

私募寿险(一)

本章要点：

- 讲解为什么高净值人士需要私募寿险
- 介绍私募寿险的发展与创新
- 介绍私募寿险的投资选择和税务优惠
- 介绍美国对私募寿险保险公司、保单和投资的监管

在前述章节中，我们学习了人寿保险的基本架构、角色、定义、类型以及在税务规划方面的功能。从这些章节中，我们了解到人寿保险在其架构属性方面的初步应用，从高净值家庭的需求出发，挑选合适的投保人、被保人和受益人，并可以和信托、私人基金会等工具结合使用。在这样的规划中，寿险不只是一个具有保障属性的产品，更是一种可以满足高净值家庭隔离保护、税务筹划等需求的规划方案，为高净值家族财富规划提供了多种多样的可能性和灵活性。

本章我们将会为大家介绍人寿保险在架构属性方面更复杂的应用——私募寿险，希望帮助读者更深入地理解：在财富规划中，人寿保险不只是一个具有保障属性和防范风险作用的产品，更是一个综合性的解决方案。理解这两者的区别是人寿保险规划的起点。

9.1 为什么高净值人士需要私募寿险

私募寿险是一种更灵活的投资型万能寿险，突出运用了寿险的免税机制和扩大了寿

险内投资的灵活性。它旨在吸引那些有兴趣用大笔保费向保单供款,并希望转入保单的保费获得投资回报的高净值人士。① 因为上述典型运作方式,私募寿险经常被称为包装(Wrapper),在英国则被称为保险债券②。对于高净值家庭来说,私募寿险不仅实现了寿险的资产保护功能,而且具有灵活投资和税务优化的功能。因此高净值人士选择私募寿险是作为一种资产持有架构的规划解决方案,而不仅是一个简单的产品。

永久人寿保险(Permanent Life Insurance)作为高净值人士的长期财富累积及税务筹划工具已经有很长一段历史了,但在过去的应用中,它无法满足定制化投资的要求。高净值人士对灵活投资的需求催生了私募寿险,他们既希望享受人寿保险税务优惠的好处,又不希望资产投资的范围被限定在保险公司提供的有限选择中。他们需要有更灵活的投资方式和更广泛的投资选择,例如一些有吸引力的高投资回报的定制化投资组合,而不只是固定收益投资。所以,私募寿险的重点不在于保险公司想要卖给客户什么样的产品,不在于保险公司现有的产品选择是什么,而更注重如何应用整个架构帮助客户满足他们的需求。

私募寿险是一种高度定制化的架构工具,用来满足高净值人士个性化的需求。当然,灵活的投资选择意味着不确定的风险。在美国,监管规定私募寿险仅适合合格投资者(Accredited Investor)和合格购买者(Qualified Purchaser)使用。根据美国《1933 年证券法》(Securities Act of 1933)501(a)条的规定,合格投资者是"个人净资产或与配偶的共同净资产超过 100 万美元(不包含主要居住的房产)的人;是在最近两年内每年的个人收入超过 20 万美元或与配偶/伴侣的共同收入超过 30 万美元,并且有理由相信在本年度达到相同的收入水平的人"。根据美国《1940 投资公司法》的规定,合格购买者是指"持有 500 万美元或以上投资的个人或由紧密家庭成员拥有的公司"。此外,满足一定条件的信托、投资经理或非家族公司也可成为合格购买者。合格投资者主要检验的是收入和净资产是否满足要求,而合格购买者则是考量基于投资的资产是否达到最低金额。经过多年的发展,私募寿险在高净值人士财富规划领域成了一个成熟的工具,客户可以通过私募寿险选择各种投资来满足自己的需求,同时兼顾风险管理和税务筹划。

9.1.1　风险管理

风险管理是寿险最重要的作用之一,客户通过寿险的架构和功能可以实现财富风险管理、资产保护、资产传承等目的。但私募寿险在风险管理方面的功能与传统寿险重点不同。传统寿险更关注人身风险和生命安全对财富的影响,通过传统寿险的高保额进行家庭风险管理,在核心家庭财富创造者去世后可以有足够的保额赔偿来保障家庭后续的财务支出。但私募寿险作为灵活投资和税务优化的工具,保额方面的风险管理功能并非其

---

① *Understanding Private Placement Life Insurance*, Mary Ann Mancini Loeb & Loeb LLP Washington, DC October 12, 2016.

② Michael Grob, The Meaning of Life Insurance, *STEP Journal*, April 01, 2015.

重点,其重点在于高净值家庭财富规划的个性需求。如果高净值家庭需要高保额的保障,则私募寿险架构设计也可满足。还是那句话,私募寿险的重点在于根据客户的不同需求来设计其架构。

① 资产保护。在私募寿险之下,资产在一个隔离账户中,不再属于自然人,同时独立于保险公司的自有账户。自然人仅作为寿险的保单持有人,享有支取现金价值或者保单贷款的权利。在某些司法管辖区,债权人无法执行保单的现金价值或身故赔偿金。[①]

② 资产传承。私募寿险将资产集中在一起,并通过指定受益人的方式实现资产的顺利传承。相较于资产分散在各处,资产集中更有利于简化传承规划,并且通过私募寿险的架构,最终以身故赔偿金的方式传承至后代。

9.1.2 税务筹划

在很多高税负司法管辖区,终身寿险是税务规划的重要工具,详见第6章。在美国和某些欧洲司法管辖区,包括英国、法国、意大利和瑞典,私募寿险也被广泛用于税务筹划[②],在拉丁美洲私募寿险也逐渐被广泛应用。在遵照当地税法要求的前提下,人寿保险内的投资也可以免税增长,不会即刻产生所得税、资本利得税,在支付身故赔偿金的时候也能实现税务筹划功能。需要关注的是,各司法管辖区税法对于人寿保险的规定要求各不相同,私募寿险如果想要达到税务筹划的功能则必须满足当地司法管辖区的具体要求,这部分我们会在后面的小节详细介绍。

> **例9.1**
>
> 一位高净值人士有5 000万美元可投资资产,如果该高净值人士个人直接持有投资,在美国联邦个人所得税累积最高税率是37%。假设投资年回报率为5%,1年投资回报收益为250万美元,不考虑累积区间税率及州税,仅以最高税率37%来计算个人所得税为92.5万美元。这仅是一年需要缴纳的税款,而在私募寿险保单中,这些投资增长均不需要缴纳所得税。累积10年、20年计算复利增长,将会是一笔不可小视的收入差异。

9.1.3 投资规划

灵活的投资选择和税务优惠是私募寿险发展的最初动力。相较于仅能提供固定收益投资、参与分红的寿险产品,以及有限的基金选择而言,私募寿险为人寿保险架构内的投资

[①] Garrett R. D'Alessandro, Eliminate Taxes Using PPLI, a High-Net-Worth Investor's Best Strategy, February 21, 2008.

[②] Michael Grob, The Meaning of Life Insurance, STEP Journal, 01 April 2015.

提供了多种多样的选择。当然,这些投资选择在不同司法管辖区也会有不同的规定限制。例如,美国有保险专用基金(Insurance Dedicated Fund,IDF)和独立管理账户(Separately Managed Account,SMA),同时还有投资者控制限制(Investor-control Limitations)和投资多样化(Diversification)要求,而在离岸地区的私募寿险投资选择则更加宽泛灵活。然而,我们也要意识到灵活的投资选择同样带来了更高的投资风险。私募寿险是面向成熟投资者和高净值家庭的工具。在美国,私募寿险仅面向合格投资者和合格购买者开放。在高净值家族资产配置中,一般70%会选择流动性高的资产来满足工作生活和退休养老的需求,另外30%会选择长期投资来作为财富的增长和传承。需要注意的是,私募寿险在投资规划方面的功能并非全盘适用,一些用来满足生活和退休养老的资产配置并不适合由私募寿险来持有。那些用来长期持有,有着潜在高收益和高税负的投资才是私募寿险最擅长持有的投资类型。

9.2 私募寿险的发展

9.2.1 私募寿险的市场需求

私募寿险最初诞生的时间点并不明确,学界观点认为其大致范围在20世纪90年代中期。起初,仅有几家小公司提供私募寿险,但几年后美国寿险市场的主流服务商开始加入进来。这些公司的加入也促进了私募寿险的进一步发展。最初私募寿险仅作为一种工具应用于美国公司持有的人寿保险(US Corporate-Owned Life Insurance,COLI),通过极大规模的机构交易非正式地为员工福利计划提供资金,之后扩展到更多私人财富规划领域。这一过程要从美国退休计划的沿革讲起,最初在美国员工退休计划中的固定福利计划(Defined-Benefit Plan)都有年度供款限额,对于许多高收入的高管来说,这部分退休金仅能占到他们工资非常少的比例,不能满足其退休后的生活安排。这一需求催生了更多的福利计划,例如非限定递延报酬(Non-Qualified Deferred Compensation,NQDC)计划和其他涉及现金价值人寿保单的应用。寿险公司在20世纪80年代为企业创造了COLI,作为非正式的为员工和行政人员的福利计划提供资金的工具,COLI产品也因其高固定回报率而颇具竞争力。在20世纪90年代,保险公司开始将COLI产品与投资型万能寿险合并,COLI提供有固定回报率的收益,投资型万能寿险提供更多的投资选择。

此后,高管退休金水平逐渐提高,这个细分市场逐渐变得成熟,其竞争也逐渐激烈。市场需要一种高度定制化的产品来满足更灵活多样的福利计划的需求,这就要求保险公司提供更灵活、更创新、对用户更加友好并为更多退休市场范围提供选择的产品。正是COLI产品对于投资的灵活选择需求和复杂性创造了私募寿险。私募寿险为COLI提供了更多灵活的投资选择,不再受限于传统保险公司提供的投资选项,并且私募寿险的设计满足了美国国税局(Internal Revenue Service,IRS)对于多样化和投资者控制限制的要求,这就意味着私募寿险同样享受美国国税局的税务优惠政策。除此之外，私募寿险还为福利计划市场提供了更多的构建方式，来满足其各种各样的需求。由于灵活的构建方式深受 COLI 市场的喜爱，私募寿险大约占据 COLI 市场 50% 的份额。在此之后，私募寿险从退休金市场规划逐渐扩大到私人财富规划。

9.2.2 寿险内投资范围的创新

私募寿险本质上是一种可以根据客户需求定制的人寿保险。如要追溯私募寿险的产生，就必须先了解人寿保险的投资范围的创新沿革。

人寿保险有两种基本类型——定期型和永久型人寿保险。定期型人寿保险是一种短期可提供高效基础保障的寿险计划，利用较低的保费获取较高的寿险保额，这对于希望用少量现金流获取高额保障的家庭来说是非常好的选择。但是定期寿险仅满足部分保障需求，高净值客户无法在定期型寿险中存放更多的保费用来投资，定期寿险也无法满足高净值客户税务筹划的需求。永久型寿险相较于定期型寿险而言不仅提供了身故赔偿金，而且提供了现金价值。现金价值的增加对于高净值财富规划而言，将寿险工具的功能从单纯的风险管理和传承规划扩展到具备投资属性的架构规划。现在，区分不同寿险产品的一个重要衡量指标即是现金价值投资回报的来源和灵活性。最简单的寿险产品并不能为保单持有人提供灵活的投资选择，甚至不提供选择。寿险市场发展到今天，有越来越多成熟且多变的寿险产品为保单持有人提供灵活多样甚至定制化的投资选择。

永久型寿险的几种主要类型中，投资型万能寿险和私募寿险的投资灵活度相比分红型终身寿险和万能寿险更高。

9.2.2.1 分红型终身寿险

分红型终身寿险是一种比较常用的终身寿险，每年必须支付固定的保费，以获取有保证的身故赔偿金，以及不同方式的分红。分红型终身寿险的现金价值通常投资于保险公司分红基金的一般账户中，该账户由保险公司内部管理，可比作黑箱。黑箱投资的结果是每个保单持有人获得相同回报的分红，而分红是根据保险公司公布的年度分红利率来确定的。分红型终身寿险保单最重要的缺点是，保单持有人无权选择保单内投资，分红型终身寿险缺乏对保单基础成本的披露。

9.2.2.2 万能寿险

相较于分红型终身寿险而言，万能寿险在保险架构方面有更大的灵活性。它有灵活的缴费方式和可调整的身故赔偿金。当你资金充足时，可以选择多放些保费；当你资金不足时，可以选择少放些保费，甚至当年不支付保费而万能寿险仍然有效。不仅如此，万能寿险在现金价值投资选择方面也更具灵活性。如果把分红型终身寿险比作黑箱，万能寿险则是玻璃箱，透过它可以清晰透明地看到保险公司的收费金额，并且它完整披露了关于保险公司在未来可以收取的保证最高收费。保单现金价值可以在一些限定范围内投资，也可以选择回报率挂钩指数。但是保单持有人仍然无法自由灵活地投资,其仅能在保险公司提供的范围内进行选择。

9.2.2.3 投资型万能寿险

在分红型终身寿险和万能寿险的基础之上,保险公司创造了一种叫作投资型万能寿险的新产品,它为保单持有人提供了一个独立的账户来持有现金价值,这也为现金价值的投资提供了更灵活的选择。独立账户中的现金价值不受一般账户的限制,其投资范围不限于保险公司提供的限定范围的基金。保单持有人可以选择债券、股票、共同基金等进行投资,这些投资选择可以由保险公司或由保险公司指定的外部顾问来管理。当然,在美国,这些投资仍然需要遵循《国际财务报告准则》第817条的多样化和投资者控制限制的规定。另外,美国的投资型万能寿险销售对象没有合格投资者及合格购买者的限定,因此投资型万能寿险不能投资于对冲基金,因为对冲基金只能接受上述合格人士的投资。

9.2.2.4 私募寿险

相较于前几种传统寿险的架构,私募寿险是在投资型万能寿险基础之上发展出来的一种高度定制化的寿险,其支付保费方式灵活,保额定制灵活,保险内投资增长免税,在投资选择范围方面可谓是极度灵活。在延续了投资型万能寿险独立账户的基础之上,私募寿险架构要求合格投资者才可使用,仅为更成熟的投资人提供了选择。私募寿险的投资选择不仅可以包括上述提到的债券、股票、基金,而且包括对冲基金,甚至是公司股权、实物资产。

私募寿险的产生根本而言是寿险内投资范围的创新,并且由于其应用越来越偏向灵活投资和税后回报,对于传统保额的高额成本而言,高净值家族们更愿意要一个满足免税要求的最低保额,用最低的成本来实现免税增长的财富规划。于是私募寿险在保费和保额方面的灵活设计最大限度地满足了高净值财富规划中的个性化需求。但是需要注意的是,由于私募寿险非常突出的投资属性,其内部的保额过低,这样的产品有触发相关司法管辖区内一般反避税原则的风险,并导致其最终丧失税务优化的作用。私募寿险与投资型寿险的比较见表9.1。

表 9.1 投资型寿险和私募寿险

	投 资 型 寿 险	私 募 寿 险
投资配置控制	持有人可以指示保险公司将现金价值分配到一系列经批准的投资选项中,并允许定期重新配置	持有人可以指示保险公司将现金价值分配到一系列经批准的投资选项中,并允许定期重新配置
收 费	零售级别	机构级别
投资规模	通常情况下少于100万美元	通常情况下大于500万美元

续　表

	投资型寿险	私募寿险
资　格	一般来说,任何完成了申请程序并符合医疗条件的人都可以申请	保单持有人必须是合格投资者和合格购买者
产品基础	通过招股说明书提供的注册证券	由私募发行提供的非注册证券
投资选择	只有注册基金,通常只做长线的策略	可以包括注册和非注册基金,包括对冲基金、结构性产品和私募股权策略

对于没有任何商业实质的交易或安排,如果这种交易的唯一目的是通过应用一般反避税原则实现税务优惠,那么当地的税务部门可以否定这种交易或安排的税务优惠。

9.3　私募寿险内的投资选择与税务优惠

9.3.1　私募寿险内的投资选择

私募寿险的投资选择一般遵循以下两个规则。

(1) 选择长期持有的投资。

高净值家庭的资产配置,一般会根据需求分为短期、中期和长期投资。短期投资用于工作生活的花销,中期投资用于退休生活的养老金,长期投资用于财富创造和遗产继承。私募寿险架构下的投资组合为保单持有人的长期需求服务,旨在满足高净值家庭流动性需求的计划通常不会由私募寿险来实现。

(2) 选择高收益的投资。

私募寿险的现金价值非常适合投资具有高回报潜力的投资产品,高回报、所节省的高税负成本让私募寿险的长期税务递延功能更加突出。当年度投资收益所面临的税负成本都在私募寿险内税务递延,并持续复利收益,让私募寿险更加具有吸引力。私募寿险的常见投资选择包括对冲基金、私募股权和风险投资。如果没有私募寿险架构,则在资产配置中盲目追求高风险和高回报将产生较大的税务后果。然而,除了具有丰厚回报的投资外,对于拥有大量固定收入并在最高税率范围内纳税的高净值人士来说,在投资产生大量固定股息、利息或租金收入等情况下,私募寿险也可以提高他们的税后回报。

理论上,私募寿险的投资范围基本覆盖大部分投资选择。但是从实际操作角度而言,除了上述两大规则之外,私募寿险的投资选择还受许多其他因素的影响,如私募寿险发行地的监管要求、保险公司自身的规定等。

(1) 私募寿险发行地的监管要求。

私募寿险是由注册在某一司法管辖区的保险公司发行的,不同司法管辖区的保险公司在发行产品时需要遵循当地监管的要求。在美国包括税法、税务裁决（Revenue Ruling）、财务部法规（Treasury Regulation）、证券法（Securities Act）等，均对投资型保险合同有所规定。例如，投资者控制原则、坚持多样化投资、寿险基金的选择等均对私募寿险内可做的投资选择范围有影响。多样化要求私募寿险内的投资不能集中在某一两个投资项目，即必须做到分散投资，保险专用基金限制对保险内投资的投资组合也提出了明确的要求。若在美国发行私募寿险，则这些监管要求必须满足，否则私募寿险将会失去税务优惠等功能及人寿保险的实质。离岸司法管辖区对税法和保险组合的监管要求则相对宽松得多，例如百慕大相关的监管规定包括《1978年保险法》（Insurance Act of 1978）和《2000年独立账户公司法》（Segregated Accounts Companies Act 2000）。但要注意的是，一个高税负司法管辖区的税务居民并不能简单通过到离岸地购买私募寿险来回避其个人在美国税法下的税务责任，因为其本人依然受到美国税法的规制。

（2）保险公司规定。

满足当地司法监管要求之后，各保险公司也会对各自的私募寿险产品给出相应的产品投资选择范围，这主要是由于各家保险公司产品和客户群体定位的差异。有些保险公司会更偏好对冲基金的投资，因为其背后的发行公司以对冲基金投资为核心业务，这在私募寿险公司是很常见的一种架构。另外，有些保险公司会接受广泛的投资选择，包括股权、实物资产等。然而保险公司会对私募寿险保单中投资的流动性和可估值性有一定要求。流动性用来满足其年费及收费，可估值性用来满足保险公司现金价值和身故赔偿金的计算。当然，不同保险公司会有不同的规定，比较常见的要求是：证券类资产每季度进行评估，房产和企业股权则每年度进行评估。对于私募寿险保单内的投资选择，有保险公司甚至规定保单持有人可自由选择投资经理，而保险公司在这方面不作任何推荐，同时不负相关责任。私募寿险是一个高度节税投资和税务优惠的包装，并且赋予成熟投资者更多的投资选择自由度。

9.3.2　私募寿险在税务筹划方面的优势

许多投资人在计算投资收入回报时会意识到税后收入才是一个准确的衡量标准。美国高额的所得税和遗产税促使很多富人寻找合适的方案来减少税务风险，这也是私募寿险产生于美国的其中一个重要原因。私募寿险可以实现税务筹划的重要原因在于：

① 私募寿险属于有现金价值且有独立账户的永久型人寿保险，它同样有身故赔偿金、退保、保单贷款或现金支取等其他保单操作。

② 私募寿险的保额比较低且可以灵活定制，所以私募寿险在纯保险部分的金额并不多，只需要满足当地监管机构对人寿保险的最低要求即可。这部分的保额设定可以让私募寿险保持其人寿保险的性质，不被穿透视为理财投资，进而可以享受各司法管辖区给予寿险内投资的税务优惠，包括对所得税、资本利得税和可能产生的遗产税的递延、减少和避免。

9.3.2.1　所得税

美国联邦所得税法对不同类型的投资收益征收不同的税。一般来说，长期资本利得

(持有一年以上)的税率为0%或15%或20%,取决于个人的收入和申报方式。短期资本利得(持有时间少于一年)包括在全年的应税收入中,并按个人所得税率纳税。大多数利息收入按累计所得税征税,2023年最高为37%(仅为联邦税),具体的税务计算非常复杂。为了举例说明,我们假设所得税率为37%。

例9.2

Jonathan在资产配置中一大部分选择了短期交易频繁的证券,并且实现了平均年回报率10%。这一部分资产配置的收入主要由短期资本利得产生,所以37%的收入应该上缴联邦政府。如果Jonathan所在的州有个人所得税,他不仅要就这部分的收入缴纳联邦所得税,而且要缴纳州所得税。假设Jonathan的综合税率为40%,那么他的税后年回报率就只有6%(10%-4%)。Jonathan的税后回报率将只有他税前回报率的60%。

符合税法相关条件和标准的私募寿险,其内部的投资得以在保险架构中免税增长。针对那些高投资回报但高税收和产生大量固定收益的投资项目,私募寿险提供了一种有效的税务筹划,从而大幅增加税后收益的方案。正如上述例子所示,Jonathan税后投资回报率仅剩6%。若该部分投资于私募寿险,则税后投资回报率等于税前投资回报率,也就是10%。这部分在私募寿险内的增长和收益不属于保单持有人所得税的纳税范围。如果投资在私募寿险内产生了资本利得,也是同样的原理。

如图9.1所示,高收益高税收的资产如对冲基金和风险投资,放在私募寿险内和放在其他应纳税架构中有着明显的差异。

9.3.2.2 遗产税

遗产规划中涉及的赠与税、遗产税和隔代税(Generation-Skipping Tax)是非常复杂的问题,且不同司法管辖区对于这些税种的规定各不相同,有些司法管辖区目前还没有开征遗产税(如中国内地),有些司法管辖区虽然没有遗产税,但在传承过程中可能会发生资本利得税(如加拿大、澳大利亚),所以私募寿险在遗产税方面的功能在各司法管辖区也不尽相同。私募寿险在遗产税方面的税务筹划效果,主要体现在大部分司法管辖区对于保单或身故赔偿金通常予以免税的优惠。例如,在加拿大和澳大利亚,保单的身故赔偿金给予受益人是免税的;但是在美国,身故赔偿金有可能触发遗产税的问题。在美国,对遗产税常见的有效规划方案,是将信托与私募寿险相结合。信托委托人通过在生前利用赠与税的免税额度,将部分资金不可撤销地赠与有合适架构的信托,而私募寿险能使这部分资产集中并投入高回报的投资收益中获得免税增长。相关资产和收益在未来最终通过信托分配至受益人时,这部分资产不再属于捐赠者的遗产,从而避免触发遗产税。

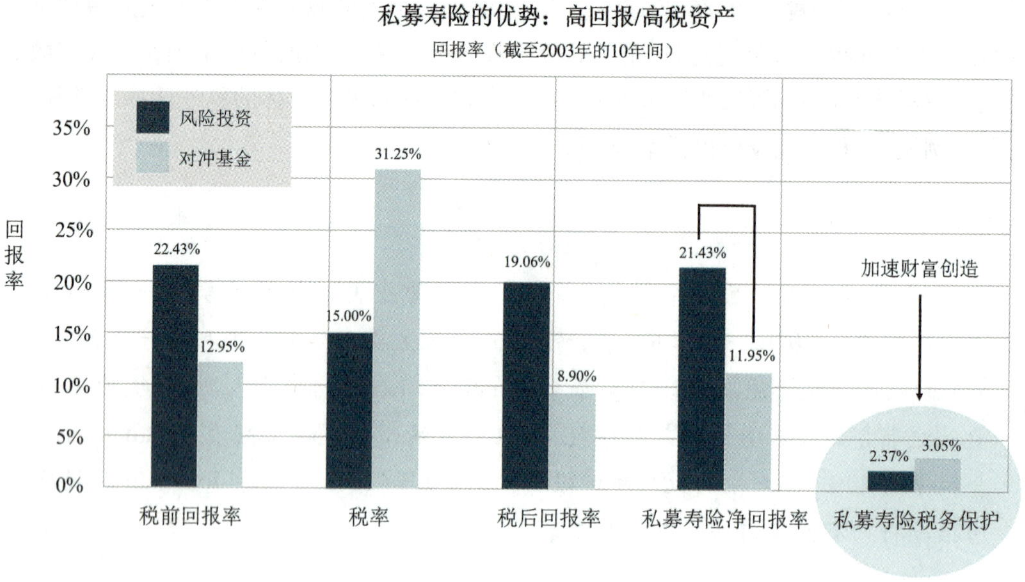

私募寿险的优势：高回报/高税资产

回报率（截至2003年的10年间）

	税前回报率	税率	税后回报率	私募寿险净回报率	私募寿险税务保护
风险投资	22.43%	15.00%	19.06%	21.43%	2.37%
对冲基金	12.95%	31.25%	8.90%	11.95%	3.05%

加速财富创造

图 9.1　私募寿险加速财富创造

来源：www.lnvestworks.com；Spencer Trask Asset Management；HFR Corp.

9.4　美国对私募寿险的监管

私募寿险最初产生于美国，美国成熟的税法体系对私募寿险监管规定也非常完善，对私募寿险保险公司、私募寿险保单、私募寿险内的投资和私募寿险的投资管理等多方面均有相关规制。

9.4.1　美国对私募寿险保险公司的监管

在美国，根据税法（IRC）第816(a)条，保险公司要满足以下要求：

① 其一半以上的业务是发行保险或年金合同，或对其他保险公司承保的风险进行再保险；[1]

② 公司总准备金的50%以上必须包括人寿保险准备金，以及未赚取的保费和保证可续保的意外和健康险保单的未付损失（以不包括在人寿保险准备金中为限）。"寿险准备金"在第816(b)条中被定义为：根据公认的表格和假定的利率计算或估计的金额，为清偿寿险合同产生的未来预计索赔而留出的金额，以及法律要求的金额。[2]

就联邦税务而言，如果一个离岸保险公司想做一项可以符合美国规定并被按此对待的美国业务，它就需要做出第953(d)条的申报。第953(d)条要求只适用于在任何特定

---

[1] Rev. Rul. 83-132, 1983-2 C. B. 270.
[2] IRC Section 816(a)(b).

的美国州开展业务的情形,如果一个离岸保险公司不做美国业务,那么该法规就不适用于该保险公司。在离岸保险公司做出第953(d)条的申报后,为美国业务签发的保单需要满足美国的合规政策。

① 第953(d)条的申报允许境外保险公司在美国所得税方面被视为美国国内公司,即使它不在美国开展业务。

② 第953(d)条的申报很重要,因为如果没有这个申报,保险公司在保单中的独立账户从美国境内的来源收到的金额将根据第871(a)条的规定以30%的税率缴纳预提税。

③ 此外,如果离岸保险公司不做出第953(d)条的申报,保单持有人将缴纳1%的联邦消费税,这是从支付给保单的保费中收取的。

9.4.2　美国对私募寿险保单的监管

私募寿险的实质是投资型万能寿险,并且前文提到私募寿险的保费和保额可以根据客户需求在满足当地司法规定要求之下进行高度个性化定制。在满足这些司法规定要求后,当地税局将认为投资型保险合同中的投资属于保险公司而非保单持有人,从而可以享受税务优惠。在美国,私募寿险若想实现其税务优惠的功能,则需要满足美国税法下的两大规定。

(1) 符合人寿保险的条件。

最高保费准则基于《美国国内税收法典》7702条款规定的测试——基准保费测试和现金价值累积测试。根据这两种测试,可以支付给合同的保费有一个最高数额,以避免保单合同违反7702条款的规定,避免其成为MEC。详情见第6章。

(2) 符合投资型保险合同的条件。

该条件主要涉及第817条的规定,该规定是为了将人寿保险内收益计算在保险公司名下,而非保单持有人名下,从而避免由保单持有人直接承担相关税务责任。

9.4.3　美国对私募寿险内投资的监管

私募寿险架构下的投资需要满足各司法管辖区对寿险投资的基本要求,这也是私募寿险存在的基础。在美国,如果一项投资要符合保险投资组合的要求,就必须满足特定的标准。这里需要特别介绍3项规则,因为它们直接影响投资选择。

9.4.3.1　规则1:多样化测试

第一条规则是多样化测试(Diversification Test)。在1984年的税收改革法案中,第817(h)条规定,如果一份投资型保单不满足该条的多样化规则,那么该保单将不被视为第72条和第7702(a)条下规定的人寿保险[1],因此该保单在美国将不属于合格的人寿保

---

① Mary Ann Mancini Loeb & Loeb LLP Washington DC, Understanding Private Placement Life Insurance, October 12, 2016.

险。如果私募寿险保单未能通过多样化测试,那么寿险的所有税务优惠都将丧失。多样化规则要求:寿险保单内的投资,单项投资不能超过总资产价值的55%;两项投资之和不能超过总资产价值的70%;三项投资之和不能超过总资产价值的80%;四项投资之和不能超过总资产价值的90%。根据上述要求,一张保单内至少要有五种投资。

美国国会于1986年修订了第817(h)条,增加了第817(h)(4)条:透视规则(Look-through Rule)。如果透视规则适用,则保单内的独立资产账户可以通过它所持有的资产,如某基金份额,来查看是否满足分散规则。例如,如果保单内独立资产账户所持有的基金本身以符合第817(h)条规定的方式分散的,那么这张保单就有资格适用透视规则,视为已经满足充分分散的要求。

9.4.3.2 规则2:保险专用基金

第二条规则是美国国税局在保险专用基金投资组合中与对冲基金部分的相关规定:保单内独立账户中的资金只能投资于符合保险专用基金要求的对冲基金。对于满足要求的保险专用基金(Insurance Portfolio),其中的价值增长不被视为保单持有人的当期收入而承担相应税负。这个规定也让一些高净值客户对满足合规要求的保险专用基金投资充满期待。在保单持有人向保险公司支付保费后,保险公司首先将保费转入一个独立账户,该账户由保险公司为保单持有人持有。在与保单持有人讨论后,保险公司将现金价值分配投资到一个或多个保险专用基金,但需要提醒的是,保险专用基金经理必须有充分的自由裁量权,不能让保单持有人影响有关保险专用基金投资的决定。保险专用基金的架构如图9.2所示。

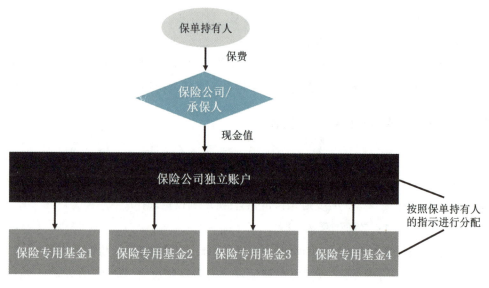

图9.2 保险专用基金架构

9.4.3.3 规则3:投资者控制裁决

在20世纪70年代,美国国税局开始大力审查保险公司提供的高现金价值和灵活投资的人寿保险产品。为了规范市场,美国国税局还发布了一系列裁决,以确保仅向符合税收合规规定的保险合同提供税务优惠。这些裁决被称为投资者控制裁决(Investor-control Rulings)或包装性裁决(Wraparound Rulings),因为美国国税局认为某些投资者选择某些保险安排的主要原因是为了用保险包装这些投资资产,以便他们能够享受投资型保险合同的税务优惠。在这些裁决中,美国国税局描述了不同的投资型保险合同安排,包括几个典型案例操作。例如,保单持有人直接控制保险公司名下的投资型保险合同的分立账户,保险公司在投资型保险合同下的投资可直接由保单持有人在不购买该保险合同的情况下直接获取。这些安排都反映了投保人对这些资产拥有不适当的投资者控制权[①]。如果保单持有人违反了上述规则,美国国税局将认为投资型保险合同中的投资属于保单持有人而不是保险公司,其结果是,保单持有人将为这些投资中产生的收入承担纳税义务。

---

① Kirk Loury (2015). *The PPLI Solution* (Chapter 12). Bloomberg Press.

CHAPTER 10 私募寿险（二）

> **本章要点：**
> - 解释如何构建私募寿险
> - 介绍私募寿险信托，并区别私募寿险与信托
> - 探讨私募寿险的不同保单持有人
> - 介绍私募寿险架构中的服务提供者
> - 解释如何为高净值人士构建私募寿险

10.1 如何构建私募寿险

私募寿险本质上是寿险，且是一种灵活定制的寿险。与传统寿险不同的是，私募寿险更注重税务筹划和灵活的投资选择，而非身故赔偿金和风险管理。正因如此，私募寿险不是保险公司预先设计的标准化零售产品，而是一个反映个人客户需求的个性化定制产品。私募寿险的架构因人而异，没有单一的规定架构，因此被称为开放式架构。私募寿险最突出的定制特征包括保费支付方式、现金价值和身故赔偿金。

10.1.1 保费支付方式

保费的支付方式多种多样，有1年付、5年付、10年付、20年付、30年付等方式。在离岸地区常见的做法有1年付、5年付、10年付；而在岸地区，受制于税法的要求，缴纳期限

通常会比较长,相对来说10年、20年、30年期比较常见。在美国,为避免保单成为MEC,保费支付期限一般会在7年以上。

在传统寿险中,分红型终身寿险的保费支付方式一般是固定的或者有定额保证保费(Level Guaranteed Premium)。不同于分红型终身寿险,万能寿险、投资型万能寿险和私募寿险的保费支付方式是非常灵活的。私募寿险的现金价值和身故赔偿金也会随着所选择的支付方式而变化,这就是为什么选择正确的支付方式是定制私募寿险保单以获得最佳财务结果的关键步骤,特别是在税务筹划方面。

寿险内的现金价值免税增长,以现金价值为抵押的保单贷款同样不需要纳税,这些税务优惠均以保单符合税法的诸多限制为前提。以美国为例,如第6章所介绍的,在一张私募寿险保单被认定为MEC的情况下,如果此时保单持有人从保单中获取现金价值,那么他可能面临相应的税务负担。详情请见本书第6章内容。

在其他司法管辖区规划私募寿险需要咨询当地的税务律师和专业人士,以实现利益最大化并确保合法合规。

10.1.2 现金价值和身故赔偿金

为了满足风险管理的需要,传统人寿保险的架构通常是扩大风险净额(Net Amount Risk),减少保费,从而达到提高身故补偿的目的(见图10.1)。在构建私募寿险时,常见的策略是将风险净额最小化并将保费最大化,这样可以最大限度地享受税务优化效果,并使投资灵活性最大化(见图10.2)。

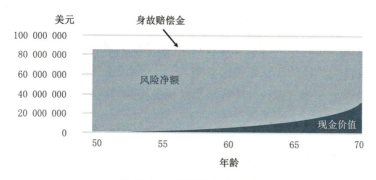

图10.1 传统寿险注资方式

由于寿险特殊的税务优惠政策,在许多司法管辖区针对人寿保险内的现金价值都有着不同的规定,以避免寿险成为逃避税收的工具。例如,美国税法第7702条包含一个现金价值通道的规定:死亡赔偿金应不低于一定比例的退保现金价值。这一限制背后的原因主要是为了避免寿险沦为避税工具,使得投保人将超过合理限度的投资资产作为保单现金价值放入寿险中。寿险内现金价值应与合理的身故赔偿金相对应。

私募寿险保额部分的定制是为了满足其寿险本质,继而享受寿险所带来的一系列税

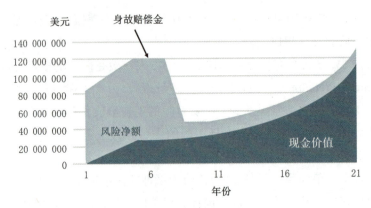

图 10.2　私募寿险注资方式

务优惠。在离岸免税地区政策会相对比较宽松，例如仅要求现金价值的 101%~110% 为身故赔偿金即可满足寿险的定义（见图 10.3）。

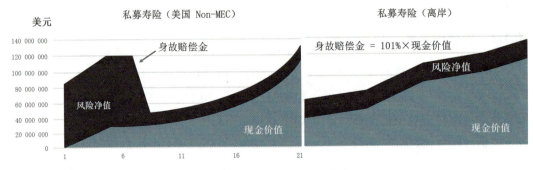

图 10.3　美国 Non-MEC 和离岸

具体到不同的司法管辖区，现金价值与身故赔偿金之间的关系均有不同的规定，由于这部分与不同司法管辖区的税法相关性紧密，涉及不同司法管辖区私募寿险架构规划时，现金价值与身故赔偿金的具体设计应征求当地税务律师的税务意见。

10.2　私募寿险信托

在高净值财富传承规划领域，人寿保险和信托是两大主要规划工具。私募寿险和信托在传承规划中的应用有何分别，又如何结合使用呢？

10.2.1　比较私募寿险和信托

人寿保险和信托是传承规划领域常见的两项工具。私募寿险是一种人寿保险，本质上是保险公司和保单持有人之间的合同；信托是受托人和受益人之间的一种法律关系（一种衡平法的义务）。在私募寿险架构中，承保人对保单持有人/财富创造者的利益负责；而在信托中，受托人只对受益人的利益负责。

我们还可以从更多维度来深入了解私募寿险和信托。

10.2.1.1 主要角色和相互关系

私募寿险的主要角色包括保单持有人、付款人、被保人、投资顾问和受益人,保单持有人、被保人和受益人之间应当有可保利益(见图10.4)。

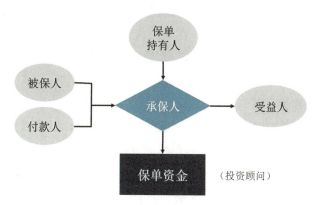

图 10.4 私募寿险的主要角色和相互关系

信托的主要角色包括设立人、保护人、投资顾问和受益人。设立人和受益人之间应当有一定的合理关系(家人、生意伙伴、高管等),见图10.5。

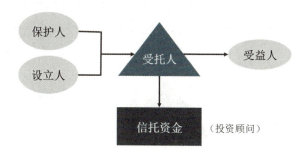

图 10.5 信托的主要角色和相互关系

10.2.1.2 权利保留

私募寿险:保单持有人可在保单现金价值支取、保单贷款、受益人变更、保单转让、保单取消等方面保留权利,可以设置不可撤销的受益人,在需要时制约保单持有人的权利。

信托:在信托管辖法允许的前提下,设立人或保护人可以保留变更受益人、分配信托资产、指定投资等方面的权利。然而,在信托中保留过多权利通常被认为是不具备真实的设立信托的意愿,并有可能被认定为虚假信托,从而导致信托无效。

10.2.1.3 资产获取

私募寿险:保单持有人可以通过各种方式获得保单的现金价值,如在保单有效期内提款、保单贷款和部分退保。如果被保人去世,则受益人有权获得身故赔偿金。

信托:对于不可撤销信托而言,只有受益人可以通过分配、费用支付、贷款或其他方式获得信托资产。对于一个可撤销信托,委托人还可以通过撤销信托的方式,将资产重新拿回到自己手上。

10.2.2 私募寿险信托

私募寿险具有寿险所有的功能,包括风险管理、传承规划、税务优惠等。上文已介绍:私募寿险的保单持有人享有多种权利,并可获取现金价值;私募寿险的受益人在被保人去世之后可一次性获得大额身故赔偿金。在相关权益由个人直接享有的情况下,个人的风险总会在一定程度上与其享有的利益绑定;而信托与私募寿险的结合,则可使高净值家族财富规划更安全、更长久。

10.2.2.1 信托作为私募寿险的保单持有人

人寿保单的资产保护功能,在不同的司法辖区均有差异。以中国为例,最高人民法院和多地省高院均发布过审判指引,确认保单内的资产可分割、可执行;以新加坡为例,由以配偶和子女为受益人设立的信托持有的人寿保单才能免于沦为破产财产[①];而在美国,更是可能面临不同州之间的法律规定均有差别的情况。虽然当地法律规定会有差别,但一般来说,在人寿保单的基础上搭配使用信托,以信托作为保单持有人,都可以加大资产保护的力度,避免自然人保单持有人的风险连累保单资产的安全。

需要注意的是,并非所有的信托都天然具备足够的资产保护功能,并非在资产上加上一个信托即可高枕无忧。想要设立一个有足够资产保护功能的信托,也是一门复杂深奥的学问,需要综合考虑信托的类型、信托内的权利机制设计、信托适用法律等多方面的问题(如图 10.6 所示)。

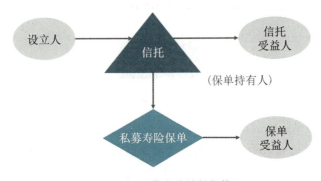

图 10.6　私募寿险信托架构

10.2.2.2 信托作为私募寿险的受益人

用信托代替个人持有保单,是为了避免保单持有人的风险累及保单内现金资产的安全。除此之外,我们还需要关注保单的身故赔偿金的安全:如果受益人欠债,那么他获得一笔巨额身故赔偿金之后,极有可能就需要以该笔资金偿还债务。但如果在寿险架构中以信托代替个人作为保单受益人,那就可以进一步加强寿险架构的资产保护功能(如图 10.7 所示)。

---

① https://io.mlaw.gov.sg/bankruptcy/information-for-stakeholders/information-for-creditors/.

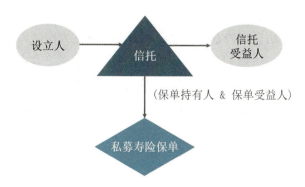

图 10.7　信托作为私募寿险的受益人

此外,信托作为私募寿险的受益人,还可以实现更长远的家族资产规划和家族治理的目标。很多创富者有这样的担心:如果家族后代一次性获取巨额赔偿金,他们可能无法驾驭财富,轻则挥霍资产,重则沾染恶习。此时,以信托作为受益人就是一个更理想的选项,届时巨额赔偿金将先进入家族信托,进而根据信托的规则,按照一定的时间、标准、要求和限制,有序地发放给信托受益人(可以是家族成员,也可以是家族企业,还可以是慈善项目)。如此一来,家族成员既能获得保障、享受财富,又可避免与巨额资产相伴的风险。这样的安排也更有利于受益人的税务筹划:虽然经妥当设计的寿险架构的身故赔偿金通常是免税的,但如果受益人是高税区的税务居民,其获得该笔资产后,相应的增值和收入将马上面临税务负担。通过信托规划,则有机会、有空间实现更好的税务规划。若设计得当,则家族企业可以获得必要的资金周转,慈善事业可以得到延续。

10.2.3　私募寿险的不同保单持有人

以下我们来综合对比不同架构作为私募寿险保单持有人的优缺点。

10.2.3.1　自然人保单持有人

自然人作为保单持有人,投保流程简单,审核资料简单,权利集中在保单持有人手中(如图 10.8 所示)。这样的架构优势在于成本低、控权大,但劣势在于资产保护效果较弱。因此,这样简单的架构适合成本敏感,且对资产保护效果要求较低的客户。

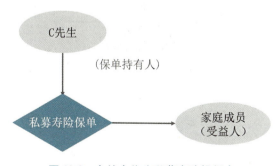

图 10.8　自然人作为私募寿险投保人

10.2.3.2 公司保单持有人

什么情况下会考虑由公司持有保单呢？一方面是税务方面的考虑（详见第 6 章和附录税务意见的内容），另一方面则是某些保险公司的强制要求。与自然人投保相较而言，通过公司投保，流程和资料会更烦琐；此外，日常保单的管理流程也相对复杂，因为公司需要通过董事会决议等方式做出决策，而非像个人一样可以直接发出命令（详见图 10.9）。

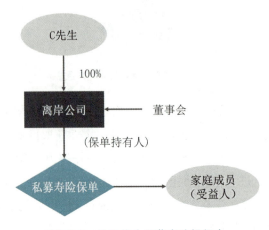

图 10.9　公司作为私募寿险投保人

10.2.3.3 信托保单持有人

信托作为私募寿险保单持有人，是三种架构中投保流程最复杂和最烦琐的，但其资产保护效果又是最出色的。所以，实践中可考虑先用自然人投保，投保成功后再更换信托作为保单持有人，此举可以加快投保的效率。信托作为保单持有人的常见架构有两种：信托直接持有私募寿险保单，或信托通过离岸公司持有私募寿险保单。二者在资产保护和传承规划方面的功效相似，在具体操作流程和费用方面则稍有区别。

（1）信托直接持有私募寿险保单。

用信托直接持有保单，受托人作为保单持有人，针对保单的具体操作和权利保留需依照信托契约的约定，归属于各个相关角色（设立人、受益人等），并由相关角色做出决策（如图 10.10 所示）。

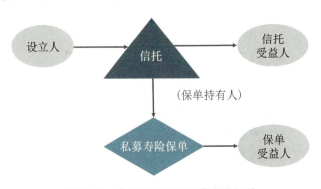

图 10.10　信托直接持有私募寿险保单

（2）信托通过离岸公司持有私募寿险保单。

信托通过离岸公司持有私募寿险保单，成本上首先需多设立并维持一个离岸公司。具体架构上，保单的直接持有人为离岸公司，而离岸公司的股东为信托受托人。在此架构下，对保单的具体操作管理权利保留在离岸公司层面，由公司董事会董事决议决定（如图10.11所示）。

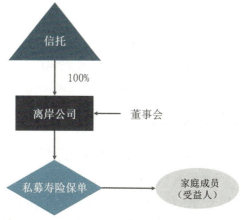

图10.11　信托通过离岸公司持有私募寿险保单

离岸公司由于一般不用来开展实质运营，而更经常为了特定的架构和目的服务，因此常常被称为特殊目的公司（Special Purpose Vehicle，SPV）。在信托与私募寿险架构规划中，离岸公司常用的功能有以下几种（如图10.12所示）。

（1）持有信托资产。

在海外信托的常见架构中，为了便利信托资产的区分和管理，受托人通常不会直接持有信托资产，而是通过离岸公司持有。

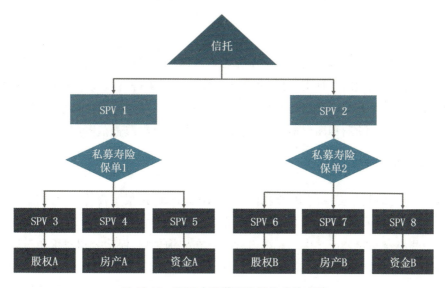

图10.12　SPV在私募寿险架构中的应用

(2) 持有私募寿险保单或资产。

在私募寿险投资架构中,根据投资的对象或目标的不同,常会设立不同的特殊目的公司持有资产或开展业务,如持有被动资产(房地产、游艇、艺术品等)、持有子公司的股份、开展在岸贸易业务、持有投资基金,以及买卖有价证券等。

10.3 私募寿险架构中的服务提供者

设计搭建架构是一个系统工程,涉及众多角色和供应商。当一个高净值家族决定使用私募寿险架构来进行规划时,其中涉及的各类服务的提供者有如下几种。

10.3.1 顾问团队——国际寿险架构师配合律师或会计师

顾问团队需要为客户介绍相关方案并进行全面的资产尽职调查,分析客户的需求,介绍私募寿险的架构和功能,设计所有权和受益人架构,并完成设立程序,以满足客户的具体需求。顾问团队还应向相关司法辖区的保险、信托、税务领域的法律和税务专家咨询有关税务和服务提供者的建议。在获得专业建议后,顾问团队将寻找和征集服务提供者,以启动和管理客户的投资项目。

10.3.2 投资经理

私募寿险架构中很重要的一部分在于投资规划,需要由投资经理与客户共同配合讨论决定合适的投资方案。客户需让保险公司知晓投资经理的人选,然后由投资经理与保险公司签订书面合约。在与保险公司签订投资管理合约后,投资经理将负责相关保单资产的投资决策。具体投资架构的安排需要满足各司法管辖区对保单投资资金的监管要求。

10.3.3 保险公司

在完成核保过程后,保险公司将接受私募寿险保单,通过一个独立的账户持有每份保单,与客户和投资经理协作管理账户,并在合同期内向保单持有人提供保单价值报告。据不完全统计,全世界有20家至30家私募寿险保险公司在不同层面上从事私募寿险业务。其中大多数在美国、欧洲和离岸地,从本地市场到国际市场,覆盖范围广泛。

10.3.4 再保险公司

在私募寿险的服务提供商中,再保险公司(Reinsurer)是很重要的一个角色。一方面,是因为涉及高额的承保;另一方面,许多私募寿险保险公司并非百年历史的巨头保险公司,而是一些小众保险公司。由于私募寿险重点在架构规划,保险公司对保单分隔账户中的资产并不负责具体运营和管理,而是配合投资经理和客户的运营管理。这样的架构模式不需要私募寿险保险公司做太多的资产管理,而是重在架构设计。所以,高额承保部分常由再保险公司配合完成。

10.3.5 托管银行

高净值家庭配置传统保险时,将保费支付到保险公司的银行账户中即可,在保单运行过程中根据保险公司提供的月度或年度结算知晓保单中现金价值的增长。但私募寿险的资产不是统一归保险公司的一般账户管理,而是放在每一个客户保单下的独立账户中,其托管银行则可能不同,具体根据不同保险公司和客户的投资决策而定(详见图10.13)。

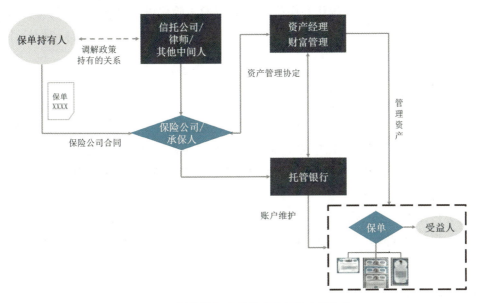

图 10.13 托管银行在私募寿险架构中的角色

10.4 如何为高净值家庭设计私募寿险架构

为高净值家庭设计私募寿险架构是一个复杂的过程,不同的客户情况会有不同的影响和考量。以下我们从大流程和基本原则上给些参考(详见图10.14),客户实际情况还

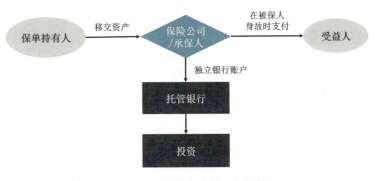

图 10.14 私募寿险的一般架构

应具体问题具体分析。请记住,私募寿险架构设计最重要的是满足客户不同的需求,所以世界上的私募寿险架构往往不尽相同。

在私募寿险架构中,需要考量的因素有以下 7 种。

10.4.1 保单持有人

保单持有人的选择会涉及由个人、公司还是信托持有,以及税务居民身份的考量。不同税务居民身份作为保单持有人会有不同的税务影响,高税负国家的税务居民,如美国、加拿大、澳大利亚税务居民等作为保单持有人,私募寿险保单架构设计需要符合当地税务合规要求,才可满足保单内投资免税增长的功能。不同司法管辖区的具体架构设计需获得当地税务律师和专业人士的意见。

10.4.2 被保人

被保人的选择主要考量私募寿险保单核保的要求:

保险核保:在私募寿险保单的整体计划中,如果被保人健康状况良好,并且没有带来核保负担,那么保险费用会相对便宜。如果被保人的健康或年龄是一个问题,顾问就需要更积极地与客户进行协商。

财务核保:考虑到所涉及的大额身故赔偿金,承保保单的主要承保人将身故赔偿金的大部分保给再保险公司。高保额的私募寿险保单比一般规模的保单需要更长的时间来完成投保。

10.4.3 受益人

受益人架构选择会比较灵活,主要考量家族受益需求和受益人选;另外,综合上文所述,可考量自然人直接当受益人还是选用信托架构作为受益人,以做更长久的传承规划。

10.4.4 保费

保费支付的金额、方法和形式是可以定制的。私募寿险与普通保单很重要的一个区别在于,前者可以接受非现金类的资产作为保费,比如公司股权、房地产等。

10.4.5 保单资产配置

保单内现金资产的投资配置由客户指定的投资经理负责,该部分需由专业投资顾问给出意见,非现金类资产的管理则由持有资产的公司董事会经营管理。

10.4.6 税务后果

整体架构设计的税务因素考量是非常重要的内容,架构中不同角色的税务居民身份和保单资产所在地的特殊要求等都需要纳入考量。满足各项税务要求才能使私募寿险架构实现其应有的功能,每个案例均应获得具体的税务意见,以保证每一个私募寿险架构的税筹功能实现。

10.4.7 费用

私募寿险架构设计及落地过程中整体架构需花费的成本也是高净值客户关注的重点之一。在私募寿险架构设计中涉及的费用包括如下5类。

① 国际寿险架构师设计费:架构设计过程中,需要拥有寿险、税务、信托综合知识且能够和律师、会计师、投资顾问等通力合作的专业人士来牵头组织,由此产生了费用。

② 律师、会计师或税务师费:架构设计过程中,需要完成资产尽职调查并提供相应建议和税务意见,这会产生额外的咨询费用。

③ 私募寿险保险公司架构费:包括一次性设立费(通常根据保费的金额而定)、年度架构使用费、保险成本(但这部分会在被保人去世后通过身故赔偿金赔偿至其受益人)以及私募寿险架构中更换投资和操作的服务费等。

④ 投资管理费:和正常投资一样,私募寿险保单内的保费投入其他投资机构会产生相应的投资管理费,如若在托管银行进行投资则会有相应的投资管理费和托管费产生。

⑤ 评估公司费用:因需要对保单内资产进行定期估值,所以会产生评估费用。

下面,我们通过一个案例来了解高净值家庭私募寿险架构的设计思路。

例 10.1

Jonathan,男士,57岁,是一位成功的企业家,且是一位投资高手。Jonathan一家均有美国身份,妻子 Anna 55岁,三个孩子均已长大成家。最近他希望为后代家庭做好传承规划,希望三个孩子的家庭可以平均获得财富。他准备把名下的5 000万美元的现金为三个孩子做好传承规划。在规划中,他希望尽量考量灵活的投资机制和税务筹划,如果可以,最好投资收益部分可以作为他的部分养老资金。

由于 Jonathan 是一位成熟的投资者,且希望在规划中满足灵活投资和税筹结合,因此私募寿险规划非常适合他。我们建议由 Jonathan 设立一个资产保护信托(持有5 000万美元),并同时作为被保人,三个孩子的家庭可分别作为信托受益人。保费分5~10年放入私募寿险保单中,这样也可通过美国 MEC 测试,从而达到灵活支取保单资金而不产生税务问题的目的。具体私募寿险保单内的投资配置可与 Jonathan 沟通,选择好投资经理,在适合的范围内挑选适合的投资标的,满足 Jonathan 灵活投资的要求。

保险市场结构及监管机制

本章要点：

- 了解人寿保险市场的结构和法规
- 讨论保险公司的核保流程，客户实名认证及反洗钱，投资法规和《共同申报准则》，以及《海外账户税收合规法案》要求
- 讨论保险申请人的购买资格，即保险公司对居民身份、健康状况及财务资格的要求
- 介绍保险中介人的资质、监管和长期后续服务
- 介绍保险推荐人、保险转介活动和转介监管

传统上来说，一个商品市场大体上由商品的供给方、需求方和中介方构成，保险市场也是一样，保险商品的供给方(保险公司)、保险商品的需求方(保险申请人)，以及保险商品的中介方(保险中介人)三方共同组成了我们现在看到的保险市场。除此之外，还有一类一般不被归类为保险市场的正式主体，但往往在保险市场实际交易中发挥重要作用的群体——保险推荐人，或者叫作保险转介绍人。

对于这四类保险市场的参与方，各个司法管辖区均通过法律法规施以相应监管，以保证保险市场正常、稳定、有序地运行。各国的监管机制对这四个角色提出了不同的要求和标准，而相同之处在于这些规则都必须被严格遵守，否则轻则可能导致保单无效，重则可能违规违法。

国际寿险架构师有可能是持有所在地保险执照的保险中介人，也有可能是家族办公

室员工、律师、会计师等财富领域的专业人士,并非一定持有保险执照,但同样被客户信赖和依赖。在为客户挑选出合适的司法管辖区和产品类型后,将客户推荐给持有保险执照或获得授权的从业者,让他们为客户具体设计和实施方案,直到完成客户的需求,这时候国际寿险架构师更多承担的是保险推荐人或保险转介绍人的角色。

作为国际寿险架构师,以国际视野为高净值客户设计规划保险架构时,必须对世界范围内几大主要保险市场的监管机制有所了解,才能联合各地的从业者,为客户提供合规、可行且有益的筹划方案。本章将以保险市场的四个主体为切入点,介绍目前世界上几大主流司法管辖区的保险监管机制。

11.1 保险公司

保险公司是发行保单的主体。通常而言,保险公司需要获得当地有关部门的牌照后方能开展保险业务,且在运营管理的过程中,也需要严格遵守当地的法律法规。作为金融机构,保险公司和银行、信托公司等一样,需要承担反洗钱、反恐怖主义融资等义务,也需要遵守包括《共同申报准则》及《海外账户税收合规法案》在内的金融信息交换的义务。

本节将根据保险公司的业务流程,依次介绍保险公司在核保、客户尽职调查、投资及金融信息互换各环节的监管要求。

11.1.1 核保

当保单申请文件提交后,保险公司开始核保。核保可以简单描述为:保险公司为保险申请人提供保障或决定采用什么保险条款而进行的风险评估。核保主要是从身体健康、财务状况、居住旅行和税务身份方面进行考量。

11.1.2 客户实名认证及反洗钱流程

反洗钱金融行动特别工作组(Financial Action Task Force on Money Laundering,FATF)是成立于1989年的跨政府与国界的组织,其设立核心是为了打击洗钱制定国际准则,以及打击恐怖分子资金筹集活动。该组织目前已拥有38个会员国成员和9个区域组织关联成员,包括美国、加拿大、澳大利亚、新加坡、中国香港、中国内地等以及涵盖离岸地区如百慕大和开曼群岛的加勒比金融行动特别工作组(Caribbean Financial Action Task Force,CFATF)。所有FATF成员都有责任和义务遵守并实施FATF订立的相关规定。简言之,各国各区域的保险公司所执行的客户实名认证,包括对于客户基本身份证明信息的采集及分析、针对已知高风险名单(如高敏感政治人物)的筛查核对,以及对申请相关保险产品可能涉及的违法行为所做的风险评估和预防,旨在就反洗钱、打击资助恐怖主义采取有效的监控和防范措施。

例如,在美国发行或承保可能会带来较高洗钱风险的产品的保险公司必须遵守《银行保密法》(Bank Secrecy Act, BSA)和《反洗钱》(Anti-Money Laundering, AML)计划的要求。涵盖产品包括：

① 团体年金合同以外的年金合同；
② 永久性人寿保单，而非团体人寿保单；
③ 具有现金价值或投资功能的一切其他保险产品。

保险相关法规仅适用于保险公司，不包括中介机构和代理人/经纪人。但是，保险公司有责任遵守上述计划，将其中介机构和代理人/经纪人纳入反洗钱计划中。

保险公司必须针对上述涵盖保险产品可能涉及的风险，制定书面的 BSA/AML 合规流程。该流程至少必须包含以下功能：

① 有指定的合规官负责有效实施计划；
② 持续培训包括保险代理人和经纪人在内的适当人员；
③ 为机构的反洗钱风险量身定制政策和内部控制流程；
④ 为持续监督合规性，对保险中介机构和代理人/经纪人进行独立测试。

除实施适当的 BSA/AML 计划外，保险公司还必须遵守可疑活动报告 (Suspicious Activity Report, SAR) 的要求。保险公司必须向美国财政部下辖的金融犯罪执法局 (Financial Crimes Enforcement Network, FinCEN) 提交 SAR。保险公司必须从中介机构、代理人/经纪人和其他来源获得相关的客户信息，以报告此类交易。

此外，作为 FATF 成员的加拿大，以及世界及亚洲金融中心代表之一的中国香港和新加坡，也分别制定了各自所辖区域的反洗钱条例，所涉各类金融机构都必须充分了解在相关条例下的责任及应履行的义务，并严格遵守执行。任何违规行为都可能面临行政处罚甚至刑事处罚。

11.1.3 投资监管

部分人寿保单带有较强的投资属性。从由谁掌握投资决策权这一点，可以将这种人寿保单分为两类：一类由保险公司直接负责投资，比如常见的终身寿险和传统型万能寿险；另一类则由保单持有人自行决定投资（或者自行决定聘任投资顾问），比如投资型万能寿险、私募寿险（可参见本书第 9 章及第 10 章的内容）。

11.1.3.1 保险公司自行投资

保险公司的投资行为将有可能极大地影响保单持有人/受益人的利益，因此，各司法管辖区会对保险公司的投资行为进行严格监管。

以加拿大为例，保险公司同时接受联邦和省级的双层监管，与加拿大其他非证券金融机构一样，在联邦层级的金融监管机构是加拿大金融机构监管署 (Office of the Superintendent of Financial Institutions, OSFI)，负责管理外国保险公司及在联邦注册的加拿大保险公司，并对保险公司的偿付能力、保险准备金的提存及保险公司的投资范畴等做出规定，其监管核心是保证保险公司的偿付能力，要求加拿大人寿保险公司都符合最低总资本充足率(Life Insurance Capital Adequacy Test, LICAT)在90%及以上,以维持保险公司正常的商业活动要求及履行对保单持有人的承诺。另外针对保费投资方面,加拿大也要求保险公司必须按照加拿大保险法(Insurance Corporation Act, ICA)中第Ⅸ部分规定的投资限定规则进行险资投资。

同理,对比美国、中国香港和新加坡的保险公司,各地相关监管机构也对保险公司的资产负债的风险情况计算最低资本要求,要求其在业务经营中必须依法留存充足的准备金,以确保保险公司的偿付能力和健康的财务状况,从而最终能够保障保单持有人的利益。对于保费的投资范围,各司法管辖区的监管部门虽然标准不尽相同,但也都严格制定了相关的投资类别、投资比例/金额及险资的运用结构等。比如新加坡强调保险投资的分散性,对单一投资板块、投资标的、单位信托、存款机构都有投资度的上限要求,避免过于集中带来的风险。中国香港保险投资监管侧重保险投资的地域管理。在美国,由各州的保险监管部门对险资投资进行规范管理和监督,通常允许保险公司投资的对象为美国政府债券、州或市政府债券、加拿大债券、抵押贷款、高质量的公司债券、限额的优先股和普通股等。同时,规定了各种投资形式运用的资金占其总资产的比重不得超过一定比例。对于保险公司发行以投资为基础的寿险保单,如指数型万能寿险等万能寿险,还有额外投资限制规定。

11.1.3.2 投保人自行决定投资(或自行决定聘任投资顾问)

如前文所述,受制于不同司法管辖区或者不同保险公司的要求,私募寿险或投资型万能寿险一般允许保单持有人自行决定投资,或允许自行聘任投资顾问。

私募寿险中的投资可以完全独立于保险公司的投资管理及投资限定要求(美国私募寿险产品会有一定的投资限定要求),投资的资产可以是金融类资产,也可以是非金融类资产,如股权、房产、不动产等,保险公司仅对投资的资产收取一定比例的管理费,而资产的投资管理决策、相关交易等,完全由保单持有人指定的投资机构或关联机构予以决定和实施。

11.1.4 《共同申报准则》和《海外账户税收合规法案》

对于所属司法管辖区为《共同申报准则》参与成员的特定保险机构,保险机构所发行的具有现金价值的保险合同(Cash Value Insurance Contracts)和年金合同(Annuity Contracts)均属于共同申报准则(CRS)要求披露的金融资产。保险公司有责任核证保单申请人的税务身份,并视其披露信息来判断该份保单合同的相关基本信息,包括保单的持有人、被保人、受益人、产品类别及保单现金价值等是否属于CRS交换信息范畴。

实践中,有些司法管辖区的保险公司仅收集申报保单持有人的信息。以加拿大终身寿险的保单申请为例,申请表中都会有专门的部分对保单持有人的税务身份进行核证(见图11.1);或者要求保单持有人填写加拿大国税局(CRA)指定的表格(RC518/RC519-Declaration of Tax Residence for Individual-s/Entities)。

Are you a U.S. citizen or resident for tax purposes (FATCA)?

☐ Yes - provide details below.   ☐ No

Your U.S. Taxpayer Identification Number(TIN)

Are you a resident of any other jurisdiction other than Canada and the U.S. for tax purposes (CRS)?

☐ Yes - provide details below.   ☐ No - skip to question 2.8.

Your jurisdiction of tax residence	Your Taxpayer Identification Number(TIN)

If you do not have a Taxpayer Identification Number, check a box to give the reason:
☐ You've applied for one but haven't received it yet.
☐ Your jurisdiction of tax residence doesn't issue TINs.
☐ Other-provide details:

图 11.1　保单持有人的税务身份核证

目前发行国际寿险保单的主要代表司法管辖区,包括中国香港、新加坡、百慕大等,均是 CRS 的参与成员;因此,履行特定保险合同的信息交换是各司法管辖区必须遵循的基本准则。

而美国的《海外账户税收合规法案》(FATCA)可以说是 CRS 的"前世今生",或者"美版 CRS"。其实施细则要求外国政府所辖金融机构向美国国税局提供美国税务居民的境外账户信息,包括美国纳税人的姓名、地址、纳税识别号、账号、账户余额或价值,以及账户总收入与总付款金额等,否则该外国政府所辖金融机构来源于美国的收入将被扣缴 30% 的惩罚性预提税(通常来说,在签有双边税收协定的情况下,该类收入的预提所得税率最高不会超过 10%)。该条例旨在打击美国税务居民(公民、绿卡持有者、符合条件的美国税务居民)利用海外金融账户和/或投资隐瞒海外资产及收入申报的避税行为。FATCA 主要采用单边/双边信息交换机制,而 CRS 则采用多边信息交换机制。

以具有投资价值的保险合同为例,由于美国目前尚不在 CRS 范围内,非美居民(美国境外人士)购买的美国保单信息,美国保险公司暂时无须向未与美国签订 FATCA 双边协议的居民所属国家/地区交换披露。反之,对于美国税务居民所购买的美国境外具有现金价值的保单合同或年金合同,在其合同价值超过一定金额后:一方面美国居民需要进行 FBAR① 申报及/或 Form 8938② 海外金融账户申报;另一方面,该保单所辖地国家/地区的

---

① FBAR,全称是 Report of Foreign Bank and Financial Accounts,也是人们常称的"肥爸条款",其目的是严查美国报税人的境外所得有否完整申报。

② Form 8938,全称是 Statement of Specified Foreign Financial Assets,对应的是 2014 年 7 月开始实行的《美国海外账户税收合规法案》(Foreign Account Tax Compliance Act),也就是人们常说的"肥咖条款"。

保险公司,也需根据与美国签订的 FATCA 双边协议细则履行相关披露义务,包括提供保单持有人的姓名、地址、纳税识别号、保单号码、保单现金价值。

对美国本地保险公司,非居民客户投保时需填写 W-8BEN[①] 或 W-8BEN-E,[②]以识别保单持有人的税务居民身份和对应司法管辖区的税号。

11.2 保险申请人

对于保险申请人,各司法管辖区的监管机制和保险公司主要从居民身份、健康状况以及财务资格方面提出要求。

11.2.1 居民身份

传统上来说,各国的寿险产品主要面向本国居民销售并提供承保。伴随全球家庭国际化的大趋势,留学、移居、移民、双国籍身份持有者增多,很多国家和地区也开始面向不同居民身份的人士提供寿险保障。总体来说,离岸地如百慕大,以及中国香港、新加坡等地因其地理位置和市场特点,对保单申请人的居民身份没有太多限制;美国绝大部分公司是面向本地居民发行保单,同时也对符合一定条件的非居民开放;而加拿大和澳大利亚等地则在此方面相对严格,基本上只对本地居民开放。

11.2.1.1 美国

美国保险公司主要依据保险申请人的国籍、居民身份、在美居住时间、跟美国实质关联、旅行记录等来判定保险申请人属于"本国"还是"外国"申请人,并以此区分投保要求和核保难度。需要明确的是,保单申请中对申请人身份的划分与我们日常生活中移民身份或税务居民身份的划分不能完全画等号,例如美国公民或者税务居民在保险申请角度上来说不一定也被算成本国居民。在实践中,对于居民身份的判断往往有很多主观的成分,最后的结论经常是依据诸多客观条件形成的主观性判断,往往需要个案分析,不能生搬硬套。美国不同保险公司有具体的标准,普遍来说美国保单申请人的身份被分为以下两类。

(1) 本国申请人。

美国保险公司主要秉承着重实质而不重形式的精神,主要以与美国是否有生活上足够的实质关联来考核一个人是否是保险意义上的本国人。一般来说,美国公民和美国永久居民(持有绿卡者)可以完全按照本国人的标准来申请保单,但也有例外情况,例如长期居住在海外的美国公民或永久居民也会被认为属于外国人,或有些公司(非

---

① W-8BEN 是美国扣缴税款的受益所有人的外国身份证明,外国人使用该表格来建立外国身份和受益所有权,并就除个人服务补偿以外的其他收入要求获得所得税条约优惠。

② W-8BEN-E,全名为 Certificate of Foreign Status of Beneficial Owner for U.S. Tax Withholding,即美国预扣税和申报受益所有人的外国身份证明,由非美国实体提交。

全部公司)会将临时绿卡持有者认定为外国人。持有长期签证(如 H-1B 等)在美国合法工作、长期居住的人因其在美国有信用和健康记录,大多也会被认定为本国申请人;而持有学生或学者签证(如 F-1、J-1 等)虽然长期在美居住,从税务角度也是美国税务居民,但仍需视保险公司的具体规则而定,多数保险公司倾向于认为此类身份属于外国申请人。

本国申请人一般无额外特殊要求,只需满足正常的健康及财务核保条件。

(2)外国申请人。

部分保险公司不将学生签证持有人认定为本国申请人,而作为特殊的一个申请类别看待,因为大多数留学生暂时没有工作收入而无法承担保费,或者认为留学生签证不是真正的长期居住签证,未与美国建立足够的永久性的实质关系。即便允许学生投保的保险公司,也会要求审查父母或在美监护人的财务能力及与学生的可保利益,确保保单是有必要、合规且能够正常支付保费的。

最常见的外国申请人则是持有旅游/商务签证即 B-1/B-2 签证短期访美的非居民外国人,此类申请人往往与美国仅有有限的关联性(如在美持有房产、孩子在美留学、持有美国银行账户、经常赴美出差等)或完全没有关联性。对于这种纯外国的申请人,审批要求中的核心点是其在美资产状况。许多信用评级高、资产规模大、具有全球风险承担能力的保险公司会对高净值的外国申请人开放部分或全部产品,投保人因此可以享有与美国本国投保人一样的产品。该类申请人需在美国境内完成销售、体检、申请表签字提交等全套流程;需要注意的是,很多从业者往往会在本国对潜在的客户进行产品和计划书的演示和销售,并且往往还是由不具美国从业执照的人员进行解说和演示,此类行为是严格违反保险公司要求而不被允许的。对外国人的审批保险公司会主要考量以下两个方面。

① 美国关联。简言之,就是申请人与美国的关系,主要是指经济关系和亲属关系。申请人在美国有房产、银行存款(通常存有至少 50 万美元并已存款一定时间)、投资账户,或入股美国公司、在美国公司担任职务获得薪资收入,或者有直系亲属、配偶长期居住工作在美国等,都是这类申请人申请美国保险的加分项,仅仅是投资美股或美国基金一般不被视为足够的美国关联。部分保险公司也会将美国境外的资产纳入考量,但核实手续会更复杂,包括进行电话访谈、要求提供第三方资产证明等。

② 申请人平均一年在美国居留时长或到访美国的次数。不同保险公司对于这一点的要求不尽相同,有些公司会要求申请保险前每年在美国至少居留 15 天或以上,也有公司会要求申请人有因购买保险以外的其他原因到访过美国。

不论申请人身份如何,所有美国保险公司都要求申请人在美国本土进行体检和保单申请签字,同时要求保险经纪人或代理人只能在美国境内进行保单讲解和销售。美国保险公司一般只接受从美国境内的银行账户以 EFT(Electronic Funds Transfer)或支票的形式来支付保费,不接受美国境外银行的付款或信用卡、现金等方式。

11.2.1.2 加拿大

加拿大永久居民和加拿大公民在通常情况下有资格申请加拿大保险公司在加拿大境内发行的全线保险产品。当然,如果此两类身份的申请人长期生活在加拿大境外,则可能会受限于部分保险产品对其加拿大境内居住要求的基本规定。

对于加拿大工作签证和学生签证持有者,部分保险公司也会根据工作签证持有者所从事行业,学生签证持有者所学专业、学历层级及在加拿大留学时长等因素,提供保额上限设定(通常不超过200万加元)的寿险保障;对于已提交了加拿大移民申请,并获得省提名计划批复的准移民,部分保险公司也会提供保额上限设定(不超过200万加元)的寿险保障。

非加拿大居民一般无法在加拿大境内投保,部分加拿大保险公司在离岸地区如百慕大的子公司通过设计国际寿险保单来承接非加拿大居民的购买需求,但此类保险是在其他司法管辖区发行的,不属于加拿大本土产品。该类寿险产品特别针对非美国公民及居民、非加拿大居民、非百慕大居民发行,同时在产品类别和产品运用方式上加以扩充和延展,能提供比加拿大本土更加丰富的产品类型。

11.2.1.3 中国香港

中国香港是全球金融中心之一,一直对全球的个人和企业投资者开放(部分被制裁和战乱国家居民除外)。除少部分特殊产品之外,一般的中国香港人寿保险产品均对非中国香港居民开放,只要申请人本人抵港,根据来港见证制度(包括见证投保人本人,核实相关身份证件、家庭关系证件、入境记录等),通过正规渠道(保险公司代理、保险中介人公司或者银行保险渠道)投保,在中国香港确认投保的产品细则并完成相应的体检/审批要求,最终批核的保单都是合法合规的。

11.2.1.4 新加坡

除政府公积金医疗险、部分受地域限制的医疗险和寿险外,新加坡保险公司发行的许多产品(主要为定期寿险、万能寿险、储蓄险等)都对非新加坡居民开放,且也采用同新加坡居民一样的保费标准来核算。

对于非新加坡居民提出的保单申请,传统上来说,新加坡金融管理局要求投保人、被保人亲自到新加坡完成体检,申请表签字,核证相关身份文件、家庭关系文件等流程,以确保保单的合法效力,保护保单中各个角色的权益;同时,和中国香港保险申请一样,来新加坡投保时,需保留好过关盖章并有签名的入境白卡,以供保险公司做好入境记录备案。但近年来为了满足海外投保人对新加坡保险的需求,市场上也出现了很多无须亲赴新加坡即可完成投保的寿险产品——以性价比较高的小额定期寿险和不超过一定保额的指数型万能寿险为主。如遇到需要体检的情况,部分保险公司也允许被保人在海外符合保险公司资格的医疗机构体检。保险公司会不定时地调整相关政策,需以最新的相关政策为准。

11.2.1.5 离岸地

以百慕大、波多黎各和巴巴多斯等司法管辖区为代表的离岸地也是活跃的国际保险市场。由于其自身远离大陆的地理位置,以及瞄准全球范围的市场目标,这些离岸地的保险公司通常不会将保单申请人的身份限制为当地居民(但有可能出于税务原因将某些高税区的居民排除在外),全球大部分未受制裁国家的居民均可申请离岸地的人寿保单,且并不会要求保单申请人入境签署保单。与在岸司法管辖区有所区别的一点是,离岸地的保险公司通常要求由离岸公司、离岸信托或者保险公司提供的集成信托子信托或集合账户的子账户来持有保单,并不接受个人直接持有保单;投保人则通过这些架构间接控制保单,离岸公司和信托一般需要额外的成本,保险公司提供的持有架构则一般免费。

11.2.1.6 澳大利亚

在澳大利亚,以生命为标的的寿险保单的唯一价值就是转移风险,通俗地说,就是当有风险发生时能及时拿到钱。澳大利亚和其他国际保险主流司法管辖区在寿险保单上的最突出差异是:自1992年澳大利亚政府强制引入养老金体系,并赋予该体系灵活的投资方式和保障形式选择后,具有投资性质的终身寿险就基本被定期寿险取代了。

澳大利亚保险公司通常要求保单申请人为澳大利亚永久居民或公民,并且长期居住在澳大利亚。也有部分保险公司可以接受澳大利亚非居民的寿险申请,但需要满足几点通用标准,并结合各保险公司各自的审核要求最终决定是否批复保障。

客观地说,对于移居或者移民澳大利亚的高净值客户,由于目前澳大利亚寿险产品的功能单一、选择较为有限,因此仅将寿险作为单纯的风险抵御工具,还不能完全满足家族在资产保护、保值、传承和税务筹划等方面的需求。为实现家族财富综合规划的需要,高净值客户可以通过了解/运用其他司法管辖区发行的兼具投资、传承和税务优化等综合功能的国际寿险产品来实现规划目标。

11.2.2 健康状况和财务资格

无论在哪个司法管辖区购买寿险产品,申请人在提出购买申请时,除了需要具备符合要求的身份资格外,保险公司还会对申请人的身体健康状况,以及与申请保额/保费相匹配的财务资格进行审核。

健康状况审核主要视被保人的年龄、申请的险种、保额等因素决定是否需要体检,回答健康问卷,或确定体检项目细则等。不同司法管辖区会规定不同的健康等级,比如不抽烟的等级由高到低分为优选+(Preferred Plus)、优选(Preferred)、标准+(Standard Plus)、标准(Standard)、不合准(Substandard);而抽烟一般只有两个等级,即优选和标准。为了确认健康等级,被保人通常需要进行体检。对于不同年龄段的被保人,保险公司通常会提出不同的体检要求,通常而言,年龄和保额越大,体检项目的要求越多。各司法管辖区要求的体检项目比较相近,常见的体检项目包括医疗测试、全血档案、尿检、心电图等。目前,一些司法管辖区如美国、加拿大、新加坡和离岸地的部分保险公司会免除一定保额(300万美元以内)保单的体检要求,仅要求填写健康问卷、披露健康状况。

在岸地和离岸地在体检上的规定略有区别,在岸地一般规定只能在其司法管辖区内的医疗机构进行体检,但可将申请人过往的海外医疗记录作为核保参考。离岸地则可接受在全球不同国家和地区进行体检,只要该医疗机构在保险公司认可名单内即可,因此离岸保单的申请人可就近在自己所在的地区进行体检。

财务资格审核则视申请险种、申请人身份、申请保额/保费等核证申请人的财务状况,并可能要求申请人提供相关的资产证明文件,以确保申请人的保险申请符合其保险需求,能够充分证明其未来持续支付保费的财务能力。每家保险公司在财务核保方面的具体要求不同,通常需要考察投/被保人的收入、净资产,以确认能够购买的保额上限。

以美国为例,根据年龄不同,最大保额可以达到收入的10倍至30倍(不同保险公司和险种会有所不同)。有些司法管辖区的保险公司和再保险公司合作,甚至可以批核高达2亿美元保额的保单。根据被保人的健康状况和财务状况,最终的核保决定可能是核准(Approve)、加费(Rating)、延缓(Postpone),或拒保(Decline)。

不同地区对于收入和资产所在地也有一定的要求,如离岸地、中国香港和新加坡等地区一般认可保单申请人全球的收入和资产,但像美国、加拿大和澳大利亚这种大的在岸地国家,财务核保主要还是以其境内的收入和资产为主,海外收入和资产为辅,如美国大部分对外国人开放的保险公司仍然要求保单申请人在美国有可证明的资产,有些公司明确提出需证明保单申请人大部分的资产在美国境内,而少部分公司则只要求在美国有少部分资产即可。

11.3 保险中介人

保险中介人是国际寿险架构师的重要构成成员,是客户与保险公司的沟通桥梁,更是长期陪伴客户的保险服务提供者。保险中介人通常包括保险经纪人(Insurance Broker)和保险代理人(Insurance Agent),两者均需获得其所在司法管辖区的相应牌照或资质后方可从业,执业期间也必须严格遵守相应的法律法规与行业规范。在不同的司法管辖区内,保险中介人的执业模式也有区别,有些司法管辖区要求保险中介人必须受雇于某一机构(比如受雇于保险公司、经纪公司或者银行),有些司法管辖区允许保险中介人独立执业,更多的地方则是两种方式并存。

以下将从各个司法管辖区的保险中介人的资格认证、监管机制和对客户的长期后续服务三个方面展开介绍。

11.3.1 保险中介人的资格认证

为使保险行业健康有序稳定发展,各司法管辖区对保险中介人都有严格的监管,以确保保险中介人的职业操守,从而充分保障客户的权益。

11.3.1.1 美国

美国是一个联邦制国家,保险业务主要由各州政府监管,美国没有全国性的保险执照考试,一般由各州自行管理。在美国从事保险业务,需要首先通过居住地所在州政府认可的培训机构完成相应的持证前教育课程,一般为30个小时以上的线上或线下课程。课程完成后可参加州一级的居民执照考试(Resident License),成功通过考试和满足其他要求后即可获得从业资格;保险中介人可以选择只申请寿险业务的执照或同时也申请财险等其他类型的保险执照,不同保险类型分别有其对应的教育和考试要求;在美国不同的州从业,均需申请所在州的执照,一旦获得主要居住州的居民执照后即可申请其他州的非居民执照(Non-Resident License),无须再次进行考试。

获得执照的保险中介人必须完成一定小时数的继续教育课程以维持执照,例如包括得州和加州在内的许多州都要求保险执照持牌人需要每两年完成24个学时的继续教育课程,课程需由所持执照类型的管理委员会批准。

美国寿险市场的中介人一般分为两大类:保险代理人和保险经纪人。

保险代理人是代表保险公司向保险申请人介绍、销售、甄选适合其需求的保险产品的从业者。其中专属代理人仅代表一家保险公司,而独立代理人通常可以代表多家保险公司。代理人独立执行保单申请直至保单生效,一般属于保险公司的员工,可从保险公司获取一定底薪和福利待遇,再按销售表现获取佣金提成。

保险经纪人是代表并协助保险申请人研究保险产品的保障范围、条款和价格等,以寻求最适合其需求的产品组合。由于经纪人不代表保险公司,因此在保险产品的购买及申请中,经纪人需通过与保险公司的合约,帮助保险申请人完成保单申请直至生效。

保险代理人和经纪人之间的主要区别是:代理人代表的是保险公司,而经纪人代表的是保单申请人(即客户)。代理人可以获得一家或多家保险公司的任命,独立完成整个保单申请;而经纪人则需要通过保险代理人或保险公司获得约定函(Binding Letter),完成保单申请。

11.3.1.2 加拿大

加拿大保险中介人要获得从业执照,首先要通过保险理事会认可的课程提供者,完成人寿保险资格证书课程(Life License Qualification Program,LLQP)。在完成LLQP课程后的一年内,成功通过牌照所要求的LLQP考试单元。人寿保险代理人牌照需要完成所有四个考试单元:人寿保险(Life Insurance)、意外和疾病(Accident and Sickness)、职业道德与专业实务(普通法)[Ethics and Professional Practice(Common Law)]以及保本基金和年金(Segregated Funds and Annuities)。

考试合格后有一年的时间可以申请牌照,在申请之前需要获得代表保险公司的合约或通过保险公司的担保和提名、确保有一名合资格的寿险代理人主管在获发牌照的头两年期间监督工作、提供无犯罪记录、购买职业保险等后方可最终申请获得从业执照。在不同省份执业也需要先获得不同省份的保险执照,如果在魁北克省执业,还需参加额外的考试及职业培训。在获得从业执照后,需通过每年的保险执照年审,包括获得最低要求的继续教育学分以及职业保险的更新和续费。再作细分,加拿大的保险中介人根据公司管理方式和代理产品不同,主要有以下三种类型。

(1) 代理人(Career Agent)。

代理人是隶属于保险公司的保险中介人,通常只销售该保险公司的产品。收入构成是底薪加佣金,保险客户属于保险公司,经纪人离开保险公司后没有独立权利直接带走保单和客户。

(2) 经纪人(Broker)。

经纪人是最常见的独立保险中介人,可以代理多家保险公司发行的保险产品,一般在总代理(Managing General Agent, MGA)处获得代理合同,赚取保单的佣金,为客户及其保单提供独立的服务。

(3) 银行保险经纪人(Bank Insurance Broker)。

银行保险经纪人是隶属于银行系统的保险中介人,只代理银行销售的保险产品,其运作模式类似于第一类职业代理人。

11.3.1.3 中国香港

根据中国香港《保险业条例》,从事保险中介业务的人员和机构被称为持牌保险中介人,主要分为持牌保险代理人和持牌保险经纪。具体来说,持牌保险代理人主要指的是持牌保险代理机构、持牌个人保险代理和持牌业务代表(代理人),而持牌保险经纪则是持牌保险经纪公司和持牌业务代表(经纪)。这五类中介人牌照中的两类主要颁发给公司,而另外的三类则是个人可获得的牌照。

从个人可获得的牌照来看,持牌个人保险代理和持牌业务代表(代理人)均为保险代理人,代表保险公司寻找客户、销售保单,并提供售前售后和索赔等服务。其主要区别是个人保险代理是作为任何授权保险人的代理人,而持牌业务代表(代理人)是作为任何持牌保险代理机构的代理人。

保险代理又分为独立代理及受雇代理。中国香港的独立代理根据《保险业条例》及《保险业(获授权保险人的最高数目)规则》不可同时代表超过四家保险公司,其中最多两家为人寿保险公司;而受雇代理仅限于为一家保险公司工作。保险代理人受中国香港保险业监管局监管,在保监局的持牌保险中介人登记册中可以查询有关保险代理人的发牌详情。

持牌业务代表(经纪)则是以任何持牌保险经纪公司的代理人身份,进行受规管活动的个人;保险经纪与保险代理人最显著的不同之处在于,经纪代表的是客户,可以和多家保险公司签订合约代理其产品,保险经纪在保险产品选择的多样性中占据优势,有助于申请人掌握更多市场信息,并利用其专业性及从业经验,为保单申请人寻找最合适的保险产品配置。同样,持牌业务代表(经纪)也受到中国香港保险业监管局监管,在保监局的持牌保险中介人登记册中也可以查询有关持牌保险经纪的发牌详情。中国香港保险中介人的牌照类别如表11.1所示。

表 11.1 中国香港保险中介人的牌照类别

持牌保险中介人	
持牌保险代理人	持牌保险经纪
持牌保险代理机构	持牌保险经纪公司
持牌个人保险代理	持牌业务代表（经纪）
持牌业务代表（代理人）	

无论是代理人还是经纪,都需要考取同样的保险牌照并受到保监局监管,在中国香港境内从事的销售和签单活动都是合法有效的。希望获得中国香港保险牌照的人士,需要参加中国香港保险中介人资格考试（Insurance Intermediaries Qualifying Examination for Insurance Brokers,IIQE）。该考试包括两个部分:第一部分是所有在中国香港的保险中介人都必须应考的考试,即保险原理与实务;第二部分则是视具体从事的保险业务类别进行相应的考试,包括一般保险、长期保险和投资连结长期保险。非投资型的人寿保险在中国香港属于长期保险的一种。通过考试不代表能获得牌照,还需满足学历要求和令人信纳的信誉及财务状况。任何身份的人士都可以在中国香港参加考试,但只有具有中国香港身份的人士才能在通过考试后申请执业牌照。

取得牌照的中介人,有的分布在保险公司,有的在独立的经纪公司,有的则在银行。无论与哪个渠道的保险中介人对接,每个投保人购买同一产品的保费、条款、服务及索赔流程都是相同的。保单由保险公司直接签发,而索赔服务也由保险公司向客户直接提供。

11.3.1.4 新加坡

新加坡保险中介事务由新加坡金融管理局负责管理,取得在新加坡销售保险的资格需要满足 MAS 订立的一系列要求。首先需要满足基本条件,其中就包括必须是新加坡公民/永久居民和基础的教育要求。一旦满足上述条件,就需要决定要通过哪家保险公司或保险经纪公司代理产品销售。下一步则是在新加坡保险学院（Singapore College of Insurance,SCI）注册新加坡资本市场和金融咨询服务考试（Singapore Capital Markets and Financial Advisory Services,CMFAS）,根据不同的险种参加对应科目的考试。如主要从事与个人医疗险、年金险、人寿险等相关的业务,则需要通过"模块5:金融咨询法律法规""模块9:人寿保险和投资连结保险""模块9A:人寿保险和投资连结型保险Ⅱ"以及"医疗保险模块"四门考试,一般至少需要三个月到半年的准备时间。在通过考试并且经背景调查查实无不良记录或不当背景后,才可以正式获得资质。

新加坡保险中介人通常分布在三种销售渠道中。

（1）在新加坡注册的保险公司。

由于金融监管严格,因此在新加坡注册的保险公司绝大多数是世界级的大型保险公司,它们直接销售产品和提供后续服务,从申请人购买保险产品的角度来说是最安全快捷的途径,同时服务期限也更稳定和长久,不会因代理人的变动而影响长效服务。隶属于该渠道的中介人,通常会获得底薪、佣金并参与职业福利计划,保险公司以此来留住优秀中介人。

(2) 新加坡独立经纪公司。

独立经纪公司可以代理多家保险公司的产品。但由于新加坡金融监管严格和保险公司的自我保护,大部分独立经纪公司因为拿不到世界级大型保险公司的代理权,所以会相对缺乏更有竞争力的产品,对于在此平台上开展业务的保险中介人也有一定的挑战性。

(3) 新加坡保险公司授权的银行代理。

银行的销售人员通常被称为客户经理(Relationship Manager),其主要工作是产品销售和客户关系维护。除了向客户推荐投资型的产品如股票、基金、债券和期权等衍生品外,他们也会向客户推荐保障类产品如各类保险和年金等。新加坡银行和保险公司多是战略合作伙伴关系,一家银行通常只代理一家保险公司的产品。在银行系统的保险中介人,通过银行自有的庞大客户库可获得可观的业务,省略了市场开发的要求,所以佣金方面比前两种销售渠道要低。

11.3.1.5 离岸地

离岸地的保险公司通常将其保险业务代理权颁发给其他司法管辖区的保险中介机构,以便在海外市场开展业务。当然,也有当地的保险中介人机构拥有保险销售许可。以百慕大为例,根据其1978年保险法的规定,保险中介人包括保险代理人、保险经纪人、保险经理(Insurance Manager)和保险市场提供者(Insurance Marketplace Provider)。保险代理人和保险经纪人在其他司法管辖区也很常见,这里不再赘述。保险经理指不受雇于任何保险公司,但以一个或多个保险公司的经理身份出现的人;保险市场提供者是指从事保险市场(为购买、销售或交易任何类型保险合同而建立的平台)业务的人。百慕大的保险中介人也需要注册,并且需要遵守一系列法律法规和职业操守。

11.3.1.6 澳大利亚

澳大利亚的保险中介人也分为保险代理人和保险经纪人。其主要区别也与其他司法管辖区类似,前者代表保险公司,后者则代表客户,是客户与保险公司之间的桥梁。澳大利亚保险经纪人必须在澳大利亚证券和投资委员会(Australian Securities and Investment Commission, ASIC)注册。ASIC 是联邦监管机构,负责维护与定期人寿保险(包括审批金融服务提供商执业许可)相关的市场完整性和对消费者权益的保护。通过参加不同级别要求的保险基础课程(Foundational Courses)及证书课程(Diploma Courses),并在符合要求的已持牌保险中介人监督指导下完成一定时数的实际工作后,才能最终获得澳大利亚金融服务执照(Australian Financial Services License, AFSL)。该执照是成为一名成熟的持牌保险中介人的入场券。持牌保险中介人在获得执照后,每年也要满足一定学分的专业能力及执业标准培训,以维持执照有效。

11.3.2 保险中介人的监管机制

11.3.2.1 美国

美国保险行业经过两百多年的发展,已经形成完备又严格的监管体系。如第 11.3.1 小节所述,美国保险行业的监管权主要在各州,联邦政府起辅助作用。

联邦一级的监管机构主要有三个,分别是联邦保险局(Federal Insurance Office, FIO)、联邦保险咨询委员会(The Federal Advisory Committee on Insurance, FACI)和全国保险专员协会(The National Association of Insurance Commissioners, NAIC)。联邦保险局在联邦一级监管保险行业和保险公司;联邦保险咨询委员会是咨询机构,为前者的职责提供支持;而1871年成立的全国保险专员协会则会制定涉及保险行业方方面面的准入条例和相关规范,具体工作包括规范美国保险业财务、技术、数据等业务细节标准及信息共享,以及协助每个州和地区的保险监管部门、提高保险公司市场竞争力、增强保险公司财务偿付能力及经营稳健性、确保保险公司为消费者提供优质服务等。

美国各个州均有自己的保险法规和管理机构。州一级的监管执行部门主要为州保险监管部。州保险监管部在不同州的名称不尽相同,但其职责均是类似的,其最高负责人一般被称为保险专员(Insurance Commissioner)。州保险监管部是各州直接负责监管保险行业的执行部门,其职责还包括监督薪酬系统、保护消费者等。例如,得州保险部(Texas Department of Insurance)在其网站列明的主要职责就包括:规范得克萨斯州的保险业务、保护并确保消费者的公平待遇、确保保险业公平竞争及培育竞争市场、依据得州劳动法规定管理得州的工人赔偿制度和确保保险法以及有关保险和保险公司的其他法律得到执行。

保险中介人的制度设立和日常管理同样属于州保险监管部门的职责,保险公司在不同州开展业务均需要满足所在州的要求,保险中介人在不同州开展业务也需单独获得所在州相对应的执照。州保险监管部门负责认定保险中介人必须具备的执业资格和条件、佣金管理及日常执业行为监督等,并对其违规行为进行处罚。除了执照以外,所有保险中介人均需投保职业责任保险。

11.3.2.2 加拿大

同样作为联邦制国家,加拿大在保险业的监管上也分为联邦和省两级管理,两者不是隶属关系,而是互相配合,在不同层面进行协调和管理。联邦一级的监管机构是加拿大金融机构监理总署(The Office of the Superintendent of Financial Institutions, OSFI),负责对加拿大联邦监管的金融机构和养老金计划进行审慎监管,对保险行业的监管职责包括管理在加拿大注册的本土和海外保险公司,重点关注保险公司的偿付能力、风险准备金和投资行为。

省一级的监管机构是金融服务管理局,主要管理在当地开展业务的保险公司。省级部门的监管重点是保险公司等金融机构的市场行为,各省根据自己的保险法,对保险代理人、保险经纪人的批准以及保险合同条款做出具体规定。例如，众多保险公司总部所在的安大略省的保险监管机构为安大略省金融服务监管局(The Financial Services Regulatory Authority of Ontario, FSRA)，其宣称的主要职责为促进高标准的商业行为、培育可持续有竞争力的金融服务业、快速响应市场变化、促进保险和养老金计划的良好管理和鼓励创新等。

加拿大保险中介人在从业过程中，需要按照当地监管部门、保险公司、保险总代理的合规要求，严格执行相关从业合规文件。同时，监管部门和保险公司每年会对保险中介人进行抽查年审，通常此类抽查的内容都非常详细，保险中介人不仅要积极配合调查，还要根据修改意见及时改正。

11.3.2.3 中国香港

中国香港的保险行业监管机构为保险业监管局(Insurance Authority，简称保监局)，于2015年12月7日成立，是一个独立于政府的新保险业监管机构。保监局于2017年接替昔日为政府部门的保险业监理处，规管保险公司，并于2019年9月起取代原有的三个保险业自律规管机构(中国香港保险业联会所成立的保险代理登记委员会、中国香港保险顾问联会和中国香港专业保险中介人协会)，规管保险中介人，统一管理中国香港逾10万名保险中介人，包括订立发牌和监管要求、审批牌照、进行监察和调查，以及实行纪律制裁。

在新的规管制度下，保监局根据多项明确准则，对所有保险中介人进行更为严格的审核后发照，准则包括中介申请人的最低学历要求、专业资格和/或工作经验、品格和诚信度，及财务状况/偿付能力等，以加强对投保人的保障。在持续专业培训方面，保监局也将每年培训的时数由每年10小时增加至15小时，并加强了培训课程的内容，包括新增"道德或规例"课程，以进一步提升保险中介人的专业水平。同时，保监局网站上的"持牌保险中介人登记册"便于公众通过开放透明的电子化系统查阅保险中介人的资料，包括姓名、牌照号码、可经营业务范围等，有助于投保人清楚了解中介背景，确保投保过程更放心。

11.3.2.4 新加坡

新加坡保险监管由隶属金融管理局(简称金管局)的保险署负责。除了金管局之外，非营利行业组织新加坡人寿保险协会和由金管局发起、独立运营的新加坡金融业争议调解中心(Financial Industry Disputes Resolution Centre, FIDReC)也在新加坡寿险行业的发展中起到了重要的规范作用。

新加坡对于保险公司和保险代理人的管理相当严格，包括安排神秘顾客访问、抽查行业行为、严肃处理投诉和违规事件。金管局通过颁布306号规章，在规范精简代理机构组织架构的同时严格保险业的从业标准，并改革代理佣金制度以使其充分透明化，确保保险中介人诚信经营，不误导销售。保险中介人必须满足最低学历要求，经过严格的资格认证考试，以及政府对其背景的各项调查后才可以正式入职，公众也可以在金管局官网查到任何一个新加坡保险中介人的信息，公开透明。

新加坡在2000年后对外开放了保险市场，吸引了越来越多的海外投保人。新加坡金融业争议调解中心的服务范围也包括来新加坡投保的外国人,为申请人的合法权益提供有力保障。保险中介人如有伪造或者欺瞒客户的情况,轻则吊销执照,重则将面临高额罚款和高达 2 年的牢狱监禁。

11.3.2.5 澳大利亚

澳大利亚主要的保险监管机构是澳大利亚审慎监管局(The Australian Prudential Regulation Authority,APRA)与澳大利亚证券和投资委员会,保险公司需要同时从两个监管机构获得执照才能在澳大利亚开展保险业务。全国保险经纪人协会(National Insurance Brokers Association,NIBA)则作为澳大利亚保险业最具代表性的行业协会,为会员制定独立管理和监控的保险中介人行为守则。

个人客户主要通过两种销售渠道购买寿险产品。一种是通过网络或电话形式直接联系保险公司购买,即通用建议(General Advice);另一种是通过保险中介人购买,即个案建议(Personal Advice)。前者为保险公司的代表性业务,仅限于提供产品的一般信息,优势是购买产品快速便捷,但缺乏定制化需求分析;后者则会根据客户需求进行产品比较分析,定制适合客户的个性化产品方案,并可提供后续长期的服务。

根据澳大利亚证券和投资委员会的数据统计,通用建议销售的退单率要高于个案建议销售,因此其认为需要规范监督通用建议销售行为,包括对网络、纸媒等市场媒体渠道,对保险产品内容描述的准确性、客观性、全面性进行审核,以避免信息误导购买行为;同时对电话销售录音进行复听,要求保险公司代表仅限于提供通用建议,若涉及客户的个案,需要征询个案建议,即保险中介人或财务规划师的建议。澳大利亚证券和投资委员会就保险中介人的行为准则加以更新,对违反行为准则的行为制定了严苛的处罚措施。

11.3.3 保险中介人的长期后续服务

保险中介人的服务,不只售前的保单规划、售中的保单申请,更重要的是售后的长期服务。当人寿保单签发后,保险中介人所提供的售后服务主要包括以下几个方面。

11.3.3.1 保单变更服务

① 行政管理上的变更,包括如保单持有人变更、邮寄地址变更、缴费账户信息变更等,有些司法管辖区发行的产品甚至允许变更被保人;

② 撤销原受益人及指定新受益人的变更;

③ 保费支付频率、支付路径及方式、支付年限等的变更;

④ 减额缴清保单,移除附加保障,调整保障级别等的变更;

⑤ 可能涉及额外核保的变更,包括吸烟状况/健康状况改变、保额增加、红利提取方式、增加保费额外供款,或增加附加保障条款等。

11.3.3.2 保单转让服务

(1) 保单的绝对转让(Absolute Policy Assignment)。

在绝对转让下,保单持有人将保单合同的法律所有权,包括所有的权利和义务,全部转让给受让人。一旦交易完成,原保单持有人对保单不再有任何的控制权或经济权益。

(2) 保单部分转让(Partial Policy Assignment)。

使用保单作为抵押去贷款要求保单持有人进行抵押转让,这种方式就属于部分转让。保单持有人虽仍持有保单,但该种方式允许受让人/出贷方阻止保单持有人进行任何降低抵押价值的行为,比如从保单中取钱,或者不支付保费及贷款利息等。若保单出险而贷款尚未偿还,则出贷方对身故赔偿金享有优先权利;若保单持有人恶意拖欠贷款本金和利息,则出贷方可以强制退保,收回尚未偿还的贷款余额及利息。

11.3.3.3 提取保单现金价值服务

① 提取红利。直接提取保单已实现的红利。

② 部分退保。降低保单基本保障额度,将现金价值按比例退回。

③ 提取保费储蓄账户。部分保险产品附加储蓄账户,可留存资金支付未来保费,也可随时支取使用。

④ 保单贷款/抵押贷款。拥有现金价值的保单即可申请保单贷款或抵押贷款,并可随时偿还全部或部分保单贷款。

11.3.3.4 保单取消、退保及保单复效服务

① 取消保单。保单持有人可通过终止支付保费从而让保单失效的方式来取消保单。但对于终身寿险或万能寿险保单来说,因保单中的现金价值可以采用保单自动贷款或现金价值自动抵扣的方式来支付保费,单纯终止支付保费不能立刻取消保单。因此,若保单持有人确定希望取消保单,则建议以书面方式提前申请。

② 退保。对于终身寿险或者万能寿险的保单持有人来说,取消保单通常被称为全额退保(Fully Surrender)。当保单持有人完全退保时,其放弃保单合同赋予的所有权利,退保后,身故赔偿金不会赔付。保单持有人也可以通过支取部分现金价值的方式部分退保(Partially Surrender)。在此情况下,保单合同的权利继续,被保人去世后,身故赔偿金仍然会赔付。无论是完全还是部分退保,都可能对保单持有人产生税务后果。

③ 复效。保单一旦失效,可以在2年之内申请复效(有些保险公司允许3年内申请复效)。复效申请可能要求再次核保,通过后需要补齐所欠全部保费和相关利息。保单2年的争议期也会从复效日期开始重新计算。

11.3.3.5 保单替换服务

因保险中介人帮助客户购买新保单时可获得佣金收入,所以当用新申请的保单去替换现有已生效保单时,可能会存在利益冲突的情况。各地保险监管条例均严格要求保险中介人,只有在以客户利益最大化为目的的前提下,才可以推荐客户将现有已生效保单替换成新的保单。

若保险中介人故意使用不完整的信息或者虚假陈述来说服保单持有人更换现有生效保单,或者通过取消现有保单来获取现金价值以购买新的保单,保险中介人就违反了从业行为准则中的受信义务。若新保单和现有保单均是由同一家保险公司发行,则上述欺骗

性的行为被称为诱导重复申请或以旧购新(Churning);若新保单和现有保单由不同的保险公司发行,则上述行为被称为诱导转保(Twisting)。

11.3.3.6 保单索赔服务

一旦被保人去世,保单的受益人或者继承人(未指定受益人的情况下)就会成为索偿人。保险中介人在索赔程序中起到支持作用,需及时协助索偿人准备相关证明文件,并协助填写索赔表格、选择支付方式等。对于身故索赔,主要证明文件包括被保人的死亡证明(Proof of Death)、保单正本、遗嘱认证函(如继承人被指定为保单的受益人)、主治医生声明、被保人的年龄和性别证明,以及保单受益人/受托人、遗嘱执行人的身份证明等。如涉及健康医疗住院险方面的索赔,还需根据保单条款要求,额外提供包括医疗检验报告、诊断报告、治疗记录、住院账单等相关凭证文件。

在进行索赔赔付安排时,除了一次性领取身故赔偿金,索偿人还有其他选择,例如用赔付款项购买定期年金或终身年金。保险中介人可在被保人去世时提供相关协助,与索偿人讨论这些赔付的支付安排,并提供相关的产品报价。

11.3.3.7 根据客户需求变化的动态服务

保险中介人还应时刻关注客户的需求变化,向客户提供动态的后续保单服务、管理及专业建议,包括对家庭新生子女成员的保障及受益权的赋予,家庭成员婚姻状况改变所需做的保单安排,家庭成员因就业变化、资产变化或经营企业变化所需进行的保单内容及结构类型的调整。

在当今时代,特别是高净值家庭,无论"钱"还是"人"都可能是动态的。伴随高净值客户家庭资产全球化分布的状况,保险中介人应该结合客户在资产保护、资产传承、资产安全保值、税务筹划方面的需求,帮助客户推荐/选择全球范围内的保险产品组合。比如客户一旦移民,税务居民身份就发生改变,原有的保单可能会给他带来一定的税务后果。此时就需要根据客户的实际情况和需求对保单架构做出调整,比如更换保单持有人、被保人或者使用私募寿险来持有资产。任何涉税问题,都建议寻求相应司法管辖区的税务专家的意见。前文所提到的各种长期后续服务都属于常规服务,而拥有相关税务及信托认知已经越来越成为服务高净值家庭的必备能力,而且是不易获得的能力,这也是国际寿险架构师的独特价值所在。

11.4 保险推荐人

保险推荐人(Insurance Referrers)又称保险转介绍人,是指在保险交易活动中将保险申请人转介绍给保险中介人,进行居中介绍的人士。

11.4.1 保险推荐人和转介绍活动的认定

众所周知,转介绍是保险销售中最有效的客户来源方式。传统上来说,保险转介绍并没有特别清楚的定义,也很少被正式拿上台面进行讨论,广义上认为保险申请人转介绍或者推荐保险中介人和保险公司的行为都属于保险转介绍。保险转介绍在真实的保险市场交易中起到了显著的作用,在很大比例的实践案例中都可以发现,保险申请人和保险中介人往往是通过一个或者多个中间人,也就是保险推荐人,来快速认识和建立信任的。

根据不同地区从业者的经验,保险市场的转介绍活动可以被归为三类。

第一类为现有客户或亲朋好友为他们认可的保险中介人转介绍其他客户,主要依靠口口相传,没有形成固定的模式和酬劳方式。此种方式具有偶然性、一次性和非专业性等特点。比如一位客户对为自己服务的保险中介人十分满意,因此在朋友需要购买保险时向朋友推荐了该保险中介人。在此种方式下,推荐人为现有客户或亲朋好友等,很多情况下可能不涉及转介绍的酬劳或者涉及很小金额的转介绍礼物作为感谢。

更为常见的转介绍活动则是第二类,即通过更有计划地安排如转介绍协议、合作协议等,由相关行业专业人士如信托、法律、投资和会计从业人员将其客户转介绍给保险中介人。此类转介绍活动占据了保险市场交易生态中很大的比例。比如,一位加拿大的会计师定期将自己的客户推荐给一位加拿大的保险经纪,或房产经纪将自己的客户推荐给保险经纪。此类转介绍往往会涉及转介绍费(Referral Fee 或 Finder Fee)。

第三类转介绍活动则是保险中介人转介绍客户给另外一位保险中介人。同一司法管辖区的保险中介人因为均可合法直接服务客户,很少有动力或者有必要与其他保险中介人合作服务客户,所以此种转介绍经常发生在跨司法管辖区的保险中介人之间。随着近年来客户的需求逐渐国际化和多元化,单个司法管辖区的产品和方案已经无法解决客户全部的需求尤其是跨国需求,客户往往需要不同地区的专业人士来服务。大部分司法管辖区都要求持牌的保险中介人必须是本国居民,保险中介人往往无法同时取得多个司法管辖区的执业牌照,因此最好的服务客户的方法就是将客户转介绍给其他司法管辖区的持牌或授权保险中介人。例如,一位中国内地保险经纪的客户希望在中国香港配置一份保险,那么该经纪通常会将客户转介绍给其认可的一位或多位中国香港保险经纪。

拥有全球视野、专业知识和解决方案资源的保险中介人往往扮演着客户与全球专业人士的桥梁,有能力为客户初步分析需求,再转介绍给客户需求所在地的保险中介人。例如,如果客户的需求横跨多个在岸地国家,那么除了将客户转介绍给这些司法管辖区的保险中介人以外,还需要为客户考虑离岸地区的解决方案。总之,为客户提供一个基于全球而不是某一特定司法管辖区的方案,通晓不同地域法律、税务、保险和信托知识已成为国际寿险架构师的使命。

综上所述,不管是以上哪一种转介绍活动,其核心是推荐人一般都不持有方案目的地司法管辖区的保险牌照,即便在一国是合法持牌的,但在涉及另一国的方案中其角色也不是保险中介人,只是起着介绍和撮合作用的推荐人,绝对不能涉及当地具体的保险专业推荐、产品讲解、保单申请和服务等受到规管的活动。不同的司法管辖区对能否跨国支付介绍费和能支付多少介绍费有其各自的规定。

11.4.2 对保险推荐人和转介绍活动的监管

各司法管辖区的保险监管部门对保险推荐人一般没有清晰的认定和监管措施,因为从理论上来说保险推荐人并不是保险市场的正式参与者,不需要获得任何牌照或准入门槛即可成为推荐人。监管部门对保险转介绍活动的要求更多的是体现为对保险中介人的约束,从保险中介人与推荐人的合作要求、是否可以或如何支付及支付多少转介绍费,以及转介绍活动的记录和审查等方面间接实现对转介绍活动的规管,其本质精神还是要将转介绍限定在不涉及保险具体事务的居中介绍,而严禁推荐人涉及具体保险业务和其他必须由持牌或授权保险中介人才有资格进行的工作,这也是规范行业发展、保护消费者的必要措施。

保险推荐人应时刻将客户的利益置于第一位,基于客户的需求为其进行推荐和转介绍。而对于接受转介绍的保险中介人而言,则应该严格遵守监管部门的规定,甚至以高于法规标准的自我要求来实践规范转介绍业务。对于有长期合作协议的转介绍业务,保险监管部门会更加审慎地看待和提出行为准则。以中国香港为例,中国香港保险业监管局在 2022 年 11 月 30 日对全港所有持牌保险中介公司负责人发布的《现场检查及非现场监测中的常见发现》(Common Findings From On-site Inspection and Off-site Monitoring)信件的附件 1 中就指出,接受保险转介绍业务的保险经纪机构应遵循以下良好实践。

① 与推荐人签订书面转介绍协议,规定转介绍安排的管理条款以及协议下各方的权利和义务,并明确禁止推荐人进行受规管活动。

② 实施控制措施,确保推荐人在转介绍过程中没有实质上进行受规管的活动。这些措施可以包括以下控制措施:

- 向推荐人提供"该做什么和不该做什么"清单,以便他们知道自己可以做什么或不能做什么;
- 抽查客户(或者进行客户调查或获取反馈),了解推荐人在进行推荐时向客户告知的内容;
- 定期提醒推荐人不要进行受规管的活动;
- 建立"危险信号"系统,识别推荐人可能在哪些地方提供了未经许可的受规管建议,然后跟进客户进行查证。在此情况下,此类"危险信号"是指客户提到他们从推荐人那里获得的保险建议。

(3) 持牌保险经纪公司也须按照中国香港保险业监管局颁发的《持牌保险代理人操守守则》C 部分标准及实务 5.5 条的要求,向转介客户提供清晰格式的披露声明。

CHAPTER 12

不同司法管辖区人寿保险公司的非寿险产品

> **本章要点：**
> - 以美国、加拿大、中国香港和中国内地为例，介绍各司法管辖区人寿保险公司发行的寿险以外的产品

全球主要司法管辖区的人寿保险公司主要有三大传统业务，即人身保险（包括人寿保险、健康保险、重疾险和意外保险等）、退休计划（包含年金等）以及储蓄和投资业务（包含储蓄计划、共同基金、交易型开放式指数基金等）。本章主要讨论高净值人士较常使用的非寿险产品如年金，以及带有保障功能的投资产品如分隔基金。

年金是各大寿险公司除人寿保险以外最重要的业务之一。人寿保险虽然在近年来发展出了更多保障以外的功能，但传统上来说还是为了保护人们过早离世所带来的财务风险；年金则与人寿保险相反，要解决的是人们活得太久而带来的一些财务上的挑战。因此人寿保险与年金在个人和家庭的财务规划中都起到了重要作用。

从定义上来看，年金是保险公司支付年金持有人终身（或一段时间内）保证收入的一份合同，年金可以立即开始或在未来某段时间内提供稳定和确定的现金流。常见的支付频率包括年付、半年付、季付或月付。年金产品的两个重要功能包括："保证"的资金增值策略和"保证"的终身（或一定时间内）领取现金流。

从不同维度来考量，年金可以被划分成不同类型：

① 按年金的主要目的，年金可分为收入年金（Income Annuity）和累积年金（Accumulation Annuity）；

② 按年金被保人的个数，年金可分为个人年金（Single Life Annuity）和联名年金（Joint Life Annuity）；

③ 按缴付保费的方式，年金可分为趸缴年金（Single Premium Annuity）和期缴年金（Flexible Premium Annuity）；

④ 按开始领取收入的时间，年金可分为即期年金（Immediate Annuity）和递延年金（Deferred Annuity）；

⑤ 按领取收入的时间长度，年金可分为终身年金（Life Annuity）和定期年金（Term Certain Annuity）；

⑥ 按领取收入的金额是否变化，年金可分为定额年金（Fixed-Income Annuity）和增额年金（Increasing-Income Annuity）；

⑦ 按投资收益来源，年金可分为固定年金（Fixed Annuity）和投资型年金（Variable Annuity）；

⑧ 按是否有权获得额外红利，年金可分为参与型年金（Participating Annuity）和非参与型年金（Non-Participating Annuity）。

除以上的类型之外，年金还有很多其他功能上的分类，一款年金产品往往是不同维度的组合，并非所有的司法管辖区和保险公司都会提供所有类型的年金产品。

除了年金以外，部分司法管辖区的寿险公司依据当地法律法规和市场特点还推出了将保险和投资相结合的产品，如加拿大的分隔基金。此类产品在投资方面非常类似于共同基金，在提供多种投资选择、具有较高收益潜力的同时还增加了保险（完全或部分保障本金并可以安排指定受益人）的特点，形成了独特的产品风格。

下面将分别介绍美国、加拿大、中国香港和中国内地相关产品的情况。

12.1 美国

美国拥有全世界最大的年金市场，根据美国全国保险委员会协会发布的《人寿保险和意外伤害保险行业分析报告》中提供的数据，2022年美国年金产品的总保费达到了3 860亿美元。

根据美国税法的相关规定，美国的年金可在合资格计划（Qualified Plan）或非合资格计划（Non-Qualified Plan）下购买，两者税务上的相关规定差异较大。本节主要探讨非合资格计划下的情形。

美国是年金产品设计最为先进、产品种类最为齐全的市场。美国常见的年金产品主要包括三大类。

12.1.1 固定收益年金

固定收益年金是一种从保险公司获得固定利息的非投资型年金，保费可以是趸缴或期缴,领取时间既可以是即期领取,又可以是递延领取,美国市场最常见的则是趸缴型或期缴型的递延年金。固定收益年金是较常见的一种年金类型,是各种衍生年金类型的基础。在固定收益年金中,保险公司以投保人支付的保费进行投资,投保人本身无法参与投资标的的选择。

对于固定收益年金,最形象的一个比喻就是,它是豪华版本的定期存款。在我们把钱存入保险公司那一刻,就已经知道了当年的固定收益率,而这个收益率往往比银行定期存款高。以2023年12月为例,美国不同银行储蓄账户平均利率在0.57%,小型或网络银行利率可达4%~5%,固定收益年金收益率则大多在4%~6%。与银行利率一样,年金产品的收益率同样会随着市场利率的变动而调整。

多年保证收益年金(Multi-Year Guaranteed Annuity)是固定收益年金的一种。它像固定收益年金和定期存款的结合体,也像一个多年期存款产品,用来解决"传统固定收益年金的利率可能会发生变化"这一问题。

固定收益年金的利息,跟银行的存款利息一样,会受美联储基准利率的影响。如果美联储降息,那么固定收益年金保险的利息,也会和银行存款利率一样下调。

多年保证收益年金,可以在一个"保证"的时间段里,确定一个"保证"的固定利率不变。这个"保证利率"的期限通常是2~10年。

截至2023年12月底,根据保险公司品牌实力和保证期限的不同,多年保证收益年金的收益率大致在3.5%~6%。多年保证收益年金适合50岁以上(临近退休年龄)、不愿意资金承受市场风险、需要保证收益率和高确定性现金流的投资人。

12.1.2 指数型年金

指数型年金(Fixed Indexed Annuity)是美国比较独特的一款产品,在其他市场不太常见;其在美国国内先于指数型万能寿险诞生,是美国保险公司发行的最早的指数型产品之一。指数型年金虽然有很强的投资属性,但在美国属于非投资型的产品,不受美国证监会的监管。按上文提到的维度进行分类,指数型年金属于期缴保费递延领取的固定年金。

相对于高风险的投资型年金,指数型年金的最大特点是其投资表现与股市指数表现挂钩,在指数表现为正时收益有封顶,在指数下跌时提供保本的保障,本金不会受到损失。为增加市场竞争力,一些指数型年金产品允许投保人自主额外选择承担一定风险和成本,换取较高的封顶收益率。指数型年金的投资部分和收益获取原理与指数型万能寿险非常类似,同样涉及指数选择、封顶收益率、参与率和保底利率等因素,具体细节可参考第3章关于指数型万能寿险的介绍。

指数型年金适合不愿意本金亏损,又希望追求市场收益潜力,距离退休还有一定年份的群体。

12.1.3 投资型年金

随着美国证券市场的蓬勃发展,1952年出现了投资型年金产品。投资型年金也称变额年金或证券型年金,在美国属于投资产品,受到美国证监会的监管。投资型年金在美国大多为期交保费的递延年金。相对于固定年金,投保人可以在投资型年金的账户里自行选择不同的基金进行投资。投资型年金的特点是,投保人承担风险,收益随市场浮动,不保证本金。

投资型年金的相关费用较高,可能是市面上能购买到的最昂贵的年金产品之一。以2022年美国个人投资型年金市场份额位居前列的一款产品为例,相关费用可分为以下几类。

(1)死亡率费用。

这是保险公司为了提供身故赔偿金而收取的费用,年金的身故赔偿金通常是一个保证支付给受益人的金额,该金额最少等于支付的保费。变额年金的死亡率费用(Mortality Expenses)一般是每年保单价值的0.5%~1.5%。

(2)账户费/保单费。

许多投资型年金都有单独的账户或保单收费,费用每年几十美元至一百多美元(每张保单)。一般来说,当资产达到一定量级后,此费用可被免除。

(3)底层投资费用。

在投资型年金中,被称为子账户的基金和债券投资将被收取投资管理费,其金额为该账户每年价值的0.25%~2.50%。

(4)附加条款额外费用。

附加条款是投资型年金保单的额外功能,可以提供额外的保障或身故赔偿金。根据保障范围的不同,附加条款每年的保费可达保单价值的0.3%~1%。

(5)退保费用。

与固定收益年金类似,投资型年金同样会有提前退保罚金的相关规定。如果提前支取超过可自由支取的额度,超过的部分将按一定的比例缴纳退保费用。退保费用的适用期限从3年到15年不等,具体收取的费用比例一般从8%~10%开始,逐年下降直至退保费用收取期结束,这将限制年金保单的灵活性。如果投保人自身情况发生了变化,比如离婚,则投保人可能需要支付退保费用才能分割其账户。

投资型年金适合愿意承担市场风险博取高收益潜力,距离退休至少还有10年的群体。

年金通常被认为是长期投资,虽然美国市场的年金有诸多优点,但也存在以下重要限制:

(1)流动性有限,过早提取可能需缴退保费。

一般来说,美国的年金产品不能完全任意支取,在退保收费期(Surrender Charge Period)内,各家公司普遍会让投保人享有每年10%的自由支取额度,如果超过当年的额度则需按照提早退保罚金的相关百分比收取相关手续费,因此年金产品更适合长期持有。

(2) 59.5 岁前提取有罚款。

美国国税局规定,在 59.5 岁之前从年金中提取的收入通常要被额外征收 10% 的收入税罚金,由此也可看出,年金在美国被定位为退休后使用的产品。

(3) 开始提取后可能需缴税。

一般来说,在非合资格计划下的年金是用税后的钱缴付保费,其税收递延属性有利于增长,但一旦开始提取,即使提取金额还未超过全部本金,提取金额中的一部分就会被视为收入,需要进行缴税。因此,提取金额在税务上会被认为有一个应税部分(收益)和免税部分(本金),具体的比例由免税比例(Exclusion Ratio)来确定。合资格计划下的年金,视不同具体的计划,保费可以是税前的钱,如个人退休账户(Individual Retirement Account,IRA)计划;也可以是税后的钱,如罗斯个人退休账户(Roth IRA)计划。因此提取时该如何缴纳个人所得税,应依据具体计划的规定。

涉及年金的税务规定相对复杂,在购买前建议咨询美国税务专业人士。

12.2 加拿大

12.2.1 年金

根据加拿大人寿和健康保险协会提供的数据,全加拿大共有超过 900 万人拥有包括年金在内的退休储蓄产品。2022 年年金保费的总供款为 622 亿加币,团体计划和个人保单的占比分别为 70% 和 30%。

与美国的合资格计划和非合资格计划类似,加拿大的年金可通过两种形式购买,不同购买形式税务政策有较大差异:

(1) 注册账户(Registered Account)的资金来购买年金,称为注册年金;

(2) 非注册账户(Non-Registered Account)的资金来购买年金,称为非注册年金。

加拿大市场的年金主要按使用目的来分类,可分为收入年金(Payout Annuity)和累积年金。顾名思义,收入年金的主要目的是向年金持有人提供持续性的收入,而累积年金则像一种有到期日的长期储蓄,非常类似于加拿大的定期存款(Guaranteed Investment Certificates)。加拿大市场更多使用的是收入年金。加拿大收入年金的结构大致如图 12.1 所示。

12.2.1.1 收入年金的特点

(1) 终身年金或定期年金。

不同的年金产品可以只是在未来一段时间内领取收入或是终身领取收入。

(2) 个人收入年金或联名收入年金。

个人收入年金可以让年金持有人在有生之年获得稳定的定期收入,一旦被保人去世就收入停止。联名收入年金也被称为幸存者年金,与配偶退休金计划相似,在本人或配偶的有生之年可以获得稳定的定期收入。当其中一人身故,在世的配偶可继续领取收入,直到去世。

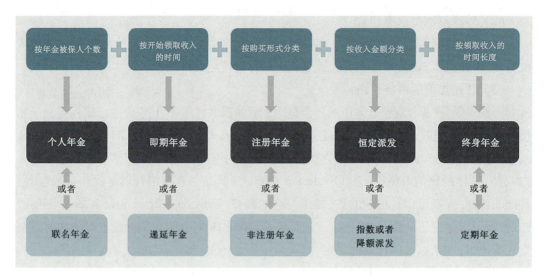

图 12.1 加拿大收入年金的常见结构

来源：Segregated funds and annuities：Life Licence Qualification Program（LLQP）Exam Preparation Manual，E-313-9th Edition，2022.

（3）即期或递延领取收入。

投保人必须选择何时开始领取年金收入，当趸缴全部保费后即开始领取年金收入称为即期型；也可选择递延到某个时间再开始领取，称为递延领取型。递延型收入年金分为累积和分配两个阶段，在累积阶段投保人持续支付保费或保费存储在保险公司以供后续分配使用，累积阶段结束后则开始分配年金收入，最长可累积时间由不同公司政策和产品决定，一般为 10 年左右。

（4）最低保证支付年限。

部分产品具有最低保证支付年限供投保人选择，这一附加条款可保障被保人如不幸在保证年限到期前去世，其受益人依然可以以定期派发或者一次性赔偿金的形式从保险公司获得最低保证支付年限应该获得的收入。最低保证支付年限视不同公司和产品而不同，一般为 0~40 年。

（5）多种收入金额可供选择。

投保人可根据需要选择不同的收入派发金额，例如：

① 恒定派发——每一期派发的收入都一样；

② 指数派发——每年派发的金额以固定百分比增长；

③ 降额派发——每年派发的金额以固定百分比降低。

12.2.1.2 风险和限制

（1）利率与通胀风险。

加拿大年金的收益率与利率环境有紧密的联系，尤其是在低利率时购买的年金将有可能遭遇利率风险，因为年金是以售出时的利率为基础来计算收益率的，年金售出后将无法再获得利率上涨的好处。通货膨胀风险跟利率风险高度相关,如果利率增加,生活成本变高,那么终身收入年金和长期的定期收入年金都会受到通胀的影响。

(2) 本金损失风险。

对于终身收入年金保单,如果没有保证期相关的条款,则有可能会因投保人过早离世而无法拿回全部本金。

(3) 提取及退保限制。

一般来说,加拿大的收入年金不允许进行部分退保或完全退保,也没有现金价值,因此收入年金不能通过除既定收入以外的方式从保单提取资金,灵活性受到较大限制。累积年金相对比较灵活,可以部分退保提取资金,但可能会影响到市值调整;同时,也可在任意时间点完全退保,拿回当前的现金价值。购买年金之前需要仔细了解年金合同的相应规定,从业者也应对客户进行充分的风险揭示。

12.2.1.3 适合人群

加拿大年金最适合以下人群:

① 即将退休或已退休人士;

② 担心退休收入/养老金不够用;

③ 担心已有的养老积蓄在金融市场表现不佳时缩水;

④ 寻求稳定的收入来源以支付基本生活开支;

⑤ 补充已有的退休收入;

⑥ 希望将累积的注册储蓄计划的资金转换为固定的收入来源。

12.2.2 分隔基金

分隔基金(Segregated Fund),又称保本基金,是由人寿保险公司发行的具有保障功能的投资类产品。之所以被称为分隔基金,主要是因为保险公司将分隔基金下的资产与公司其他资产分隔开来管理。分隔基金的法律术语叫个人变额保险合约(Individual Variable Insurance Contract,IVIC),这一名词可以更好地表达其投资产品的属性。

分隔基金类似于有保障功能的共同基金,保险公司根据保单持有人的不同投资选择将投保人支付的保费汇聚在一起进行集中投资管理,基金内的现金价值将会根据投资标的的表现和基金的费用进行涨跌。当合约到期或者身故时,投保人可获得当期的现金价值或是合约保证的最低保障金额(一般为本金的75%或100%)。

此类产品使得投资组合兼备增长潜力、灵活性,同时通过其保证条款为投资人和受益人提供保障。每个分隔基金均有专业管理的资金池,投资分散在不同领域,通过分散投资达到多样化,并且保障其免受市场不景气带来的影响。

同时分隔基金可依投保人的需求量身定制,帮助保障初始投资本金及积蓄。

12.2.2.1 分隔基金的优点

① 保障投资本金。当合约到期或者身故时,依不同产品可选择保障本金的75%

或100%。

② 终身收入保障。可选择终身保障收入,分隔基金的表现不佳也不会减少收入金额。

③ 保障遗产。可确保特定受益人享有优先于债权人索偿的权利,即在特定条件下具有防债权人追讨的功能。

④ 财富传承。可以指定受益人,身故赔偿金将直接支付给受益人,而无须经过遗产认证和支付认证费用。

⑤ 投资选择丰富。不同保险公司可提供上百至数千只不同基金供投保人选择。

⑥ 专业管理。基金的投资和管理均由专业的管理团队负责。

⑦ 流动性。可方便提取资金,或通过完全及部分退保获得资金。

12.2.2.2.2 分隔基金的缺点

① 基金的选择过于冗余且高度同质化。

② 部分分隔基金有较高管理费用(Management Expense Ratio),包括销售费用和持续的管理费。

与年金一样,加拿大分隔基金也可用注册账户或非注册账户持有,其税务政策区别较大,在购买相应产品时应先咨询相关税务人士。

12.3 中国香港

年金业务在中国香港同样被归属于长期保险业务,但相对于保险市场每年新增上千亿港元保费来说,中国香港的年金市场规模较小。根据中国香港保监局发布的数据,截至2022年底,年金业务的有效保单共有1 078 841份,而2022年新造个人年金业务共售出49 590份新保单,带来76.85亿港元的保单保费。

中国香港年金产品有多种类型,按领取开始时间可分为即期年金和延期年金,按领取持续时间可分为定期年金和终身年金,按领取金额来看则可分为定额年金和递增年金。与美国等年金市场最发达的司法管辖区对比来说,中国香港的年金产品基本上都是非投资型的,并且也没有与指数挂钩的产品,绝大部分是固定收益型或者是分红型的年金。固定收益型的产品通常会有底利率,再按保险公司厘定的利率派息;而很多分红型年金产品的现金价值增长类似于中国香港的储蓄分红险,因此其领取的年金收入通常也被分为保证和非保证部分。

虽然中国香港的年金在投资选择权方面不如美国的同类产品丰富,但中国香港作为中西文化交流的中心,在产品设计上充分考虑了华人客户特定的需求。在参考了西方发达国家同类产品基本形态的前提下,中国香港部分保险公司在其年金产品上也推出了之前在储蓄分红险上才具有的一些独特功能。例如,投保人可选择8种货币进行投保并在满足一定条件下把原有保单货币转换至新保单货币,充分满足中国香港客户国际化的需求。此外,部分产品还允许在保单生效期无限次更换投被保人,以更好地满足华人客户重视传承的需求。

与美国和加拿大类似,中国香港居民可通过税务优惠计划来购买年金,获得一定的税务扣除优惠。具体政策可咨询相关税务专业人士。

12.4 中国内地

12.4.1 年金保险的功能

年金在中国内地市场也被称为年金保险,是指在被保人生存期间,保险公司按照合同约定的金额、方式,在约定的期限内,有规则地、定期地向被保险人给付保险金的保险。年金保险在中国内地的发展历史不算太长,其主要应用是从资产配置的角度被当成一个低风险但收益相对确定的理财产品。近几年在银行理财、信托等资管产品安全性及收益性均降的情况下,年金保险因其可在利率较好时锁定未来长期的收益而获得了很大的关注。

与海外市场不同的是,中国内地的投资者选择年金主要是偏重理财属性,而忽视年金的本质即养老功能。随着经济发展阶段和居民资产配置意识的变化,有理由相信中国内地的年金产品在设计上将会提供更多保障功能和投资选择,更加注重长期的增值和养老需求。

年金保险在中国内地主要有以下功能:

① 养老保障:年金保险可以在达到一定年龄后按期领取固定的养老金或生活津贴,确保被保人退休后有稳定的收入来源。

② 分散风险:年金保险是一种无风险的理财产品,不受市场波动的影响,可以作为其他投资渠道的补充。

③ 锁定收益:年金保险的收益是确定地写在合同里面的,不会随着利率变化而变化,可以在利率下行的趋势下保持较高的收益率。

④ 享受税优:部分年金保险产品可通过个人养老金账户购买,作为个人所得税的专项扣除项目,按照规定每年可以扣除 12 000 元。

⑤ 财富传承:年金保险可以在被保人死亡时给予受益人一定的赔付金额,或者在合同期满时返还剩余本金和收益。

⑥ 强制储蓄:年金保险需要缴纳一定的保费,可以帮助人们养成良好的储蓄习惯,避免消费过度或者投资失误。

如图 12.2 所示,中国的年金保险与海外的年金产品类似,可按不同的维度组合成为多种类型。

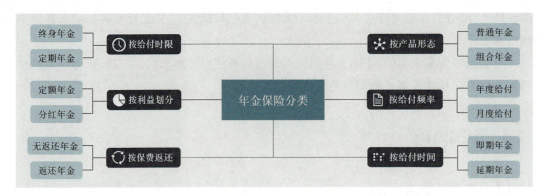

图 12.2　中国年金保险分类

12.4.2　年金保险的特点

（1）不同期限产品并存。

中国内地的年金保险存在多种保障期限，短期年金保险一般保障期限为 5~8 年，也有保障 10~20 年的中期产品和终身保障的长期产品。中短期产品更像安全性较高的定期存款或两全保险，养老的成分较小；长期产品则更像海外同类产品，提供长期收入。

（2）附加万能账户。

短期保障的年金产品因其收益往往较低，因此大多可搭配万能账户，通过年金保险的分红或领取后可将资金转入万能账户，获得更高的收益。万能账户的保证利率视不同产品而言一般在 1.75%~3.5%（受监管制约，持续下降中），当前利率则由保险公司定；依照 2023 年底的数据，大多数保险公司的当前结算利率在 4% 以上。如第 5.6.5 小节所述，此类万能账户与海外的万能寿险虽然名字类似，但实质上有较大的区别。

（3）领取年金及保证收益率。

长期保障的年金保险与海外年金类似，在一定年龄如 55 岁或 60 岁后，投保人可开始领取终身或定期的退休金收入，有更强的养老属性，同时部分产品也允许任意支取现金价值内的金额，给予更高的灵活性。长期保障型年金保险的收益也分为保证利率和非保证利率，保证利率通常会按不同投资选择来设定，实际结算利率则同样由保险公司定期公布。目前，因监管不断调低产品预定收益率，2023 年四季度开始流行类似港险的年金加主险分红产品，收益率突破监管上限 3%，很多公司陆续推出此类产品并成为热销优势产品。

附录 A：美国税务意见

US Tax Opinions

Butler · Snow | *2024.01.10*

Memo 1: US International Tax Concepts in General[①]

1.1 Tax resident status

1.1.1 Criteria for Determining Whether an Individual is a US Person

Generally, a "US Person" is taxed by the United States on their worldwide income. For example, income earned by a US Person living and working solely in Singapore still must pay US taxes on the income earned in Singapore. Additionally, a US Person is subject to certain disclosure obligations for certain non-US assets (e.g., ownership of non-US companies, corporations, and partnerships) and foreign bank accounts (i.e., Report of Foreign Bank and Financial Accounts).

The four ways to determine whether someone is a US Person is:

i The individual is a US citizen (i.e., someone who holds or is entitled to hold a US passport);

[①] For clarity, US state and local taxes are not within the scope of this memo. Further, except as otherwise indicated, we are not considering situations where a life insurance policy is issued by a US life insurance company and held by a non-US Person.

ii The individual holds a US green card (the "**Green Card Test**");

a However, an individual with a green card could escape being a US Person if such individual is entitled to be treated as a resident of a foreign country under an income tax treaty with the US (the "**Treaty-tie Breaker Exception**"). US tax advisors would need to be involved to determine whether an individual with a green card qualifies for this exception.

iii The individual has a substantial presence in the US for the current year(the "**Substantial Presence Test**"). This test depends on how much time an individual spends in the US and looks at the number of days such individual is in the US over a 3-year period, including the current year and the two years before that. An individual must meet both requirements below to become a US Person under the Substantial Presence Test:

a The individual must be in the US for at least 31 days for the current year.

b The individual has been in the US for a total of 183 days or more over the past three years. Here, each day from the current year counts as 1 day, each day from the year before counts as 1/3 of a day, and each day from two years ago counts as 1/6 of a day.

c However, if an individual becomes a US Person under the Substantial Presence Test, such individual can avoid US Person status if such individual qualifies for the "**Closer Connection Exception**". One of the basic requirements of this exception is that the individual must have stayed in the US for fewer than 183 days in the current year. Since there are other more nuanced requirements to qualify for this exception, US tax advisors would need to be involved to determine whether an individual qualifies for this exception.

iv The individual chooses to be treated as a US Person through a special election. We will not dive into this election because it is rare for an individual to make this election. We sometimes see individuals making this special election when he or she is married to a US Person.

Scenarios demonstrating the rules above:

i X, an individual who holds a US passport, lives and works in Canada and only stays in the US for 30 days annually. X is a US Person because she is a US citizen.

ii Y, an individual who has a green card, lives and works in Singapore and only stays in the US for 30 days annually. Singapore does not have an in come tax treaty with the US. Y is a US Person because he holds a green card.

iii B is an individual who is not a US citizen and does not hold a green card. She lived in the US for 120 days in 2023, 120 days in 2022, and 120 days in 2021. For 2023, based on the formula of the Substantial Presence Test, B has resided in the US for less than 183 days from 2021 to 2023 (120 days in the current year (2023) + 40 days (120 days in 2022 times 1/3) + 20 days (120 days in 2021 times 1/6) = 180 days).

Therefore, even though B stayed over 31 days in 2023, B is not a US Person under the

Substantial Presence Test in 2023 because she stayed in the US for fewer than 183 days from 2021 to 2023.

1.1.2　Criteria for Determining Whether a corporation is a US Person

Generally, a corporation is a US Person if it was incorporated under the law of the United States or of any State (a "**US Corporation**"). If a corporation is incorporated in the US, the location of the corporation's offices or business operations would not affect its US Person status.

Interestingly, corporations formed in US territories such as Puerto Rico are not considered "incorporated under the law of the United States or of any State."

Lastly, certain non-US corporations could be treated as US Corporations if such non-US corporations went through an inversion transaction. Generally, an inversion transaction happens when a US Corporation becomes a subsidiary of a non-US corporation and the shareholders of the non-US corporation are the same shareholders of the US Corporation. US tax advisors should be involved to determine whether a non-US corporation is treated as a US Corporation.

1.1.3　Criteria for Determining Whether a Trust is a US Person

- Grantor trusts

To determine whether a trust is a US Person, it is necessary to first determine whether the trust is a grantor or nongrantor trust. A grantor trust is treated as a flow-through entity and not as a separate taxpayer. This means all the US tax liability and reporting obligations still belong to the grantor (e.g., the person who transferred property or cash to the trust). In a grantor trust, the relevant question would be whether the grantor is a US Person. Highly complex rules determine whether a trust is a grantor or nongrantor trust. US tax advisors must be involved in making this determination. Generally, if a US Person beneficiary receives disributions from a grantor trust, such beneficiary would not have to pay US taxes on the distribution but would have an obligation to report the distribution on their tax filings. But, if the grantor is a "Covered Expatriate" (discussed in this memo below), then the distribution would be subject to US taxes.

- Nongrantor trusts

If a trust (or any portion thereof) does not qualify as a grantor trust, it will be classified as a nongrantor trust for US income tax purposes and taxed as a separate taxpayer. A nongrantor trust generally calculates its taxable income in the same manner as an individual, subject to several modifications, which allocate the trust's income, gains, deductions, and credits between the trust and its beneficiaries. As such, it is relevant to determine whether a nongrantor trust is a US Person. US Person beneficiaries of a nongrantor trust are generally subject to US income tax on distributions received from such trust.

- US trust or non-US trust

Atrust is classified as a "US trust" and thus a US Person if it meets both the "court test" and the "control test." When a trust fails either one of the tests, the trust is classified as a "non-US trust." A trust meets the "court test" if a court within the United States can exercise primary supervision over the administration of the trust. A trust meets the "control test" if one or more US Persons have the authority to control all substantial decisions of the trust. In other words, if the terms of a trust provide that the administration of the trust is governed by the law of a jurisdiction that is outside of the United States, or if a non-US Person has the power to control any substantial decision of the trust, the trust is classified as a foreign trust.

- Foreign grantor trust planning

Typically, individuals who are not US Persons but have children or grandchildren who are US Persons set up a foreign grantor trust ("FGT") to prevent the application of US estate taxes (discussed below) by keeping their wealth in the trust. By transferring assets to a trust rather than directly to descendants, the individual protects his or her assets from the punitive US estate and gift tax regime (discussed below).

Once the individual who created the FGT passes away, the FGT automatically becomes a foreign nongrantor trust, and additional structuring is necessary to manage income taxes and penalties associated with foreign nongrantor trusts.

Because of the highly complex nature of FGT planning, individuals typically work with professional trustees and US tax counsel to structure FGTs.

1.2 US estate and gift tax

The three types of transfer taxes in the US are:

ⅰ gift tax, which applies to property given away while someone is alive;

ⅱ estate tax, for property transfers at and after death; and

ⅲ generation-skipping transfer tax ("**GSTTax**"), for gifts made to people at least one generation younger than the giver, like grandchildren.

Which tax applies depends on the individual giving the gift or property. This individual can be a US citizen, a US domiciliary, or neither.

1.2.1 US estate and gift taxes for US citizens and domiciliaries

The estate and gift taxes are like special fees on the action of passing on wealth. These taxes are charged to the person giving the wealth (the transferor) and are based on the total value of what's being given away. If the transferor is a US citizen or domiciliary, they are taxed on property transfers anywhere in the world regardless of where the property is located. As of 2023, they can transfer up to $12.92 million tax-free during their lifetime or at death. In 2024, the exemption amount will increase to US $13.61 million. Amounts over this limit are taxed up to 40%. This exemption will fall to $5 million adjusted for inflation at the beginning of 2026 if Congress does not extend the current law beyond 2026. An additional yearly gift exclusion per recipient is available to everyone, regardless of citizenship status. In 2023, the gift exclusion amount is $17,000.

- Definition of a US citizen

US citizenship from birth is determined by two key principles: jus soli (right of the place of birth) and jus sanguinis (right of bloodline).

i Jus Soli, citizenship by birthplace: This rule says that anyone born within the US becomes a citizen automatically. This covers all 50 states, the District of Columbia, and most US territories. However, in American Samoa and Swains Island, people are usually US nationals, not citizens.[①] It is important to note that children born in the US to foreign diplomats do not get citizenship through jus soli.

ii Jus Sanguinis, citizenship by parentage: Under this principle, a child born outside the US can be a US citizen if one or both parents are US citizens at the time of the child's birth. The specific rules for this depend on a few things: whether the parents are married, how long the US citizen parent lived in the US before the child was born, and the year of the child's birth. For instance, if a child is born outside the US to married parents, where one is a US citizen and the other is a US national, the citizen parent must have lived in the US for at least five years, including two years after they turned fourteen.

Jus Soli and Jus Sanguinis often create "**accidental Americans**", individuals who are US citizens but are unaware of their US citizenship and are disconnected from American culture, politics, general way of life. Accidental Americans are obligated to pay US taxes even though they may never have lived in the US and may not even possess a US passport.

- Definition of a US domiciliary

The determination of whether a person is considered a US domiciliary is based on both their physical presence in the US and their intention to stay in the US indefinitely. Various factors are considered by the IRS to evaluate this intent, including:

i Duration and Frequency of Stay: The length of the individual's stay in the US, as well as the frequency of travel between the US and other countries, areevaluated.

ii Homes and Dwellings: The location, size, cost, and nature of the individual's homes or other dwellings are considered, as well as whether these places are owned or rented.

iii Location of Personal Possessions: The location of valuable and cherished personal possessions may indicate a person's intention to reside in a particular place.

---

① US nationals do not have as many rights and privileges as US citizens. For example, US nationals cannot vote in federal elections.

ⅳ Family and Friends: The location of an individual's family and close friends can suggest where the individual intends to stay.

ⅴ Community Ties: The places where the individual maintains church and club memberships and participates in community affairs can also show intent.

ⅵ Business and Professional Relationships: The location of the individual's business and professional relationships (e.g., legal, accounting, financial, etc.) can indicate where the individual plans to reside.

ⅶ Declarations of Residence or Intent: Declarations made in visa applications, wills, deeds of gift, trust instruments, letters, and oral statements are considered.

ⅷ Motivations: Personal motivations such as health, pleasure, and the desire to avoid war or political repression are also taken into account.

These factors are not exhaustive, and no single factor is determinative. The IRS looks at the totality of the individual's circumstances to assess their intent and therefore their domicile status. US tax advisors shouldbe involved to determine whether an individual is a US domiciliary.

Green card holders are legally "lawful permanent residents" of the US and may find it challenging to escape a US domicile. US tax advisors may sometimes assist with helping a green card holder arguen on-US domicile even though such a person possesses a green card.

1.2.2　US estate and gift tax for non-US citizens and domiciliaries

If an individual is neither a US citizen nor domiciliary, such individual only has to pay US estate and gift taxes on the transfer of property that is considered to be situated in the US ("**US-Situated Assets**"). The definition of US-situated assets (or US situs assets) can vary between US estate tax and US gift tax.

Examples of US-Situated Assets for estate tax:

ⅰ Real estate in the US: This covers all types of real property, like residential houses, commercial buildings, and, in some situations, leases.

ⅱ Tangible personal property in the US: These are items you can touch and see, like cars, artwork, jewelry, furniture, and collectibles in the US.

ⅲ Shares in US Corporations: Stocks of US Corporations are considered US-Situated Assets, no matter where the stock certificate is.

ⅳ Certain debts owed by US people or entities: This includes money owed by US citizens, companies, the government, or any state or territory in the US. But, if the interest on the debt qualifies for a special exemption from income taxes called the "portfolio interest exemption," then the debt will not be treated as a US-Situated Asset.

v   Cash in specific US bank accounts: Depending on the account type, money in US banks may be US-Situated Assets.

Examples of US-Situated Assets for gift tax:

i   Real estate in the US: Like the estate tax rule, this includes both residential and commercial properties.

ii   Tangible personal property in the US: Like the estate tax rule, physical items like cars, art, jewelry, and furniture in the US fall under this category.

iii   Intangible property: Unlike the estate tax rule, generally, intangible property is not considered to be a US-Situated Asset for gift tax. For example, shares in US Corporations are usually not US-Situated Assets for gift tax purposes.

These differences create planning opportunities. For example, an individual who gifts away US shares while he or she is alive does not have to pay US gift tax. However, if the same individual instead bequeaths US shares in his or her Last Will and Testament, such US shares would incur US estate tax.

1.3   US expatriation planning

US citizens or green card holders who held their green card for eight[①] of the last fifteen years ("**long-term green card holders**") are subject to US expatriation rules when they give up their US passport or green card. The expatriation tax rules currently in effect were introduced in mid-2008, effective for any individual whose "expatriation date" is on or after 17 June 2008. If they violate these rules, they would be considered as a "covered expatriate" and subject to the following taxes when they expatriate:

i   a mark-to-market "exit tax"

a   When someone becomes a covered expatriate, it's as if they sold everything they own in the world for its market value the day before they gave up their US citizenship. If the profit from this hypothetical sale is more than \$866,000[②], they have to pay US income tax on the amount that's over \$866,000.

ii   a current or withholding tax on deferred compensation items such as pensions and individual retirement accounts, and

iii   a withholding tax on taxable distributions from certain trusts.

Also, if a US citizen or US domiciliary receives a gift or inheritance (either directly or indirectly) from a covered expatriate, they have to pay an inheritance tax on it. This tax is

---

① Special rules apply in calculating the eight years.
② This exemption figure is indexed to inflation and changes annually. The \$866,000 figure is relevant for 2024.

charged at the highest rate for US estate tax, which is currently 40%.

1.3.1 Definition of a covered expatriate

A "covered expatriate" is defined as any US citizen who relinquishes his or her citizenship or any long-term green card holder who terminates his or her lawful permanent residency, if such an individual has:

i a net worth of USD $2,000,000 or more (the "**Net Worth Test**"),

ii had an average annual net income tax of more than USD $201,000 (this amount is adjusted for inflation so it will change over the years) over the five tax years before giving up their US citizenship or residency (the "**Tax Liability Test**"), and

iii cannot or do not confirm, under the penalties of perjury, that they have met all their US federal tax and reporting duties for the 5 years before giving up their US citizenship or residency (the "**Tax Certification Test**").

The decision if someone is a covered expatriate is made based on their status on their "expatriation date." This date is either when they officially give up US citizenship or, for long-term green card holders, when they stop being a lawful permanent resident for US federal income tax purposes.

For a US citizen who meets the Net Worth Test or the Tax Liability Test, there are two specific situations where they won't be classified as a covered expatriate.

i Exception for minors: If someone gives up their US citizenship before they turn 18.5 years old, and they haven't lived in the US for more than 10 tax years (as ascertained by the substantial presence test) before they give up their citizenship, they won't be considered a covered expatriate.

ii Exception for certain dual citizens: If a person was born with both US citizenship and the citizenship of another country, and they still have the non-US citizenship and pay taxes as a resident of that other country at the time they give up their US citizenship, and they haven't lived in the US for more than 10 out of the last 15 tax years (again, based on the substantial presence test) before they give up their US citizenship, they won't be considered a covered expatriate.

However, it is important to note that neither of these exceptions will apply if the person fails the Tax Certification Test-that is, if a person cannot show that he or she has complied with all US tax laws for the five years before giving up his or her citizenship, these exceptions will not avail him or her to a tax-free exit from the US.

1.4 Taxation of death benefit payouts from life insurance policies

For purposes of this section, we will assume that the life insurance policy discussed is

(1) compliant with section 7702①, (2) not a Modified Endowment Contract, (3) has not been previously "transferred for value," and (4) not under "investor control."②

Generally, under US tax law, death benefit payouts to a beneficiary of a life insurance policy are tax-free under section 101(a) regardless of whether the beneficiary is an individual, a limited liability company (an "**LLC**"), or a corporation. But any interest paid on the death benefit payouts is taxable.

An LLC formed in the US has a unique advantage when it comes to choosing how it is taxed in the US. This flexibility is one of the LLCs' key features. When an individual creates an LLC, by default, the LLC is treated as a "flow-through" entity for tax purposes.③ This means that the LLC itself does not pay taxes on its income. Instead, the income "flows through" to the owners (members) of the LLC, who then report and pay taxes on their share of the income on their personal tax returns. However, an LLC can choose to be taxed like a corporation instead. To do this, the LLC files a form with the IRS to elect corporate tax status. Once this election is made, the LLC pays corporate income tax on its earnings, and any dividends paid to members from those earnings can be taxed again on the members' personal tax returns. This ability to choose between flow-through taxation and corporate taxation gives LLCs significant flexibility to optimize their tax situation.

Example A.1

David is the sole member of a US LLC that does not make an election to be treated as a corporation for US tax purposes. The US LLC purchases life insurance on behalf of the life insured with the US LLC as the beneficiary. When the life insured passes away, the death benefits received by the US LLC are directly viewed as David's income since the US LLC is a flow-through entity that does not need to pay taxes itself. Because death benefits payouts from a life insurance policy are tax-free, David would not be taxed on the payout. The distribution of the payout to David from the US LLC would also be tax-free because it already "flowed through" to David upon the US LLC's receipt of the payout.

i Assume the same facts as the above example except that the US LLC makes an election to be treated as a corporation for US tax purposes. The death benefit payout to the US LLC would still be tax-free. But the distribution of payout to David could be

---

① Except as otherwise indicated, all section ("§") references herein are to sections of the U.S. Internal Revenue Code of 1986, as amended (the "Code"), and all regulation references are to the U.S. Treasury regulations promulgated ("Treas. Reg.") or proposed thereunder.

② More complex insurance concepts will be addressed in the next part.

③ The default characterization rule for foreign limited liability companies differs from US LLCs. Generally, foreign companies in which all their shareholders/members have limited liability would be treated as a corporation for US tax purposes by default. Such foreign entities can elect to be treated as a flow-through by filing a form with the IRS.

subject to tax if the distribution is treated as a dividend. A distribution by a corporation is treated as a dividend to the extent of the corporation's current and accumulated earnings and profits.

1.4.1 Employer-owned life insurance contracts

The general rule that death benefit payouts are tax-free does not apply to employerowned life insurance contracts ("**EOLIC**") unless the business meets specific conditions and keeps up with certain reporting requirements. If the business does not meet those conditions and requirements, the tax-free amount is limited to what the business has paid in premiums and other payments for the EOLIC.

Generally, an EOLIC is a life insurance contract that: (1) is owned by a person engaged in a trade or business under which that person (or a related person) is directly or indirectly a beneficiary under the contract; and (2) covers the life of an insured who is an employee with respect to the trade or business of the policyholder on the date the contract is issued.

If an EOLIC meets certain notice and consent requirements as discussed below, the limitation on tax-free death proceeds does not apply to:

i if the person who died (the insured) was connected to the policyholder (the business owning the policy) as:

a an employee at some point in the 12 months before they died, or

b at the time the policy was taken out, they were an officer, director, "highly compensated employee" (which includes independent contractors), or a highly compensated individual.

ii or if the money from the insurance policy, after the insured person's death, is used in either of these ways:

a paid to a family member of the insured, someone chosen by the insured to get the money (as long as it's not the business itself), a trust set up for the family or chosen person, or the insured person's estate, or

b used to buy part of the business (like shares or ownership interest) from anyone in (ii)(a) directly above.

The notice and consent requirements mandate that before the issuance of the contract:

i the employer must let the employee know in writing that they plan to insure the employee's life, including the highest amount the insurance could cover when the policy begins,

ii the employee must agree in writing to be insured under this policy and also agree that the insurance can continue even if they leave the job, and

iii the employer must tell the employee in writing that, if the employee passes away, the employer (as the policyholder) will get the money from the insurance.

US tax advisors should be involved in determining whether an insurance contract is an

EOLIC and whether the death benefits of such EOLIC can still qualify for tax-free treatment.

1.5 Relevant US income tax concepts for non-US Persons

Unlike a US Person who must pay US income tax on all their income from around the world (this includes capital gains), a non-US Person only has to pay US income tax on two specific types of income:

i Certain US-source income: This is known as fixed, determinable, annual, or periodical income that comes from the US ("**FDAP Income**"). An example is dividends from a US Corporation. Interest from a US Corporation falls within this type of income unless the interest qualifies for a special exemption from income taxes called the "portfolio interest exemption." However, this usually does not include capital gains.

ii Income connected with a US trade or business: This includes any income (like capital gains or profits from selling US real estate) that is effectively connected with a US trade or business, known as effectively connected income or "**ECI**", no matter where the income is earned.

When a non-US Person earns FDAP Income, this income is taxed by the US at a rate of 30% on the gross amount (that means the total income before any deductions). But, this rate can be reduced or even eliminated through narrow exceptions under US law or an applicable income tax treaty.

On the other hand, if a non-US Person earns ECI, this is taxed on the net amount, which is the total income minus any deduction.

It is important to note that the application of US income tax on non-US Persons is extremely complex. This summary cannot cover all the rules and nuances of US income tax for non-US Persons.

Memo 2: Explanation of Certain US Federal Tax Concepts[①]

2.1 US tax benefits of a life insurance policy

Here are several US tax benefits of a life insurance policy:

i Tax deferral: For certain life insurance policies with an investment component, the gains from the investments and reinvestment of the gains within the insurance policy are

---

① For clarity, US state and local taxes are not within the scope of this memo. Further, except as otherwise indicated, we are not considering situations where a life insurance policy is issued by a US life insurance company and held by a non-US Person.

generally not taxed until the policyholder surrenders the policy or withdraws the money. In contrast, if a US Person[①] held the investments directly, the US Person would have to pay US income taxes on the gains from the investments upon the sale of the investments. Thus, the increase in the cash value of the policy because of the investment component of the policy provides tax deferral.

ii Death benefit payouts: As discussed in Section 1.4 of the Previous Memo, the death benefit payouts to the beneficiary would not be subject to *US income taxes* regardless of who purchased the policy, who the insured individual is, or who the beneficiary is. However, if the policy was previously transferred for value as discussed in section 2.6.3 below, then the death benefit payouts to the beneficiary could be subject to US income tax.

iii Mitigating US tax issues for ownership of certain non-US entities for policyholders: US Persons must report ownership of certain non-US entities[②], and in certain situations, such US Persons would have a US income tax liability for the income earned by such non-US entities or would be subject to punitive anti-deferral rule upon the sale of such non-US entities collectively, the **US tax burden for owning non-US entities**. However, if the US Person owns a life insurance policy that holds non-US entities in the investment component of the policy, such US Person would generally not be subject to the US tax burden for owning non-US entities. Note that this benefit can only be achieved if the policy satisfies the "investor control" requirement discussed below.

2.2　General anti-avoidance rules for life insurance policies

Due to the benefits discussed above, life insurance policies are occasionally misused as covert investment vehicles, potentially allowing individuals to evade taxes on investment income. To counteract this misuse, many leading onshore countries, such as the US, have implemented various anti-avoidance regulations. These rules aim to preserve the fundamental difference between insurance policies and investments. The following outlines key anti-avoidance measures in the US concerning life insurance policies:

2.2.1　Section 7702[③]

Section 7702 was enacted to ensure that life insurance policies are primarily used for their

---

① Defined in the Memo 1

② For example, any foreign entity that is considered a "passive foreign investment company" or a "controlled foreign corporation" under US tax rules. The rules to determine whether a foreign corporation is a passive foreign investment company or a controlled foreign corporation are beyond the scope of this memo.

③ Except as otherwise indicated, all section (" § ") references herein are to sections of the U.S. Internal Revenue Code of 1986, as amended (the "**Code**"), and all regulation references are to the U.S. Treasury regulations promulgated ("**Treas. Reg.**") or proposed thereunder.

intended purpose-providing a death benefit-rather than as taxadvantaged investment tools. If a contract qualifies as a life insurance contract under §7702, its death benefit is usually not subject to income tax. Also, any interest or other earnings that build up in the contract's cash value are typically not taxed until there is a distribution (like a withdrawal or loan) before the insured person's death.

For a life insurance policy to be treated as a life insurance policy for §7702 purposes (and thus be eligible for all the tax benefits discussed above), it must first qualify as a "life insurance contract"[①] according to applicable laws, and then it must pass one of two specific actuarial tests discussed below. Because "applicable law" includes foreign law, a contract issued in a foreign country would need to be a life insurance contract under the laws of that foreign country.

Additionally, a life insurance contract must meet one of the following two actuarial tests to qualify as a life insurance contract for US tax purposes:

 i The Cash Value Accumulation Test("**CVAT**"): Acontract will satisfy the CVAT if, by the terms of the contract, the contract's cash surrender value ("**CSV**") does not at any time exceed the net single premium ("**NSP**") that would be required to fund the contract's death benefits. For example, when a life insurance contract starts, there must be no possibility that uncertain factors like dividends, extra interest, or lower-than-expected charges could make the contract's CSV go higher than its NSP at any point. Also, the policyholder should not have any rights in the contract that could let the CSV exceed the NSP at any time. Even though the CVAT mainly looks at the terms of a life insurance contract, it is also essential that the actual performance of the contract sticks to these terms. This is to make sure that the contract's CSV never goes above its NSP. If the contract is operated in a way that's not outlined in its terms, this alone can lead to a failure under the CVAT. Also, if in practice the CSV ends up exceeding the NSP, the contract will not meet the CVAT requirements, even if its terms seem compliant on the surface. This test essentially limits the amount of cash value that a policy can accumulate relative to its death benefit.

 ii The Guideline Premium Limitation ("**GPL**") and Cash Value Corridor ("**CVC**") test: The GPL/CVC test, different from the CVAT, does not require specific terms in the contract. Instead, it needs to be met through the actual operation of the contract at all times. Due to this feature, many consider the GPL/CVC test as the default test. If a contract's terms do not pass the CVAT, then it automatically falls under the GPL/CVC test to decide if it

---

 ① In this memo, we will use "contract" and "policy" interchangeably. However, it's important to note that the official term used in the Code is "life insurance contract."

should be treated as a life insurance contract for US tax purposes and when any noncompliance might occur. Specifically, the contract must satisfy the following two requirements:

a Guideline premium requirements: This sets limits on the premiums that can be paid into the policy in relation to the death benefit. It ensures that the premiums paid do not disproportionately exceed the amount needed to support the death benefit. A contract meets the guideline premium requirements if, at any point, the total premiums paid do not go over the GPL set for that time. A contract's GPL is the larger amount between the "guideline single premium" and the total of the "guideline level premiums." The guideline single premium is the initial premium payment that covers the future benefits under the contract. The guideline level premium, subject to specific minimum rate computation rules, is a consistent yearly amount. The specific formulas to calculate the guideline single premium and the guideline level premiums are beyond the scope of this memo.

b CVC: This requires that a contract's death benefit be at least a specified percentage of its CSV. To meet the CVC, a life insurance contract's death benefit must be at least a certain "applicable percentage" of its CSV. The "applicable percentage" is determined based on a specific table provided in Section 7702(d)(2).

Note that both CVAT and the GPL/CVC test are actuarial tests and would require an actuary to determine whether a policy would satisfy either of the two tests.

If a contract subject to § 7702 is a life insurance contract under applicable law and fails the requirements of § 7702, it loses the usual tax deferral benefits that life insurance contracts get. In such a case, the income on the contract, as defined in § 7702(g), will start to accumulate each year from when the contract first failed to comply. Income on the contract for this purpose is defined as the excess of the sum of the increase in the net surrender value during the taxable year and the cost of life insurance protection for such year, over the premiums paid during such year. Also, in the year when the contract fails to comply, all the income that has built up in previous years is considered as received or accumulated by the taxpayer (and thus subject to tax). However, the net amount at risk in the contract, which is the difference between the death benefit payout and the net surrender value, is still not taxed under § 101. This means that part of the death benefit payout from such noncomplying contracts is still tax-exempt to the extent it exceeds the cash surrender value, just like it is with contracts that do comply with § 7702.

2.2.2 Modified Endowment Contract and Distributions Prior to Death

As discussed above, if a contract is a life insurance contract as defined in § 7702, its death benefit generally will be tax-free from an US income tax perspective, and interest and other earnings accruing on its cash value generally are not taxed unless a distribution, transfer, or withdrawal is made before the insured's death. The application of taxes to any distributions taken out of a life insurance policy before the insured's death depends on whether the policy is a modified endowment contract ("**MEC**") under §7702A. Accordingly, life insurance contracts that satisfy the requirements of §7702 can be of two types: MECs or non-MECs.

A MEC has the same tax-free treatment for death benefits as life insurance policies, but the way it handles distributions (including loans) is less favorable. Congress created MEC rules to differentiate tax treatments between life insurance contracts that are funded quickly (and are more investment-focused) and other types of life insurance contracts.

Specifically, when an individual takes money out of a MEC, tax law regards such withdrawal as first a withdrawal of income then second as a recovery of the investment in the contract. This is the opposite for non-MECs, where the law treats distributions first as a recovering of the investment in the contract. Accordingly, distributions from a MEC would be taxable income to the extent the contract's cash value exceeds its investment in the contract. This also applies to any loans taken from a MEC, as well as when the policy is assigned or pledged as collateral. Additionally, if distributions are made within two years before a contract becomes a MEC, they are treated as if they were made by a MEC. Further, an additional 10% penalty tax may apply to distributions of income from a MEC.

The definition of a MEC mainly hinges on whether the premiums paid into the policy are faster than what is allowed under a "7-pay test" under §7702A(b). The 7-pay test generally provides that a contract will fail this test (and thus the contract would be considered a MEC) if the accumulated amount paid under the contract at any time during the first seven contract years exceeds the cumulative sum of the net level premiums which would have been paid to that time if the contract provided for paid-up future benefits after the payment of seven level annual premiums.①

Additionally, two other rules often come into play when applying §7702A:

i Reduction in benefits rule (§7702A(c)(2)): This rule requires the 7-pay test to be reapplied retroactively if there's a reduction in the policy's benefits. Basically, if the benefits under the contract decrease, the 7-pay test is recalculated based on these lowered benefits.

ii Material change rule (§7702A(c)(3)): If this rule applies, the contract is treated as if it's a new policy for the purposes of the law. This means the 7-pay test starts over. This rule kicks in if there's a significant change to the policy, like an increase in coverage or other major amendment.

---

① An in-depth discussion of the calculations for the 7-pay test is beyond the scope of this memo.

2.2.3 Investor control

The "investor control" doctrine posits that if a policyholder has enough control or rights ("incidents of ownership") over the assets in a separate account tied to a variable life insurance, then the policyholder, not the insurance company, will be seen as the owner of those assets for US tax purposes. If this doctrine applies, the policyholder would not be able to mitigate the US tax burden for owning non-US entities assuming the policy holders non-US entities.

The IRS has issued several revenue rulings identifying that the critical "incident of ownership" is the power to choose the specific investments in the account. The general policy is that the policyholders must not control individual investment decisions. Other "incidents of ownership" identified in these rulings include the power to vote on securities in the separate account, exercise various rights or options related to these investments, withdraw or otherwise take money out of the account, and gain other forms of "effective benefit" from the assets.

Here are some examples from the IRS revenue rulings:

i In Revenue Ruling 81-225, the IRS considered five situations. In the first four situations, mutual fund shares were accessible for the general public to purchase, not limited to just policyholders who purchased an annuity contract with the life insurance company. In these cases, the policyholder had the ability to initially choose the fund for the separate account's investments and had the flexibility to change their investment among the selected funds periodically.

In these four situations, the IRS found that the insurance company acted mainly as a go-between for the policyholders and their mutual fund shares. Since the policyholder's situation was almost the same as if they had bought the mutual fund shares directly, the IRS determined that the policyholder had enough control over the investments to be considered their owner for US tax purposes.

However, the IRS reached a different conclusion in the fifth scenario. In this case, the insurance company controlled the investments in the mutual fund shares, which were solely meant as an investment tool for the insurance company to fulfill its annuity contract obligations. Since these shares were not open to the general public and could only be accessed through buying an annuity contract, the IRS viewed the insurance company as the actual owner of these assets.

ii In Revenue Ruling 82-54, the IRS examined a case where the segregated account tied to variable policies included three funds, each investing in different assets: common stocks, bonds, and money-market instruments. The insurance company managed these funds, which were not open for sale to the general public. Policyholders were allowed to choose and change their investments among these three funds.

The IRS stated that "for the insurance company to be considered the owner of the mutual fund shares, policyholders must not control individual investment decisions." Based on this principle, the IRS determined that the insurance company was the actual owner of the assets in the separate account. The reasoning was that the policyholders' ability to select among general investment categories like stocks, bonds, or money market instruments (at the initial purchase or later) did not amount to enough control over specific investment decisions to attribute ownership of the mutual fund shares to the policyholders.

iii In Revenue Ruling 2003-91, a life insurance company offered variable life insurance and annuity contracts funded by a separate account divided into 12 subaccounts. Each subaccount had a distinct investment focus, like moneymarket, large company growth, telecommunications, international growth, or emerging markets. These funds weren't sold to the general public and met the diversification requirements of §817.

The policyholder could change how their premiums were divided among these subaccounts at any time and could transfer funds between them. However, all the investment choices for the subaccounts were made by an independent investment manager hired by the insurance company. The IRS made it clear that policyholders couldn't choose or suggest specific investments for the subaccounts, communicate with investment officers about selecting investments, or have any deal with the insurance company or investment manager about the investment strategy or assets in a subaccount.

In summary, while the policyholder could decide how to distribute funds among the subaccounts, all decisions about the actual securities in each subaccount were made solely by the insurance company or its investment manager. Under these conditions, the IRS determined that for US income tax purposes, the insurance company was considered the owner of the assets in the separate accounts. This ruling was meant to provide a "safe harbor" for taxpayers to follow.

Even though IRS revenue rulings are generally not binding authority, US courts would still provide a certain level of deference to the rulings. Also, several court cases follow the investor control doctrine. For example, in Webber v. Commissioner[①], the court held that the taxpayer's level of control over the investments in the separate accounts of the life insurance policies was such that he was effectively the owner of those assets normally accorded to life insurance contracts for US tax purposes. As a result, the tax benefits normally accorded to life insurance contracts were lost.

The determination of whether the investor control doctrine applies depends on the facts

---

① 144 T. C. 324 (2015).

and circumstances. As such, the client should be proactive in consulting US tax advisors regarding the application of this doctrine.

2.3 Tax implications of the life insurance policy in America

2.3.1 Application of US estate tax on life insurance proceeds[①]

Section 2042 deals with the inclusion of life insurance proceeds in the estate of the deceased. It applies to the following situations:

i Ownership at death: If the decedent owned any life insurance policies on their life at the time of death, the proceeds of those policies are included in the gross estate. This means that if the deceased person had the right to change beneficiaries, surrender or cancel the policy, borrow against it, or otherwise control the policy, the proceeds are considered part of their estate for estate tax purposes.

ii Life insurance on another person: If the decedent had any incidents of ownership in a life insurance policy on someone else's life, the proceeds from that policy are also included in the decedent's gross estate. This is less common but can happen in certain business or family planning arrangements. Note that the incidents of ownership in this context differ from the incidents of ownership under the investor control doctrine discussed above.

iii Transfers of life insurance policies under §2035: If a decedent transfers ownership of a life insurance policy within three years of their death, the proceeds from that policy are included in their estate if the policy would have been subjected to §2042 in either of the situations described above assuming the decedent held the policy on the decedent's date of death.[②]

Generally, this only applies to US citizens or domiciliaries but there may be rare situations where this could apply to non-US citizens or domiciliaries. The executor of the client's estate should seek US tax advice regarding this issue.

2.3.2 Application of US gift tax on life insurance proceeds

US gift tax could apply to the value of the life insurance proceeds. For example, if Daughter is the owner of a $2 million insurance policy on Mother's life and has named herself and Brother as equal beneficiaries, and assuming Mother has successfully divested herself of all incidents of ownership in the policy (and has lived for three years following the divestiture), there won't be an estate tax issue for Mother upon her death. However, at Mother's death, it would be considered as though Daughter has made a $1 million dollar gift to Brother. This outcome is because Daughter, being the policy owner, had the option to be

---

[①] Note that a discussion of the "Generation Skipping Transfer Tax" is beyond the scope of this memo.
[②] A detailed discussion of §2035 is beyond the scope of this memo.

the sole beneficiary but chose to include Brother, thereby effectively transferring half the proceeds to him at Mother's death. No gift is considered to have been made by Daughter before Mother's death since she could change beneficiaries at any time before that, assuming the beneficiary designation was revocable.

2.3.3 Cash value withdrawals and policy loans

Generally, if a life insurance contract is not a MEC, cash withdrawals up to the amount of the premiums paid (the policy's "basis") are typically tax-free. However, withdrawals that exceed the policy's basis are taxed as ordinary income. Additionally, policyholders can often take out loans against the cash value of their life insurance (assuming it is a non-MEC). These loans are generally not taxable as long as the policy is in force. However, if the policy lapses or is surrendered while there's an outstanding loan, the loan amount exceeding the policy's basis becomes taxable. Also, if the loan is not considered bona fide debt for US tax purposes, then it may be considered a distribution or withdrawal.

If a client wishes to withdraw cash or obtain a policy loan, the client should seek tax advice and fully understand the potential tax consequences before withdrawing cash or obtaining a loan.

2.3.4 Transfer of policy ownership

Transferring ownership of a life insurance policy could be subject to US taxes depending on the facts and circumstances.

Application of US gift tax

US gift tax would apply if a policyholder transferred a life insurance policy with cash surrender value to a third-party that is not the spouse of the policyholder. The cash surrender value would be the value of the gift and if such value exceeds the annual gift tax exclusion[①], the policyholder would have a US gift tax filing obligation (and potentially a US gift tax liability if the policyholder already used up their lifetime exemption amount[②]) if the policyholder were a US citizen or domiciliary. If the policyholder is a non-US citizen or domiciliary and the third-party is a US Person, the third-party may have a US tax filing obligation if the value exceeds a certain threshold[③].

Application of US income tax

US income tax would apply if a policyholder sold their policy to a third-party for valuable consideration. The policyholder would recognize income to the extent the consideration exceeds the policyholder's adjusted basis in the policy.

---

① This exclusion is discussed in Section 1.2.1 of the Previous Memo.
② The lifetime exemption amount is discussed in section 1.2.1 of the Previous Memo.
③ See Form 3520 and the related instructions.

Example A.2

B, a US Person, sold his life insurance contract to C for $50,000 on Date X. As of date X, B held his life insurance contract for over one year and paid total premiums of $40,000 under the life insurance contract. Also, the contract had a cash surrender value of $46,000.

Accordingly, B must recognize $10,000 of income. Under the "substitute for ordinary income" doctrine, B would have ordinary income of $6,000 because the inside build-up under the contract ($46,000 cash surrender value minus $40,000 basis). B would have long-term capital gains of $4,000 ($10,000 income minus $6,000 ordinary income).

The transferred for value rule

Generally, a beneficiary does not include amounts received (whether in a single sum or otherwise) under a life insurance contract as income, if such amounts are paid by reason of the death of the insured as discussed above and in Previous Memo. However, the "transferred for value" rule of § 101 (a) (2) generally provides that in the case of a transfer for valuable consideration, by assignment or otherwise, of a life insurance contract or any interest therein, the amount excluded from income shall not exceed an amount equal to the sum of the actual value of the consideration paid and the premiums and other amounts subsequently paid by the transferee (i.e., the person who purchased the contract from the original policyholder). This rule does not apply in the case of a transfer involving a carryover basis or in the case of a transfer to the insured, a partner of the insured, a partnership in which the insured is a partner, or to a corporation in which the insured is a shareholder or officer.

Example A.3

On June 15, 2009, Y, a US Person, purchased from X, a US Person, for $20,000 a life insurance contract (satisfying the requirements of § 7702) on the life of X. The contract was originally issued by IC, a US corporation, to x on January 1, 2002. The contract was a level premium fifteen-year term life insurance contract without cash surrender value. At the time of purchase, the remaining term of the contract was 7 years, 6 months, and 15 days. The monthly premium for the contract was $500, due and payable on the first day of each month. Y named himself as the beneficiary because Y had the right to change the beneficiary as the owner of the contract.

Y had no insurable interest in X's life and, except for the purchase of the contract, Y had no relationship to X and would suffer no economic loss upon X's death. Y purchased the contract to profit. The likelihood that Y would allow the contract to lapse by failing to pay any of the remaining premiums was remote.

On December 31, 2010, X died, and IC paid $100,000 under the life insurance contract to Y because of X's death. Through that date, X had paid monthly premiums totaling $9,000 to keep the contract in force.

Because Y purchased the contract from X in exchange for $20,000, Y's acquisition of the contract was a "transfer for a valuable consideration" within the meaning of § 101 (a)(2). None of the exceptions to § 101(a)(2) applies. Accordingly, § 101(a)(1) excludes from Y's gross income the amount received because of X's death, but § 101 (a)(2) limits the exclusion to the sum of the actual value of the consideration paid for the transfer ($20,000) and other amounts paid by Y ($9,000), or $29,000. Y therefore must include in gross income $71,000, which is the difference betweenthe total death benefit received ($100,000) and the amount excluded under § 101 ($29,000).

Further, the $71,000 of income would be treated as ordinary income because neither the surrender of a life insurance or annuity contract nor the receipt of a death benefit from the issuer under the terms of the contract produces a capital gain.

2.3.5 Tax issues arising from changes in the policyholder's or beneficiary's tax status

For example, if a policyholder who is a non-US Person living outside of the US immigrates to the US and becomes a US Person, the policyholder would have complex US tax liability and compliance issues if the policy were captured by any of the antiavoidance rules discussed above in section 2.2 of this memo. Before immigrating to US, clients are recommended to have a proactive discussion with their tax advisor about the subsequent tax issues of the policy in force. Many US tax advisors provide this "pre-immigration" service.

2.4 Tax implications of the foreign life assurance policy

2.4.1 The insurance excise tax

Foreign-issued insurance products encounter an additional challenge due to the US excise tax mandated by § 4371. This tax applies to a wide range of insurance and reinsurance contracts. Specifically, for life insurance contracts, the tax is set at 1% of the paid premiums, as stipulated in § 4371(2). This rate is also valid for reinsurance contracts that provide coverage for life insurance policies or annuity contracts.

The excise tax is typically levied on policies issued by a "foreign insurer," defined in § 4372(a) as an insurer or reinsurer who is either a nonresident alien individual, a foreign partnership, or a foreign corporation. However, this definition excludes foreign governments, municipal entities, or other corporations that exercise taxing power.

Life insurance policies that may be subject to this excise tax are those made, continued, or renewed concerning the life of a US citizen or resident, as outlined in § 4372(e).

Nevertheless, there are exceptions to this excise tax. It does not apply to any amount effectively connected with the conduct of a trade or business in the US, except when the amount is exempt from §882(a) due to a treaty with the US, as mentioned in §4373(1). Moreover, the tax also does not apply to entirely foreign retrocessions, which are premiums paid on reinsurance policies issued by one foreign reinsurer to another foreign insurer or reinsurer.

2.4.2 Report of Foreign Bank and Financial Accounts

The regulations under the Bank Secrecy Act of 1970, as updated, require US persons (excluding foreign subsidiaries of US persons) with financial interests in or authority over foreign financial accounts, including bank and securities accounts, to report these relationships to the IRS Commissioner annually. This reporting is done using FinCEN Form 114, commonly known as the FBAR (Report of Foreign Bank and Financial Accounts). This form must be filed electronically by October 15 each year for accounts that exceed $10,000 at any time during the previous year. Failing to file the FBAR timely can result in substantial IRS penalties.

Furthermore, the definition of "other financial account" was expanded in regulations finalized in February 2011 to include life insurance policies with a cash value. Therefore, if a US person holds a cash-value life insurance contract from a foreign insurer, this is considered an interest in a financial account. If the combined value of all the US Person's accounts exceeds $10,000 at any point during a year, an FBAR filing is required. For these purposes, the account value is generally based on the contract's cash value, typically not considering any surrender charges. The obligation to file the FBAR lies with the policyholder, not the beneficiaries[①].

If the client is a US Person, the client should discuss the reporting requirement of their ownership of foreign-issued life insurance with a US tax advisor.

2.4.3 Reporting under §6038D

Section 6038D, introduced by the Hiring Incentives to Restore Employment (HIRE) Act of 2010, effective for tax years after March 18, 2010, mandates reporting requirements for US Persons holding interests in "specified foreign financial assets" if the total value exceeds certain threshold amount during the tax year. The threshold amount differs depending on several factors including where the US Person is located and whether the US Person is married[②].

The scope of "specified foreign financial assets" is quite broad, potentially including cash-value life insurance contracts held for investment purposes, especially those with issuers or counterparties that are not US persons. This broad definition aligns with the FBAR requirements,

---

① For more detailed information, you can refer to the specific regulations and guidance provided by the IRS and the Financial Crimes Enforcement Network (FinCEN).

② See the IRS website (FAQ regarding Form 8938): https://www.irs.gov/businesses/corporations/do-i-need-to-fileform-8938-statement-of-specified-foreign-financial-assets (last visited Jan 6, 2024).

under which cash-value life insurance contracts are also reportable. Regulations confirm that both FBAR and Section 6038D encompass reporting of these financial vehicles.

If the client is a US Person, the client should discuss the reporting requirement of their ownership of foreign-issued life insurance with a US tax advisor.

Memo 3: Application of US Federal Income Tax in Certain Scenarios①

3.1 Assumptions

Before we dive into the scenarios, we will be making the following assumptions about all the scenarios:

• The life insurance policy (the "**Policy**") is treated as a life insurance policy under local law and does not have a net surrender value;

• The Policy neither allows for cash withdrawal or loans against the Policy (including using the Policy as collateral);

• The "investor control" doctrine as discussed in section "investor control" does not apply;

• The policy owner is not a US domiciliary as discussed in section "Definition of a US domiciliary" of the Memo 1;

• The policy owner purchased the Policy directly from the life insurance company;

• None of the persons in the scenarios are "cover expatriates" as discussed in the Memo 1; and

• The Policy is not considered an "employer-owned life insurance contract" as discussed in Memo 1.

3.2 Scenario 1

The Policy:

It is a life insurance policy issued by a Bermuda Life Insurance Company.

Policy Owner:

a Non-US Person②, who is also the payor of the Policy.

Beneficiary:

a US Person as defined in Memo 1.

---

① For clarity, US state and local taxes are not within the scope of this memo. Furthermore, this should not be construed to be tax advice and cannot be relied on by any persons.

② the definition of a "US Person" can be found in Memo 1

Questions:

Regardless of whether the Policy is § 7702① compliant or not, would the US beneficiary be subject to US income tax upon the receipt of any amount paid on the death of the insurance under the Policy②?

Under § 7702(g)(2), US income tax should not apply to the death benefits paid out in this scenario assuming the insured is also the policy owner.

3.3　Scenario 2

Same facts as Scenario 1 except that: (1) the insured of the Policy is a US Person who is not the owner or the beneficiary of the Policy, and (2) the beneficiary of the Policy is a non-US Person.

Since the beneficiary is a non-US Person, US income tax should not apply to the death benefits paid out in this scenario. Further, even if US income tax somehow did apply, § 7702(g)(2) should still be applicable to eliminate any US income taxes in this scenario.

The insurance excise tax may apply in this situation. Please see the section "The insurance excise tax" of Memo 2.

3.4　Scenario 3

Same facts as Scenario 2 except that: the beneficiary of the Policy is a US Person.

Under § 7702(g)(2), US income tax should not apply to the death benefits paid out in this scenario. However, in cases where the policy owner can change the beneficiary, US gift tax may apply in a situation where the policy owner, the insured, and the beneficiary are different people. Please see the section "Application of US gift tax on life insurance proceeds" of Memo 2.

The insurance excise tax may apply in this situation. Please see the section "The insurance excise tax" of Memo 2.

---

① Except as otherwise indicated, all section ("§") references herein are to sections of the U.S. Internal Revenue Code of 1986, as amended (the "**Code**"), and all regulation references are to the U.S. Treasury regulations promulgated ("**Treas. Reg.**") or proposed thereunder.

② We have assumed that the question refers to US income taxes because US estate and gift tax applies to the estate of the deceased or the person making the gift and not the beneficiary.

附录 B：加拿大税务意见

Canadian Tax Opinions

Stephen Harwood | 2023.12.17

1 Tax Resident Status

1.1 Criteria for determining the tax residency of an individual in Canada

Canadian tax residents are subject to Canadian income tax on worldwide income. Relief from double taxation is provided through Canada's international tax treaties, as well as via foreign tax credits and deductions for foreign taxes paid on income derived from non-Canadian sources. In addition, Canadian tax residents are subject to reporting obligations under the Income Tax Act (Canada) (the "Act"). For example, Canadian tax residents who own foreign investment properties whose total cost exceeds CAD100,000 must file an information return (Form T1135) each year they own such properties.

Exceptions apply to certain types of assets, such as those held in a foreign pension plan. Canadian-resident individuals, corporations or trust must file an annual information return (Form T1134) if they own any a foreign affiliate (FA) at any time during the tax year. If a Canadian tax resident has received distributions or loans from a non-resident trust, a Form T1142 must be filed for each non-resident trust.

In effect, an individual will be deemed to be a resident of Canada throughout a taxation year (other than special cases such as the year a person becomes or ceases to be tax resident, the taxation year for individuals in Canada is generally a calendar year ending 31 December) if the person:

- is physically present in Canada in the year for 183 days or more; this test will catch stays of a temporary nature so the reason for the stay will not be relevant; or
- was ordinarily resident in Canada during that year.

The principle of "ordinarily resident" is a question of facts and has been interpreted by Canadian courts to mean residence in the course of the customary mode of life of the person concerned, as contrasted with special or occasional or causal residence (Thomson v. M. N. R., 2 D. T. C. 812 (S. C. C.)). In determining an individual's ordinary residence, all relevant facts must be considered. Residential ties of particular significance include the maintenance of a dwelling place available for the individual's occupation even during his absence from Canada and the residence of the individual's spouse and dependants. Secondary factors include social and business ties and personal property, such as memberships in clubs and religious organisations, directorship in a Canadian corporation, Canadian driver's licenses, vehicle registration, and provincial medical insurance coverage.

Finally, an individual can be considered to be a resident of both Canada and of another country under that country's domestic tax laws. In these cases, Canada's tax treaties often provide "tie-breaker" rules for determining residency, such that an individual is considered resident in the jurisdiction with which the individual has closer personal, economic and social connections although other factors may be relevant too. If an individual "tie-break" into a country which has entered into a tax agreement with Canada, the individual would be treated as a non-resident for all purposes of the Act. For example, the "tie-breaker rules" in the Canada-China Income Tax Agreement primarily rely on the following tests and are applied progressively until a determination can be made:

- permanent home test;
- centre of vital interests test;
- habitual abode test; and
- nationality test.

Example B.1

Mr. A holds a Canadian passport, but he and his family live and work in Hong Kong year-round. Mr. A does not live in Canada and does not have any Canadian property, bank accounts, or other assets, nor does he have Canadian provincial medical insurance coverage or a Canadian driver's license. In this case, it is likely that Mr. A is not a Canadian tax resident, but a Hong Kong tax resident.

1.2 Criteria for determining the tax residency of a corporation in Canada

A corporation will be deemed to be a resident of Canada if it was incorporated in Canada after 26 April 1965 pursuant to subsection 250(4) of the Act.

A corporation which is incorporated outside Canada will be considered a resident of Canada for purposes of the Act (and hence its worldwide income would be subject to Canadian tax) if its central management and control is exercised in Canada. Determining the location of the central management and control is a question of facts. The place where meetings of directors are held to conduct the business of the corporation and the residency of the directors are given substantial weight.

A corporation incorporated outside of Canada but with its central management and control situated both in and outside Canada will be deemed to be a non-resident of Canada if it qualifies as a non-resident of Canada under the applicable treaty tiebreaker rules in Canada's tax treaties. Each of the Canada-China Income Tax Agreement and the Canada-Hong Kong Income Tax Agreement provides if a corporation is considered to be a resident of both Canada and of another treaty jurisdiction, the competent authorities should determine the corporation's tax residency by mutual agreement.

1.3 Criteria for determining the tax residency of a trust in Canada

A trust is a Canadian resident for tax purposes if the powers and discretions of the trustee are exercised in Canada. This is a question of facts. In most cases where the trust is discretionary in nature and the affairs of the trust are indeed managed and administered by the trustee, the residence of the appointed trustee is the sufficient basis for determining the residence of the trust.

Notwithstanding that a trust is managed from outside Canada, a non-resident trust will be considered to be a Canadian resident pursuant to subsection 94(3) of the Act and will be taxable on its worldwide income associated with the resident portion of its assets for its 2007 and later taxation years if the trust has a "resident contributor" or a "resident beneficiary" at a "specified time".

In this regard, a "resident contributor" is defined in subsection 94(1) of the Act to mean a Canadian resident person who has made a "contribution" to the trust.

On the other hand, the definition of a "resident beneficiary" requires that two conditions be satisfied:

- there must be a "connected contributor"; and
- there must be a beneficiary of the trust who is a Canadian resident.

A "connected contributor" is defined to mean any person who has made a "contribution" to the trust other than persons who would not be considered to be contributors if "contributions" made by them during a "non-resident time" were ignored. In order to fit into the "non-resident time" definition, a person must not have been resident in Canada at any time during the period of 60 months prior to the contribution to the trust. "Specified time" means the end of the taxation year of the trust unless the trust was terminated during the year, in which case the specified time means the time that is immediately before such termination.

A transaction which falls under the definition of "contribution" in subsection 94(1) or the deemed contribution rules in subsection 94(2) of the Act will be considered a contribution to a trust. Generally, a "contribution" means a transfer or loan of property to the trust by a particular person, other than a transfer or loan on arm's length terms.

Due to the complexity of the rules, it is beyond the scope of this chapter to summarize all the transactions that may constitute deemed contributions under subsection 94(2) of the Act. However, the following examples will illustrate how these rules are intended to operate:

- Paragraph 94(2)(a) of the Act deems a transfer of property (other than an "arm's length transfer") to be a direct transfer to a trust if the property is transferred from one person to another and, as a result of the transfer, the fair market value of the property of the trust increases or the liabilities of the trust decrease.

- Paragraph 94(2)(c) of the Act deems a transfer or loan of property from a person to another person (referred to as the "intermediary") to be a direct transfer to a trust where the trust holds property the fair market value of which is derived from property held by the intermediary if certain conditions apply.

- Paragraph 94(2)(f) applies where any service (other than an "exempt service") is rendered after 22 June 2000 by a person to, for or on behalf of another person. In these circumstances, the person rendering the service is deemed to have transferred property to the other person unless either (a) the service rendered is an "exempt service" or (b) the relevant trust is an "exempt foreign trust".

- Paragraph 94(2)(n) stipulates that where a particular trust makes a contribution to another trust, the contribution is deemed to have been made jointly by the particular trust and each person or partnership that is a contributor to that particular trust.

Example B.2

1. Mr. A is a tax resident of Singapore. He has never been a Canadian tax resident and does not plan to relocate to Canada. His son B has immigrated to Canada with his wife and children. Mr. A settled a discretionary trust under the laws of Singapore and does not reserve any powers as the settlor. The trustee of the trust is a resident of

Singapore. The beneficiaries are B and his children who are all tax residents of Canada. If the Canadian resident beneficiaries do not make any contributions to the trust and do not play any role in the trust other than being appointed as the discretionary beneficiaries and subject to the application of general anti-avoidance rules under the Act, it is likely that trust will not be considered to be a Canadian resident pursuant to subsection 94(3) of the Act. This trust is typically known as a "Granny Trust".

2. If however Mr. A moves to Canada to reunite with his son two years after the settlement of the trust, the trust will become a tax resident of Canada.

2　Estate and Gift Tax

There are no federal or provincial inheritance, estate, orgifttaxes. However, a Canadian tax resident is deemed to have disposed of any capital property immediately before death. This can result in a capital gain tax. In addition, most provinces impose probate fees or administrative charges for probating a will.

The death benefit payment from a life insurance policy to an individual beneficiary can help fund the Canadian tax liability of an estate and may help to prevent the liquidation of the estate assets in order to pay capital gain taxes on death.

3　Tax Implications of the Life Insurance Policy in Canada

3.1　Cash value

For insurance policies with investment attributes, the policy's cash surrender value will fluctuate with investment returns. In most cases, the policy's cash surrender value will grow year over year, as life insurance policy investments are generally chosen for their high stability and low risk. For this part of the investment appreciation, life insurance policies can play an important tax planning role by deferral of taxable income. This is because, if the policy appreciates in value due to increased investment returns, the policy owner is not subjected to tax on the appreciation in value unless he or she surrenders the policy prior to death or requests a policy loan from the insurer under the insurance policy.

It should be noted that, if the policy is issued by Canadian insurance companies to Canadian residents, the policy is likely to comply with the exempt policy Regulations under the Income Tax Act (Canada), since such Regulations are monitored by Canadian insurers, and the policy owner will enjoy the benefits of tax deferral. If the policy is issued by insurance companies outside of Canada to Canadian residents, there is a much greater concern that the policy will not be compliant with the exempt policy regime and, if the policy is not an exempt policy, the policy owner may be subject to Canadian taxation on annual accrued growth.

3.2 Cash withdrawal

As discussed above, while the investments within a life insurance policy continue to grow in value, the investment earnings are usually sheltered from taxation provided the policy is an exempt policy. At what point do these deferred taxes need to be paid? If the policy owner wants to withdraw cash from the policy through a policy loan or to partially or fully surrender the policy, he or she may face a significant Canadian tax burden. This issue cannot be avoided by purchasing a policy issued in a low-tax jurisdiction, as policy owners are liable for income taxes imposed by their jurisdiction of tax residence.

Taxation laws and methods may vary from country to country, so when a client intends to withdraw cash from his or her policy, an international life insurance counselor should help the client to thoroughly assess and evaluate the potential tax consequences.

3.3 Transfer of policy ownership

Depending on the specific provisions of local tax laws, policy owners may find themselves liable for income tax when transferring a policy. For example, in Canada, the general rule, with certain exceptions, is that a transfer of a policy is subject to tax to the extent the proceeds of disposition received for the policy are greater than the policy's ACB. Therefore, if a client intends to transfer a policy to another person, the client should seek tax advice and fully understand the potential tax consequences before deciding.

3.4 Policy loan

The policy owner can use the policy as a pledge to apply for a loan. The loans in Canada can be divided into two categories:

• Policy loan-the policy owner can directly apply for a loan from the insurance company, in which case, the loan amounts are required to be compared with the ACB of the policy each year. Even if the interest generated from the policy loan is paid every year, the policy owner may be required to pay tax for this policy loan if the policy loan exceeds the ACB of the policy.

• Collateral loan-the policy owner can also use the policy as collateral to apply for a loan from banks or other financial institutions. This type of loan arrangement usually would not result in taxation even where the amount of the loan exceeds the ACB of the policy.

Therefore, when a client wishes to obtain a policy loan, it is important for the client to thoroughly understand their needs and to work with a professional advisor to help obtain the loan in the most tax-efficient manner.

3.5　Death benefit

Usually, the beneficiary of the insurance policy is exempt from paying taxes on the death benefit if the policy satisfies the definition and requirements of an exempt life insurance policy under Canadian tax law. If, however, the policy is not an exempt policy a Canadian resident beneficiary may be liable for taxes on the death benefit received. Under these circumstances, it is important for the client to consult a professional tax advisor before making decisions.

3.6　Residency status of policyholder

If a client who is a Hong Kong resident purchases an insurance policy in Hong Kong for his family members and then subsequently immigrates to Canada, the client may be liable for foreign property reporting responsibilities under Canadian tax laws and the policy, if not exempt, would be subject to ongoing taxation in respect of its investment component.

Before immigrating to Canada, the client is, therefore, recommended to have a proactive discussion with his tax advisor about the subsequent tax issues of the policy in force and whether or not the policy owner should be changed.

4　Taxation in Business-Owned Life Insurance

In Canada, private companies use a notional CDA (Capital Dividend Account) to record certain tax-free surpluses accumulated by the Company including, among other items, the 50% of capital gains that is not subject to tax under the tax law, some or all of the death benefit from life insurance and capital dividends received from other corporations. Companies with a CDA account can elect that dividends be treated as tax-free capital dividends to the extent of the CDA account.

It is important to note that a CDA is a notional account, which means it does not actually hold funds like a bank account, but simply records the tax-free elements of certain corporate transactions or corporate receipts. The CDA records the balance of funds that a company can distribute to shareholders tax-free. When a company has a positive CDA balance and sufficient assets on hand, it can choose to designate a dividend to shareholders as a tax-free capital dividend. When the company distributes the capital dividend, the CDA balance is reduced by the same amount. The CDA account is also reduced by capital losses of the Company.

For life insurance, only the portion of the death benefit that exceeds the policy's ACB (Adjusted Cost Basis) of the policy to the company immediately prior to death is included in the CDA and can ultimately be distributed as a tax-free capital dividend. Death benefits from exempt life insurance policies are not taxable to the company.

---

* Our discussion is based on the Income Tax Act (Canada) (the "Act") and regulations thereto effective as at December 15, 2023 as well as our understanding of the administrative position of the Canada Revenue Agency ("CRA") as available to the public as at as at December 15, 2023, but does not consider the application of the general anti-avoidance rules or any other anti-avoidance provisions in the Act. It is a summary only and is not intended to be specific legal advice and may not be relied upon as such.

附录 C：澳大利亚税务意见

Australian Tax Opinions

JD Advisory Group | 2023.12.15

1 Tax Resident Status

1.1 Criteria for determining the tax residency of an individual in Australia

The determination of whether a person is an Australian tax resident is assessed and achieved by considering the person's facts and circumstances in light of certain common law and statutory tests.

• Common law test-An individual is assessed to be an Australian tax resident if the individual resides in Australia according to the ordinary meaning of that word (subsection 6 (1) of the Income Tax Assessment Act 1936 (ITAA 1936)) and to the statutory definition of that word (section 995-1 of ITAA 1936). All the facts and circumstances that describe an individual's behavior in Australia are relevant. Particularly, the following factors are useful in describing the quality and character of an individual's behaviors:

- intention or purpose of presence;
- family or business and employment ties;
- maintenance and location of assets; and
- social and living arrangements.

No single factor is necessarily decisive, and many are interrelated. The importance and weight given to each factor varies depending on individual circumstances.

• Statutory tests-If an individual fails the common law test of residency, the individual is still considered to be an Australian tax resident if the individual satisfies one or more of four statutory residency tests in subsection 6 (1) of the ITAA 1936:

– residence according to ordinary concepts;

– the domicile and permanent place of abode test;

– the 183-day test; and

– the Commonwealth superannuation fund test.

The definition states that a resident means a person who resides in Australia. If the individual resides in Australia under ordinary concepts, residency status is established and the other three tests in the subsection 6 (1) definition need not be considered.

The domicile and superannuation fund tests apply to individuals who are usually residents of Australia but during the income year are not living in Australia. Domicile and the concept of permanent place of abode are addressed in Taxation Ruling IT 2650.

The 183-day test to be applied is, subject to certain conditions, physical presence in Australia for more than half the financial year in which the income the subject of assessment is derived. This test is necessary in order to eliminate the great difficulties which occasionally arise in establishing to the satisfaction of a decision that a person is resident in any particular country.

Example C.1

Vicky leaves Australia to work in Korea as a teacher of English. Vicky has a one-year contract after which she plans to tour China and other parts of Asia before returning to Australia to continue work here. Vicky lives with a family in Korea during her time there and rents out her property in Australia. Vicky is single. Her parents live interstate and her brother has moved to France.

Vicky is an Australian resident for tax purposes even though she is residing in Korea because, under the domicile test:

1. her domicile is in Australia (as she is a resident who has lived in Australia and will generally retain a domicile here when absent overseas), unless she chooses to permanently migrate to another country;

2. her permanent place of abode remains Australia.

Example C.2

Lily, an Australian resident, receives a job offer to work overseas for three years, with an option to extend for another three years. Lily, her husband and three children decide to make the move. They rent out their house in Australiaas they intend to return one day. While overseas they rent a house with an accommodation allowance provided under Lily's contract. Lily is unsure if she will extend her contract to stay for another three years. She will decide later depending on how the family like life.

Lily is a foreign resident for tax purposes because she does not satisfy 'the resides' test. This is due to:

1. the length of her physical absence from Australia;

2. other circumstances not being consistent with residing in Australia, even though she has retained the family home-such as:

- establishing a home overseas with her family;
- renting out her family home in Australia.

Lily has also not satisfied the domicile test, as:

1. her permanent place of abode is outside Australia due to:

- the length of time committed to being overseas
- the establishment of a home overseas
- her family going with her overseas

2. the fact that she won't be selling the family home in Australia, although relevant, is not persuasive enough to overcome the finding on the basis of the other factors;

3. it can be argued that she has abandoned her home in Australia for the duration of her stay, by renting it out.

1.2 Criteria for determining the tax residency of a corporation in Australia

Under the Corporations Act 2001, corporation defines as an organization which can be a company, body corporate, or a certain kind of unincorporated body. Among these, company is the most widely used structure.

According to subsection 6(1) of the Income Tax Assessment Act 1936 (ITAA 1936), a company is a resident of Australia if:

- it is incorporated in Australia, or
- although not incorporated in Australia, it carries on its business in Australia and has either its:

— central management and control in Australia, or

— voting power controlled by shareholders who are residents of Australia.

In TR 2018/5, Australian Taxation Office (ATO) provided some detailed guidance on the central management and control test of corporate residency. This ruling identifies four relevant matters, along with corresponding criteria:

- Does the company carry on business in Australia? -To be considered a resident under the central management and control test of residency, a company must carry on business in Australia. However, it is not necessary for any part of the actual trading or investment operations of the company's business to take place in Australia. This is because the central management and control of a business is factually part of carrying on that business.

- What does central management and control mean? -Central management and control refers to the control and direction of a company's operations. The key element here is the making of high-level decisions that set the company's general policies, and determine the direction of its operations and the type of transactions it will enter, which is different from the day-to-day conduct and management of its activities and operations.

- Who exercises central management and control? -Identifying who exercises central management and control is a question of fact. It cannot be determined solely by identifying who has the legal power or authority to control and direct a company. The crucial question is who controls and directs a company's operations in reality.

- Where is central management and control exercised? -A company will be controlled and directed where those making its high-level decisions do so as a matter of fact and substance. It is not where they are merely recorded and formalised, or where the company's constitution, bylaws or articles of association require it be controlled and directed, if in reality it occurs elsewhere. This will not necessarily be the place where those who control and direct a company live.

It is also emphasized in TR 2018/5 that whether a company is a resident under the central management and control test of residency must be determined by reference to all the facts and relevant case law. To assist foreign-incorporated companies and their advisors to apply the principles set out in this ruling, PCG 2018/9 provided some practical examples. Here is one of them about exercising central management and control vs day-to-day management of a company's operations:

Multinational Co is incorporated in Ostasia and carries on business solely in Australia. The shareholders and directors of Multinational Co are residents of and live in Ostasia. Its directors hold board meetings and perform their duties as the company's high-level decision-makers in Ostasia.

Multinational Co's board of directors establish an overarching framework and policies for how its operations are to be run. It also appoints an Australian-based manager to manage its Australian business activities and gives them wide authority to do so under its supervision. This includes the authority to make decisions on major contracts, as well as financing and general trading policies for its Australian business. Despite the wide authority granted to the

Australian manager, the board retains the power to override any proposed decisions before they are made. It also retains the power to direct the Australian manager on how they are to conduct the Australian operations.

During board meetings, the board makes high-level decisions about Multinational Co's Australian business. The board reviews Multinational Co's Australian business and the Australian manager's performance. The board concludes that the business and Australian manager are performing competently and in line with how it wants the business run. The evidence shows that the board has the power to, has historically, and is prepared to intervene if it is not satisfied with the decisions of the Australian manager, or how they are running the business. Where the board deems it necessary, it further directs the Australian manager on how to conduct the business.

Multinational Co's central management and control is exercised by its board of directors in Ostasia, not the Australian manager. It is therefore not a resident of Australia under the central management and control test of company residency.

2 Tax Implications of the Foreign Life Assurance Policy (FLP) in Australia

The tax opinions below are based on the understanding of the relevant background facts as set out below:

- The policyholder is an Australian resident for tax purpose.
- The policyholder holds a foreign life assurance policy in relation to which the date of commencement of risk is after 27 August 1982.
- The insured and the beneficiary are both Australian residents for tax purposes.
- After the policy takes effect, the premium paid each year does not exceed 125% of the premium paid in the previous assurance year.

2.1 Income tax implications of FLP before 2010-2011

For taxpayers before 2010-2011, the FIF measures applied to income and gains accumulating in foreign companies that were not controlled by Australians. A taxpayer had an interest in a FLP if they have legal title to the policy and therefore, the FIF measures would then apply.

However, the FIF measures have been repealed and do not apply to taxpayers from 2010-2011. For taxpayers after 2010-2011 who are involved with FLPs, only section 26AH of the Income Tax Assessment Act 1936 (ITAA 1936) would be taken into consideration.

2.2 Income tax assessment 1936 section 26AH

According to ITAA 1936 sub-section 26AH (6), the tax treatment on the bonus received by a policyholder is defined as follows:

'Where, during the eligible period in relation to an eligible policy, a taxpayer receives an amount (in this subsection refered to as the relevant amount) under the policy as or by way of a bonus, being an amount that, but for this section, would not be included in the assessable income of the taxpayer of any year of income, the assessable income of the taxpayer of the year of income in which the relevant amount is received shall include:

(a) if the relevant amount is received during the first 8 years of the eligible period-an amount equal to the relevant amount;

(b) if the relevant amount is received during the ninth year of the eligible period-an amount equal to two-thirds of the relevant amount; or

(c) if the relevant amount is received during the tenth year of the eligible period-an amount equal to one-third of the relevant amount.'

Based on the background facts, it is reasonable to consider that the policy in this specific scenario is an eligible policy because of the absence of a detailed definition on the percentage of the investment component occupied in a FLP. ATO reserves the right to deny the treatment of eligible FLPs.

Tax treatment on bonus received

Assuming the policy in this specific scenario is not denied by ATO as an eligible policy, ITAA 1936 sub-section 26AH (6) applies in determining the tax consequences of receiving bonuses on this policy. More specifically, we have reached some conclusions as the following:

• After the foreign life assurance policy takes effect, the policyholder does not need to declare and pay tax to the Australian Taxation Office for the increase in the cash value of the policy every year, unless he actually receives the bonus.

• According to Paragraph 10 of IT2346, to ensure that bonuses or other amounts in the nature of bonuses are not subject to tax unless the total amount received by the policyholder exceeds the premiums paid under the policy, a term of "relevant amount" is raised in respect of calculating the amount of bonus the policyholder received that would be included in the assessable income.

• Under IT2346, as a general rule, the "relevant amount" to be included in assessable income under ITAA 1936 sub-section 26AH(6) is to be calculated in accordance with the formula:

$$'(A/B)[(B+C)-(D+E)]$$

where-

A = the amount withdrawn from the policy

B = the surrender value of the policy immediately prior to the withdrawal

C = the sum of any earlier amounts paid out under the policy

E = the sum of previous "relevant amounts" plus the sum of any previous bonuses taxed under any other provision of the Act e.g., paragraph 26(i)

The gain [(B + C)-(D + E)] represents the difference between the policy value and the gross premiums paid with an adjustment in respect of earlier withdrawals.'

- During the 1st to 8th years of the eligible period, an amount equal to the relevant amount would be included in the assessable income for the policyholder if the policyholder received an amount under the policy as or by way of a bonus.

- During the ninth year of the eligible period, an amount equal to two-thirds of the relevant amount would be included in the assessable income for the policyholder if the policy holder received an amount under the policy as or by way of a bonus.

- During the tenth year of the eligible period, an amount equal to one-third of the relevant amount would be included in the assessable income for the policy holder if the policyholder received an amount under the policy as or by way of a bonus.

- After the foreign life assurance policy takes effect and the eligible period (10 years) has passed, from the 11th year onwards, any bonus the policyholder received on surrender or maturity of the life assurance policy would not be included in the assessable income.

Example C.3

A taxpayer takes out a life assurance policy after 7 December 1983 with an annual premium of $1,200 payable at the commencement of each assurance year. Assume that immediately before the end of the eighth year the policy is worth $10,139 (Original premiums-Management costs + Bonus). The policyholder has three partial surrenders each of $2,500 immediately before the close of the eighth, ninth and tenth years.

- 8th year

The 'relevant amount' = (2,500/10,139)×[(10,139+0)-(9,600+0)] = $132

As the 'relevant amount' was received during the first 8 years of the eligible period, the assessable income of the taxpayer of the year of receipt includes an amount equal to the relevant amount-i.e., $132.

- 9th year

Assuming at the end of the ninth year and immediately before the partial surrender in that year (i.e., withdrawal of $2,500), the value of the policy is $9,382 after accounting for a further premium payment of $1,200 at the commencement of the ninth year.

The 'relevant amount' = (2,500/9,382)×[(9,382+2,500)−(10,800+132)] = $253

As the 'relevant amount' was received during the ninth year of the eligible period, operates to include in the assessable income of the taxpayer of the year of receipt 2/3rds of the relevant amount-i.e., $168.

- 10th year

At the end of the tenth year and immediately before the partial surrender (i.e., withdrawal of $2,500), the value of the policy is $8,556-a further premium payment of $1,200 having been made at the beginning of the tenth year.

The 'relevant amount' = (2,500/8,556)×[(8,556+5,000)−(12,000+132+253)] = $342

The amount to be included in assessable income is 1/3rd of the 'relevant amount'-i.e., $114.

- Year 11 and later

If a further withdrawal had taken place, or the whole of the policy had been forfeited, surrendered or otherwise terminated, any amounts received as or by way of bonuses would not be subject to tax.

Restarting of the Eligible Period

The rule of restarting the eligible period is defined in ITAA1936 subsection 26AH (13) as follows:

'(13) Where the amount of the premiums payable under an eligible policy in relation to an assurance year (in this subsection referred to as the premium increase year) exceeds by more than 25% the amount of the premiums payable under the policy in relation to the immediately preceding assurance year, the eligible period in relation to the policy shall, for the purposes of..., be reckoned from the date of commencement of the premium increase year.'

The term of 'premiums payable' is used to differentiate between policies with single premium and policies with regular premiums, which leads to the following different scenarios.

When the policyholder is not contractually obligated to make a fixed premium payment annually, the premium payable in relation to an assurance year is the total amount paid on the policy during that year. In this case, the eligible period will restart if the policyholder pays a premium into the policy which exceeds by more than 25% of the premium paid in the previous assurance year.

When the policyholder is contractually obligated to make a fixed premium payment annually, the eligible period restarts if the premium payable in an assurance year exceeds by more than 25% the amount of the premiums payable under the policy in relation to the immediately preceding assurance year. For example, when the amount paid by the policyholder in a certain year does not meet the required amount for some reason, the overdue premium paid in the next year will not be counted in the premium payable in the second year. However, if the premium paid in respect of the next year exceeds by more than 25% the amount of the premium payable in respect of the immediately preceding year, the eligible period will restart.

Example C.4

A policy commenced on 1 June 2010, with an initial payment of USD $200,000. Therefore, the ten-year eligible period would be due to end on 31 May 2020.

On 1 July 2013 (Policy Year 4), an additional investment of USD $250,000 was paid into the policy. As no additional investments were made in Policy Year 3 (1 June 2012-31 May 2013), the ten-year eligible period would re-start from 1 June 2013 (i.e. the start of Policy Year 4).

As a result, the ten-year eligible period will now run from 1 June 2013 to 31 May 2023.

Residency Status of Policyholder

The analysis above is based on the assumption that the Policyholder, Insured and Beneficiary are all Australian residents for tax purpose. We will continue to talk about the potential tax consequences when the policyholder is not an Australian resident while others remain unchanged. The key to this circumstance is to determine who will be considered as the bonus recipient.

According to ITAA 1936 sub-section 26AH (4) & (5):

'(4) *For the purposes of this section, but subject to subsection (5), a taxpayer shall be taken to have received an amount under or in relation to an eligible policy although the amount is not actually paid to the taxpayer but is reinvested or otherwise dealt with on his or her behalf or as he or she directs.*

(5) *Subsection (4) does not apply in relation to an amount in relation to an eligible policy if the amount is re-invested or otherwise dealt with on behalf of the taxpayer or as the taxpayer directs so as to increase the amount that might reasonably be expected to be received under the eligible policy on a surrender or maturity of the eligible policy.* '

Even though there is no specific distinguishment between policyholder and beneficiary in ITAA 1936 section 26AH, the fact that a bonus is paid to a beneficiary can be considered as the bonus is dealt with as the policyholder directs. As a result, the bonus is deemed to be received by the policy owner. This opinion was also confirmed by the ATO in our communication. Since the policyholder is not an Australian resident for tax purpose and the bonus received is not from an Australian source, the Australian tax law has no jurisdiction over the policyholder's income. As for the beneficiary (Australian tax resident), an amount he receives shall be considered as a gift and is not assessable. In conclusion, no Australian tax consequence is resulting from this event.

2.3 Australia's anti-avoidance rules on insurance policies

- 'Policy penetration' under general anti-avoidance principles

Broadly, the definition of an eligible policy is limited under ITAA 1936 section 26AH, which provides an arbitrage opportunity to the ATO's advantage. The purpose of holding eligible policies is often subjective and hard to prove. The policy structure interrelates with the purpose of holding an FLP.

- Project Wickenby

If an Australian tax resident's passive investment income accounts for a relatively high proportion of the income from FLPs; or he surrenders the policy several times before the maturity of the policy, the ATO has a reason to concern that the person holds the insurance policy with a purpose of liquidating investment or even evading tax liability. Separate tax assessments on relevant policyholders and even beneficiaries of the policy may be conducted and penalties may apply. This is referred to TA 2009/17, Project Wickenby and the communication with ATO. The determinants of the final decision are not disclosed by the ATO.

- Interest-free or Low-interest Loan against an Eligible FLP

ITAA1936 sub-section 26AH (11) provides guidance on the tax treatment of advance or loan a policyholder receives in relation to an eligible policy:

'(11) Where, in relation to an eligible policy, a taxpayer receives an amount from the assurer, or from another person at the request of, or under an agreement with, the assurer, by way of an advance or loan in respect of which interest is not payable or in respect of which interest is payable at a rate less than the rate of interest that could reasonably be expected to be payable in respect of a loan of the same amount made on similar terms and conditions by the assurer or the other person, as the case may be, to a person with whom the assurer or that other person was dealing at arm's length, the amount shall, for the purposes of subsection (9), be deemed to be an amount to which paragraph (9)(a) applies.'

Whilst entering an interest-free or low-interest loan agreement may not obviously be recognized as a partial surrender of the policy-no statement contractually outlined that the amount borrowed consists of accrued bonuses, it shall still be deemed to an amount that has been received as a way of bonus, considering the nature that the parties were not dealing at arm's length. Therefore, the advance or loan the policyholder receives would be included in his assessable income.

2.4 Tax treatment for private placement life insurance (PPLI)

The definition of 'eligible policy' is defined under ITAA1936 sub-section 26AH (1):

'..."eligible policy" means a life assurance policy in relation to which the date of commencement of risk is after 27 August 1982, other than a funeral policy (as defined in the Income Tax Assessment Act 1997) issued on or after 1 January 2003.'

According to IT2346, ITAA 1936 section 26AH may apply to amounts received under any form of life assurance policy, including those called unbundled life assurance contracts (referred to as "unbundled insurance policies" in this ruling). The two main categories of unbundled policies are investment account policy and investment-linked policy. The general characteristics of unbundled policies are as follows:

'Investment account policy

A contract providing a death benefit plus some type of identifiable savings account or investment account, the balance of which usually becomes the benefit payable in certain circumstances, most commonly after a number of years when a balance has accumulated in the account. Source: Life Insurance Commissioner Annual Report 1985

Investment-linked policy

A contract providing a death benefit, and an investment account the value of which is directly linked to the performance of a specific investment portfolio. The value of the policyholder's interest will rise and fall with the movements in the value of the portfolio. Source: Life Insurance Commissioner Annual Report 1985'

The private placement life insurance has the characteristics of an unbundled policy. According to the existing information, the private placement life insurance in this specific scenario is considered to fall within the definition of 'eligible policy' under the ITAA regulations and all eligible policies are subject to ITAA1936 section 26AH and there is no difference in tax treatment. However, ATO reserves the right to deny the treatment of eligible FLPs. Each policy needs to seek for independent advice from relevant authorities based on certain facts and backgrounds.

3 Taxation on FLPs with Different Policyholder Structures

3.1 Australian resident trust

With the recognition of eligible FLPs, the tax treatment of bonus received by the beneficiaries of the Australian Resident Trust ('the Trust') as a result of the surrender of eligible FLPs will be the same as the treatment of Individual holding status.

The word 'Taxpayer' used in s 26AH has the definition defined in s 202A, along with the other sub sections in s 26AH, the Trust is allowed to hold the eligible FLP with the same tax outcome for the Bonus received.

As the ATO's claim on the Bonus which is deemed to be received by the policyholder regardless of whether the Bonus was transferred to the beneficiaries directly or not. If the policyholder is the Trust, and there is an eligible FLP is held by the Trust. In Australia, the Trust will not be taxed at the Trust level but the beneficiary level. The tax obligation then falls to the beneficiary level.

After the 10th of year, the Bonus received by the surrender of the eligible FLP will be distribute to beneficiaries and the nature of such Bonus remains the same. Under s 26AH, the Bonus received by beneficiaries after the 10th of year, will not be assessable.

3.2 Overseas/Non-Resident trust

The tax opinions below are based on the understanding of the relevant background facts as set out below:

- There is an eligible FLP.
- The FLP can be a standard FLP or a Private Placement Life Insurance (PPLI).
- The FLP is holding by an Oversea/Non-Resident Discretionary Trust (T1).
- The Trustee of T1 is a wholly foreign-owned trustee company.
- The Tax Residency of the beneficiary and the person who indirectly control the trust are Australian Tax Resident with Australia Residency under Australian Citizenship Act 2007 or Migration Act 1958.
- The eligible FLP is acquired in the time period after this document is issued by using T1.

Non-Resident trust as the holding structure

i With a non-resident trust as the policyholder, the key issues to be considered are the recognition of the eligible of FLP as an asset, the residency of the trust, and whether the trust is a Controlled Foreign Trust (CFT).

ii Assumptions in this case are set as partially or wholly surrender of the FLPs before the 10th of the year.

Asset category

iii The FLPs can be defined as eligible FLPs or investment instruments by the ATO's interpretation in relation to both the FLP's structure and the intention of holding the FLP. The asset category highly impacts the final tax obligation position for the policyholder and the beneficiaries who received the Bonus.

iv In relation to s 108.5 ITAA 1997, with the background facts mentioned above, the eligible FLPs fall into the definition of a Capital Gain Tax asset (CGT asset).

v Considering the trust holds the standard FLP as an asset with no surrender before the 10th year, the increase in the value of the investment component of the asset would rather be considered as the valuation surplus, not the profit for accounting and taxation purpose.

vi Broadly, the definitions of an eligible FLP are limited under s 26AH ITAA 1936 which provides an arbitrage opportunity towards the ATO's advantage. The intention of holding FLPs is often subjective and hard to prove. The policy structure interrelates with the purpose of holding an FLP.

vii From the facts, an investment focused standard FLPs or a PPLI could be defined as an investment instrument under the coverage of Life Assurance Policy because of the absence of detailed definition on the percentage of the investment component occupied in a FLP. ATO reserves the right to deny the treatment of eligible FLPs.

Trust residency and CFT

viii Trust residency and the CFT conceptcould highly impactthe final tax obligation of the individual who eventually received the money.

ix The tests of the residency of the trust[①] should be initiated in order to assess the tax obligation carried by the trust.

x From the facts, the trustee of the trust estate is a foreign company and the central management and control (CMC) of the trust will not be able to be physically in Australia at any time during the years of income (s 95(2) ITAA 1936). The trust is therefore defined as non-resident trust.

xi In order to further assess the tax obligation of the non-resident trust, with controlling interests in that trust which can be established from the background facts, the CFT concept needs to be examined.

---

① Paragraph 1, Exhibit A.

xii The existence of non-resident trust ('T1') has been proved. As the definition of CFT[①] isclearly setin ITAA 1936, the wording of each condition will become the key determinant of assessing the CFT provision. Tests of the existence of CFT need to be conducted through both s 342 (a) and s 342 (b) ITAA 1936.

xiii From the facts, the acquirer (not T1) could nominate the beneficiaries and control the distribution of the profits or corpus. These characteristics can be considered as the power of trustee. By all means, the control position of the trust is satisfied.

xiv With the definitions and interpretations of phrases employed in ITAA 1936 and the understanding of s 342 and s 347 ITAA 1936, the CFT tests are satisfied, and the non-resident trust is a CFT.

FLPs as eligible FLPs holding by CFT

xv With the recognition of eligible FLPs, the tax treatment of Bonus received by the beneficiaries as a result of the surrender of eligible FLPs will be the same as the tax treatment of Individual holding status.

xvi Considering the Trust holds the standard FLP as an asset with no surrender before the 10th of year, the increase in the value of the investment component by aligning the positions of investment components of the asset would rather be considered as the valuation surplus, not the profit for accounting and taxation purpose.

xvii For example, the T1 holds an eligible FLP, the Bonus received by the beneficiaries at any point of time, as a result of surrender the eligible FLP, will be assessed under s 26AH ITAA 1936.

FLPs as investment instruments holding by CFT

xviii The investment focused FLP is quite sensitive. If the structure and intention of holding an FLP does not satisfy the requirements of an eligible FLP, we should assess all the income received by the beneficiaries as investment income, and s 26AH ITAA 1936 will no longer be the suitable section to assess such income.

xix To the extent of unfavorable decision where ATO denied the existence of FLPs, the purpose of holding FLPs would be generally defined as the investment of Mthe trust.

xx Considering the trust holds an investment focused FLP or a PPLI which is defined by the ATO as an investment asset, the investment gain will be treated as assessable income under beneficiaries' individual tax position regardless of the reinvestment of the investment gain into the FLP or the PPLI after the initial or the multiple disposals.

xxi For example, the T1 held an investment instrument asset, and T1 disposed parts of

---

① Paragraph 2, 3, 4, 5&6, Exhibit A.

the investment components (e.g. Shares in some listed companies) and received the principal amount and a capital gain as a result of such disposal. The T1 subsequently reinvested all the proceeds received into the asset without actually paid out to the beneficiaries. Such capital gain is required to be taxed under Income Tax Assessment (1936 Act) Regulation 2015 (ignore exempted income here) regardless of actually distribution of such gain.

xxii In relation to the Section 3 of foreign income return form guide 2020 provided by the ATO and the Income Tax Assessment (1936 Act) Regulation 2015, the exemption of Accrual Tax System exists where CFT is a tax resident of one of the Listed Countries and received the Eligible Designated Concession Income (EDC).

xxiii For example, T1 is registered in the United States of America (USA)[①]. For the income or profits to be exempted from assessing in Australia, all the conditions must be met. To the extent of our interpretation, the most crucial point is, the income or profits generated must not be taxed in the USA.

Summary of non-resident trust as a policyholder

xxiv The main determinants of tax treatments for the Bonus received after the surrender are the asset category, trust residency and CFT concept.

xxv The tax treatment for Eligible FLPs held by CFT would be the same as the Individual holding status.

xxvi The tax treatment for Investment Instruments (Non-eligible FLPs) held by CFT would be much more complicated depends on different situations, and the s 26AH ITAA 1936 will no longer be the suitable section to assess such income.

Tax treatment of surrender in the 11th Year

i The Asset Category concept impacts significantly on the tax treatment of Bonus/Investment Gain received from the FLP/Investment Instrument.

ii As mentioned above, the CFT will be subjected to the Accrual Taxation system at the very beginning of the policy became effective if the ATO defined the investment activities under an investment focused FLP or a PPLI as an investment instrument by the trust which associates with the income or profits generated from such activities.

iii In relation to the circumstances mentioned in (i), ATO defines the investment focused FLP or the PPLI as an investment asset, all the investment gain receives from the disposal of such asset will be treated as assessable income by referencing Income Tax Assessment (1936 Act) Regulation 2015.

iv Any Bonus gained by the eligible FLP other than the situation mentioned in (i),

---

① Paragraph 7 & 8, Exhibit A.

after the 10th of the year, will be determined under s 26AH ITAA 1936, where the Bonus will not be assessable.

Tax issues arising from Australian tax resident receiving the distribution

i In relation to analysis above, the income will become assessable under certain circumstances.

ii If the ATO defines the investment focused FLP or the PPLI as an investment asset, the operation relating to such asset conducted by the trust which associates with the income or profits generated from such activities, the amount of the profit will be assessed under the beneficiaries who received or deemed to receive (beneficial interests in T1) the distribution as an income by referencing Income Tax Assessment (1936 Act) Regulation 2015 regardless of the realization status or the holding period.

iii For example, the T1 held an investment instrument asset, and T1 disposed parts of the investment components (e.g. Shares in some listed companies) and received the principal amount and a capital gain as a result of such disposal. The T1 subsequently reinvested all the proceeds received into the asset without actually paid out to the beneficiaries. Such capital gain is required to be taxed under Income Tax Assessment (1936 Act) Regulation 2015 (ignore exempted income here) regardless of actually distribution of such gain.

iv After the 10th year, if the trust surrendered the eligible FLPs other than the situation mentioned in (ii), the Bonus will be non-assessable under s 26AH ITAA 1936.

v For example, T1 holds an eligible FLP, the Bonus received by the beneficiaries after the 10th of year, as a result of surrender the eligible FLP, will be assessed under s 26AH ITAA 1936.

Tax residency of settlor

i In relation to the different Trust Acts in different states of Australia, the tax residency of the Settler of the trust does not affect the situations and analysis mentioned above in Australia. Whether the Settler has different power under overseas relevant Trust Acts, please consult relevant professions.

Interest bearing loan against an eligible FLP

i The interest rate needs to be determined with arm-length basis or otherwise be treated as a way to receive of the Bonus.

Tax treatment for PPLI

i For example, T1 holds an eligible FLP (either a standard FLP or a PPLI), the Bonus received by the beneficiaries at any point of time, as a result of surrender the eligible FLP, will be assessed under s 26AH ITAA 1936.

ii In relation to the investment focused FLPs or PPLIs where the tax treatment and the determination of the investment activities with any kind of income or profits, the Income Tax Assessment (1936 Act) Regulation 2015 applies.

iii For example, the T1 held a PPLI which is defined as an investment instrument by ATO, and T1 disposed parts of the investment components (e.g. Shares in some listed companies) and received the principal amoun tand a capital gain as a result of such disposal. The T1 subsequently reinvested all the proceeds received into the asset without actually paid out to the beneficiaries. Such capital gain is required to be taxed under Income Tax Assessment (1936 Act) Regulation 2015 (ignore exempted income here) regardless of actually distribution of such gain.

3.3 Overseas master trust

In relation to the specific holding structure, Overseas Master Trust holding structure, we believe the tax treatment will be the same as what we analyzed and concluded above.

For example, the sub Trust under the Master Trust is a CFT, and the FLP is an eligible FLP, the Bonus received by the FLP beneficiaries will be determined under s 26AH ITAA 1936.

In contrast to the situation mentioned above, the sub Trust remains as a CFT, the FLP is defined as an investment instrument (a non-eligible FLP), the Income Tax Assessment (1936 Act) Regulation 2015 applies.

4 Taxation in Business-Owned FLPs

Usually, holding offshore policies with a local company in Australia and using the company's undistributed profits to pay the premiums may save the dividend tax on undistributed profits to individuals. Other tax issues arising from holding the FLP with a company will be discussed below.

4.1 Cash value of an eligible FLP

With the policy's cash value growing year over year, it will not trigger tax issues for the company itself (for example, a local company in Canada holding too many passive assets may result in it losing the qualification for enjoying low tax rate on the first CAD 500K profits).

If the FLP falls within the scope of the rules in Section 26AH (commonly referred to as insurance bonds) the tax on investment earnings in an investment bond are paid by the bond issuer and after ten years from the start date, the return of the investment is free of income tax in the hands of the investor (the policy owner) when surrendered.

Furthermore, the growth of cash value of the policy can still realize the benefits of tax deferral for the reasons that: the tax on investment earnings in an investment bond are paid by the bond issuer and after ten years from the start date, the return of the investment is free of income tax in the hands of the policy owner when surrendered.

4.2　Cash withdrawal from an eligible FLP

From the 11th year of the eligible period onwards, if a withdrawal is taken place, or the whole of the policy had been forfeited, surrendered or otherwise terminated, any cash received as or by way of bonuses to the firm account would not be subject to tax.

However, it should be noted here that the ten-year eligible period will recommence to the start of any policy year in which the amount re-invested plus the amount of any other premium paid in that same assurance year exceeds by more than 25% the premium paid in the previous year.

4.3　Interest bearing loan against an eligible FLP

A non-resident withholding tax obligation will be raised if the company obtains a loan from the non-resident entity and pays interest to the non-resident company. No deduction can be claimed for the interest by the Australian company until the withholding tax obligation has been met, referring to Section 26-25 ITAA 1997.

The withholding rate is generally 10% although this depends on whether the client is a resident of a country that has a double tax agreement with Australia.

Further, the interest will also be non-deductible if the borrowed funds are used to generate exempt income under subsection 51(1) of the Act.

4.4　Death benefits distribution to shareholders

When the company is the beneficial owner upon the insured's death, the received death benefit is considered non-assessable. This is because a life assurance policy is a CGT asset for the purposes of the CGT provisions. Section 118-300 of the ITAA 1997 specifies that any capital gain or loss is disregard if the taxpayer is the original beneficial owner of the policy.

Insurance proceeds can be taxed on revenue account if:

- The proceeds are intended to replace lost income; or
- The proceeds are intended to cover the operating expenses of a business.

Neither of those seem likely to apply if the company does not carry on business and only holds the policy.

When the company distributes the death benefit as dividends to the shareholders, the shareholders are supposed to declare dividend income in their personal tax return. Furthermore, whether there is franking credit attached to the dividends distributed dependson whether the company has paid any tax on other income. If the company does not have other income, the dividend should be unfranked given that the death benefit is non-assessable to the company.

4.5 Potential fringe benefit tax

If the company is only the policy owner of the life insurance component and not the beneficiary that receives 100% of the death benefit from the policy, it will trigger the Fringe Benefit Tax (FBT). The tax system in Australia aims at the ultimate benefit whether it is received by the party who invested in at the first place. A company as a separate legal entity, it is entitled to receive full benefit from assets it invests, otherwise, the expenses used to generate the benefit where others are the beneficiaries, the FBT applies.

Reference:

i Related Rulings/Determinations:
- TD 94/82
- TR 2004/3(W)
- TA 2009/17
- IT 2346
- IT 2504
- Private Ruling 55355
- Private Ruling 1051187190539
- Income Tax Assessment (1936 Act)

ii Legislative References:
- ITAA 1936 23AK
- ITAA 1936 26AH
- ITAA 1936 95
- ITAA 1936 317
- ITAA 1936 347
- ITAA 1936 342
- ITAA 1997 108(5)
- NSW Trustee Act 1925
- QLD Trusts Act 1973
- Powers of Attorney Act 2003
- Income Tax Assessment (1936 Act) Regulation 2015

Our income tax advice is based on current taxation and as at the date our advice is provided.

Our advice does not consider the application of the general anti-avoidance rules or any other anti-avoidance provisions.

You will appreciate that the tax laws are frequently being changed, both prospectively and retrospectively. A number of key tax reform measures have been implemented, a number of other key reforms have been deferred and the status of some key reforms remains unclear at this stage.

Unless requested to do so, this advice will not be updated to take account of subsequent changes to the tax legislation, state duty laws, case law, rulings and determinations issued by the Australian Commissioner of Taxation or other practices of taxation authorities. It is your responsibility to take further advice, if you are to rely on our advice at a later date.

We are, of course, unable to give any guarantee that our interpretation will ultimately be sustained in the event of challenge by the Australian Commissioner of Taxation.

These comments are made specifically based on provided background facts.

Accordingly, neither the firm nor any member or employee of the firm undertakes responsibility in any way whatsoever to any person or company other than for any errors or omissions in the advice given, however caused.

附录 D：英国税务意见

UK Tax Opinions

Stephenson Harwood | 2024.8

1 Background

1.1 This memorandum addresses the specific questions which are replicated below in blue for reference.

1.2 The information provided in this memorandum is based on English law as applied by the English courts and our understanding of the current practice of HM Revenue & Customs ("**HMRC**") at the date stated on the front of this note. This note does not consider the legal or tax implications in any other jurisdiction.

1.3 As the advice provided is based on current tax laws and as tax legislation is subject to change, it is crucial to consult with us again in relation to any specific case and/or before any planning is undertaken to ensure that the advice provided remains accurate and applicable to the specific situation.

1.4 The following terms are used throughout this memorandum：

1.4.1 "**Policy Owner**" means the person who takes out the life insurance policy and who can enforce the rights under the contract with the insurer, also known as the "policyholder". Where the Policy Owner is two or more individuals, then usually the rights to the policy will automatically accrue to the surviving individual（s）. As there is a contractual relationship between the Policy Owner and the insurer, the Policy Owner's entitlement is governed by that contract. In the case of an investment-linked policy, which is the focus of this memorandum, the Policy Owner is not beneficially entitled to any underlying investments. Generally, it has also been assumed in this memorandum that the policy is held by a UK resident individual, rather than (for example) a trust although we make some preliminary comments regarding policies held in trust where relevant.

1.4.2 "**Life Insured**" means the named person(s) on whose life the insurance policy is based on. Under English law, a life insurance policy is only valid if the person effecting the policy has an insurable interest.① In practice, policies are typically written on the lives of multiple family members, and the lives assured may include not only the initial Policy Owner, but also any spouse, any children, and any grandchildren. Having multiple Life Insured extends the duration of the policy, and it means that the policy will not, by default, terminate on the death of the original Policy Owner. This may be important for UK tax purposes as the termination of the policy is one of the "chargeable events" that can give rise to a UK income tax charge, as mentioned below.

1.4.3 "**Beneficiary**" means the individual(s) designated to receive the death benefit proceeds upon the death of the (last) Life Insured provided the policy has not been surrendered or lapsed without value. This may include family members or trustees of trusts. If nothing further is done when a new life policy is purchased, on the death of the (last) Life Insured, the death benefit will be paid to the Policy Owner's personal representatives and will form part of his/her estate. A grant of representation will be required before the proceeds are available, and the sum may be liable to inheritance tax ("**IHT**") if the proceeds are left to a beneficiary other than the deceased's spouse (or charity). In order to avoid this, the policy can be written in trust or assigned to one or more individuals outright.

1.4.4 "**Irrevocable Beneficiary**" means the individual(s) appointed to receive the death benefit on the death of the Life Insured, however, the selection is irrevocable. This means that the Policy Owner cannot change the Irrevocable Beneficiary or the terms of the policy or cancel the policy without the Irrevocable Beneficiary's consent. This provides them with a more secure interest in the policy.

1.5 Given the nature of the questions asked, this memorandum refers to several important UK tax concepts including tax residence, domicile, deemed domicile, the remittance basis of taxation, the temporary non-residence rules, the taxation of trusts and IHT. This memorandum therefore assumes a foundational understanding of these topics although separate further advice

---

① Sections 1 and 3 of the Life Assurance Act 1774.

on these areas of UK tax law can be provided, if desired.

2 Summary

2.1 Whilst there is no statutory definition of life insurance policies, for UK tax purposes, a distinction is made between "qualifying" and "non-qualifying" policies. Foreign policies will, however, always be non-qualifying policies. In addition, most UK policies taken out by wealthy individuals are likely to be non-qualifying policies since there is an annual premium limit of no more than £3,600 across all qualifying policies. Furthermore, the single premium investment "bond" which is commonly used in the UK context for investment purposes is not a qualifying policy as the premiums are not paid annually or more frequently. The rules for non-qualifying policies (explained in section 5 of this note) are therefore more likely to be relevant in practice.

2.2 Investment linked policies are treated the same as other types of life insurance policies, although there are separate anti-avoidance rules that apply to "*personal portfolio bonds*". These anti-avoidance rules create an annual deemed tax charge where the Policy Owner can control investment strategy and, in doing so, can select investments other than typical managed fund investments. These types of policies should therefore be avoided for UK connected Policy Owners and/or structures established by them or for their benefit.

2.3 The UK tax regime which applies to life insurance policies is known as the "chargeable event" regime. The regime effectively defers any UK tax to when a "chargeable event" occurs. Common chargeable events include, for example, the death of the last Life Insured giving rise to benefits under the policy, the surrender of the policy, and the maturity of the policy. Under the chargeable event regime, the "chargeable event gain" is subject to UK income tax (which has a higher rate of up to 45% as compared to capital gains of up to 20%).

2.4 In broad terms, the chargeable event gain is the value over and above the premiums paid. This is charged to income tax regardless of whether the underlying profits have been generated by income or capital gains.

2.5 Where the Policy Owner is an individual, the time that the chargeable event gain arises is particularly important as a gain arising to a non-resident is not taxable.

2.6 Where the Policy Owner is a trustee, the creator of the trust (i.e. the settlor) will be taxed on the gain. This is the case unless the trustees are UK resident and the settlor is absent (i.e. non-UK resident or deceased), in which case the trustees will be subject to tax instead.

2.7 If the settlor and trustees are non-UK resident, then the trustees will not be liable, but a UK tax charge could arise when a UK resident beneficiary receives a benefit from the trust under complex anti-avoidance rules.

2.8 When the death benefit is paid to the Beneficiary, the Beneficiary can usually receive this amount free of UK tax. However, for non-qualifying policies, the payment of the death benefit is a chargeable event and therefore the Policy Owner triggers an income tax charge immediately before their death, resulting in an income tax liability for their estate if they were UK resident at the time of their death.

3 Definition of the Policy

3.1 For the purpose of UK tax laws, is there any definition of "Life Insurance Policy"? If yes, what is the definition?

3.1.1 There is no statutory definition of "life insurance policy" or indeed even "insurance" in UK tax legislation.

3.1.2 According to the Life Assurance Act 1774, a policy of life insurance is simply an insurance policy "*upon lives*".

3.1.3 The case of *Prudential Insurance Company v IRC*[1] sets out a useful description of "insurance" that can be a helpful starting point (our emphasis in bold):

"*a contract of insurance, then, must be the **contract for the payment of a sum of money**, or for some corresponding benefit … **to become due on the happening of an event**, which event must have some degree of uncertainty about it and must be of a character more or less adverse to the interest of the person effecting the insurance*".

3.1.4 Moreover, HMRC guidance states (or emphasis in bold)[2]:

"**There is no legal definition of insurance** but the dictionary definition used in the VAT insurance manual describes insurance as:

the act, system, or **business of providing financial protection against specified contingencies such as death**, loss, or damage. Life insurance is widely referred to as assurance although the words are interchangeable."

3.1.5 If a policy therefore pays benefits on the death of an individual, then it is likely to be considered a policy of life insurance. It is not relevant for UK tax purposes that the policy may also provide insurance against other risks, such as disability and critical illness.

3.1.6 In practice, life insurance policies are used in two main contexts in UK tax planning:

---

[1] Prudential Insurance Company v IRC (1904) 2 KB 658.
[2] IPT03600-Overview and the law: what is regarded as insurance?

(a) **Liquidity to pay for IHT charges** – First, insurance can sometimes offer a practical way of dealing with potential IHT charges. For example, a gift of an asset by an individual to another individual may be subject to IHT if the donor dies within seven years. Term insurance can often be taken out relatively cheaply to cover the tax charge.

(i) **Term insurance**: Term insurance is a type of policy that insures a person's life for a specific sum and for a specific length of time, typically for a period up to 20 years. If the insured person dies within the term of the cover, the insurance company will pay out the sum. This type of insurance provides protection only, and there is no investment element.

(ii) **Whole of life**: In contrast, a whole life policy will pay out a sum on the death of the Life Insured, whenever that death occurs, in return for a premium. This is also commonly used to protect against IHT exposure on death but can be used as for investment purposes too. Premiums are generally paid monthly or annually throughout the life of the Life Insured or until they reach a certain age, when premium payments can stop but the cover can continue on what is termed a 'paid up' basis, with the policy accruing no additional value attributable to the unpaid premiums. The death benefits payable under the policy can either be unit-linked (i.e., valued by reference to the performance of unitised investments in a fund established by the insurance company) or 'with profits' (i.e. valued on the basis of bonuses declared by the insurance company from its general funds). Whole life policies may also be 'guaranteed', meaning the policy provides a set level of cover.

(b) **Investment "wrapper"** – Second, life assurance contracts issued by non-UK life insurance companies may be used as an investment "wrapper" to shelter income and gains arising on investments. It is typical to see whole of life policies that serve as an investment product rather than a life insurance policy taken out in respect of a specific risk or eventuality. Although they have an insurance element, in practice, it may be relatively small (for example, 105% of the policy value) and the insurance premium is invested such that the surrender value of the policy grows over time. The insurance company is in a tax-efficient offshore centre so the investments can grow virtually tax free. Commonly, there will be just a single initial premium paid in respect of the policy, rather than regular annual premiums. It is even possible to transfer existing assets (such as an investment portfolio) as a premium payment in kind. In the UK market, these are often known as 'offshore bonds'. These are often split into several different policies so that different policies can be surrendered equally or just a few specifically. The Policy Owner can then access the investment either by regular withdrawals, by part of full surrender, or via a fixed account for a loan.

3.1.7 Despite the lack of statutory definitions in relation to life insurance policies, a distinction is made between "qualifying" and "non-qualifying policies" for UK tax purposes.

In brief, if a policy is a qualifying policy, most profits thereon will not be taxable in the hands of the Policy Owner. The rules of whether a policy is a qualifying one are set out in statute.① The main conditions are as follows:

(a) The policy term must be ten years or more②.

(b) Premiums must be payable yearly or more frequently③.

(c) The level of premiums must be reasonably smooth, which effectively means the premiums paid in any 12-month period must not exceed (i) twice the premium in any other 12-month period, or (ii) $1/8^{th}$ of the total premiums paid for a period of 10 years or its specified term④.

(d) For policies taken out on or after 1 April 1976, if the policy has a surrender value, the sum assured must be not less than 75% of the premiums payable during its term or within a specified premium payment term⑤.

(e) The policy must be issued by a UK company or through a UK branch or permanent establishment of an overseas resident insurer. ⑥

(f) For policies issued or varied from 21 March 2012, annual premiums payable under all such policies must not exceed £3,600⑦.

3.1.8 In practice, the appropriateness of qualifying policies is likely to be greater for individuals looking for lower levels of overall cover as opposed to wealthier individuals able to pay higher premiums to obtain a higher level of cover given the £3,600 annual premium limit for qualifying policies. In addition, the familiar single premium investment 'bond' is not a qualifying policy as the premiums are not paid annually or more frequently.

3.2 Does the jurisdiction of the issuer of the Life Insurance Policy (a UK issuer or a foreign issuer) have any impact on whether a Life Insurance Policy could satisfy the definition under UK tax laws (if any)?

3.2.1 As noted above at paragraph 3.1.7(e), a qualifying life insurance policy must be issued by a UK company or through a UK branch or permanent establishment of an overseas resident insurer. Therefore, most foreign policies will be non-qualifying life insurance policies.

3.2.2 Life insurance policies issued by a non-UK resident company or forming part of

---

① Schedule 15 of the Income Tax and Corporation Taxes Act 1988.
② Paragraph 1(2)(a), Schedule 15 ITCTA 1988.
③ Paragraph 1(2)(a), Schedule 15 ITCTA 1988.
④ Paragraph 1(2)(b), Schedule 15 ITCTA 1988.
⑤ Paragraph 1(1), Schedule 15 ITCTA 1988.
⑥ Paragraph 24, Schedule 15 ITCTA 1988.
⑦ Paragraph A3, Schedule 15 ITCTA 1988.

the overseas life assurance business of a UK insurer are defined as "foreign policies".①

3.3 Does whether the Life Insurance Policy is investment-linked or not have any impact on whether a Life Insurance Policy could satisfy the definition under UK tax laws?

3.3.1 An investment linked policy is one in which the benefits are determined by reference to the value of investments that are broadly identified and to which the return is linked. Whilst the sum payable may ultimately depend on the value of the linked investments, their nature and value are not directly relevant to the tax charged to the Policy Owner. As such, investment linked policies are treated the same as other types of life insurance policies, subject to the application of the personal portfolio bond rules, which are referred to below.

3.3.2 Broadly speaking, an investment-linked policy that gives the Policy Owner the ability to select the property or index concerned beyond "whitelisted" indices is known as a "personal portfolio bond". These supplemental rules are anti-avoidance rules, which deem an annual tax charge for the Policy Owner regardless of any actual economic gain realised on the underlying investments. This deemed gain is intended to prevent the placement of personal assets into life insurance policy contracts to benefit from tax deferral.

4 Qualifying Policies

In general, for a Life Insurance Policy, that meets the definition under the UK laws (if any) (the "Qualifying Policy"):

4.1 What tax liabilities would the Policy Owner have as a UK tax resident?

4.1.1 The specific tax treatment for the Policy Owner can depend on the type and terms of the policy, the Policy Owner's residence status throughout the lifetime of the policy, and the nature of the "chargeable event" that triggers the tax charge.

4.1.2 The UK operates a specific tax regime for life insurance policies known as the "chargeable event" regime②. The effect of the chargeable event regime is to defer any UK tax liability to the point where a "chargeable event" arises. The legislation provides that the Policy Owner becomes liable to UK income tax on gains (known as the "chargeable event gains") arising from the policy.③

4.1.3 In general, "qualifying" policies only give rise to chargeable events in restricted circumstances. A chargeable event will arise for a qualifying policy if within 10 years

---

① HMRC manual IPTM3330.
② This regime can be found at Chapter 9, Part 4 of Income Tax (Trading and Other Income) Act 2005 (ITTOIA 2005).
③ Section 461 ITTOIA 2005.

from the making of the insurance policy, or if sooner, within three-quarters of the term for which the policy is to run if not ended by death or disability, any of the following events occurs[①]:

(a) surrender or assignment of all rights under the policy;

(b) an 'excess event' where a 'periodic calculation' shows a gain; or

(c) the end of the insurance year in which a 'part surrender or assignment event' gives rise to a gain.

4.1.4　Qualifying policies therefore have a special tax status, and the proceeds can be provided free of tax if the policy has been held to maturity. However, it should be remembered that foreign policies are not qualifying policies and many UK policies exceed the threshold for premiums and therefore these rules may be less relevant in practice.

4.2　What tax liabilities would the Life Insured have as a UK tax resident?

4.2.1　The answer to this question depends on the precise identify of the Life Insured. If the Life Insured is neither the Policy Owner nor the Beneficiary, they would not have any UK tax liability in respect of the policy.

4.2.2　If the Life Insured is the Policy Owner, as noted above, qualifying policies usually have a special tax status that does not trigger a chargeable event on the death of the Life Insured. As long as the policy is held to maturity, the proceeds from the policy can be received by the Beneficiary without giving rise to a chargeable event gain for the Policy Owner.

4.3　What tax liabilities would the Beneficiary have as a UK tax resident?

4.3.1　As noted above, chargeable events occur very rarely for qualifying policies, and therefore where proceeds are received from a qualifying policy that has been held to maturity, those proceeds are usually received free of tax. If a chargeable event were to occur, then the Policy Owner would be charged to UK income tax (explained further below).

5　Non-qualifying Policies

In general, for a Life Insurance Policy that does not meet the definition under UK tax laws (if any) (the "Non-qualifying Policy", the "NQP"):

5.1　What tax liabilities would the Policy Owner have as a UK tax resident?

5.1.1　Since non-qualifying policies are more common in practice and it is the Policy Owner who usually suffers the UK tax charge, the answer below considers the UK tax rules in more detail.

---

① HMRC manual IPTM3310.

Who is liable under the chargeable events regime?

5.1.2 The UK chargeable event regime only charges an individual if they are UK resident in the tax year in which the gain arises, and:

(a) **the individual beneficially owns the rights under the policy or contract**-in most cases, the Policy Owner will be the person beneficially entitled to the rights under the policy. However, for example, if a bare trust or nominee arrangement is used, then the legal owner of the policy may hold the beneficial interest in the contract for another person; or

(b) **the rights under the policy or contract are held on non-charitable trusts which the individual created**-where the Policy Owner establishes a non-charitable trust (e.g. a family trust) to hold the life insurance policy, then they will still be chargeable under the chargeable event regime as the creator (i.e. the settlor) of the trust; or

(c) **the rights under the policy or contract are held as security for the individual's debt**-this category imposes the tax charge where the economic ownership lies. It is less common in practice as in most cases the Policy Owner will be the person assuming the debt and the Policy Owner in most cases is the beneficial owner of the rights under the policy.[①]

What is a chargeable event gain?

5.1.3 For non-qualifying life insurance policies, a chargeable event occurs when there is[②]:

(a) The surrender of all rights under a policy or contract.

(b) The assignment for value in money or money's worth of all the rights under a policy or contract.

(c) The maturity of a life insurance or capital redemption policy.

(d) A death giving rise to benefits on a life insurance policy, or payment of a capital sum on a life annuity where the annuity was made on or after 10 December 1974.

(e) An 'excess event' where 'periodic calculations' show gains.

(f) A 'part surrender or assignment event' where transaction-related calculations show gains.

(g) A 'personal portfolio bond event' where annual personal portfolio bond calculations show gains.

(h) For life annuity contracts only, the taking of a capital sum as a complete alternative to the, or further, annuity payments.

5.1.4 If a chargeable event occurs, any chargeable event gain can be charged to UK

---

① Section 465 ITTOIA 2005.
② Section 484 ITTOIA 2005.

income tax.

Residence[①]

5.1.5 As noted above, the Policy Owner will only be chargeable to UK income tax if they are UK resident. An individual is UK tax resident if they satisfy the UK "Statutory Residence Test".

5.1.6 A person who is UK resident and UK domiciled will be chargeable to UK income tax on an arising basis. This means that even if they receive funds outside the UK, they will still be liable to UK income tax.

5.1.7 By contrast, individuals who are UK resident, but non-UK domiciled (and not deemed domiciled) can (at present) benefit from the "remittance basis of taxation". This means that they only pay UK tax on their foreign investment income and gains if they are brought to or remitted to the UK. Importantly, the remittance basis does not, however, apply to chargeable event gains. Therefore, if a remittance basis user is charged under the chargeable events regime, an income tax charge will still arise even if the policy is a non-UK policy and even if those funds are never remitted to the UK. It is worth noting that the current UK government intends to abolish the remittance basis from 6 April 2025 so this point may not be relevant for much longer.

5.1.8 Note that there are wider anti-avoidance rules that can apply to individuals who are "temporarily non-resident". The chargeable events regime has a specific rule that treats any chargeable event gain arising during a short period of non-residence as being charged to UK income tax when the individual returns to the UK.[②] These anti-avoidance rules avoid the situation where individuals will become non-UK resident for a short period of time, realise a gain free of UK tax, and then return to the UK immediately after.

Calculating the chargeable event gain

5.1.9 As for calculating the gain chargeable to income tax, where the whole of the rights are given up, the chargeable event gain is equal to the excess of the total policy benefits received during the life of the policy over premiums paid, less any earlier policy gains.

5.1.10 For example, if premiums paid over the life of the policy were £100,000, and the benefit received under the policy was £500,000, and there have been no earlier chargeable event gains under the policy, then the gain would be £400,000.

5.1.11 Where there is a part surrender or assignment, the event gain is equal to (i) the excess of the total value of part surrenders or assignments so far, over (ii) an allowance at a

---

① We are not providing advice on resident, domicile or other key UK personal tax concepts in this note, but can provide further details separately, if required.

② Section 465B ITTOIA 2005.

cumulative 5% annual rate on each premium paid so far, starting with the insurance year of payment and ending at the end of the insurance year of calculation, subject to a maximum of 20 years of allowances.

5.1.12 For example, if the premiums under a policy are £10,000 per year, then the 5% allowance is capped at £500. If a part surrender is made of £2,000 then there is £1,500 in excess of the 5% allowance which would be a chargeable event. If premiums have been paid for 2 years, then the allowable element is $2 \times 5\% \times £10,000 = £1,000$. Therefore, the gain would be £1,500 - £1,000 = £500.

Reliefs

5.1.13 For UK policies, in most cases, individuals and trustees within the scope of UK tax are treated as having paid tax on the gain at the basic income tax rate (currently 20%).[1] This means that the notional tax does not have to be paid by the Policy Owner, but anything above the basic rate will need to be paid.

5.1.14 The second relief available is known as "top slicing relief".[2] This relief is available where the taxpayer would be liable to tax at a lower rate of income tax, were it not for the inclusion of the chargeable event gain in their income for that tax year. Effectively the relief allows the gain to be annualised so the Policy Owner pays tax at a rate equivalent to the rate that would have applied if the gain had been taxable in each year it was made.

5.1.15 For example, if a Policy Owner were to receive a £100,000 gain on a policy in one year this would mean they are subject to UK income tax at the highest rates. If the gain was accrued over 10 years, then the annual equivalent would be £10,000, which may be taxed at a lower rate of tax.

Foreign policies

5.1.16 As noted above at paragraph 5.1.2, a Policy Owner can only be chargeable to UK income tax if they are UK resident at the time the chargeable event gains arise. In addition to this residence requirement, where the gain arises from a foreign policy, that gain is reduced if the Policy Owner was not UK resident throughout the entirety of the policy period. This is referred to as "time apportioned reduction".[3] Therefore, it is necessary to consider the period in which the Policy Owner was UK resident and not UK resident on a time apportionment basis, even if they are UK resident at the time the chargeable event occurs.

5.1.17 Unlike UK policies, foreign policies cannot in most cases be treated as though

---

[1] HMRC manual IPTM3810 and section 530 ITTOIA 2005.
[2] HMRC manual IPTM3820 and section 535 ITTOIA 2005.
[3] HMRC manual IPTM3730.

basic rate tax has been paid on any gains. ①

5.1.18 In addition, for top slicing relief, to prevent excessive relief, the number of complete years by which a gain on a foreign policy is divided under the top-slicing relief provisions is also reduced if the Policy Owner was not UK resident throughout the policy period.

5.2 What tax liabilities would the Life Insured have as a UK tax resident?

5.2.1 Once again, it is necessary to consider whether the Life Insured is also the Policy Owner and whether they are, therefore, the relevant person chargeable under the chargeable event regime.

5.2.2 It is common for individuals to have multiple Life Insured so that the life insurance policy lasts for longer. Furthermore, it is common for the Life Insured to be different to the person who receives the benefit under the life insurance policy contract. As such, it is important that the terms of each contract are considered carefully.

5.3 What tax liabilities would the Beneficiary have as a UK tax resident?

5.3.1 The Beneficiary will receive the death benefit on the death of the (last) Life Insured. This can be received free of UK tax as it is the Policy Owner who potentially suffers the UK liability under the chargeable event regime assuming the Policy Owner was UK resident at the time of their death.

6 Specific Scenarios

6.1 Suppose that the Policy Owner, a UK tax resident, who purchases and holds a Non-Qualifying Policy ("NQP"), will he be subject to any tax liabilities when:

6.1.1 the Policy Owner purchases a NQP and pays the premium;

(a) In general, there are no immediate UK tax implications for a UK resident Policy Owner paying premiums for a non-qualifying life insurance policy held in the Policy Owner's personal name.

(b) If the policy is written into trust, for the purpose of ensuring that the proceeds from the policy do not form part of the Policy Owner's estate for IHT purposes, then payments to the trust to fund the premium payments could give rise to an immediate IHT charge at a rate of 20% to the extent the payments are above the Policy Owner's 'nil rate band' (currently £325,000).

(c) The easiest way to avoid this IHT charge is to ensure that the premiums are paid out

---

① HMRC manual IPTM3720 and section 531 ITTOIA 2005.

of surplus income during the lifetime of the Policy Owner. This is because there is an exemption for IHT purposes for lifetime gifts made from excess income.[①]

(d) In order to qualify for the IHT exemption, the payments must be paid out of income on a regular basis. Importantly the Policy Owner must have sufficient income remaining to maintain their usual standard of living.

(e) Where a Policy Owner is non-UK domiciled (and not deemed domiciled) and the policy is a non-UK policy, then this IHT charge will not be a concern. This is because (under current rules) a non-UK domiciled Policy Owner can settle a non-UK policy on trust and there would be no IHT issues as the policy is non-UK situs. Furthermore, if the Policy Owner uses non-UK situs funds to fund the trust to pay the premiums, there will be no potential IHT charge on those settled funds. Please note that the IHT rules are potentially changing from 6 April 2025. It is proposed that domicile is no longer the connecting factor and instead if a person has been UK resident for 10 years or more, their overseas as well as UK assets will be within the scope of IHT.

(f) Another key point for UK resident and non-UK domiciled Policy Owners who are currently (or have been) taxed on the remittance basis of taxation relates to the payment of any premiums. The payments should be paid using "clean capital". It is important that the funds used to pay the premiums do not represent foreign income and gains that arise at a time when the Policy Owner was UK resident, as they would be taxed if they are remitted to the UK.

6.1.2 the Policy Owner holds a NQP;

(a) Holding a non-qualifying policy is not a taxable event in itself. A Policy Owner can only be charged under the chargeable event regime if a chargeable event arises and there is a gain which can be charged to the Policy Owner.

6.1.3 the cash value increases and accumulates within the NQP;

(a) Non-qualifying policies benefit from tax deferral, so that generally there is no immediate UK tax charge on any income and gains arising within the policy itself. It is only at the point in time that a chargeable event occurs will there potentially be a tax charge on that profit.

(b) However, if the policy is instead a "personal portfolio bond", then the separate anti-avoidance regime will apply. This will deem the Policy Owner to make a gain on an annual basis, and therefore no tax deferral will be available.

6.1.4 the Policy Owner loans against the NQP (including using the policy as collateral);

---

① Section 21(1) Inheritance Tax Act 1984.

(a) An individual will be chargeable to UK income tax under the chargeable event regime where the rights under the policy or contract are held as security for the individual's debt (see paragraph 5.1.2 above). Therefore, if the Policy Owner uses the non-qualifying policy as security for personal debt, then they can be charged to UK income tax when a chargeable event arises (albeit this charge would arise in any event since the Policy Owner is usually the beneficial owner of the rights under the policy).

(b) A UK income tax will still only arise as and when a chargeable event occurs. The use of the policy as collateral is not a chargeable event in and of itself, and therefore there will be no immediate charge to UK income tax when the loan is made by the Policy Owner.

(c) However, it should be noted that the making of a loan by an insurer in connection with a life insurance policy will be treated as a part surrender of the policy, and therefore a chargeable event.①

6.1.5 the Policy Owner transfers the NQP to other person;

(a) It is assumed for these purposes that "transfer" here means a transfer for consideration. An assignment of the whole or part of the non-qualifying policy to another person for money or money's worth is a chargeable event.

(b) As such, to the extent there are any chargeable event gains arising on the assignment, the Policy Owner may be required to pay UK income tax.

6.1.6 the Policy Owner gifts the NQP to other person;

(a) An assignment not for value (i.e., by way of gift) is not a chargeable event under the chargeable events regime. As such, a gift of the non-qualifying policy will not give rise to a UK income tax charge.

(b) It should be noted that to the extent the Policy Owner has not used the 5% allowance (see below) during their ownership of the policy, then the donee will be able to benefit from the unused allowance following the gift.

6.1.7 the Policy Owner partially or wholly surrenders the NQP;

(a) The partial or whole surrender of all rights under a non-qualifying life insurance policy is a chargeable event for the purposes of the chargeable event regime. Therefore, the Policy Owner will be liable to UK income tax on any chargeable event gains arising on the surrender.

(b) There is a specific rule known as the "5% deferral rule"② which allows partial surrenders or assignments of up to 5% of accumulated premiums made with any tax charge

---

① HMRC manual IPTM 3400 and section 484 ITTOIA 2005.
② Section 507 ITTOIA 2005.

postponed until maturity or a later realisation. As such, the Policy Owner can withdraw up to 5% of the accumulate premiums per annum without incurring an immediate UK income tax charge.

(c) Any unused "allowance" can be brought forward and used in the following year. As such, this effectively allows the Policy Owner to withdraw the entirety of the premium payments within 20 years of the establishment of the life insurance policy.

6.1.8 the Policy Owner receives bonus/dividends from the NQP;

(a) The receipt of a "bonus or dividend" from the non-qualifying policy above the 5% allowance noted above at paragraph 6.1.7(b) will be treated as a surrender of the rights of the policy. As such, this will be a chargeable event to which a chargeable event gain may arise.

6.1.9 the Life Insured dies and the Beneficiary gets the death benefit;

(a) On the death of the (last) Life Insured, two events occur: (i) there is a death benefit pay out to the Beneficiary, and (ii) the life insurance policy matures or terminates. As such, there will be a chargeable event for the purposes of the chargeable event regime.

(b) Where this occurs, the Beneficiary will be able to receive their death benefit free of UK tax. However, the Policy Owner will pay any UK income tax on the chargeable event gain. If the Policy Owner was also the Life Insured, then the chargeable event gain will be treated as arising immediately prior to their death. Therefore, their estate will pay the required UK income tax charge.

(c) It also worth noting that as the policy will form part of the estate of the Policy Owner, this will have implications for IHT purposes (where the Policy Owner is UK domiciled or the policy is a UK policy). The Policy Owner's estate will be required to pay IHT at a rate of 40% on the value of the policy. It is therefore important to establish if the policy has a surrender value at the time of death. If it does, it would make sense to plan around this potential IHT liability.

6.1.10 In the above scenarios, does the tax residency of the Life Insured or the Beneficiary have any impact on the tax liability of the Policy Owner?

(a) Assuming they are different persons, the tax residency of the Life Insured or the Beneficiary will not impact the tax liability of the Policy Owner as the Policy Owner is the relevant taxable person under the policy contract. It will be residence position of the Policy Owner which is relevant.

(b) Individuals can only be charged under the chargeable events regime if they are UK resident in the tax year in which the gain arises (subject to the temporary non-resident rules). An individual is not liable to tax under the chargeable event regime on any gains arising in any tax year in which the individual is not UK resident.

(c) There are additional rules which apply where a life insurance policy is held on trust. These are considered briefly below.

6.2 Suppose that the Life Insured of the NQP is a UK tax resident:

6.2.1 Will the Life Insured be subject to any tax liabilities?

(a) If the Life Insured does not receive any benefits from the policy, and does not benefit from any rights whatsoever, then there should be no UK tax liability for the Life Insured.

(b) As noted above, the Life Insured will only be subject to UK income tax under the chargeable events regime if (i) they are also beneficially entitled to the rights under the policy; (ii) they are the creator of a trust which holds a life insurance policy, or (iii) they have used the policy as collateral for a personal loan. For these to apply, this usually means the Life Insured and the Policy Owner are the same person.

6.2.2 Does the tax residency of the Policy Owner or the Beneficiary have any impact on the tax liability of the Life Insured?

(a) The tax residency of the Policy Owner or the Beneficiary would not impact the tax liability of the Life Insured. If the Life Insured is taxable under any of the three facets noted above, they will only be chargeable to UK income tax if they themselves are UK resident in the tax year in which the gains arise.

6.3 Suppose that the Beneficiary of the NQP is a UK tax resident:

6.3.1 Will the Beneficiary be subject to any tax liabilities when the Life Insured dies and the Beneficiary receives the death benefit?

(a) The Beneficiary will receive the death benefit free of UK tax but the Policy Owner will usually be charged to UK income tax on the chargeable event gain.

6.2.2 Does the tax residency of the Policy Owner or the Life Insured have any impact on the tax liability of the Beneficiary?

(a) The person chargeable to UK income tax under the chargeable event regime is only taxable to the extent they are UK resident in the tax year in which the gain arises. The residence status of any other person does not affect the tax status of the chargeable person.

(b) Given the Beneficiary will usually receive the death benefit free of UK tax, the tax residence of the Policy Owner or the Life Insured would not usually affect this.

(c) One circumstance in which this might affect the Beneficiary is where the policy is held on trust in a non-UK resident trust settled by a non-UK settlor (i.e., the Policy Owner). In this case, the receipt of a distribution or benefit by a UK resident beneficiary from the non-UK resident trust could trigger a UK income tax charge for the beneficiary of the trust.

6.4 Suppose that the Irrevocable Beneficiary of the NQP is a UK tax resident (the

Irrevocable Beneficiary is appointed by the Policy Owner, and the Policy Owner could not withdraw, surrender, transfer, or loan against the policy without the Irrevocable Beneficiary's consent):

6.4.1 Will the Irrevocable Beneficiary be subject to any tax liability while the NQP is in force?

(a) The Irrevocable Beneficiary's liability to UK income tax under the chargeable event regime will depend on whether they are a relevant taxable person as noted at paragraph 5.1.2.

(b) Where the Policy Owner is chargeable to UK income tax, then the Irrevocable Beneficiary will not be charged to UK income tax even if they are required to provide their consent for the Policy Owner to benefit from the policy. This is because the Policy Owner will remain the beneficial owner of the rights under the policy contract, even if the Irrevocable Beneficiary's consent is required. Furthermore, on the death of the Life Insured, the life insurance policy will terminate, so the consent powers effectively become redundant.

6.4.2 Will the Irrevocable Beneficiary be subject to any tax liability when the Life Insured dies and he/she gets the death benefits?

(a) On the death of the (last) Life Insured the policy would end, and assuming the Policy Owner is beneficially entitled to the proceeds under the policy contract, the Policy Owner will be charged to UK income tax on the chargeable event gain. The Irrevocable Beneficiary will receive any death benefit on the death of the Life Insured free of UK tax.

6.4.3 Does the tax residency of the Policy Owner or the Life Insured have any impact on the Irrevocable Beneficiary's tax liability?

(a) Generally, the tax residency of the Policy Owner or the Life Insured will not affect the UK tax position of the Irrevocable Beneficiary where the policy is held in the Policy Owner's personal name.

(b) However, if the policy is held in a non-UK resident trust settled by a non-UK settlor (being the Policy Owner), then the Irrevocable Beneficiary could be charged to UK income tax if it were to receive a distribution or benefit from that trust whilst resident in the UK.

6.4.4 Does the proportion of the Irrevocable Beneficiary's interest in the death benefit (from 1% to 100%) affect his tax liability?

(a) The Irrevocable Beneficiary can receive their interest in the death benefit free of UK tax. However, the Policy Owner (being UK tax resident) is charged to UK income tax under the chargeable event regime.

(b) As noted at paragraph 6.4.3(b), if an Irrevocable Beneficiary is charged to UK income tax by virtue of receiving a distribution from a non-UK trust, then the distribution would be charged to UK income tax to the extent it is matched to the relevant income within the trust itself. If the trust only holds the life insurance policy, this will mean the distribution is matched to the chargeable event gains. Therefore, the Irrevocable Beneficiary will be taxed in relation to their proportional interest in the benefit.

7 Life Insurance Policies and Tax Planning

7.1 Under UK tax law, how can a UK tax resident make use of a NQP for tax planning?

7.1.1 There are specific tax benefits to UK residents purchasing non-qualifying life insurance policies.

7.2 Deferred UK tax

7.2.1 Broadly, the taxation of life insurance policies and the chargeable events regime as compared to holding investments personally is that, provided there is no chargeable event, the Policy Owner would not have to pay UK income tax on dividends and interest arising from the policy's underlying investments. Nor would they pay capital gains tax on disposals when the underlying investments are altered.

7.2.2 Therefore, non-qualifying life insurance policies provide a mechanism for tax deferral during the lifetime of the Policy Owner.

7.2.3 If the Policy Owner intends to become non-UK tax resident in the future, then as long as they surrender their rights under the policy during a time when they are not UK resident (and not temporarily non-resident) then there will be no UK tax charge at all.

7.3 5% tax-free withdrawal allowance

7.3.1 As mentioned above, life insurance policies subject to the chargeable events regime allow Policy Owners to make tax-free withdrawals of up to 5% each year from accumulated premiums, without triggering a chargeable event. This means that over a 20-year period (or longer), they can extract the full amount of the premium without exposure to an immediate tax charge in the UK.

7.3.2 This is the most effective method for drawing on the policy and these drawdowns can be accumulated and drawn down in future at a single event, at such time as the withdrawal is required.

7.4 Change in ownership versus a change to the life/lives assured

7.4.1 The Policy Owner can gift the life insurance policy to another individual entirely free of UK income tax. However, if the Policy Owner is UK domiciled or the policy is a UK policy, this will be treated as a gift for UK inheritance tax purposes. Whilst gifts are not immediately chargeable to inheritance tax, the Policy Owner would need to survive seven years from the date the gift is made to avoid an inheritance tax charge on death in relation to the gift.

7.4.2 Alternatively, the Policy Owner could change or expand the individuals insured under the life insurance policy. However, this would give rise to a chargeable event, and therefore a UK income tax charge for the Policy Owner.

7.4.3 The key chargeable event outside the Policy Owner's control is the death of the last life assured. By choosing multiple life assured, there is therefore the possibility of the policy continuing after the Policy Owner's death, as the first life assured, which can defer the policy's termination and delay a chargeable event until the death of the surviving life assured. If those inheriting the continuing policy are non-UK resident, then they could surrender the policy without a UK tax charge if they wished.

7.5 There are a number of ways that life insurance policies could be held including: (1) personal ownership, and (2) ownership through a trust:

7.5.1 Personal ownership

(a) In personal ownership, the life insurance policy is directly owned by an individual.

(b) Policy Owners who are UK tax resident may be liable for tax on chargeable event gains arising from the life insurance policy. Therefore, chargeable event gains from a life insurance policy would be subject to income tax in the tax year they occur.

(c) The value of the policy will form part of the Policy Owner's estate (if they are UK domiciled or the policy is UK situs) unless for example the policy is written in trust from which the Policy Owner is excluded. It is commonplace for policies to be written into trust where the Policy Owner is subject to inheritance tax.

7.5.2 Trust ownership

(a) Trust ownership involves placing the life insurance policy into a trust, where a trustee holds and manages the policy on behalf of the beneficiaries. The trust would typically be a discretionary trust, the beneficiaries of which would be the Policy Owner's spouse and/or children. It is also common for individuals to use bare trusts for the benefit of their minor children.

(b) This structure provides control, flexibility, and potential estate planning benefits. However, the suitability and availability of this option may vary based on local laws and regulations, as not all jurisdictions allow life insurance policies to be held in trust.

(c) If the Policy Owner is UK tax resident and they settle the life insurance policy onto trust, they will still be treated as a person chargeable under the chargeable event regime. This applies even if the Policy Owner cannot benefit from the trust.[①]

---

① S465(1A) ITTOIA 2005.

(d) Furthermore, if the Policy Owner is UK domiciled and charged to UK inheritance tax on their worldwide estate, they will need to ensure that premium payments made to the trust are paid using excess income to avoid an immediate inheritance tax charge of 20%.

(e) Policy Owners who are non-UK domiciled (and not deemed domiciled) could contribute their non-UK funds to the trust to enable the premium payments to be made by the trustee.

(f) If a UK resident Policy Owner settles a UK resident trust, but then either becomes non-UK resident at the time a chargeable event occurs, or the chargeable event takes place following their death, then the UK resident trustees will be liable to UK income tax.

(g) However, if a life insurance policy is held in a non-UK resident trust, and the settlor/Policy Owner is non-UK resident or deceased at the time the chargeable event takes place, then there is no immediate charge to UK income tax. Instead, an income tax charge would arise when a UK resident Beneficiary receives a distribution or benefit from the trust under complex anti-avoidance rules.

7.6 As such, there are options available for UK resident Policy Owners regarding the life insurance policy itself and how the policy is held to ensure that the structure is as tax efficient as possible.

附录 E：日本税务意见

Japan Tax Opinions

Tagaki Law Office | 2024.08

1　Background

1.1　General rules of income tax and corporate income tax

1.1.1　Taxpayer

Under Japanese tax law, individuals and corporations are ordinary taxpayers. Resident individuals and domestic corporations are subject to Japanese income tax on world-wide income, and non-resident individuals and foreign corporations are subject to Japanese tax on Japan source income.① Non-permanent residents who are not Japanese nationals and who live in Japan for a period of not more than 5 years within the past 10 years will be subject to tax on Japan source income and non-Japan source income transferred to Japan or paid in Japan.

Each taxpayer will pay income tax (for individual taxpayers) or corporate income tax (for corporate taxpayers) separately. The individual tax rate is progressive, and the marginal tax rate is 55%, including local tax of 10%. Corporate income tax is approximately 30.62% (large

---

① Income Tax Law Art. 2 Para. 1 Item 3 and Item 5, Income Tax Law Art. 7 Para. 1 Item 1 and Item 3, Income Tax Art. 164, Corporate Tax Law Art. 2 Para 1 Item 3 and Item 4, Corporate Income Tax Law Art. 141.

corporation), including local tax of approximately 6.5%. Non-residents and foreign corporations are exempt from local tax, unless they have a permanent establishment in Japan.①

In the case of a certain domestic "family corporation," where 50% or more of the shares in the company is owned by three or fewer shareholders, the company is subject to an additional 10 to 20% of corporate income tax on the undistributed income②. In the case of a family corporation, including a foreign one, the tax authority is granted the right to re-characterize or re-calculate the income of the company and/or the shareholders, if the original transaction or calculation unduly reduces the tax due③.

Also, if a majority of shares in a foreign corporation are owned by a resident individual and/or a domestic corporation, and the effective tax rate in the country where such foreign corporation is located is lower than 20%, the income of such foreign corporation will be aggregated with the income of the domestic taxpayers unless such foreign company has substance of business④.

Even if the taxpayer has not violated any of the specific rules above, there are general anti-avoidance rules such as rules on "substance over form" or "denial of valuation of asset for tax avoidance purposes" that give wide tax adjustment powers to the tax authority⑤.

1.1.2　Free transfer of assets

A gift (or inheritance) from one individual to another is subject to gift or inheritance tax.⑥ Non-resident donees and heirs are "limited taxpayers" where they are subject to Japanese gift/inheritance tax on the assets located in Japan.⑦ Japanese nationals will not be limited taxpayers unless they and the donor/deceased are both non-residents at any time in the ten years prior to death or gift.⑧ Non-Japanese nationals will not be limited taxpayers if the donor/deceased or done/heir were residents at any time in the ten years prior to death or gift. Non-Japanese nationals staying in Japan with Type 1 temporary visas will be limited taxpayers. Gifts or bequests to a person who is conducting charitable activities are not subject to gift tax if it is certain that such person will use the asset for a charitable purpose.⑨

---

① Income Tax Law Art. 2 Para. 1 Item 4, Income Tax Law Art. 7 Para. 1 Item 2.
② Corporate Income Tax Art. 67, Corporate Tax Law Art. 2 Item 10.
③ Corporate Income Tax Law Art. 132 Para. 1 and Art. 147, Income Tax Law Art. 157 Para. 1, and Inheritance and Gift Tax Law Art. 64 Para. 1.
④ Special Taxation Measures Law Art. 40-4 and Art. 66-6.
⑤ Income Tax Law Art. 12, Corporate Income Tax Law Art. 11, Basic Circular regarding Valuation of Asset, Art. 6.
⑥ Inheritance and Gift Tax Law Art. 1-3 Para. 1 Item 1 and 1-4 Para. 1 Item 1.
⑦ Inheritance and Gift Tax Law Art. 1-3 Para. 1 Item 3 and 1-4 Para. 1 Item 3.
⑧ Inheritance and Gift Tax Law Art. 1-3 Para. 1 Item 2 and 1-4 Para. 1 Item 2.
⑨ Inheritance Tax Law Art. 12 Para. 1 Item 3 and Art. 21 Para. 1 Item 3 Inheritance Tax Law Enforcement Ordinance Art. 2 and Art. 4-5.

Status of heir, donee, beqeustee Status of deceased or donor		Resident		Non-resident		
		Temporary resident with Type 1 Visa	Others	Japanese person who was resident in the past 10 years	Other Japanese national	Non-Japanese national
Resident	Temporary resident with Type 1 visa	L	U	U	L	L
	Others	U	U	U	U	U
Non-resident	Resident in the past 10 years	U	U	U	U	U
	Resident in the past 10 years. However, non-Japanese national (inheritance tax), or less than 10 years as resident in past 15 years (gift tax), or more than 2 years after became non-resident (gift tax)	L	U	U	L	L
	others	L	U	U	L	L

L: Limited Taxpayer. U: Unlimited Taxpayer.

On the other hand, the free transfer of assets between two corporate taxpayers will not be subject to gift/inheritance tax. The transfer is subject to corporate tax at the recipient corporation (donation income) and the donor corporation (denial of the loss for corporate income tax purposes).[1]

Free transfers from individual taxpayers to corporate taxpayers are not a matter of gift/inheritance tax in ordinary situations. A free transfer will create a deemed capital gain if an individual donor transfers appreciated assets to a corporate taxpayer.[2] Such deemed capital gain will be exempt if the donee is the government or certain public interest organizations[3]. The recipient corporate taxpayer is subject to corporate income tax on the value of the transferred asset. In the case of a gift from an individual to a family corporation, the transfer will be considered a gift to the shareholders to the extent of the value of the shares increased

---

[1] Corporate Income Tax Law Art. 22 Para. 2 and Art. 37.
[2] Income Tax Law Art. 59 Para. 1.
[3] Special Taxation Measures Law Art. 40.

by such gift①. Then gift tax will be imposed on the shareholders, in addition to the tax on the corporation itself.

In the case of a gift or bequest, including an initial gift or bequest for establishment, to an association or foundation without juridical personality, which has provisions for a representative or administrator, gift tax is imposed on the association or foundation②. This gift tax will be exempt if such association or foundation is conducting charitable activities under certain conditions③.

Furthermore, in order to prevent use of gifts by a corporation without ownership interest to avoid gift or inheritance tax, a contribution to a corporation without ownership interest is subject to gift tax if it results in an unfair reduction of gift or inheritance tax of the family or relatives of the founder④. The enforcement ordinance provides that a gift to such a corporation shall be treated as an unfair reduction of gift or inheritance tax of family or relatives unless (i) the operating organization is properly managed and the Articles of Association provide that the number of family directors should not exceed 1/3 of the total number of members of the board, (ii) the corporation shall not provide special benefits regarding use of facilities, operation of funds, distribution of residual assets, loans, assignments or salary to the donor, bequestor, founder, member, director etc. or their family or relatives, (iii) the Articles of Association provide that the residual assets at the time of dissolution shall go to the government or other public interest organizations, and (iv) there is no violation of laws, concealment or forgery of accounting documents, etc. regarding such corporation⑤. Even if a corporation without ownership interest itself is not treated as a gift and inheritance taxpayer by this rule, if such corporation provides a special benefit regarding use of facilities, operation of funds or distribution of residual assets to the founder, member, director, etc. or their family or relatives, the gift or bequest to such corporation shall be treated as a gift or bequest to the person who receives the special benefit⑥.

Finally, the free transfer of assets from a corporate taxpayer to an individual taxpayer will be treated as a non-deductible expense for the corporate taxpayer and occasional income for the individual taxpayer who received the gift from the corporation⑦.

---

① Inheritance Tax Basic Circular Sec 9-2.
② Inheritance Tax Law Art. 66 Para. 1 and Para. 2.
③ Inheritance Tax Law Art. 12 Para. 1 Item 3 and Art. 21 Para. 1 Item 3 Inheritance Tax Law Enforcement Ordinance Art. 2 and Art. 4-5.
④ Inheritance Tax Law Art. 66 Para. 4.
⑤ Inheritance Tax Law Enforcement Ordinance Art. 33 Para. 3.
⑥ Inheritance Tax Law Art. 65.
⑦ Corporate Income Tax Law Art. 22 Para. 2 and Art. 37 Income Tax Law Art. 34 Income Tax Law Basic Circular Sec. 34-1.

The valuation of the asset for purposes of the inheritance and gift tax is provided in the circular issued by the tax administration①. The basic valuation of unlisted shares will be determined by the net asset value method or a combination of the net asset value and the comparable share price methods②. However, shares in certain companies such as "designated stock holding companies", "designated land holding companies" or companies incorporated within 3 accounting years are evaluated by the net asset value method only③. Land is basically valued by the road side price method, which is approximately 70%–80% of fair market value④.

1.1.3 Source of income and location of asset

In order to determine the taxable income of a non-resident individual or a foreign corporation, the Income Tax Law and Corporate Income Tax Law have detailed rules about the source of income⑤. For example, dividends from a Japanese corporation, and rent and capital gains from Japanese real property shall be Japan source income. Also, the Gift Tax Law provides rules about the location of an asset in order to determine the tax duty of a limited taxpayer⑥. For example, money in non-Japanese accounts is located in the country where the account exists. The treatment of an asset in a trust account is not clearly provided in the law, but the location of the account is considered to be the location of the entrusted asset itself by the majority of practitioners.

1.2 Taxation of foundations in general

Under Japanese law, a foundation is considered to be a legal entity where the basic fund was contributed for the principal purpose determined by the founder. Establishment of a foundation is a taxable event for a person who is contributing assets, with regard to the appreciated value of such assets (deemed capital gain). If assets were non-appreciated, there is no deemed capital gain. On the other hand, the foundation is treated as an ordinary corporation if it is not exempt under Japanese law. Therefore, the amount of the contribution shall be subject to corporate tax at the foundation as corporate income. If such foundation is a non-Japanese corporation, it is subject to corporate tax on the gift of Japanese assets by the resident⑦.

---

① Basic Circular regarding Valuation of Asset, Sec 5-2 of the circular provides that assets located outside of Japan shall be valued in accordance with the rules applicable to domestic assets.
② Basic Circular regarding Valuation of Asset, Sec 179.
③ Basic Circular regarding Valuation of Asset, Sec 189-3 and 189-4.
④ Basic Circular regarding Valuation of Asset, Sec 11.
⑤ Income Tax Law Art. 161 Corporate Income Tax Art. 138.
⑥ Inheritance Tax Law Art. 10.
⑦ Corporate Income Tax Law Enforcement Ordinance Art. 178 Para. 1 Item 2.

In order to facilitate public interest activities, there are certain tax emptions for public interest foundations.

	Public Interest Association/ Foundation	Ordinary Association/ Foundation (Non-profit type)	Ordinary Association/ Foundation (Other than non-profit typr)	Approved NPO Corporation	NPO Corporation
Exemption from tax on non-prifit making activities (corporate income tax)	○	○	×	○	○
Exemption from withholding tax on interest/dividend (income tax)	○	×	×	×	×

1.3 Taxation on trusts

There are three types of taxation on the income earned by a fund contributed to a trust. These are the taxation on the beneficiary upon accrual of income by the trust (beneficiary taxation trust), taxation on the beneficiary at the time of distribution to the beneficiary (collective investment trust), and implementation of corporate tax on the trustee upon accrual of the income to the trust (corporate taxation trust). Beneficiary taxation trust is basic taxation of the trust income. Collective investment trust is applied to financial products using a trust structure, retirement pension trusts and designated public interest trusts, etc. Corporate taxation trust is applied to a trust such as one which has no beneficiary.

In the case of a basic beneficiary taxation trust, the ownership of the assets is transferred to the trustee, however, for tax purposes, the beneficiary is treated as if it is directly holding the assets, debts, income from the trust assets and expenses, and is subject to tax at the time of accrual of income. For example, if the trust assets were real property for rental, rent income shall be subject to tax in the year of accrual to the beneficiary. Whether the beneficiary actually received income from the trustee or not is not relevant. A beneficiary treated as a beneficiary to whom trust assets, debts, income and expenses are attributable shall include a person who has the right to change the trust and is able to receive income from the trust (i.e. a deemed beneficiary).

If there is no current beneficiary and no deemed beneficiary, such as a purpose trust which was established by will, the trust will be a trust without beneficiary and treated as a corporate taxation trust where the trustee is subject to corporate income tax.

The treatment of a discretionary trust is not always certain. Usually a taxpayer takes the position that despite a discretional distribution by the trustee, the beneficiary was granted beneficiary ownership of the asset in trust when he/she became a beneficiary. The tax authorities will take the same position. However, there is a lower court case against such position. In 2011, Nagoya District Court agreed with the taxpayer who argued that the beneficiary (a grandchild) was not yet a beneficiary of the trust which received money from the grandfather because the money was used to purchase life insurance, and actual distribution is subject to the trustee after payment of the insurance payment. The court also pointed out that the grandson may not be a beneficiary in the future since the father had the power to designate a new beneficiary as a protector of the trust. The appeal court and Supreme Court rejected the District Court's decision and agreed with the State, who imposed gift tax on the grandson. According to the appeal court and the Supreme Court, the beneficiary is subject to gift tax even if distribution of income is discretionary to the trustee. The court also rejected the taxpayer's argument that the trust should be treated as an insurance trust where the beneficiary is subject to tax upon payment of insurance proceeds. According to the courts, such exceptional tax treatment should be allowed only if the trust is considered to be an insurance agreement itself where there is no discretion for the trustee regarding investment and management assets and the trustee is obliged to purchase the insurance under the trust deed.

1.4 Insurance business law

According to Article 2, Paragraph 1 of the Insurance Business Act, life insurance is "insurance that promises to pay a fixed amount of insurance money upon a person's life or death and receives insurance premiums."

Under the Japanese Insurance Business Law ("IBL"), purchase of insurance with respect to a Japanese resident or Japanese property from a foreign insurance company that has no licensed branch in Japan is permissible with the prior permission of the Financial Service Agency (the "FSA") (IBL Art. 186 Para. 2). A foreign insurance company is not allowed to accept such insurance (IBL Art. 186 Para. 1). Certain types of insurance that are specifically exempt from such requirement are re-insurance and foreign travelers insurance (IBL Enforcement Order Article 19, IBL Enforcement Regulation Article 116) but other insurance, such as life insurance, is not specifically excluded from such requirement. Violation will result in the representative or an employee of a non-licensed foreign insurer being subject to a criminal penalty of up to 2 years imprisonment or fines of up to 3 million yen or both and fines of up to 3 million yen for the insurer (ILB Art. 316) and administrative fines of up to 500,000 yen for the person who enters into an insurance contract with a non-licensed foreign insurer (IBL Art 337).

Article 275 of the IBL prohibits insurance solicitation of clients who are resident in Japan except by limited persons. Violation will result in the representative or an employee of a non-licensed foreign insurer being subject to a criminal penalty of up to 1 year's imprisonment or fines of up to 1 million yen (IBL Art. 317).

However, assuming that all activities related to the execution of a life insurance contract under which a Japanese resident is an insured, including referral, solicitation, application, medical examination and execution, occur outside Japan, we are of the opinion that Articles 186 and 275 (and the appurtenant penalty clauses) of the IBL would not apply in an extraterritorial context. The reasons are three-fold.

First, a recent amendment to the IBL includes a list of the Articles of the IBL which specifically apply in an extra-territorial context. Articles 186 and 275 (and the appurtenant penalty clauses) do not appear on the list. Further, while the penalties under IBL Arts. 186 and 275 includes criminal penalties, as there is no clear indication in the law that it will apply in the circumstances. As there is no clear indication that penalty clauses in respect of Articles 186 and 275 apply in an extraterritorial context, the application of criminal sanctions in respect thereof would go against fundamental principles of Japanese law. Finally, in the ten years since the last major amendment to the IBL, there has been no attempt by the FSA to apply Articles 186 and 275 (and the appurtenant penalty clauses) on an extraterritorial basis.

Although there are certain concerns about administrative procedures and criminal fines, it should be noted that the validity of an insurance policy itself is not an issue of Japanese law. It is an issue under the law which governs the insurance agreement.

1.5 Taxation of life insurance

1.5.1 At the time of purchase of insurance policy

Payments of premiums for certain insurance is deductible for individual taxpayers up to JPY 120,000 per year[①]. Corporate taxpayers may deduct a certain portion of premium payments for life insurance for corporate directors and employees which does not correspond to the portion of the insurance proceeds accumulated as savings and refunded at maturity. Income accrued and accumulated by the insurance company is not subject to the income tax or corporate tax of the policyholder unless there is a distribution. If a distribution is made to the

---

[①] Income Tax Law Art. 76.

premium payer before the maturity of the policy, it will be considered a refund of the premiums and not subject to income tax.

1.5.2 Payment upon death of insured

Life insurance proceeds are subject to different taxes based on the relationships between the premium payer, the insured person and the recipient of the proceeds.

Premium Payer	Insured Person	Recipient	Type of Tax
A(e.g. Mr. Client)	B(e.g. Mrs. Client)	A	Income tax of A
A	A	C(e.g. children)	Inheritance tax from A to C
A	B	C	Gift tax from A to C

If the premium payer and the recipient of the insurance proceeds are the same person (A), the insurance proceeds are subject to income tax at the hand of A. Lump sum payments are treated as occasional income and annuity payments will be treated as miscellaneous income①.

If the premium payer and the insured person are the same, the insurance proceeds will be subject to inheritance tax at the hand of the recipient of the insurance proceeds since it is deemed to be received by inheritance (if the recipient were an heir) or bequest (if the recipient were not an heir)②.

If the premium payer, the insured person and the recipient of the insurance proceeds are all different people, they will be treated as a gift from the premium payer to the recipient of the insurance proceeds③.

1.6 Foreign asset reporting requirement

A foreign asset reporting requirement has been introduced from January 1, 2014 as a mechanism to require taxpayers themselves to declare their assets held overseas in order to ensure proper taxation of foreign-related income and gifts/inheritances. In accordance with this system, Japan residents who have assets in foreign countries equivalent to a total of over ¥50 million as of December 31 for any year are to be required to submit a statement (generally, attached to their income tax return) describing the type, quantity, and price, etc.

---

① Income Tax Law Arts. 34 and 35.
② Inheritance Tax Law Art. 3.
Before tax reform in 2007 non-Japanese life insurance was not treated as deemed estate. Therefore it was not subject to inheritance tax.
③ Inheritance Tax Law Art. 5.

of the foreign assets by March 15 of the following year. The penalty provisions for failing to submit a statement or forging an entry in a statement came into force in January 2015. In the case of a trust structure, the beneficiary who is treated as the owner of the assets should report the assets.

2 Definition of the Policy

2.1 For the purpose of Japan tax laws, is there any definition of "Life Insurance Policy"? If yes, what is the definition?

The Income Tax Act and the Inheritance Tax Act apply the definition of the Insurance Business Act mutatis mutandis to life insurance contracts. Therefore, life insurance is "insurance that promises to pay a fixed amount of insurance money upon a person's life or death and receives insurance premiums." for tax purpose.

However, the tax authority can apply the tax law according to the substance rather than the form of the contract. Therefore, even if it is in the form of a life insurance policy, a life contract with an extremely low death benefit may be subject to a current gift to the beneficiary and income tax to the beneficiary as an asset management contract or trust contract to the beneficiary.

In addition, Universal Life, which allows the settler to specify the degree of risk of the portfolio to the insurance company to some extent, is recognized as an insurance policy, but if the settler has complete control over the details of individual assets and can instruct the acquisition of unlisted shares or real estate, it may be judged that it is not an insurance policy.

2.2 Does the jurisdiction of the issuer of the Life Insurance Policy (a Japan issuer or a foreign issuer) have any impact on whether a life insurance Policy could satisfy the definition under the Japanese tax laws (if any)?

The Insurance Business Law distinguishes between licensed foreign life insurance companies and unlicensed foreign life insurance companies in Japan and limits the deduction for life insurance premiums to contracts with foreign life insurance companies.

The Inheritance Tax Law defines the scope of deemed inherited property as insurance contracts and other contracts stipulated by laws and regulations, and the Inheritance Tax Law Enforcement Order includes contracts with foreign insurers in other contracts stipulated by laws and regulations (Article 1-2, Paragraph 1, Item 1 of the Inheritance Tax Law Enforcement Order). Therefore, the governing law of the issuer of a life insurance policy is irrelevant in the treatment of inheritance tax law.

2.3 Does factor that whether the Life Insurance Policy is investment-linked or not have any impact on whether the Life Insurance Policy could satisfy the definition under the Japanese tax laws (if any)?

Variable insurance is a product in which the premiums paid are invested in stocks and bonds, and the amount of money received in the future fluctuates depending on performance. Insurance claims may increase depending on investment performance, but on the other hand, maturity refunds and cancellation refunds may decrease. However, for death benefits and advanced disability benefits, the basic insurance amount is guaranteed at a minimum. Variable insurance claims consist of the sum of the basic insured amount and the variable insured amount.

The basic insurance amount is the amount that is used as the basis for calculating the death benefit. In general, the basic insurance amount is determined by the age and insurance premium at the time of contract, and if the premium is paid as a lump sum, the amount of the premium paid will be the basic insurance amount.

3 Qualifying Policies

In general, for a Life Insurance Policy that meets the definition under the Japan tax laws (if any) (the "Qualifying Policy"):

3.1 What tax liabilities would the Policy Owner have as a Japan tax resident?

The owner of the insurance policy does not accrue income and does not incur income tax until he or she receives the insurance proceeds or surrender value.

3.2 What tax liabilities would the Life Insured have as a Japan tax resident?

The insured person does not receive insurance benefits, so he does not pay income tax.

3.3 What tax liabilities would the Beneficiary have as a Japan tax resident?

The beneficiary of the insurance proceeds is subject to income tax, gift tax or inheritance tax by the premium payer and the insured as described above.

4 Non-qualifying Policies

In general, for a Life Insurance Policy that does not meet the definition under Japan tax laws (if any) (the "Non-qualifying Policy", the "NQP"):

4.1 What tax liabilities would the Policy Owner have as a Japan tax resident?

Since the gift is deemed to have been made from the policyholder to the beneficiary, the policyholder is not taxed. If the beneficiary is a legal entity, deemed capital gains taxation is levied at the time of gift.

If NQP is not a Japan insurance contract but means an insurance contract with a foreign insurer, the answer is the same as 3. 1 above.

4.2 What tax liabilities would the Life Insured have as a Japan tax resident?

The insured person does not receive insurance benefits, so he does not pay income tax.

4.3 What tax liabilities would the Beneficiary have as a Japan tax resident?

The beneficiary is subject to gift tax as if he or she received the gift immediately, and may be subject to income tax when investment income accrues on subsequent investment gains.

If NQP is not a Japan insurance contract but means an insurance contract with a foreign insurer, the answer is the same as 3. 3 above.

5 Specific Scenarios

5.1 Suppose that the Policy Owner, a Japan tax resident, who purchases and holds a Non-Qualifying Policy ("NQP"), will he be subject to any tax liabilities when:

5.1.1 The Policy Owner purchases a NQP and pays the premium;

Same as 4.1 above.

5.1.2 The Policy Owner holds a NQP;

Same as 4.1 above.

5.1.3 The cash value increases and accumulates within the NQP;

Same as 4.1 above.

5.1.4 The Policy Owner loans against the NQP (including using the policy as collateral);

Same as 4.1 above. Borrowing is not income.

5.1.5 The Policy Owner transfers the NQP to a third party;

If the NQP is a trust or asset management agreement, capital gains tax will be levied on the policyholder at the time of transfer.

If NQP is not a Japan insurance contract but means an insurance contract with a foreign insurer, tax is paid when the insurance payout is received. There is no need to pay anything at the time of the change of the policyholder.

5.1.6 The Policy Owner gifts the NQP to a third party;

If the NQP is a trust or asset management agreement, capital gains tax will be levied on the policyholder at the time of transfer.

If NQP is not a Japan insurance contract but means an insurance contract with a foreign insurer, tax is paid when the insurance payout is received. There is no need to pay anything at the time of the change of the policyholder.

5.1.7 The Policy Owner partially or wholly surrender the NQP;

If the NQP is a trust or asset management agreement, capital tax will not be levied on the policyholder at the time of surrender.

If NQP is not a Japan insurance contract but means an insurance contract with a foreign insurer, tax is paid when the surrender payout is received.

5.1.8 The Policy Owner receives bonus/dividends from the NQP;

If the NQP is a trust or asset management agreement, income tax will be levied on the policyholder at the time of accrual of bonus/dividend.

If NQP is not a Japan insurance contract but means an insurance contract with a foreign insurer, tax is paid when the bonus/dividends are received.

5.1.9 The Life Insured dies and the Beneficiary gets the death benefit;

If the NQP is a trust or asset management agreement, gift tax was levied on the settlement when premium payer paid premium.

If NQP is not a Japan insurance contract but means an insurance contract with a foreign insurer, tax is levied on the beneficiary when the death benefit is received.

5.2 Suppose that the Life Insured of the NQP is a Japan tax resident:

5.2.1 Will the Life Insured be subject to any tax liabilities?

No. However, as stated above, life insurance contracts with a Japanese resident as the insured person are illegal without Japanese insurance license even if they are concluded outside of Japan.

5.2.2 Does the tax residency of the Policy Owner or the Beneficiary have any impact on the tax liability of the Life Insured?

No.

5.3 Suppose that the Beneficiary of the NQP is a Japan tax resident:

5.3.1 Will the Beneficiary be subject to any tax liabilities when the Life Insured dies and the Beneficiary receives the death benefit?

Same as 5.1.9 above.

5.3.2 Does the tax residency of the Policy Owner or the Life Insured have any impact on the tax liability of the Beneficiary?

If the policyholder is the premium payer, the recipient's tax bracket will vary depending on whether the policyholder is a resident, as discussed above.

5.4 Suppose that the Irrevocable Beneficiary of the NQP is a Japan tax resident (the Irrevocable Beneficiary is appointed by the Policy Owner, and the Policy Owner could not withdraw, surrender, transfer, or loan against the policy without Irrevocable Beneficiary's consent):

5.4.1 Will the Irrevocable Beneficiary be subject to any tax liability while the NQP is in force?

Same as 5.1.9 above.

5.4.2 Will the Irrevocable Beneficiary be subject to any tax liability when the Life Insured dies and he/she gets the death benefits?

Same as 5.1.9 above.

5.4.3 Does the tax residency of the Policy Owner and the Life Insured have any impact on the Irrevocable Beneficiary's tax liability?

If the policyholder is the premium payer, the recipient's tax bracket will vary depending on whether the policyholder is a resident, as discussed above.

The residency of the Life Insured has no impact on the Irrevocable Beneficiary's tax liability. However, as stated above, life insurance contracts with a Japanese resident as the insured person are illegal without Japanese insurance license even if they are concluded outside of Japan.

5.4.4 Does the proportion of the Irrevocable Beneficiary's interest in the death benefit (from 1% to 100%) affect his/her tax liability?

If the death benefit is less than the total amount of the premiums, it may not be considered an insurance contract.

6 Life Insurance Policy and Tax Planning

Under Japan tax laws, how can a Japan tax resident make use of a NQP for tax planning?

As mentioned above, the transfer of assets through insurance is taxed as a gift at the time of payment of the insurance premiums or as a gift or inheritance at the time of payment of the insurance benefits, so the same planning as for simple inheritance or gifts can be applied. For example, it is common to plan by donating the total amount of insurance premiums and treating any investment gains that exceed the total amount of insurance premiums as occasional income. NQP promotions are often conducted on the assumption that high investment gains from long-term management will exceed inheritance and gift taxes. On the other hand, some customers may find it better to manage the assets themselves, as the initial costs and initial surrender value are discounted.

后　记

2021年3月19日,在国际寿险架构师协会首任会长Andrade Man先生的邀请下,我走进了理事会这个国际化大家庭。大家讨论的话题是:如何打破寿险行业培训的边界?我被邀请的原因之一是:曾经在2018年12月把国际信托与遗产从业者协会的TEP[①]考试带入中国,算是有国际课程教育经验吧。

国际寿险行业在近30年里发生了很大的变化,特别是在满足高净值家庭财富管理需要方面,出现了很多"新式武器"。比如:人们可以跨境寻找保险公司,而不是局限于目前生活的司法管辖区;出现了与主流市场股指挂钩的收益实现方式;出现了可以用人寿保单来持有各类资产,而过去我们只听过家族信托持有各类资产、人寿保单里只可以存入现金类资产;出现了保单和信托一起搭建的架构,从而互补短板;澳大利亚甚至有对境外合格人寿保单格外友好的税务政策;美国引领全球寿险行业的创新,当然也是第一个发起对寿险是否姓"寿"、是否可以获得税务优惠政策挑战的司法管辖区……林林总总,这么多信息、专业知识和规划空间,从业者都了解吗?

近10年,很多华人客户到中国香港、新加坡、百慕大购买跨境保单,之后很可能又改变了税务身份,比如移民到了美国或者加拿大,那他们的跨境保单将面临什么税务问题?又或者父母这一辈在本国购买了大额保单,但子女移民到了高税负国家,今后大额保单的大笔资金将因为父母离世而被子女继承后进入子女所在国家的税务管辖范围。

回到开头,这就是国际寿险架构师协会理事会每一次会议讨论的内容:打破知识的边界,学习寿险知识的同时需要学习国际税务和国际信托;打破产品的边界,不为任何司

---

① Trust and Estate Practitioners(TEP).

法管辖区,也不为任何寿险公司或者所发行的单一产品代言,而是让从业者广泛学习和了解全世界各类型产品,在规划架构和选择产品时,唯一的依据是"客户的需求",不是保险公司近期想大力推广的产品,更不是从业者可以获取的最高利润。

在初期的讨论中,大家把视线集中在寿险从业者,但很快就发现,与客户财富相关的其他从业者似乎更需要这方面知识的扩展。比如客户的投资顾问,过去可能只需要考虑如何提高回报率,但随着客户家庭成员在世界各地游走,"税后回报率"才是有效回报率,而在经济下行的环境里客户对"本金安全、稳健收益"的需求高于对高回报的追求。再比如客户的移民顾问,过去提到美、加、澳全球纳税问题时常常会建议客户在登陆移民国之前将企业股份及其他资产转给家人代持,后来发现代持产生的问题更大!将资产转入家族信托,要么有些资产转不进去,要么转进去也不解决问题。这是一个家办思维的问题:如何合规合法合理地将移民前累积的"部分资产"与移民目的国的税务管辖相隔离。当家族成员和家族资产都在世界各地游走时,律师们则需要回答这样的问题:客户在哪里设立遗嘱能实现其继承愿望?会计师和税务师也都希望给出公平合理的规划方案,视客户如珍宝的私人银行服务更能感受到高净值家庭的多种需要。银行、信托、律师、会计师、税务师、移民顾问、投资顾问往往从来没有接触过完整的寿险知识培训,但在高净值家庭日益国际化的需求下,无视客户的相关需求等于将客户拒之门外,对本职工作也会有影响。

框定了国际寿险架构师认证课程的目标学员后,理事会的讨论又集中到了合规问题:国际寿险架构师是专业知识认证,不是寿险销售执照,每个司法管辖区对寿险销售都有严格的管理规定,因此在教材中必须有一个重要章节:保险市场结构与监管。这让学员们能够理解满足客户需求还有个大前提:合规。简单来说就是:可以给客户专业意见和方向,当遇到不能触碰的禁止行为时就要通过专业推荐来实现,比如推荐给有执照或授权的从业者完成,而不能个人"勇闯销售雷区"。

理事们的担心还有很多,在后续会议中,一边讨论教材的内容,一边担心在授课过程中授课老师会不会不小心就开始"带货"?教材是不是还要再多几次审校?是否应该和高校一起推出?首版教材会不会太难了?事实证明理事们的每一个担心都很有道理。但是2023年11月和一位客户的讨论让我"弹跳"了起来,甚至有些粗鲁地告诉理事们我所代表的中文区要行动了!

这个案例来自一家全国性的家族办公室,客户是在2022年年中时和我认识的,2023年11月再见到他时,他说他在一位中国香港保险经纪的推动下,在2022年入境美国前以保费融资的方式购买了一份中国香港保单,而他现在已经成为美国税务居民一年了。再捋一下:一位美国税务居民、个人持有一张一次性支付的美国以外保单!各位读者,如果您读到这里还没有为这位客户感到"悲痛",请一定要来这个课堂一起学习,因为这样的做法在美国税务局眼里就是投资行为,不仅保单存续期间拿不到任何延税政策,就连将来的身故赔偿金都可能面临遗产税问题!我问客户为什么做这个决定前没有来和我商量一

后 记

下？他说因为那位香港保险经纪给了他"非常满意"的回扣！听到这里我眼前满满都是捂脸的表情包！这个回扣拿得太不香了吧！在开过长达两年多的理事会后，我好想抓住这位靠回扣做业务的保险经纪走进国际寿险架构师认证的课堂！

这一番描述后，读者应该可以读到我为什么会"粗鲁地"告诉理事们，中文区不能再等待了。这股动力来自对寿险这个行业的期盼和内心的责任感。理事们很诧异：教材还在审校中，怎么就说干就干了？于是我提出了"试运行"的安排：这么大的一件事如果总是停留在会议上，而不通过试运行这样的实践，让实践告诉我们教材的问题、运营的问题、方向的问题，那么我们很长时间都无法宣布正式运行。感谢天，理事们同意了我的这个想法，但表示中文区在招生时暂时不可以使用理事们的名字。懂，爱惜羽毛是对的，毕竟理事们是会长的老友，并不是我的，他们的担心我完全可以理解，理事们还认为试运行的人数不能多，好，那就50位吧。2023年我的圣诞假期就这样泡汤了，取而代之的是打出一通通的邀请电话。参加过信知也学社信托课程的学友们的名单又来到了我的案头，罗列出了140个名单，心里其实准备好了只有大约1/3的人会说yes。不同于TEP走了30年的认证，LIC毕竟是个新认证，同事们也觉得心里没底。就在这个当口，复旦大学国际金融学院高华声院长和我讨论EMBA业界导师安排时问我LICA是否有进展，感谢高院长的这一问，有了这么多的"后来"和令人惊讶的快速推进。接受LICA试运行课程的学友们超出了预期，从50位上升到了80位，最后我以88是个吉利数字，说服理事会锁定了88个席位。

2024年1月15日，我们向88位学友推出了试运行教材，经过春节假期的预习，6堂共18个小时线上课程再加上连续2天12小时线下课程得到了学友的极大认可。随着课程的推进，LICA中文区的"两个翅膀"也都安装到位：复旦国际金融学院和LICA理事会签署合作协议、理事们的照片和简历也都公示在了网站上。英文区受到了来自中文区的鼓励，英文教材也在紧锣密鼓地修订。我在线下课上一遍遍地向88位学友表达我的感激，正是这么多位学友说yes才有中文区，乃至带动全球为国际寿险架构师认证课程按下了"start"（开始）键！接下来教学和招生都不是最难的，最难的将是全球各地国际寿险架构讲师的培养。88位学友中有半数以上报名了讲师竞聘，未来我们不是独行者，讲师队伍的壮大将会极大地推动知识的传播。

我是在上海飞往阿姆斯特丹的航班上写的这篇后记，今天已经是4月21日，88位学友在全球4个时区的4月19日完成了LIC试运行的考试，整整5个小时，学友中年龄最大的已70岁，每一位都是各自行业里的高层或机构所有者，我听到最多的话就是：打开了思路、看到了外面的世界、找到了解决客户问题的工具、我身边也有案例分析题里的类似客户……距离去年11月的冲动过去了整整5个月，请允许我利用这篇后记向所有为LICA中文区发展做过贡献的朋友们表示我最诚挚的感谢！感谢理事会过去三年的掌舵和纠偏；感谢参与中文教材编写的老师们，他们是Andrade Man、章强、李淞、方建奇、杭苏、李雯、卜晴、王晶晶、巫宁宇、康唯、苏任正，还有我自己；感谢3—4月首发讲师巫宁宇、方建奇、李淞三位老师，这可能是他们花最多时间备过的课；感谢复旦国际金融学院钱军院长、高华声副院长、李粤江书记、谢铿老师、张维老师等各位领导和老师的全力支持；感谢我在中、加两地的战友窦凤云、李略、杭苏、张念念、乔毅、喻海波及两地办公室的全体同事们，感谢长期给予学社各方面支持的名誉社长陈智晓女士和王琼博士，感谢始终信任我的信托领域里的中国信托业协会首席经济学家蔡概还老师、原银监会非银部主任资深信托专家高传捷老师、开曼战友 Alan Milgate 和 TEP 课程的两位"教头"魏楚寒、蒋镇钟老师，虽然当年我们没有拿到 STEP[①] 在中国的代理权，但是从来没有白走的路；感谢幕后的两位"小咖"——Ada Huang 和 Ally Wang，过去几个月以及未来更长的岁月，她们将会陪伴很多学员在这个平台上找到属于自己的收获。

我再次想感谢的、和我一起"吃螃蟹"的 88 位学友并非终端用户，真正的终端是我们服务的客户。没有看过世界的世界观是最糟糕的世界观，财富从业者们要想与客户游走世界的状态同步，就必须一起看世界！来吧，世界纷纷扰扰，人潮来来往往，一切刚刚好，最好的学习时机就在您捧起这本书的这一刻！LICA 国际寿险架构师协会欢迎您！

张婧媞 Janet Zhang

2024 年 4 月 21 日

于上海飞往阿姆斯特丹的航班上

---

① The Society of Trust and Estate Practitioners（STEP）.

图书在版编目(CIP)数据
国际寿险架构理论与实践/LICA 国际寿险架构师协会主编. -- 上海：复旦大学出版社, 2024.10.
(复旦卓越). -- ISBN 978-7-309-17651-3
Ⅰ. F840.622
中国国家版本馆 CIP 数据核字第 2024XH8133 号

国际寿险架构理论与实践
LICA 国际寿险架构师协会　主编
责任编辑/张美芳

复旦大学出版社有限公司出版发行
上海市国权路 579 号　邮编：200433
网址：fupnet@fudanpress.com　http://www.fudanpress.com
门市零售：86-21-65102580　　团体订购：86-21-65104505
出版部电话：86-21-65642845
上海华业装璜印刷厂有限公司

开本 787 毫米×1092 毫米　1/16　印张 17.5　字数 372 千字
2024 年 10 月第 1 版第 1 次印刷

ISBN 978-7-309-17651-3/F・3069
定价：69.00 元

如有印装质量问题，请向复旦大学出版社有限公司出版部调换。
版权所有　　侵权必究